while you were sleeping
THE WORST OF

Schiffer Publishing Ltd

4880 Lower Valley Road • Atglen, PA 19310

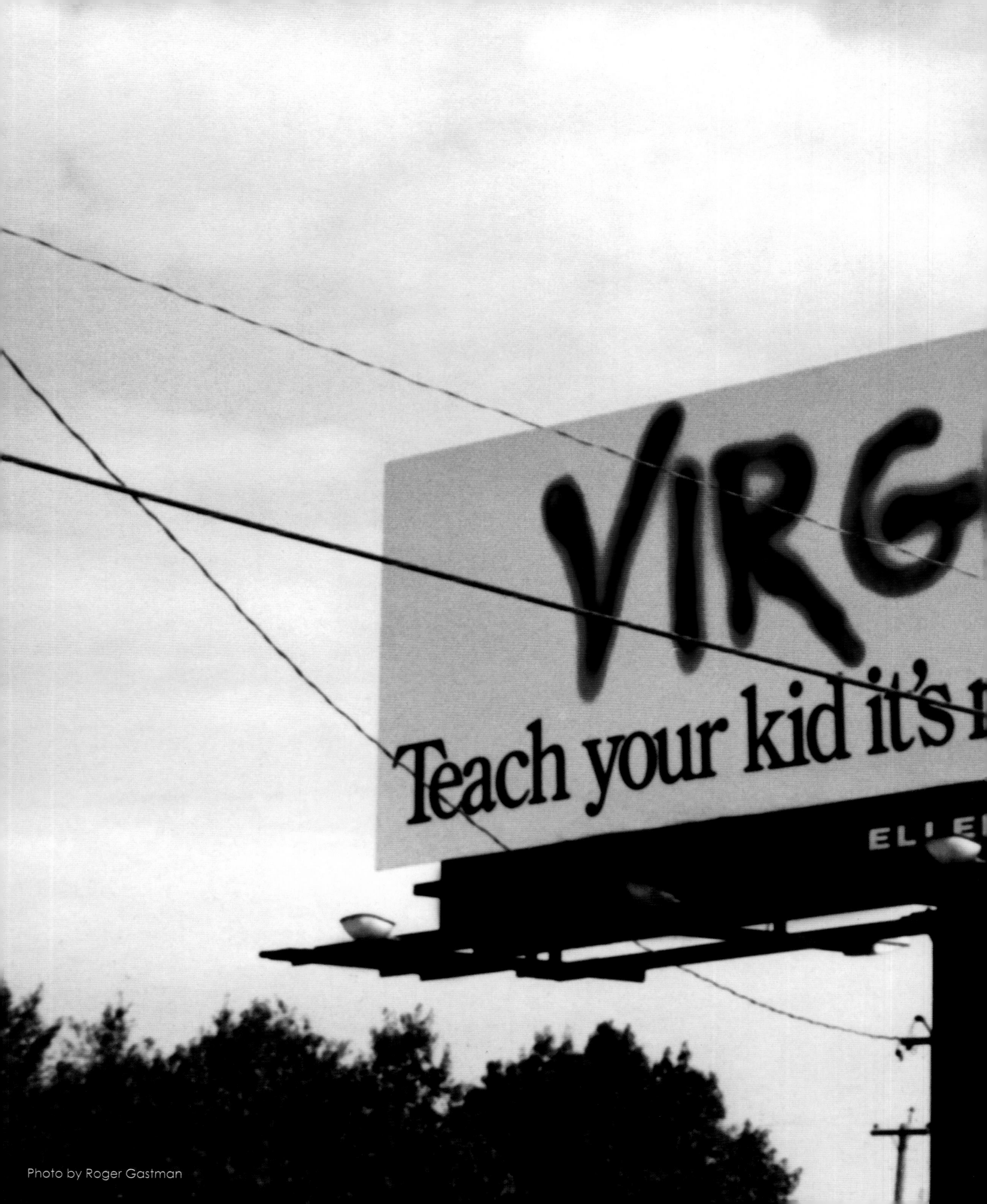

Photo by Roger Gastman

AIMER   DISCLAIM

We hope the following pages won't encourage underage drinking, drug use, teen pregnancies, senseless violence, theft, mutilation, vandalism or anything of that nature. So, don't go out and do very bad things. If you do, however, don't blame us… you should have known better. For you knuckleheads, that means don't forward us any legal bills, medical bills or any damn bills of that sort. We ain't responsible for your stupidity. But *do* feel free to write us and tell us about your mishaps and clashes with the law and/or society.

It is not OK to hurt people, break into buildings or homes, write on people's shit, do drugs or touch underage girls. Though these activities might seem fun and amusing to read about, doing them can get you into a whole heap of trouble. If you do anything and get away with it, please write and tell us about it. If you get caught, don't blame us.

WYWS realizes most of this shit is illegal. We don't care. We see "graffiti" as contemporary art, and we hope you do too. So keep painting. Fuck permission.

DISCLAIMER

while you were sleeping
THE WORST OF

While You Were Sleeping **was founded by Roger Gastman.**

The Worst of WYWS includes some of the greatest stories ever told—and many that are not so good. For this edition, we re-typed, re-scanned, re-touched and tried to fix the zillion typos that we were famous for. Yeah, we know the grammar sucks, but Zio couldn't read it anymore; it was making her dumb.

Guy in Charge of the Book: Roger Gastman
Girl Who Edited it the Best She Could: Zio Fulcher
Designer Who Worked on the Original *WYWS* and Now the Book: Shane Jessup
Coast Jumper Who Did the Production: Leon Catfish
Assistant to the Dictator Who Saw Too Many Body Parts Re-Scanning Images: Deanna Guzman
Intern I Was Too Broke to Hire: Francesca Quintano
Cover Design: Cleon Peterson & Shepard Fairey, 2000

Thanks to all of the original staff, interns, advertisers and people that put up stickers and stuff for *WYWS*. A special thanks to all of the people that I made re-visit this part of their lives and tell stories.

Without the vision and support of Morty Gudelsky *While You Were Sleeping* never would have lasted past issue 12. My sincere thanks to you, Morty.

While You Were Sleeping is owned by NorthWest Ventures, LLC.

Copyright © 2012 by R. Rock Enterprises

Library of Congress Control Number: 2012935521

ISBN: 978-0-7643-4202-8
Printed in China

OFFIC

OPEN Most d
asionally as early
as late a

WE CLOSE ab
Occasionally ab
Sometimes as la

SOMEDAYS or
aren't here at
been here i

"LIKE, 'YEAH WE HAVE A SUCCESSFUL NATIONAL MAGAZINE... YOU DON'T?'"

As you will no doubt see in this book, *While You Were Sleeping* was anything but normal. It wasn't a normal magazine. Its success wasn't normal. Its lasting influence wasn't normal. Its creator certainly wasn't normal. But it wasn't this lack of normalcy that caused *WYWS* to become such a unique entity. I think what made *WYWS* awesome was that everything seemed so absolutely normal to everybody involved. Like, "Yeah we have a successful national magazine... you don't?" It wasn't about posturing or proving anything because *WYWS* didn't need that shit. It was *WYWS* and that came with its own set of rules and logic. So here is my final written list for *WYWS*. I present you with the things *WYWS* taught me were normal (that probably weren't):

• Hanging out with Mr. T is normal.
• Cooking with porn stars is normal.
• Being regularly published in a magazine is normal.
• Being rewarded for spending your entire childhood watching TV is normal.
• Getting free shit is normal.
• Wearing a T-shirt that says "I Fucked Your Daughter" to freshman orientation is normal.
• People copy-editing crap you write is normal (this made me so lazy that I still haven't corrected the problerm).
• Inappropriate touch from a family member is normal.
• Naked pictures of people's girlfriends are normal (we sorta predicted this one becoming normal).
• Having office space is normal.
• Advertising dollars are normal.
• Having a legacy is normal.

—*Ian Sattler*

Bill's Wheels, Santa Cruz, CA

NO RULES
THE STORY OF ROGER GASTMAN'S
WHILE YOU WERE SLEEPING

It all started as a twisted dream. (I always wanted to start this way since I read the Misfits use it in a bio.)

I never wanted to be a doctor, fireman or any of the stuff kids want to be growing up. I never wanted to be a publisher either, but everything seemed to fall into place, and at age 19, that's what I wound up doing.

Now that I've been a publisher for more than 15 years, and have produced more than 30 art-related books, I figured it was time to revisit the first thing I ever published: *While You Were Sleeping*. What follows is the short version of how *WYWS* came to be, with many pictures for those who, like me, hate to read.

PART ONE

I grew up in Bethesda, Maryland, a suburban community adjacent to Washington, D.C. I got into hair metal as early as second and third grade, listening to bands such as Ratt, Van Halen (with Lee Roth) and Twisted Sister, and that quickly led me to punk. By fifth and sixth grade, I was listening to the Dead Milkmen, Sex Pistols, Naked Raygun, Mucky Pup, Gwar and on and on.

Since D.C. is the home of Minor Threat and straightedge, I soon became immersed in the hardcore scene, and thanks to John Robinson—who was in fifth grade when I was in sixth—I became friends with a lot of local bands, straightedge kids and thieves—many of whom also wrote graffiti.

One of the graffiti crews was called BTG (BIG TIME GRAFFITI). They were into hardcore, robbing houses and writing graffiti. When they got more serious about graffiti, they changed their name to NAA (NEVER ADMIT ANYTHING or NEW AGE ART). I'd see them at hardcore shows and was aware of who they were, but didn't really know any of them.

Then, the summer after 8th grade, I went to the beach for a week—everyone from the D.C. area would go to Bethany or Rehobeth beach in the summer—with my friend Meghan and her family. Meghan's brother was in BTG and introduced me to a bunch of NAA's members. I started hanging out with them, and when I got back to Bethesda, I continued to do so. I couldn't tell if the guys in NAA liked me, or if I was just some goofy little kid to them, but it didn't really matter.

I started trying out different graffiti names and, ended up with the name CLEAR in the summer of 1993. The name had no real meaning to me, but I liked the letters and it stuck. I practiced writing all the time, and every single notebook I owned was filled with tags. Pretty soon, I figured out how to steal paint. Luckily, I went to a high school that had a lot of graffiti writers in it, most of them older than me, and they would drive me to hardware stores so that I could build up my spray paint arsenal. My "regular" friends would go steal with me even more because they just liked the idea of causing trouble.

By this time, I had befriended RAGE, who went to the same school as me, was one of the leaders of NAA and a member of two bands, Ashes

and Battery. On the weekends and during breaks from school, I went on tour with RAGE and his band Ashes to such far off places as California and such shitty places as New Jersey, where I met more writers and started trading photos with them. I owe a lot to RAGE: It was because of him that I started to forge a national graffiti network.

At a punk show in a New Jersey basement, the hardcore straightedge band Strife played. I noticed tags on their equipment cases and started up a conversation with them. I learned they were from Orange County, and one of them was BUS from MSK crew. I didn't know much about L.A. graffiti or MSK at that point, I just knew I had a new friend to trade pictures with and whom I could go visit.

Looking back, it's weird to think our parents let us go all these places. Maybe it was because we were straightedge or maybe we just had cool parents, but even so, it's strange to be able to say, "Hey, mom, I'm going to California to meet up with a graffiti writer I've traded pics with," and for her to say, "OK, have fun, let me know you're alive." But that's exactly what happened, and at 15, I took a trip out to L.A. to visit BUS. He introduced me to a lot of people there, and I can definitely credit him for a lot of the L.A. connections I have today.

Back in Bethesda, I was annoyed at how hard it was to get caps—spray paint tips that allow you to control the pressure and the width of the paint—

so I tracked down a distributor in New York and started buying them from him wholesale. Since I already had a big network of graffiti artist friends around the country, many of them bought caps or told me about local stores in their areas that I could sell to. One thing led to another, and in 1995, at 17 years old, I started to add storeowners to my ever-growing graffiti network.

By the time I graduated high school in 1996, I had no idea what I wanted to do. I ended up at the University of Pittsburgh's summer program, where I went to parties, hung out with graffiti writers more than five years my senior, and wrote on stuff. I lived with two writers, NECS and SPAED, and on weekends we would take trips to Ohio to buy spray paint at flea markets, or to Milwaukee to paint freights with FCR. I was having the time of my life.

By this time, I had made friends with a lot of people who were doing graffiti magazines, which were coming out more frequently and becoming easier to get. I figured I had lots of photos from trading back and forth with all the people I had met around the country; I knew a lot of storeowners from selling caps; and I had friends that were making magazines to help me with questions—so why not start my own magazine?

PART 2

In early 1997, after less than two semesters at Pitt, I moved back to Bethesda to attend American University. It was a good school—my mom had graduated from there—and it was only a 15-minute drive from the house. I was living in my old room in my mom's house, and I decided I had to get this magazine off the ground.

I named the magazine *While You Were Sleeping*, after a common phrase my high school friends and I used to start stories with. "Last night, while you were sleeping, I…" My friend CERT used that phrase the most. He was addicted to going out; I don't know how the hell he managed to graduate.

To help startup the magazine, I reached out to my diverse group of friends. It was a serious group of misfits—cheerleaders, private-school lacrosse kids, high-school dropouts, graffiti writers—but a hilarious and creative group of misfits at that.

They didn't know how to make a magazine either, but one had a scanner, one knew how to use Photoshop and, piece by piece, the magazine started to come together.

My good friend KIER, who was a graffiti legend and a popular rave DJ in D.C., had just graduated from Corcoran. He had a graphic design job, and access to a computer, a scanner and a copy of Quark Express. After a few meetings, he became the first art director of *WYWS* (not that I knew what an art director actually did). But since KIER came from a graffiti background, he was more than just an art director, he was able to read pieces and contributed to the overall feel of early *WYWS* issues.

I also reached out to my friends in Cincinnati,

Ohio, who did *Scribble* magazine. They gave me a bunch of pointers, and even were kind enough to hook me up with their printer. With the help of all my friends, the first issue of *WYWS* hit stands in the summer of 1997, when I was just 19 years old. Issue 1 was just 24 pages—16 color and eight black-and-white—and featured two D.C. graff legends, JOKER and RUST, on the cover. The issue also included an interview I did with ESPO, whose *On the Go* magazine was a big inspiration to us, as was his graffiti. That interview, and the questions I asked, pretty much set the tone for *WYWS* forever. I don't think I ever sat down and planned to ask people weird questions that didn't have anything to do with graffiti, it just happened. I guess that's where my mind was at the time—and has been ever since.

By the third issue of *WYWS*, KIER had gotten too busy with DJing and his real job to be able to spend time on *WYWS*, which was understandable since nobody was getting paid. My friend SICK156 from Boston stepped up to the task and picked up where KIER left off.

It was 1998, and internet access and emails were still slow, so SICK156 and I mailed zip discs back and forth, and he came to D.C. a few times, and I went to Boston a few times. When issue 3 came out, it was designed in SICK156's Photoshop collage-style, and it ended up determining the aesthetic for what the graffiti pages and the logos in the magazine would look like for the next several issues. And while that was the only issue SICK156 worked on in its entirety, issue 3 marked a major turning point for *WYWS*. We added more text, stories that didn't have to do with graffiti, and—nothing against Dave's design—but it actually started to look like a real magazine.

My friend Linas, who I knew from the hardcore scene, was an awesome illustrator and was also a huge asset to *WYWS* at the time. Plus, his sense of humor was just as fucked up as mine—or worse. Linas would go on to illustrate more *WYWS* stories than anyone and played a huge part in making *WYWS* what it was.

Shortly after I had started *WYWS*, I went on a 10-day tour with EXAKTO and his straightedge hardcore band Ten Yard Fight from Boston. While on that tour, I got to know the band's bass player, John LaCroix, much better. LaCroix was responsible for a well-known hardcore fanzine called *Extent*, and was very into the tech and graphic design worlds. He was the most real designer I had met at that point. He wasn't into graffiti, but knew a lot of people who were, and liked the fact that I was making a magazine on my own terms, so he offered his design skills.

Roger Gastman & Ten Yard Fight in front of CBGB.

With issue 4, I took him up on his offer. Not only did John teach me how to design a magazine, but also how to distribute a magazine, sell advertising, edit an article, re-touch a photo, and much more. I remember when he talked JNCO into buying an ad for the back cover; that was a huge moment for us. It was probably only a $500 ad, but it was a popular brand at the time and their jeans were available in malls everywhere. It was an important steppingstone for us.

In order to work on the issues, I took many trips to Boston, and John took many trips to Bethesda. He would stay at my mom's house, and we wouldn't leave the house for days on end. When we did have free time, John would come on adventures with me and my meathead friends, diving into our odd suburban lives that served as the basis for many *WYWS* stories and resulted in more than one trip to the ER.

We also started asking most people we interviewed John's trademark question: Would you punch an alien? This got us the strangest looks—sometimes even more odd looks than asking people what things had been put up their asses.

Yes, this is autographed by Ron Jeremy.

In the fall of 1998, I was mistakenly living in Mississippi under the guise of being a baseball player eating way too much chicken on a stick and desperately searching for anything that resembled a bag of pot. I'm not sure how Roger found me, but a copy of *While You Were Sleeping* ended up in my mailbox. On the cover were two of the hottest chicks from eighth grade in miniskirts, Anna Main and Kristin Lyle. I left Mississippi two months later without the magazine. I bought a copy on eBay a couple years ago, and still have it.

—*David Wilfert, The Worlds Best Ever*

WYWS was a combination of art weirdos, jocks, meatheads, juvenile offenders and girls of questionable reputation. In the real world, the confluence of these polar opposites simply would have never happened. Somehow, someway, *WYWS* suspended the laws of nature and allowed these groups to not only coexist but meld into some bizarre perversion of nature that only Roger Gastman would create.

—*Mackie B.*

Roger is like the Steven Spielberg of graffiti.

—*SHAKEN*

WYWS was one of the first magazines to cover more than the graffiti scene in the 1990s. It covered fashion, culture and lifestyle.

—*WANE ONE*

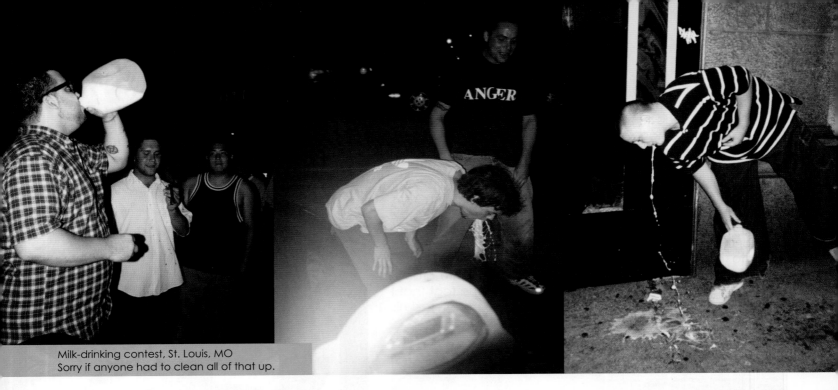

Milk-drinking contest, St. Louis, MO
Sorry if anyone had to clean all of that up.

In the meantime, graffiti had been catching on and cities started having small festivals. For some reason I still don't understand, St. Louis hosted an annual graffiti festival known as Paint Louis, for which the city invited writers to paint the walls along the river bank, and writers also ventured into the neighboring freight yard. In 1998, for the second or third Paint Louis, I decided it was time for *WYWS* to make an appearance. EVER, DASAR and I drove 16 hours from Bethesda to St. Louis in a car that was packed to the brim with merchandise for me to sell and spray paint (Kelly Lang where are you?).

We had started filming a video to go along with the magazine's madness, which included walking around in cow costumes, scaring little kids and a bunch of stupid stunts and senseless destruction, so we decided to film a milk-drinking contest while we were in St. Louis. Basically, we bought a bunch of two-liter jugs of milk, and offered $20 to anyone who could drink the whole thing in under two minutes and not puke. It's physically impossible for the body to do that, so it ended up being a bunch of people puking in the middle of the street. It was awesome.

When I got back to Bethesda, I shifted my focus toward selling ads. I had no idea how to sell ads, so my friends and I just pretended like we did. In the first few issues, some small graffiti shops advertised, but as we started to feature more music stories in the issues, record companies started to buy ads too.

Even though we were selling more ads, *WYWS* was still very DIY at this point. My friends PMD—aka the Record Idiot—and Fat Rich were the main ad salesmen; my mom was managing the subscription list; and if it weren't for me selling caps, the magazine would have never survived past the first few issues.

Besides ads, once we started writing more about music, I started to get bombarded with mail.

It wasn't just scumbag graffiti writers sending me pictures of bad graffiti anymore, but we were getting bombarded with CDs and porn (and, as someone in their early 20s, getting a lot of porn in the mail was freaking awesome).

One day, I received a postcard in the mail from a photographer named Carlos Batts. It said that he wanted to work with me in some capacity, either shooting covers or adding fashion. Carlos lived in Baltimore, which was less than an hour north, and had found the magazine through Reptilian Records. He was a bit older than me and had an impressive portfolio. He'd been printed in real magazines, shot album covers, knew models, and understood what shooting fashion meant. Plus, he had shot for every fucked up porno magazine you can imagine. So, for issue 5, Carlos shot the cover and we added a fashion spread. I had no idea if the fashion was good or bad—you can see by photos of me in this book that I'm not a very fashionable dude—but I did know it would open up the magazine to new advertisers.

Now, the clothing started coming in too. It wasn't just CDs and porn anymore, but full boxes of clothes from Puma, Adidas and all the major streetwear brands like Tribal, Haze and Kikwear. Since I didn't have money to pay people, being able to give them clothes, shoes and tickets to concerts was awesome. (They also liked free porn.)

John designed issues 4 through 7, and then, if my memory serves me right, he got a real job. By this time, I'd learned to scan pictures, sort of retouch them and use Quark Express, so I dummied out the next several issues by myself. Then friends who knew a lot more about design—like Shane Jessup, Darryl Pittman and others—would clean it up and get it ready for the printer.

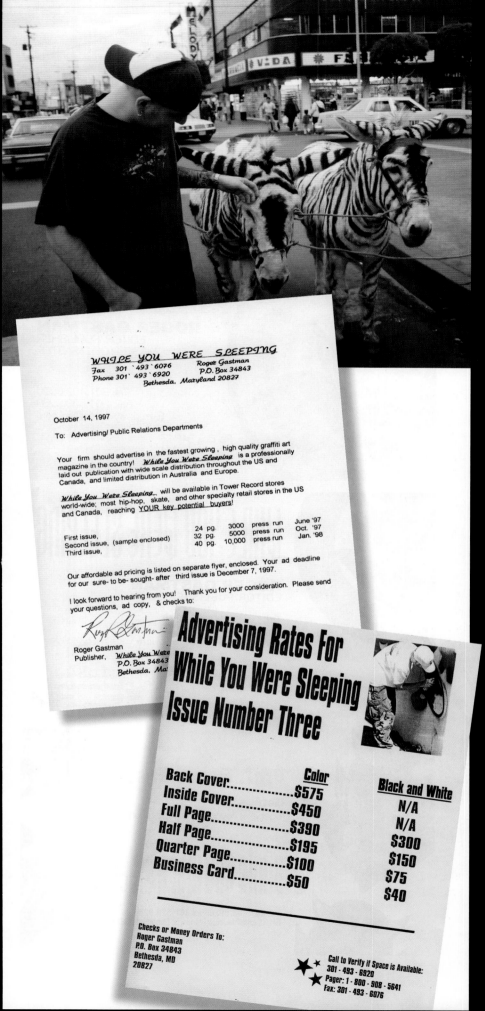

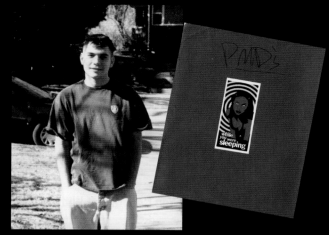

I wrote for *WYWS* in the late 1990s. I did some of my first legitimate interviews with the likes of Pete Rock and Ras Kass and did some inane rambling as a nonsensical reviewer known as "The Record Idiot."

I even did some porn reviews (don't ask me what that means) and ended up dealing with the porn industry for the first time (I went on to have an illustrious career as a regular porn watcher).

What I remember most about working for *WYWS* was spending time at the editor/publisher's house.

Oh, let me clarify. This "editor" was a friend of mine in the class above me in high school named Roger (I call him Roy). Roy was a fucking looney tune—a straightedge weirdo with crazy tattoos who used to utter gibberish-like words on repeat and some how manage to bang lots of chicks in the process.

He was also sort of a genius, though, for two reasons. One was the fact that he had a legitimate magazine with real circulation at 17 years old—funded off of his other business of being the world's largest graffiti cap distributor. Keep in mind he ran the business from his bedroom while dealing with his loving but high-strung mom screaming at him 80 percent of the day.

Roger's real genius came with women, though. Not only was Roy unattractive physically (pudgy, hairy and with a face only a loving mother could learn to like), but he was also a known scoundrel and perv in high school.

All the girls at our high school—and nearby private schools—knew exactly what Roger was about and yet he got an alarming number of them to give it up. It was amazing.

He just told these cute-ass chicks what he wanted and they gave it to him. He was unabashed about who he was and he exuded a confidence that almost no young men have—particularly, bizarre young men. It was this confidence that made weird-ass Roy so cool, and in turn made this magazine so good.

This magazine was exactly what it set out to be and had a real personality. In my humble and biased opinion, *WYWS* was the first magazine in a genre that is now chock-full of copycats—most of which have no true identity.

That all comes from the lunatic 19-year-old who started it and the weirdos he had working for him. I take pride in being one of those people.

Fun shit. Thanks, Roy.

—*Peter Rosenberg, radio/TV personality, Hot 97 NYC*

WWW.WHILEYOUWERESLEEPING.COM

INSIDE DOPE

Graf Pages *by BEN HIGA*

You CAN Take It With You

Since the days when PHASE 2 laid down the first copy of *IGT* (*International Graffiti Times*) back in the early '80s, the field was ripe for the underground media explosion that was ready to take shape. With the graffiti movement spreading to an international level, communication at local "writers' benches" gave way to more broadly disseminated "graffiti media." With publications such as *IGT* out of New York and Can Control out of L.A. setting the pace, hundreds of 'zines flooded the community following the advent of desktop publishing.

Videography and video magazines were spearheaded by former New York writer Carl Weston with his series of *VideoGrafx* throughout the past decade. The '90s brought us the technological revolution of the information highway, bringing to life a myriad of graffiti-related sites on the World Wide Web—spearheaded by Art Crimes, the largest and most comprehensive archive on the Web to date. Info: www.graffiti.org

Web New York City

@149st
Cyber Bench

With a name referencing the famous 149th Street subway station, where artists would gather to bench (watch trains), @149st is a vital documentary site authored and maintained by participants of the '70s graf movement.

Currently, the site has over 80 pages, hundreds of photographs of detailed murals, dozens of interviews and profiles on crews and artists, many of whom were neglected by the first wave of graffiti books and videos.

According to the site producers, "Documenting the history of writing is inevitably subjective. Due to the fact that it is an underground movement and the life span of works can be as brief as days, most of history is limited to word-of-mouth accounts. We of @149st have made a modest attempt to encapsulate the history. In addition to witnessing history firsthand, we have spoken directly with many participants.

"We have chosen the medium of the Web over print due to its flexibility," they explain. "Historical inaccuracy on the Web can be addressed in a matter of minutes or hours. The print medium is not so forgiving. Keep in mind that this site is a work in progress, and its aim is to build towards the truth."

Info: www.at149st.com

Zines

The real graf pages.

Big Time
With over a couple hundred graffiti magazines on the market, a few stand out. *Big Time*, L.A.'s own magazine of "urban art and expression," surviving into its second year of publication, seems to pick up momentum with every issue. The current issue features not only crispy clean graf flicks, but a spread on Estevan "Scandalous" Oriol's photographic documentation of L.A.'s Latino underground art movement. Also prominently covered are the various styles of Chicano writing, possibly the oldest known graffiti tradition to date. Info: *Big Time*, P.O. Box 11262, Glendale, CA 91226

While You Were Sleeping
For the enthusiasts on a quest for aerosol ecstasy, a group of Maryland natives brings you *While You Were Sleeping*—a unique publication blending graf flicks, porn interviews and music reviews into one graphic display of "perversion, art and noise." Scantily clad women sprinkle the pages from cover to cover among explicit interviews with well-known porn stars as well as a sex advice column for the sexually distraught. The only magazine with a hit list of interview questions for writers, ranging from sleeping with overweight females to discussions of midgets, WYWS clearly blurs the line between reality and fantasy.

Info: www.whileyouweresleeping.com

MAGAZINE

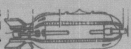

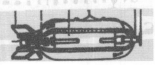

PART 3

In the late 1990s and early 2000s, Tower Records was instrumental in the distribution of graffiti magazines, and to the spread of graffiti culture. They had a magazine section unlike any other store in the country, in which every sort of subculture was represented. For whatever reason, the magazine buyers—Doug and, later, Clint—were huge supporters of the graffiti culture, and *WYWS* found nationwide distribution through them. It's safe to say that without Tower Records, *WYWS* would not have made it past the first few issues. It's also safe to say that without Tower, *WYWS* would not have been available in so many major cities, as well as smaller ones, from Sacramento to Richmond.

Even though I had my hands full with *WYWS*, I was still taking classes at American University. But as the magazine started to build up more hype, more distribution, and a few more advertisers, it was getting too difficult to keep up with both school and *WYWS*. So I had to choose between the two. I figured I could always go back to school, but I knew I wouldn't be able to pick up the momentum that I had started with *WYWS*. So I quit skool and, to this day, have never gone back.

In a way, *WYWS* was my college education. I learned much more doing it than any other college class could have provided, and I'm happy with the decision I made. (However, I'd gladly accept an honorary degree or doctorate—or an overeager intern who wants to take online courses for me.)

By issue 7, I finally moved out of my mom's and moved into my own house. It was a suburban split-level house with a two-car garage near the heart of downtown. The garage became the shipping and storage room, while the rec and TV room served as my office. The house opened up a new chapter for *WYWS*. I had definitely done many things in my mom's house that I probably shouldn't have, but now that I had my own house and office, there really were no more rules. (Just ask Jay about how he got arrested for throwing a beer bottle at a cop when we got busted for having an underage drinking party.)

Issue 7 featured our "biggest" star to date on the cover: Julie Benz, who had recently starred in *Jawbreaker* and was on *Angel*. I was so excited. In the end, her interview sucked because she is boring and doesn't do nude scenes, but Carlos Batts, who had just moved to L.A., shot her.

The next several issues kept getting bigger and things were moving faster. More advertisers, writers, random stuff in the mail, more parties, more travel, more trips to tradeshows—*WYWS* became my full-time job and I was working it 24 hours a day.

By issue 12, I was pretty worn out. It was just me, Chris Henzel and some interns—Lauren Gifford, Andrew Black and a few others—doing absolutely everything. The magazine had grown a lot, and we were putting out over 15,000 copies an issue, but cash flow was still hard. Advertisers didn't want to pay on time or at all; and it was the same deal with the magazine distributors. I was getting fed up, but at the same time, the magazine was getting more and more popular with readers. Just as I was thinking about closing up shop, an investor bought into the magazine.

Here's what I wrote about it in the introduction to issue 13:

"This issue marks a new beginning at **WYWS.** *The first seven issues were thrown together in my bedroom at my mommy's house. For issues 8 to 12, I moved into my very own house and worked out of my basement. Along the way, several people have pitched in and helped out, but, overall, it was a one-man project that ruled my life and kept getting bigger and bigger, like a fat woman at a buffet. Lucky for me, fat and stupid is fashionable once again.*

Now, who's to say 13 is an unlucky number? This little boy sure as hell got lucky. With help from some good friends, **WYWS** *has found an investor. That means the little-magazine-that-could is moving on up. Well, just down the street actually. The new worldwide headquarters is less than two miles from where I grew up.*

Now that we're a legitimate business, I no longer wake up at noon and stumble down the stairs in my boxers to work on the mag. Instead, I wake up at 9, and drive two minutes down the street to the heart of wonderful downtown Bethesda, Maryland. We landed a storefront just a stone's throw from California Tortilla, the lunchtime mecca for teenage girls in the Washington Area, and now the entire **WYWS** *staff (that's right you schmucks, I gots me a staff) sits in the window, drinks 40s, and stares at all the hot girls that walk by. Eventually, we'll get enough energy to get off our butts and talk to them. For now, grunting and hooting suffices.*

WYWS *has grown so much since its inception. Who would have thought that this magazine, in all its idiotic splendor, would touch so many souls worldwide? I never expected to be doing this crap. What did I expect to be doing? Got me. The one thing I know is that I never want to grow up. In some ways, I'm never going to have to because there is plenty more where this came from—I can be fat and stupid until I die. Enjoy it."*

Belligerent & Drunken

Congratu-fuckin-lations on your high-profile media debut in today's *Washington Post*. Now kids everywhere, not just the cool ones like me, will be studying your mag for the latest on underground fetishes, how not to get laid, and the other semi-felonious activity that is vividly portrayed on each page of your publication. I guess I would say I have to hate you, because I am afterall a player hater. But at the same time *WYWS* has found a place in my boxer briefs (no, I'm not gay). But enough of the ass-sniffing, and to the business. I am curious as to how serious you all are about accepting freelance work. My compositions and commentary are suitable for your rag as I find myself in situations that would make for great coverage in your mag (i.e. fucking senators' daughters, going to court, evading drug tests, vandalism, doing young broads, belligerent drunken antics at parties). I am returning to school in the fall, and will be able to provide you schmucks with all types of sleazy and downright immoral material. OK, that's enough from me, I would appreciate a reply as I have just wasted 10 minutes of my time.

Chris

In case you didn't know by now I'm officially famous

The Magazine Reader

A Young Man's Fantasy Between Glossy Covers

By PETER CARLSON
Washington Post Staff Writer

It's not true that Roger Gastman publishes a slick national magazine devoted to graffiti artists, porn stars, punk rockers and serial killers from a bedroom in his mother's house in Bethesda.

He did that for a couple of years but then he moved out. Now he publishes a magazine devoted to graffiti artists, porn stars, punk rockers and serial killers from a spotless little office in his *own* house in Bethesda.

The magazine is called While You Were Sleeping, and it's ... it's ... it's hard to describe. It's dumb but it's fun. It's annoying but it's also kind of impressive.

It's a full-color magazine printed on heavy slick paper just like the magazines published by actual adults who work for big corporations. But it reads like the official publica-

See MAGAZINES, C4, Col. 3

Inside the Teenage Male Mind: It Ain't Pretty

MAGAZINES, *From C1*

tion of the fraternity in the movie "Animal House."

The good thing about While You Were Sleeping is that it takes you inside the adolescent male mind. The bad thing about it is that it takes you a little too far inside the adolescent male mind.

Believe me, you don't want to know what's inside these minds, particularly if you are related to any adolescent females. Sex is what's on their dirty little minds. Sex, plus drinking. Also graffiti art, porn stars and serial killers. And sex.

Reading While You Were Sleeping makes you want to lock up your daughters and buy a shotgun.

The weird thing about this is that Roger Gastman seems like such a fine young man. At 22, he's polite and soft-spoken. He doesn't eat meat. You'd almost call him clean-cut, except for the tattoos and the earrings and the shaved head. He's hard-working and highly motivated. At an age when most kids are scrounging for a job at McDonald's, he started his own magazine and hustled to arrange national distribution.

"There's a hole in the market that I'm trying to fill," he says. "There was no magazine that had everything I was into. It's a magazine for young men—for rambunctious youth, you could say."

He put out the first issue in 1997, a little more than a year after he graduated from Bethesda-Chevy Chase High School.

He'd spent an unhappy semester at the University of Pittsburgh, then moved home to Mom's and enrolled at American University. He was a graffiti artist and the first issue of the mag was a crudely printed compendium of photographs of spray-painted buildings.

"The title is an old graffiti-writer's term,"

he says. "While you were sleeping, I was—fill in the blank."

With each issue, Gastman expanded his subject matter to other things you could do while less adventurous folks were sleeping, which accounts for the coverage of punk bands, porn stars and epic drinking bouts.

As for the serial killers, that was more of an academic interest. "One of my friends came to me and said he'd like to write about psycho killers, so I said okay," Gastman explains.

Now, the magazine features a regular column on America's most famous psycho killers. It's called "Americans I Most Admire." The title is sarcastic, Gastman explains: "It fits with the tone of the magazine." He's not endorsing serial murder, mind you, just reveling in the sickness of it.

The magazine also provides its young audience with an introduction to some of America's weirder career possibilities: It has printed interviews with tattoo artists, an undertaker, a bounty hunter, a repo man, a dominatrix and the owner of a Nevada brothel.

Despite—or maybe because of—the bizarre subject matter, the magazine thrived and expanded. Gastman dropped out of school to work on the mag full time, writing, editing, taking pictures, selling ads, hiring a national distributor.

Now, it's what he calls "an iffy bimonthly," which means it comes out every three or four months. It sells about 30,000 copies an issue, most of them at places like Borders or Tower Records.

The current issue, which is the 10th, is fairly typical. There are interviews with a porn actress, a graffiti pimp, a zoo keeper, a porn actress, a graffiti artist, several punk rockers and an electronica musician who performs naked except for a coat of bright blue paint and who calls herself "an intergalactic fertility goddess from the 16th dimension."

There's also an entertaining account of

spring break in Panama City Beach, Fla., where the drunken revelers are constantly proselytized by Christian missionaries who just won't take no for an answer.

And there's a fashion spread that shows folks modeling clothes in the macabre halls of L.A.'s Museum of Death, which makes for a bizarre fashion spread indeed.

But not as bizarre as the one in an earlier issue, in which guys modeled clothes while pretending to stuff a corpse into the trunk of a car. I think it was supposed to be a satire of idiotic fashion stories. It's hard to tell.

Speaking of death, this issue is a bonanza for psycho-killer buffs.

The "Americans I Most Admire" column is devoted to Richard Ramirez, the infamous "Night Stalker." And there's also a piece on Gilles de Rais, an aristocratic French serial killer from the 15th century. Two psycho killers for the price of one! What a bargain!

Like all issues of While You Were Sleeping—and most issues of most magazines—this one features a buxom, scantily clad woman on the cover. She turns out to be Natalie Raitano, a third-tier actress now appearing on "V.I.P.," the Pamela Anderson TV show.

Apparently, Raitano's pulchritude is so intoxicating that the interviewer, Neil Mahoney, could barely speak, causing Raitano's publicist to ask: "Who's going to write this article?"

"I am," Mahoney says.

"So you can write," the publicist says, "you just don't know how to interview?"

"Exactly," Mahoney says.

Actually, I'm not so sure about his writing ability, either. But good writing isn't the appeal of While You Were Sleeping. Outrageousness is.

It's not a bad mag, if you're in the mood for mindless adolescent high jinks. But Gastman and his perverted pals better stay away from my daughters.

PART 4

WYWS did a lot of things first. Steve Powers was the first person I interviewed, and we were the first to do stories on BANKSY, Shepard Fairey, Ron English, Atmosphere, Kaiju Big Battel, Andrew WK, The White Stripes, Mister Cartoon, Jumbo's Clown Room, Vaughn Bode, Rockstar Games/*Grand Theft Auto*, Fergie, DALEK, Richard Colman, Jamie Hewlett and the Gorillaz and more. We were too ahead of our time, and ended too soon.

Anyway, there is a lot more to this story than I'm writing here. It's still a bit too soon to tell some of the juicy details, but this is enough for you to get the gist of it. Currently, I've been messing around with film just like I messed with magazines and books, so if I live long enough, you might be able see an *American Pie*-style movie about the making of *WYWS*. And, yes, it'll be set in Bethesda.

As Big Pat would say, "Peace in da hood."

To be continued,

Roger Gastman

P.S. Would you punch an alien?

"SO I GUESS WHAT I'M TRY-ING TO SAY IS THAT WYWS STARTED OFF AS A 24-PAGE GRAFFITI ZINE. OVER THE PAST FOUR VERY STRANGE YEARS, I'VE WATCHED THE GLOSSY REINVENT ITSELF MORE THAN JUST A FEW TIMES; ALMOST ALWAYS FOR THE BETTER. GRAFFITI HAS FUNDED ALL OF THIS. IT'S REALLY SOME RETARDED SHIT, BUT I OWE IT A WHOLE HELL OF A LOT."

—*Roger Gastman,* Issue 20 Introduction

So, what does *While You Were Sleeping* mean to me? Well, it means a lot of things. It means coming up in the Washington, D.C., area in the early 1990s and hearing everyone talk about COOL "DISCO" DAN. It means showing up at high school parties 20 people deep—and not even knowing who the fuck lived at the house. It means a bunch of kids in the suburbs who weren't afraid to climb around on rooftops in Northeast D.C. at 3 a.m. It means the crew you hung out with every day thought graffiti was cool, and couldn't understand why the rest of the world didn't get it. It means getting your crib raided by the cops was a right of passage growing up. And, most importantly, it means not thinking twice about producing a video of a crack whore blowing some dude in an alley.

—*EXAKTO*

WYWS was the first graff mag I was featured in (both graff and writing), and it also featured pretty much all of my circle of friends. Roger seriously put everyone on. From writing to taking photos to being featured—this was so many people's way in. I don't think we appreciated it back then, but looking back on it, it's kind of amazing how many people who would not have otherwise been doing anything but wrecking D.C. found a different creative outlet. Check out what people are doing now for proof. There's a lot of photographers, artists and authors out there who have *WYWS* to thank.

Last thing I'll mention, *WYWS* was also unapologetically Roger. There's so much of his weird shit in there, you kind of have to respect it.

—*Gabe Banner*

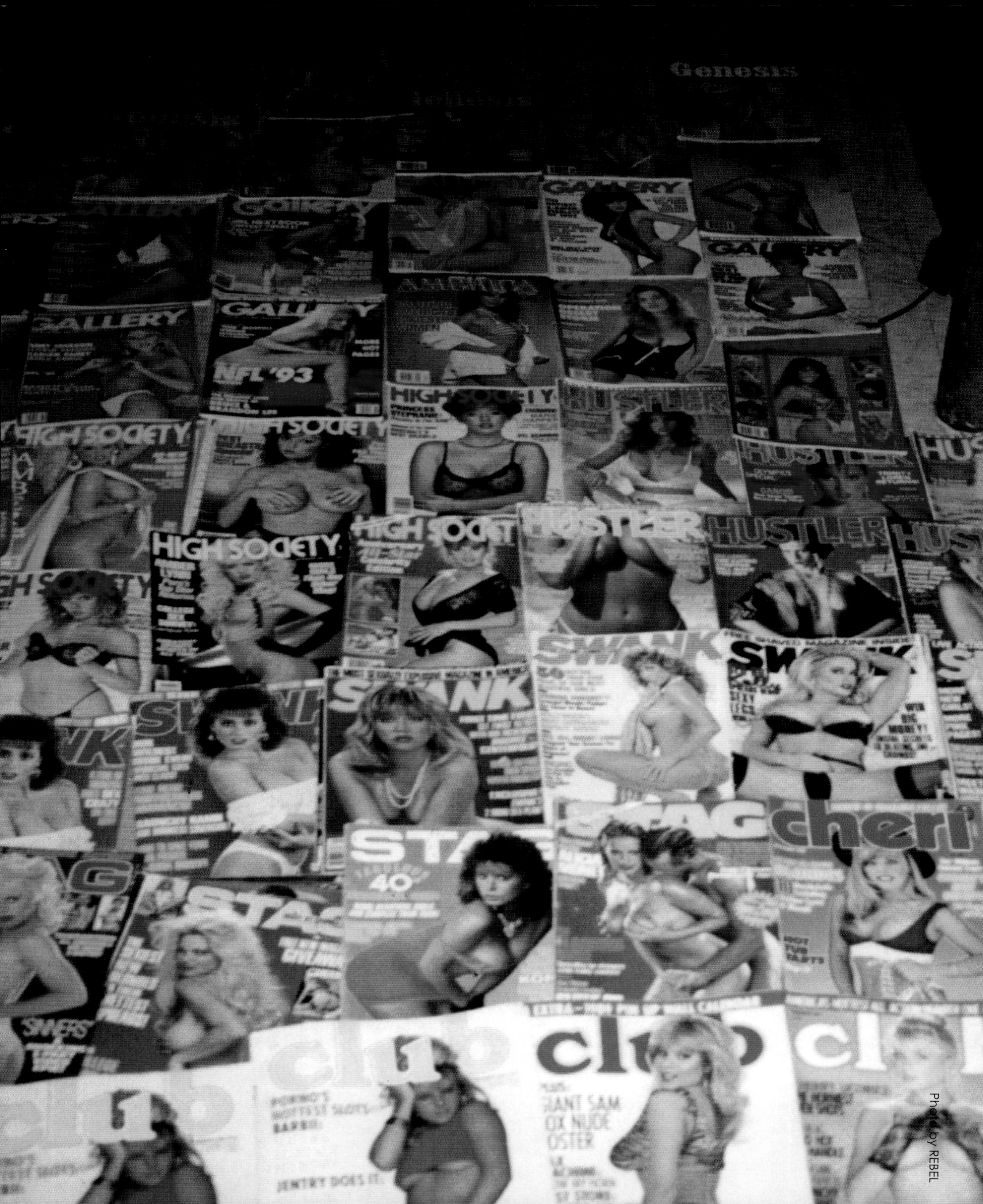

Photo by REBEL

DEAR MR. EDITOR

My dad was the quarterback at Yale for two of their best seasons, and he always gives me a hard time about not playing football. He was a legend at Yale. Dude, I hate football! And he thinks I'm gay, too. I've said to him that I'm not gay, but he doesn't respond when I tell him. What should I do to prove to my dad I'm not gay? And how should I try to make him proud?

Sincerely,
Richard
Hyattsville, MD

It sounds like you have the same problem that our intern has. We'll give you the same answer that we gave Andrew: You need to stop blowing kisses to the coach and concentrate more on your cheerleading.

Yo,
WYWS is a fresh mag. It's one of the few that I buy. But I gotta comment on your interviews—get serious! The best part of reading mags is opinions on style, bombing, legal walls, etc. Hey I gotta admit, your interviews are funny as shit, especially the Canadian one! Just an opinion.

Gray

We are working on an article of big-time writers and their favorite recipes. Who cares about opinions of graffiti when you could have a new pot roast recipe!

Dear *WYWS*,
I was thinking about mashed potatoes the other day while I was checking out the last issue. Have you guys ever seen that movie *Penitentiary 2*?

Man, there's this one scene where the bad guy, his name is Half Dead, slaps this bitch he's chillin' with and then she pulls out a straight razor and Half Dead grabs her and throws her down on the bed and then slaps her again and asks her if she likes potato salad. Then he takes this bowl of potato salad and dumps it on her face and then starts eating it off her face while he starts kissing her and shit. It was pretty intense.

Keep up the good work!
Peter
Lake Wobegon, MN

I'm assuming that you are telling us this because you wish you are the bitch that Half Dead smacked. It's OK, you can tell us the truth. We're not judgmental (freak).

Yo!
Word. Your zine is da straight up bomb! I been peeping it since day one, fool. I can get down wit all da fresh interviews you got wit all dem writers and shit. I exspecialy like dat shit you do on various rap artists and porn stars. Peep dis. Just last week me and my hommie Curve was checkin out your lastist issue and we came across dat "Klass Act" spread. That shit was the straight up bomb, bee! Yo does that chick take it up da booty hole for real? If so, damn fool!

AVENGE, FHT CREW
Buffalo, NY

Last time I checked, they spoke English in Buffalo, didn't they?

WYWS,
I am a newcomer to the mainstream of destruction. I have been down with this tagbangin' gangster art for four years though by being introduced to it through the gangsta lok DZINE. I was 12 and I sucked. I had heart though (like a mugggg), and I kept vandalizing and being careless about people's property. I am 16 and I am living in poverty with no proper guidance in life and I would like some "wreck" ognishon for my ability to be disrespectful. I have visible examples of my negative-charged energy and I would be happy if they got in your magazine that is ranked way up there with child pornography. I would just like to let all these obnoxious nuckleheadz know that I'm out here.

Peace,
SKETCH
Chicago, IL

I'm glad you look to us for guidance and recognition. We need more kids like you. If Charles Manson had a cult, why can't we? "Break it, fuck it, kill it," a wise man once told me. That wise man also looks like the Predator and likes duct tape a whole lot.

Dear *WYWS*,
Where do you guys find all of the sexy models for your magazine? Do you guys have someone on the payroll who goes out and searches for these lovely ladies or are just the luckiest group of sons of bitches in the world? You would be surprised how many luscious lovelies I see every day. There is this burrito place just down the street from my house and every day I must see a half-dozen top contenders go in there who would be perfect for the job. If you need my services or have the digits of the existing models so I might get some.

Loveless and out of work,
KAGEONE
Houston, Texas

Why do you think we started a magazine? To meet girls, of course. Not that I didn't have a nice supply to begin with. It just gave me an excuse to take pictures of them half naked.

Hey Roger—
Here are a couple of our newer releases. Several of our bands have expressed their reluctance to be in ads/ reviews in zines like yours (brought up after the spacase ad in the porn mag incident) so I'll continue to send those records that the bands are OK with. Hope you are well.
Susan

Revelation Records • P.O. Box 5232 • Huntington Beach, CA 92615-5232
(714) 375-4264 • info@RevHQ.com • www.RevHQ.com

Dear Roger & other *WYWS* criminals,
Hey, ya know what? Out of the sad, tired-ass multitude of graff-oriented mags out there, I enjoy yours the best! At least yours has something to read, and the mindset is correct. The column "Americans I Most Admire" is one of my most favorite sections in ANY periodical. Anyway, DR. REVOLT says you guys are righteous. So here's a little packet for ya. Sorry the quality is kinda lousy. I'm quite busy juggling work, girlfriends, ex-wives, etc.

Peace & Respect,
QUIK, RTW
Netherlands

You sound like a hustler. "Americans I Most Admire" is one of our favorite columns also. Just don't be getting any ideas. You probably already have, and that's why you're living in the Netherlands.

Dearest *While You Were Sleeping*,
Hello! My name is Erin McKinney. I'm writing you today to give you guys props on your mag. I just seen it this February for the first time and got hella hyped! I'm currently locked up in a wack-ass boys camp, but I was wondering if you could possibly hook me up with a copy of your magazine. I thank you very much for your support and hope to hear from you soon.

Thanks!
Erin McKinney
San Leandro, CA

Sorry, no freebies here, Erin. If you're a hardened criminal you should be able to steal a copy. What did your dumbass get caught for anyway? I hope you robbed a gas station. I've always fantasized about putting some panty hose over my head running into the local Exxon and having my way with...

Greetings from the frozen North,
I am writing you guys to inquire if you are interested in some photos of graffiti ice sculptures and tagging on igloos by some crazy young outlaw penguins from Edmonton. Actually, Edmonton's graffiti scene is booming. We even recently had some wack church group declare graffiti "detrimental" to our community and they rollered the only legal wall here. They said they will keep going over any graff, "good or bad," until the writers get tired of it. Well, that sounds like a challenge, so we are going to increase our efforts, of course, but most writers are getting up on trains and walls elsewhere anyways. Like STAGE said in issue 6's "Dear Mr. Editor" page, freight yards here are pretty low security so the scene is getting bigger. I have been writing only for about a year, but have also been taking lots of photos of walls and freights that roll through the yard near where I live. I have just started to get interested in writing for magazines, but have already done stuff for two magazines in Canada (one hip-hop mag from Toronto, and a Calgary-based skate and snowboard mag). I really like what you guys are up to, your mag covers so many interesting topics outside of graffiti. Tell me what sort of stuff you are interested in, and I will get back to you. Maybe I can send you one of our fresh Canadian beavers.

Peace,
Keith Allred

What is it with you damn Canadians and beavers? So it's your national animal. Get over it already. The only kind of beaver I want to hear about is shaved and in between a young lady's legs.

Roger,
Hi. I phoned you once but you were at some porn convention in Vegas. I was stuck in Bethesda. Whatever. I moved from Vancouver back to Montreal. Montreal is fucked. Stupid French. I like the new *WYWS*. I like less graffiti. Graffiti artists are like wrestling fans, white trash geek motherfuckers. Here's a few photographs. I finally got caught this week. And hopefully will be going to jail. 'Cause I paint trains. Fell off a train and busted my head open last week. Graffiti is all the same.

Even though Maryland is some strange strip-mall highway, you come off. It makes me happy. Come to Montreal. Topless car washes. French people are strange. Winter sucks. Highest HIV among women in North America. Graffiti artists complain about each other. It is the only fucking province where you can buy beer and wine at corner stores. In the rest of Canada you have to go to liquor stores. But who fucking cares? Keep it fake.

OTHER ONE
Montreal Canada
P.S. Come visit, we'll break things.

P.P.S. Let me work for you. Send me to the worst white trash ghetto trailer park in the States. I want to photograph them. I want to interview inbreds. Travel by Greyhound, of course. Where is the worst white trash trailer park? Florida?

I remember this phone call. I was on assignment at the Bunny Ranch. You were staying with this very attractive girl that I went to high school with. The real question is, did she get fat in the three years since I have seen her, and what have you touched?

Dear *While You Were Sleeping*,
I think you guys are awesome, the flix is alwayz off the hook, and the words is mad funny too. But yo, can you hook me up with some of them cover girls, cuz I am so tired of meetin' these fucked up bitches on the inter-web and shit. Yo, check this, I met this honey at Fatburger on Vermont Ave. and she musta been like 250 pound, not fat though, she was just big as shit, like 6'8 and diesel. I was scared that she was gonna break me ass in half if we got to fuckin'. So get me them digits of that girlie with all the fly tattoos so I can whips out the Whitesnake and get down on that shit, nigga!

Sincerely,
Jeremy Elyisson, age 12

Are you trying to impress us with your age Jeremy? It ain't gona work. If you could get with any of the lovely ladies featured in our mag I would be very impressed. Learn to spell first and maybe lie about your age at least. So far the only thing you have going for you is the Whitesnake.

Dear *While You Were Sleeping*,
Recently my 23rd birthday passed. I suppose my life is lame 'cause that is what I am led to think. Nothing really has changed since, well, seventh grade? I still have the same general interest. I listen to the same music. I do the same dumb stuff. At night I sneak out and spray graffiti on the Blue Line and the highway. While everyone else my age seems to be at home with their wives. Sure, I have kept and moved all my interest up a level in life but people tell me I still need to grow up. Mostly, what I want to know is who is in the wrong here—me or them? Them representing the people in high school that have put everything behind them to pursue an adult life, or myself that has brought everything along with me in growing, not necessarily growing up.

PS. I have one more dilemma, when you're 23 years old and straight edge, what is a good way to meet girls? I feel like a pervert for looking at 17-year-old girls in the mall, but girls my age seem to just hang out in bars, and girls from AOL just rob you and steal your computer. Please help!

Jose Phaeo

The story of my freaking life with one exception: I am still getting the 17-year-olds and don't feel like a pervert even one bit.

Hey,
I love the new perverted, buttrock, graff mag. I will send more shit soon. I'm trying to get some nasty pictures to you guys. Maybe I can get some high school girls to let me take pictures of them pissing on my face. Would you like that? I would. I'm going to go now.

Eliot
Tacoma, WA

My late friend Patrick got very drunk one night after a nice young lady with very large bosoms had taken him to her junior prom. She passed out drunk in a dark corner of the porch where the after party was being held. Patrick decided he needed to urinate. He stumbled over to that very same corner. You know the rest of the story.

Dear *WYWS*,
Your magazine sucks. There are no write-ups on female taggers, all the women are half naked and your childish writers make me want to barf with all the stupid shit they pull. You idiots are the ultimate toys, trying to be cool and down, meanwhile you spend all your time jacking off to porno and asking your mothers for money. It's about time females get the respect they deserve in this graffiti game, and I mean writers besides BARBARA and EVA, LADY PINK and QUEEN B. Where are the flix of all the TAMP-ONE pieces and PMS krew top-to-bottoms I sent you? What about it, punk? Eat me raw you bunch of faggots.

PANTY of the J-CREW
Los Angeles, CA

Test tube baby!

Hey Roger,
So, I get my *WYWS* 6 in the mail today. As always, I sat down and rolled me a joint on the cover of it and I have to say, for all you j-rollers out there, it's grade A+ to roll on!

Sagent the German
Cincinnati, Ohio

Sagent,
I also like to use the mag for purposes other than reading. Here are some of the many things you can try with your very own copy of *WYWS*:
1. Start forest fires.
2. Eat it as a light snack (sprinkle lightly with salt).
3. Create elaborate dioramas and origami swans.
4. Pretend it's your magazine and pick up hookers and high school girls. ("Hey, do you want to be in my magazine? I'll make you famous! Just take off your clothes.")
5. Use it as toilet paper.

Yo Roger, what's up
This is NEWA out here in the corn-fed, inbred Midwest. Sorry it took so long to send you some shit, the last package I was going to send kinda sucked, so wanted to wait till I had some more new shit to send. Hope you enjoy.

If you ever feel like dropping some shit out in KC let me know. I got a nice, big house, full of paint and a lot of get-over walls and trains. I'm supposed to be doing some large-ass gallery with all fake billboards and fake advertisements and shit coming this spring. Maybe I can steal you guys some plane tickets. Increase the peace...

Oh yeah, there's a video in here of me on the news. If there is not, I was too lazy to copy it.

NEWA
Blue Springs, MO

You lazy, fat fuck, of course you didn't copy the video. You were probably too busy watching reruns of *Good Times* and eating Ding-Dongs. There is only one way to redeem yourself: Fuck stealing us a plane ticket, we want the whole goddamn plane!

Why Canadians Hate You:
I was in Vancouver the other day, and your shit is like $7.50 there. I would hate you too.

And when we said that Canada is America's retarded cousin they didn't believe us...

Let's see some more of those road kill pictures! That stuff turns my old lady on!

Nate Franklin
Dallas, TX

There's really nothing I can say to this except "Wow!"

WYWS,
Look at this photo. I took her out for dinner and a movie! Those lips are better than they look. Word!

Jester
CA

And people thought I had problems.

WYWS,
I read the article on "21 Shots to Manhood," and thought that is the best way to spend your 21st birthday. So me being the poor fucking loser I am, I would like to spend my 21st b-day party with the staff of *WYWS*. So what do you say? I might even let you guys pay for my flight to Maryland. Write back and let me know soon as to what kind of things you will have lined up for me when I get there. I'll do anything. I have lots of graff pics. Since you sorry fucks have obviously made it big, I have no doubt that you can afford it so send me a plane ticket (first class preferably), I'll come up there and we can celebrate in style. Tell Tammy and Shiloh I've got some good ol' fashioned Texas jack sauce for em' and that honey on the cover of the most recent issue.

MIKRO

The *While You Were Sleeping* jet is on the way. Please hold your breath.

Hey *WYWS,*
Yo, your mag is so awesome. It always has pics of fuckin' chicks. To be honest, I like to jerk off to some of the chicks. That Natalie Raitano broad is just dope. I've jerked it to her shots more then a few times. I just wanted to tell you guys to keep up the good work and I'll keep blowing my load in the name of *While You Were Sleeping*.

Sincerely,

Bobby D
Seal Harbor, ME

You pleasure yourself with pictures of the fine ladies in our mag, huh? Well, we here pleasure ourselves to readers' letters. Readers like you.
WYWS,

You printed my email about why Canadians hate you, which is fine, but you made it look like I am Canadian I am not. I expect a full retraction and for Roger to give me a BJ (and stick his finger in my ass while he's at it).

Finn

So you're not "one of them," you just like blow jobs from guys. Right. Glad you clarified that.

Dear Editor,
I was recently going through my 12-year-old son's room and found a copy of your magazine. To say the least, I was appalled. I asked how he got it and how long he had had it and he replied, "Three months ago, slut." Well, if my memory serves me right, three months ago is when he was charged with molesting the neighbors' 10-year-old daughter, and since then we have had complaints of him busting out windows with slingshots, scratching "my stupid parents" and his nickname "Lil Chubby Chuck Rok," into three of the neighbors' vehicles, and stealing vacuum cleaners. Prior to all this, he was a straight-A student, and I am fully holding your magazine responsible.

Sincerely pissed,
Parent of the once sweet, "Lil Chubby Chuck"

Once again, our intern Andrew is having serious issues he has to deal with at home.

Yo, *WYWS*!
I picked up a mag of yours and love it, but there's one problem: There needs to be more girls and people's sisters getting naked. How about this, I know you get naked chic pics. You should do a certain column that's dedicated to people's naked sisters. Say what's up to Pat the Party Jerk. I am not kissing your ass or anything but I love this mag. Especially, the "Americans I Most Admire." Maybe I will be that American one day, stay tuned.

JR aka Not So Normal
Placenta, CA

You mention "people's sisters." That is a topic that I'm very well-versed on. Specifically little sisters. But the details people don't know would hurt them. So I'll stay quiet. Anyway, to the point. Yes, we receive countless pictures of naked girls that are probably "people's naked sisters." You're right. We need a column dedicated to them. So here is the first. Enjoy:

PEOPLE'S NAKED SISTERS

We want to see your sister! It'd be less creepy someone else sent the picture in, so do your part b popping flicks of someone else's sis. "Oooh wee oooh!" Those who send in pics receive fun prizes lik caps and stickers, but fame is its own reward.

PEOPLE'S NAKED SISTERS

bet you don't get a lot of letters from teenage girls. So
bet that by me just starting my letter like that you al-
eady have a hard on. Calm down, boys, if I can even
all you scumbags that. I'm not in high school and I'm
bout to turn 20. From the trash you write, I bet that
eans I'm off the market for the staff. Too bad, I have
nice rack, if I say so myself. At the moment I don't
ave a boyfriend and my girlfriends think I'm a tramp
or reading your magazine and sending this picture in.
Il be going off to school in the fall at GW in Washing-
on, D.C. I think that's nearby you all? Maybe I'll look
ou all up. But don't hold your breath.

Kara Mattingly
acksonville, FL

**Don't worry, we'll find you. It's not like we don't know
what you look like. We've got that school on lock.**

Dear *WYWS*,
You know those pink pads that say "While You Were
Out," and they have all those different choices of
what happened. You guys should make ones that
say *While You Were Sleeping*, and they'll say shit
like: I farted in your face, I fucked your girlfriend, we
drank your booze, the Yankees won the World Series, your momma called and we were talkin' dirty,
you took a piss, you started crying etc., etc.

Just an idea,
NDM
Los Angeles

Funny you mention that. They're at the printer right now.

WYWS,
Here's some flix. Compliments on the freshest mag
out there. I don't know how you got my Ritalin-
needing ass to read a whole magazine cover to
cover, but you pulled it off. I read a lot of issue six on
the Greyhound. Three different articles made me
pop boners and for me to get aroused on the bus is
unusual. Anyways, I was wondering what you guys
do with all those naked flix? What's up with a *WYWS*
porn mag of all them chicks? I wanna see cross-
eyed Japanese girls with markers up their asses and
paint on their titties! And some dominatrix midget
broads with crazy latex outfits on and… well, I could
go on for days. Anyway, the mag is fresh. Keep the
ugly graffiti up (illegal pieces and lotsa throwups
and high-risk shit) and the fancy shit out. The last
thing we need is another production magazine.

Chris Thrust
Los Angeles, CA

I popped a boner reading your letter.

Hey You,
The police in Connecticut are looking for MAGE because when caught catching a tag on a cash register inside an Amoco gas station, he shot the ca-
shier with a Taser gun running on two AA batteries.
There's nothing funnier then seeing a 250-pound
man get an ass kicking by a little punk graffiti writer.
Since then, my friend MAGE went back to New York
City, but not before slapping the enclosed sticker
all over the gas station.

TWOE

**I know this guy who used to tase his girlfriend when
they were fucking. He said the only bad part was
that he felt the tase too.**

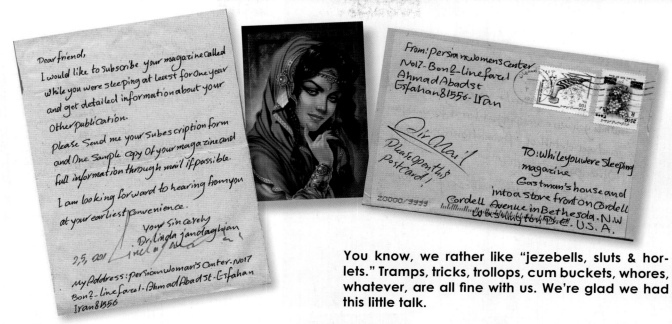

Dear friend,

I would like to subscribe your magazine called while you were sleeping at least for one year and get detailed information about your other publication.

Please send me your subscription form and one sample copy of your magazine and full information through mail if possible.

I am looking forward to hearing from you at your earliest convenience.

Your Sincerely
Dr. Linda Jandaghian

2,5, 2001

My Address: Persian Woman's Center - No 17 - Bon2 - line fare 1 - Ahmad Abad St - Esfahan Iran 81556

From: Persian Womens Center No 17 - Bon 2 - line fare 1 Ahmad Abad st Esfahan 81556 - Iran

Air Mail
Please Print this Post Card!

20000/9999

TO: While you were sleeping magazine Gastman's house and into a store front on Cordell Cordell Avenue in Bethesda N.W. Washington D.C. U.S.A.

You know, we rather like "jezebells, sluts & horlets." Tramps, tricks, trollops, cum buckets, whores, whatever, are all fine with us. We're glad we had this little talk.

Dear Perverts,

I hope you read this letta'. I'm a graph artist and have been for 10 years. I know that hip-hop is screwed up enough with drugz, alcohol and perversion. That's why I'm writing this letta'. I like your mag. You have a lot of fresh productions and graph, but you need to quit puttin' your perverted ads that I tear out when I get the mag. You need to repent of perversion. I would send you some flicks of my stuff but you probably would not put them in because they are Christ-centered. Hip-hop is about positivity, not supporting smut. I will keep anonymous because I think it will be the best thing to do as of now. There are good moral hip-hop headz in this such as HEX. One of the dopest in L.A. If you keep putting these flicks of jezebells, sluts and horlets, I will send you anotha' letta' with my work. Your foul ways need to be exposed. Your a rotten sinner who needs Jesus. Repent now before you look like an idiot on judgment day. The bible says, "Know the truth and the truth will set you free." Its obvious you need to be set free from pornography. I hope you print this in your mag instead of doing wasteful interviews with sinners like you talking about stupid crap. Why don't you print something interesting? You want to do a real interview, interview me. I'll tell you what time it is. Obviously you won't because you're scared of the truth. I use hip-hop as a tool to tell others about Christ. Like you it is pretty frank that you need to except Jesus. He died on the cross for those sins you do know. He didn't die so you could be wasting your time collecting pictures of jezebells. He wants to know you. I'm doing this because it needed to be done.

Sincerely,
Anonymous

P.S. Keep putting trash in the mag, and the name will be filled in the next letta'.

Dear *WYWS*,

My friend just did the coolest thing for my birthday and I wanted to let you guys know about it because I thought you might like it. I've been writing and hitting up parts of Northern Baltimore for a few years and I love your mag. Anyway, my best friend paid a prostitute to fuck me 'cause I'm still in high school, and was still a virgin. But that's not the best part: He paid her to pick me up from school in her 1988 Camaro! Yo, it was fucking amazing! I came out of school and she was right in front in this mini skirt and tube top looking hot as shit standing in front of her car. It was so cool leaving school with this older hot chick and everyone saw! The next day, everyone was like, "Yo, who was that hot mama who picked you up yesterday?" Anyway, that's it. I felt so much better than all those other high school fucks. Hope you dudes enjoy!

Kyle Samson
Baltimore, MD

I have a hard-on thinking about it. You lucky little fuck.

Dear *WYWS*,

Hey, you guys seem to be into the younger chicks, so I wanted to ask you guys if you think I should hit this cute little girl who is a freshman in high school right now. I'm back from college and I'm 20. The holiday break is a good time to catch up with friends and have some fun, but do you guys think she's too young?

J-Train
Pittsburgh, PA

Barring hospitalization or natural disaster, we are home at 3:15 every day to watch the seventh grader across the street get off the school bus. Does that answer your question?

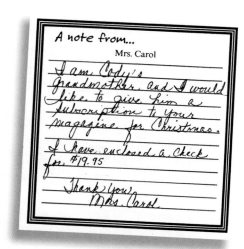

A note from...
Mrs. Carol

I am Cody's grandmother and I would like to give him a subscription to your magazine for Christmas. I have enclosed a check for $19.95

Thank you,
Mrs. Carol

Dearest *WYWS*,

OK, I finally got off my lazy ass to write you maggots. I write this letter in peace with some constructive criticism. I am just a lowlife bum that doesn't do anything, but live at home with my parents, do graffiti, and try and make it to class on time to get a fucking clue about some shit. Now, as I have recently discovered, you barnacle bobcat, bee-bee shooting midget pokers have changed your motto to "Live the Life." My opinion on this is that "Perversion, Art and Noise" is where it's at. But hey, fuck me with a sideways telephone pole, I don't write your goddamn magazine. I just think you could have came up with something a bit more creative. But I do think it is about time that some twisted fucks with half a brain decided to exercise the right to freedom of press, and speech, in order to entertain a bunch of degenerates like myself. Not to mention that your interviewees are well chosen, as well as your questions in the past mags. But I got issue nine about two weeks ago and I did not laugh as hard as I did before. Come on guys, I want to see some good damn interviews and stories about some gut-busting shit. Get off your lazy asses, beat someone up, eat a cat, tag a bridge, and choke a 12-year-old. I want to see an article on ALF the cat-eating alien. He's a funny-ass fucker, so will you do that favor you ass ticklers and write about my furry friend?

Mike

I'm sorry to report that ALF has turned down several of our interview requests. We have been given no explanation by his people. Don't worry my Melmacian friend, we will keep at it.

Yo *WYWS*!

I first started eating bark when I was about 7 or 8. I used to play in the swamp behind my house. Mostly I just dug holes. My friend and I also made traps for other kids and my parents. Then one day I tried my first bark. It was not all that special. Nevertheless, I continued to eat bark. Then I found weed. My first joint was rolled in college-rule notebook paper. Not that special. Now I smoke every day. It eases my pain. I see lots of gray spots or floaters from the acid and mushrooms. I used to smell, smoke and eat painkillers all day. Now I just smoke pot and masturbate with sandpaper. I don't really use sandpaper. That was meant to be funny. You fellows seem to enjoy publishing slightly demented views voiced by angst-ridden teens, so I thought the whole sandpaper thing would be appropriate. The last time I really used sandpaper I was in shop class and I was making this clock. The clock was in the shape of the letters H-O-T and I used a bit of fire engine red glaze to make it flaming red. I am a genius. For a while, I had all my fingernails about two inches long. I guess this was so that other people would know that I was cool and liked to stuff barbiturates up my nose. I had to cut the nails because I mauled my ex-girlfriend's private area. I also tore a muscle in her ass but that has nothing to do with fingernails. I wrote a college essay about me fornicating with farm animals and I got accepted. I also got rejected by a lot of schools. Now I go to college and I smoke pot all day. Actually, I still have trouble rolling a joint and I have been trying for 10 years. Everything in this letter is fact, with the exception of the sandpaper and penis interlude. I would like you to hire me as a freelance writer. Here is my offer: If you publish me, I will allow you to give my mother a jelly donut. I take it for granted that you young scouts are well versed in the execution of jelly donuts.

Brendan Fagan

Are you sure it was your girlfriend's ass muscle you ripped? I bet it was your mother's. Kids and their jelly donuts.

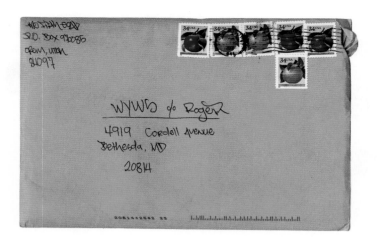

Dear Lauren,
Florida was fun, except for the lack of hot girls. I need to go back in winter, maybe more girls will be there. I've enclosed some flicks for you. If you like them, show them to Roger and maybe he'll throw them in. I'm looking forward to *Bedtime Stories* part two—part one kills! I laughed so hard I thought I was going to die. The Chevy footage made it gold. Nice job!

Sincerely,
Aaron Gombar

P.S. Are you hot? You sound cute over the phone and I'm sure *WYWS* wouldn't hire old, fat, wrinkled whores that wear thongs on Delray Beach and make me sick!

I'm 17 years old. I weigh 109 pounds. A lot of people tell me my boobs are "perky." I wish they would stop staring at them. Well, I guess I prefer they stare at them then grab my ass. Let me know if you are ever in the area. We could go out. – Lauren

Hey Roger,
Hey, Sugar Plums, how ya'll be? Anyone get laid lately? Preferably 12-year-olds or dead people. So yeah, I write, been out of it for awhile, got busted, since been a pussy, that or too busy gettin' pussy. But anyhootin'-holla, is yer new flik gimp or does it as I expect kick some major 65-year-old granny ass? Damn, I promised myself I wouldn't say this, but mad fuckin' props to yer mag, nah, fuck that, I'll show ya'll real respect. You all be a bunch of fucked up fuck-ups. You fuckin' combine everything wonderful and put it in one lil mag. All the great stories from Pat the Party Jerk, all the great interviews, ya'll really hit the shit that makes me feel all funny just talkin' bout how I like what ya write. Sure, maybe some say lay off the crack, but fuck it! Yeah, but I've said what I'm about, peace muthafuckers, I'm out.

Timmy "The Mutha Fuckin' Duck"

Have we been getting laid by 12-year-olds and dead people? What a stupid fucking question. Try 11! And as always, we've been diggin' up the graves to get the "goods."

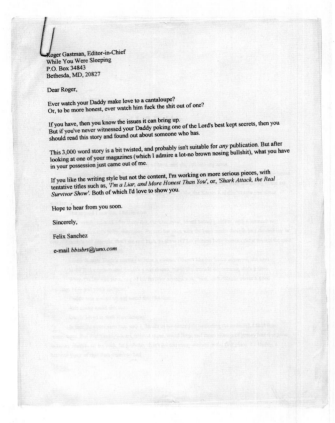

Dear *WYWS*,

All I have to say is, double farts. Getting busted for graff really sucks. Getting busted for graff and being patted down sucks even more. Getting busted for graff and patted down by an undercover DT sucks Big Poppa's big, black left tit. Getting busted for graff and patted down by an undercover DT dressed-up like a rabbi in one of the most bombed white neighborhoods in Brooklyn is 100-percent turds. But it happened to me, 10 years ago. After catching tags on the Avenue O and 16th Street underpass in Brooklyn around 1991, a big, fat Mendel rolls out of a Crown-Vic fuckin' station wagon. At first, I was expecting to hear, "Oi." But instead, we heard "Up against the wall." So Officer Gefilte whips out the badge, spreads us out, dips into my friend's Eastpak, pulls out a can of paint and says, "Can I have half a pound of chopped liver?" Just kidding. He says, "Turn around slowly." Believe me, I always thought the best way to turn a white kid into a black kid was letting him hang around shopping malls in Minnesota and listen to Rappin 4-Tay. But this guy [had a different idea and was] spewing Ultra Flat Black all over out faces, up our noses, on our clothes, sneakers, whatever. You know how you always say how great the smell of Ultra Flat Black is? Well, fuck Ultra Flat Black. I still can't get that smell out of my nose and I'm fuckin' 25. There is a bright side to the story. My friend was flapping about how ill his new Bulls Starter Jacket was before we went bombing and him and his jacket got served with paint. So today's lesson should be taken seriously. All you clowns out there wearing $150 Jordans and your favorite North Face jacket while bombing are playing with loaded guns. I learned my lesson the hard way. That is why I always go bombing in shit-stained underwear, a pair of 1986 New Balance sneakers, and a hat that says, "Shove Work, Go Fishing."

NSONE TOK, Brooklyn

The "rabbi" should have shaved your heads and spray painted yamika's on your sorry asses.

Hey Jerkoffs,
Here is a picture I had lying around, you sick fucks. It's my buddy getting a beer enema.

Jantzen
Talent, OR

You're almost a genius! But that's such a waste of beer. You could be getting the 12-year-old neighborhood girl drunk with that.

Hello all you nymphos!
I'm writing to fulfill your deepest, darkest fantasies that your mate may not think is sane! Check this, I always wanted these bangin' hoes to pee on me, but they would run at the thought. Now I ask them to pee in a 7UP bottle for me so I can pass my probation. Then I masturbate with it, drink it, or pour it on myself. I also like defecation sex. If the chick ain't with it, purchase Taco Bell, bring her into the shitter, wait about 35 seconds and say, "Oh, don't flush, you'll flood the bathroom," and her shit is yours! Got a foot fetish? Apply at Lady Foot Locker. When the nasty slobs need help, play the cut. Try shoving two Pilots in a girls anus! There is this stupid young chick-enhead around my way that wanted to get down with our crew and go out tagging. We all cummed in two Pepsi bottles for months till it was globs of cum and made her down it all. She gagged but did it. Till this day she ain't down! (Sorry PAWS.) I got the illest bootleg pics of a threeway orgy involving Jennifer Lopez and anal sex! A must-see! In conclusion, sexual exploration must really pick up. It's too damn boring. More anal, more defecation, more toe sucking, more orgies, more bisexual teenage girls taking it with no tears. More nastiness. Incorporate graff into sex. Oh yeah, I'm incarcerated for trying to destroy some herb ass toys from Jersey (MHS) that ratted me out for bombing!

Peace and love,
DESK
Adult Correctional Center, New Brunswick, NJ

You like experimentation, huh? I hope you like the experimentation your ass gets in prison fuck face.

PEOPLE'S NAKED SISTERS

Hey Roger,
My name is Daniel and I sent you pics in trade for other pics. But you didn't send me nothin'. I sent you naked pics of my sis and they were good pics. Well, here's the deal, I want pics—young girls. In the future, maybe can buy pics from you. And just to let you know, you are my supplier for caps. You're the cheapest!

Peace!
Daniel
Honolulu, HI

**Daniel,
We enjoyed your pictures, but we have to doubt they are your sister. If they are, you are truly a very sick fuck and we congratulate you. Though we hope you are practicing safe sex because the world definitely does not need more little Dannys running around. As far as buying pictures of young girls from us, we don't have any for sale. Remember, 18 is the legal age for nudie flicks. We don't want you writing us your next letter from jail. I suggest Hustler's Barely Legal.**

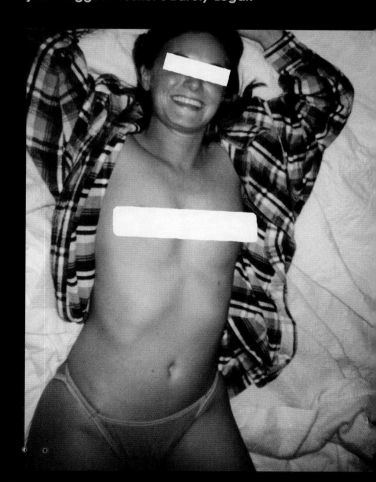

PEOPLE'S NAKED SISTERS

Dear Roger,
This is a letter written out of gratitude. From the cocaine scars in the deepest corner of my heart, thank you. Thank you for combining my favorite things in life and laying them out into one magazine. I am committed to doing all that I can to ensure that this publication of substance and vision survives the great American cultural void. I have paid for this year's subscription out of a sense of duty and I have urged those whose lives are complemented and enhanced by your magazine to do the same. Unfortunately, we live in a time and place where many people are not only unappreciative of your magazine but deeply afraid of, and threatened by, the information and images that are nicely laid out for the reader's enjoyment. These people are in fact herd animals who live by the words of people like Oprah Winfrey and spend their time degrading themselves in an attempt to resemble the people they admire on television. I want your readers to realize the importance of supporting your magazine while it's still alive and kicking people in the face. It would be a shame if one day you awoke to realize that while you were sleeping this magazine had to close up shop. Shout out to General Gau and his crispy chicken.

Matt

I think I love you.

Dear *WYWS*,

Hey, I just want to ask what's up with all the red and demon-looking stuff on the stickers. Is that supposed to be a symbolic sort of thing? Or you all are obsessed with the color red, devils and stuff? Also how the hell do ya'll get those fine-ass chicks to pose for ya'll magazine? Were they drunk or something? Yummy!

Menace4Art

We are, indeed, obsessed with devils, but most of them are dressed in cheerleaders' outfits.

While You Were Sleeping,

I have mixed feelings about your mag. Sometimes you have great articles: the ZEPHYR interview of the female writers in NYC, DAZE'S Martin Wong piece, etc. Then you have "Americans I Most Admire." I don't know if it's supposed to be ironic. I guess if the section was called "Sick, Sad Fucks" I could hang with it more. It's easy to be creepy, cruel and insane. Regardless, I bought the current issue.

Regards,
Change

If you keep buying this crap, we'll keep shitting it out.

Dear Assfucks,

I like your minds. Crazy as hell. I've probably read the last five issues 10 times each. I keep 'em at the tattoo shop and most of my customers have something bad to say about you guys being all messed up (this is a good thing, some people shouldn't understand). Now I have to say you guys are seriously lost. Naked chicks are great, graffiti is good too. Older women, young chicks and beer—all cool by me. But the "Americans I Most Admire" article on Baniszewski is seriously wack. What would make you think it's cool to portray beating and killing kids as being admirable? At some point, you should realize that selling out for an entertaining article simply makes you another gluttonous American. Wake the fuck up. Maybe you guys could focus on the positive side of life: naked chicks and booze!

Viamor

For every bad thing we do, we counteract it with something positive. Because of your letter, we started *While You Were Sleeping* bible study. Stop on by and give us a chance to redeem ourselves in the name of the Lord.

Zephyr *Exakto*

Philly

While You Were Sleeping...

Tyke • Jase • SMK • Cool Disco Dan • Wet Dream Team • Music & Much More!

WHILE YOU WERE SLEEPING

#3

While You Were Sleeping...

Issue 1
Summer 1997

Transcendead

WHILE YOU WERE SLEEPING

graffiti • killers • girls • perversion • noise

mardi gras, giant,
ever, canadians,
shepard fairey,
ron jeremy

Issue Number 4 • $5

WHILE YOU WERE SLEEPING

PERVERSION • ART • NOISE

while you
were sleeping

NIKKI SIXX
join the crue
ALISHA KLASS
no butts about it
AWR & MSK CREWS
DONDI
rest in peace
GEERTE FRENKEN
axes for breakfast
RAS KASS
uh huh
ASHES
a sixteen year old girl with a shotgun

BIRTHDAY PARTY TIPS, NAPALM STEW, ARMAGEDDON,
GREATEST AMERICAN HEROES, BOMBING FATIGUES

WHILE YOU WERE SLEEPING

PERVERSION • ART • NOISE

PETE ROCK
VANILLA ICE
BRADY DUNCAN
ROCKSTAR GAMES
GRAFFITI STUDIO 1980
SMALLY PAULIE
FRANK KOZIK
RALPH GRACIE
DENNIS HOFF
RISKY
AOK

A

A

We Missed The Bus

Innocence Can Be Sexy

"Give The Dog a Bone"

"IF THERE'S GRASS ON THE FIELD, PLAY BALL."

"YOUR MOM'S FAVORITE M

" INCLUDING: FREE PIZZA! "

MOM, NO HANDS!"

WORKING MAN'S DIGEST

WHILE YOU WERE SLEEPING

PERVERSION • ART • NOISE

GRIME
JANINE
MISFITS
IZ, THE WIZ
LUNACHICKS
RON ENGLISH
VAUGHN BODE
JULIE BENZ

ISSUE #7 $4.49 US / $7.75 CANADA

WHILE YOU WERE SLEEPING

LIVE THE LIFE 2000

Danzig
the last laugh

Mark Bode
re-invents Cheech Wizard

Wild Orchid
the trio starts off right

Rachel True
tells it like it is

John Pound
plays with garbage

Stacey Valentine
erotic bombshell

Kool Keith
the black Elvis

ISSUE #7 $4.49 US / $7.75 CANADA

Repo Men Amusement Park Disasters Morticians Graffiti

WHILE YOU WERE SLEEPING

LIVE THE LIFE

STEFFIANA DELA CRUZ
status quo dismissed

ANDY GORE
death in a snow globe

GARY COLEMAN
a different stroke

Playboy Playmate:
Stacey Fuson

NYC Graffiti Legends:
Quik & Freedom

Kurupt Bounty Hunting Bad Brains Jurassic 5 Richard Simmons Cults

WHILE YOU WERE SLEEPING

LIVE THE LIFE

AMERICAN PIMP
Rosebudd Bitterdose

THE MUSEUM OF DEATH

DEEP FOCUS
Porn: Behind the Scenes

TRIBE
L.A.'s Hottest Female Writer

NATALIE RAITANO
VIP's Resident Firecracker

ISSUE #10 $4.98 US / $7.30 CANADA

WC 7 00
333 $$4.98

BETTER THAN CHOCOLATE

PLUS BODE COMICS • THE BOSSTONES • DEL • TATTOOS • MELRODE LARRY
DWARVES • ROLLINS • PAUL BARMAN • GRAFFITI • SPACEMONKIES

WHILE YOU WERE SLEEPING

LIVE THE LIFE

BEHIND BARS
An Insiders Guide to Prison Life & Crime

FIGHT CLUB
Real Wrestling Real Blood

RON JEREMY
Dressed to Spill

STAY HIGH 149
NYC Graffiti King Returns After 20 Years

'NSYNC
Tattoo Artist Speaks Out

JILL RITCHIE
Ripe & Ready

PLUS HIGH SCHOOL CHEERLEADERS • BRAWLIN' BROADS • JIM ROSE • AFI
ALICIA WITT • SETH ENSLOW • BIG L INTERVIEW • MUGGS & ALCHEMIST

WHILE YOU WERE SLEEPING

LIVE THE LIFE

ALL EXCLUSIVE

IAN MACKAYE
Punk Rock Hero

ROAD KILL
Hit & Run Art

NY'S SEXY
Spray Can Divas

ALIENS
The Truth About Little Green People

Chris Nieratko gets down and dirty with Popular's

TAMMY LYNN MICHAELS

PLUS MOTORHEAD • SASCHA KNOPF • BLACK DAHLIA • PLEASANT GEHMAN
MARTIN WONG • SEANCES • TRASH FETISHES • DAN THE AUTOMATOR • WILLIE D
MEXICAN DEATH MAGAZINES • FEMALE WRESTLERS • OBITUARIES • DAVE WAUGH

"SORRY TO SAY BUT XXXXX REJECTED *WHILE YOU WERE SLEEPING FOR THE FOLLOWING REASONS: ANIMALS HAVING SEX, UNDERAGE CHILDREN TOUCHING EACH OTHER, NUDITY AND ARTICLE CAPTIONS USING THE F WORD."*

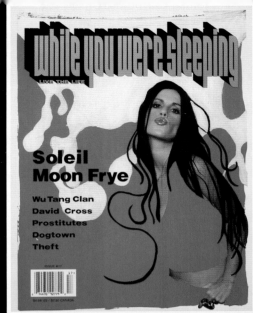

while you were sleeping
LIVE THE LIFE

Carmen Electra
#1 Ex-Girlfriend

De La Soul
Mark Mothersbaugh
Jaime Pressly
Popstars

while you were sleeping
LIVE THE LIFE

Soleil Moon Frye

Wu Tang Clan
David Cross
Prostitutes
Dogtown
Theft

WYWS
WHILE YOU WERE SLEEPING

The Fake

Puffy AmiYumi • Moby • Joe Rogan
• Stephen Powers • Gang Starr •
Summer Fashion • Gene Simmons •
Afrika Bambaataa • Mötley Crüe

Issue # 18

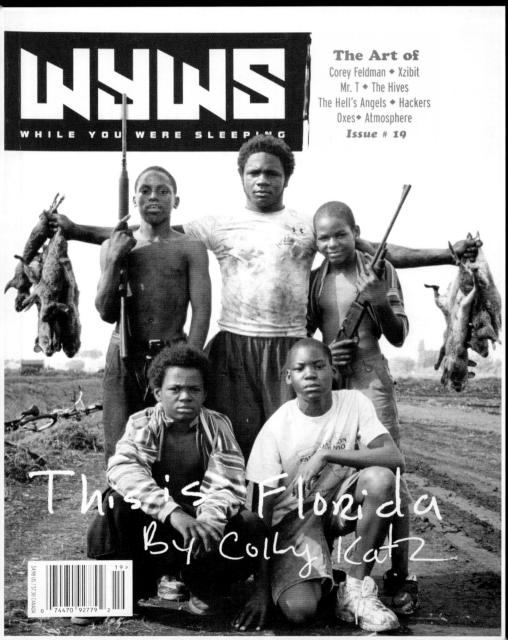

WYWS
WHILE YOU WERE SLEEPING

The Art of
Corey Feldman ✦ Xzibit
Mr. T ✦ The Hives
The Hell's Angels ✦ Hackers
Oxes ✦ Atmosphere
Issue # 19

This is Florida
By Colby Katz

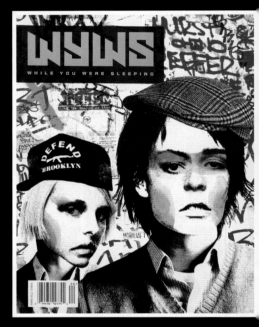

WYWS
WHILE YOU WERE SLEEPING

"THANK YOU ALL WHO ARE READING THIS FOR PAYING THE $4.98 ADMIS-SION TO MY LIFE. HAVE FUN, AND REMEMBER, USE PROTECTION."

WYWS

ISSUE #20

WYWS ISSUE #19

WYWS ISSUE #18

while you were sleeping

while you were sleeping

while you were sleeping

while you were sleeping

while you were sleeping

WYWS ISSUE#9

while you were sleeping

WHILE YOU WERE SLEEPING

WHILE YOU WERE SLEEPING

WHILE YOU WERE SLEEPING

WHILE YOU WERE SLEEPING

ART • PERVERSION • NOISE

WHILE YOU WERE SLEEPING

ISSUE #6 • $5

ISSUE #20

ISSUE #19

ISSUE #18

ISSUE #17 • $4.98 US / $7.30 CANADA

ISSUE #16 • $4.98 US / $7.30 CANADA

ISSUE #15 • $4.98 US / $7.30 CANADA

ISSUE #14 • $4.98 US / $7.30 CANADA

ISSUE #13 • $4.98 US / $7.30 CANADA

ISSUE #12 • $4.98 US / $7.30 CANADA

ISSUE #11 • $4.98 US / $7.30 CANADA

ISSUE #10

ISSUE #9 $4.98 US/$7.30 CANADA

ISSUE #8 • $4.98 US / $7.30 CANADA

ISSUE #7 • $4.99 US / $7.25 CANADA

"LOOK MOM, NO HANDS

"NOW INCLUDI

WORKIN

"YOUR M

"IF THERE'S G

INTRODUCTIONS

PETE ROCK
VANILLA ICE
BRADY DUNCAN
ROCKSTAR GAMES
GRAFFITI STUDIO 1980
SMALLY PAULIE
FRANK KOZIK
RALPH GRACIE
DENNIS HOFF
RISKY
AOK

I f any of you spent real time with Roger [left] and I [right], you'd know that *WYWS* was more a traveling three-ring circus of freaks than it was a magazine. (Notice the smoking midgetous clown between us.) The pages were merely the document of this sick world of cretans—ourselves included.

Would you punch an alien? Ever had a milkshake on a plate? Every day, I saw something new while doing this magazine, and it was all because of our ringmaster, Roger Gastman. If your dad met Roger, he'd call him a "character." But if you're a teenage girl, your dad knows to just call the cops. He's a total fucking freak, and adventure is always on his tail. Who would have thought that suburban Bethesda, Maryland, could make such a crew of basket cases like Roger and his friends? In my time visiting there, I saw Pat (the party jerk) romance a 300-pound cheerleader, random yuppie girls tried to initiate orgies with us, I spent hours in awe of all the damn mail we got, I even got a contusion in my second vertebrae while playing miniature golf with a couple underage girls. This could only happen in Bethesda when you were with Mr. Roger Gastman.

I think there's a saying about the company a person keeps. Associating with any of the people in this magazine could surely leave you with a nasty case of the something gross. Luckily, we escaped the above and continued to do our thing. The moral of the story is: Make your life the circus that ours has been, and start your own stupid magazine so I can take a nap.

—*John LaCroix, co-editor*

Originally printed in WYWS Issue #6

S o you just got your new copy of *WYWS*, probably skimmed through it, saw some pictures of girls too sexy for you to ever talk to in real life, and maybe even checked out an article or two. Now you wanted to start at page one in order to glean every bit of enlightening, life-enriching informative literature in this publication. As I'm sure you can tell, putting this thing together took more than one guy with photos running down to Kinko's for 20 minutes. A lot of time, money and man-hours go into bringing you things that most other magazines just don't offer.

WYWS is truly one man's brainchild. This is the man who loses more sleep than any other in his never-ending quest to make the perfect magazine, the man who day and night, pours his heart and soul into communicating and expressing his values and the things that he truly strands for. This man is, and could only be, Roger.

I feel like I know Roger as well as anyone. We met in sixth grade. I was the fat, awkward kid and he was the fat, weird kid with purple hair. We really didn't become friends until about eighth grade, at which time I was still the awkward kid and he had just begun to wear jester hats (like the one Flava Flav was wearing in Sean Combs' sacrilegious video for Puff 2000, the "Spanish Fly" version), and getting into the destruction of private and public property. Now for most people in eighth grade, you wouldn't ever think of talking to anyone of the opposite sex. But Roger had friends that would fight for him and with lots of planning and ingenuity, he pulled off amazingly successful feats with the ladies.

These are just a very few of the memories that I have from the "good old days," but who needs memories when not much has changed. I'm still the awkward kid and Roger is still having relations with girls whose ages I am scared to even ask, but I fear this is one thing that will be a constant for Roger well into his 60s, if not longer. Unfortunately, I don't live in Bethesda—the Washington, D.C., suburb in which we grew up and where the women are beautiful and life is good—anymore so I don't see Roger as much. But when I want to hear a story about something I wouldn't believe coming from the mouth of anyone else (much of which ends up in this very magazine), or if I just want to hear someone tell me about all of the "exotic women" they are having intercourse with, or even only to be called a "pussy" for having a girlfriend, I know Roger will come through for me. It is also always comforting to know that there is a place with countless stacks of free stuff including clothing, CDs and records that I never knew existed, porn and a malt liquor collection as big as Donald Trump's wine cellar. This place is called, Roger's house.

—*Ian Mazie*

Originally printed in WYWS Issue #7

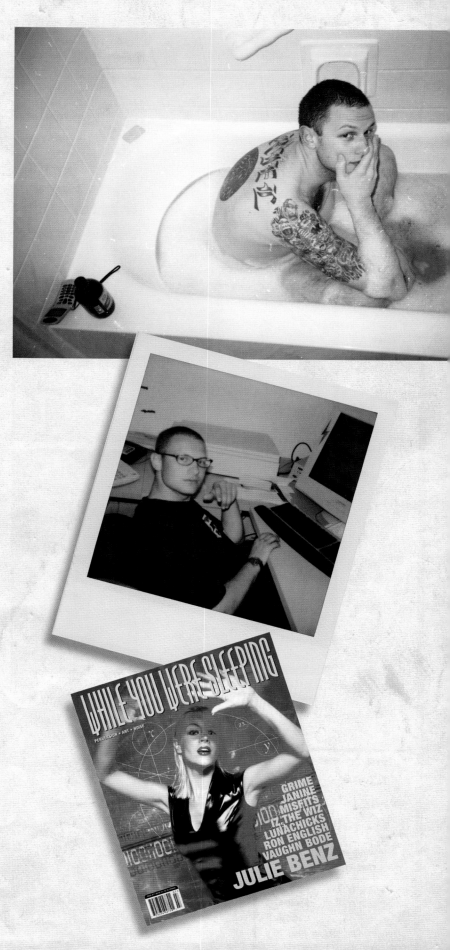

This magazine probably changed people's lives. That's what it did for me. I was spending my days dwelling in College Park, Maryland, going through the mundane routine of attending classes, hitting the local dives, and hooking up with chubby sorority girls (ain't nothing wrong with that), then I realized I had to make a change.

What better way to make that change than by doing something I love, examining our bizarre American culture? So, I somehow managed to simultaneously get credit toward my college degree and do something I love by interning for my good friend, Roger Gastman, a man whom I have yet to confirm is the devil.

I say this not out of fear, but rather due to the fact that he could get me anything I wanted. In the brief amount of time I interned for *While You Were Sleeping*, I became the proud owner of tons of pornography and clothing, and got more sexy girlies' telephone numbers than John Ritter circa *Three's Company*.

While You Were Sleeping was the finest publication you may have never read. So now is your opportunity to take a step into the realm of some seriously altered gentlemen. This is your chance to realize that this world is filled with a ton of nut-jobs, weirdos and artists. Whether they paint a wall, do the nasty on film, hack up almost half of Eastern Europe or publish a dirty lifestyle magazine, their timeless efforts and achievements deserve to be recognized.

—Andrew Black

Originally printed in WYWS Issue #8

I first started "living the life" in eighth grade when Roger, notorious for proclaiming that he was a reincarnated purple cow and his frequent "Soy el taco" outbursts in Spanish class, took me under his wing. Although I never fully accepted his ideology based on the music of the Misfits, Sex Pistols and Gwar, we became best friends.

The crux of *While You Were Sleeping* was Roger, but this magazine was fashioned by all of the people who placed a brick on Roger's own yellow brick road: the women, the younger women, the really young women, the graffiti artists, the frat boys, the brands and anyone who had been kind enough to let Roger sit back and watch them make fools of themselves.

As you flip through the pages of *WYWS*, you will notice that many of the contributors have little in common except for the fact that they like to get drunk and womanize. (Although Roger himself doesn't drink, he was always quick to pitch-in for brew, not for his own consumption, but for the female populace.) But these simplest of life's pleasures in no way brought our social circles together—Roger did. But who would Roger be without us, his most prized possessions? And who would we be without Roger?

For one thing, I would be a whole lot more innocent without Roger (whether that is a good thing or bad thing, I have yet to determine). But I like to take some responsibility for the thing known as Roger (excluding the tattoos, nipple rings and occasional gibberish). The people who have made Roger, Roger, are the same people who made *While You Were Sleeping* a fine, interesting, unique publication. We can be as entertaining as animals having sex, as volatile as Sean Penn (circa the 1980s) and as cute as Webster. Some of us, like me, can even embody all of these personas at the same time. Still, the contributors to *While You Were Sleeping* were clearly the "usual suspects." We are the people who entertain others by sacrificing our dignity, acting foolishly or spending a day with a former pimp or on the set of a porn movie.

I would like to express gratitude to all those contributors I have and haven't met (the West Coast fucks) for making my life more interesting. Without this diverse set of crazed maniacs who provided the unmatched, classy entertainment found in these pages, *While You Were Sleeping* would have been little more than Roger's escapades with young women stuck between pictures of graffiti. Thank you, and keep on "living the life."

—*Trevor Michaels*

Originally printed in WYWS Issue #10

By the time this issue is in your grubby little hands, summer will sadly be over. No more half-naked teenage girls, no more fun in the sun and, for better or worse, the time has finally come for your mother to hang up the thong. The motivated and educated crowd will be back on their respective college campuses, reaping the benefits of actually having attended class in high school.

If I had followed in the path of my peers, I would have recently graduated college and just spent the last carefree summer of my life being as lazy as I could, picking up as many chicks as I could, and just not giving a fuck. Instead, I stopped going to college toward the end of my sophomore year so I could bring you, the readers, this outstanding publication. What thanks do I get for it? Not much. While my friends are out drinking at the bars and picking up on chicks, I'm sitting here at 2:17 a.m., the night before deadline, laying out an articles. If I'm lucky, my roommates might bring some ladies home and I can snatch up their leftovers.

Whoever would have thought I would hit double digits with this sucker? Sure as hell not me. Who would have ever thought that I would get to meet Ron Jeremy? Not once, not twice, but three times (and I think he even remembered me)? Who would have thought that he would be excited about being in this issue? And who could have guessed that he would have something as ridiculous as "you guys are way sicker than me" to say? Well, it's happened.

Welcome to this ongoing circus I call my life. Hell, things could be worse. I could be out there looking for a job right now like most of my friends. I could have "sold out," and moved to work for J-Crew like our very own Pat, the Party Jerk. I could

have had to step in the ring with Incredibly Strange Wrestler the "Poontangler," and had her spray "mother's milk" all over my body—now that I think about it, I might enjoy that.

I can't even count how many times I've been fed up and quit. But who am I kidding? Who quits on himself? Especially when such tasty videos like *Brawlin' Broads* come in the mail. I swear it's important research to sit down for an hour and watch white trash tramp after white trash tramp kick the living crap out of each other. It's all just business.

Most folks don't realize all of the hard work, time and effort it takes to put out a magazine. *WYWS* could go up in flames tomorrow, but I could firmly say that I have learned more about life and the way the world turns during my tenure here than I believe I would have with a four-year college education. Who am I kidding? I didn't miss out one bit by not finishing college. Those girls are way too old for me anyway.

I would like to dedicate this issue to all of the people behind the scenes that help make this happen, and all of the girls who have passed through my bedroom. Whether you want to admit it or not, you know who you are. (Don't come to me saying that baby's mine. Bitch, I don't know you!) And thank you all who are reading this for paying the $4.98 admission to my life. Have fun, and remember, use protection.

—Roger Gastman, Editor in Chief

Originally printed in WYWS Issue #11

Halloween, my favorite holiday, just passed a few weeks ago. What did I do, you ask? I kept it real is what I did. Candy apples with razor blades, candy bars with extra special treats inside—you know the deal. All kidding aside, what I really did was go egging. Some of you are saying to yourself: "You fucking loser! You're 23 years old and you're going out egging. What are you doing?" At least, that's what my room-mates were saying. But I went. My friend Jonesy and I went.

We had 10 dozen eggs and we were ready. You would think they would have put a ban on people buying more than a dozen eggs on Halloween. Egging is a tradition. I've gone for the past eight years if you don't count 1999. (You can't rag on 1999, though, that's the year we had a dead cat.) The more people that go, the more fun it is. More hands equals more eggs thrown equals more unhappy people. We're not so cruel that we egg little kids out trick-or-treating with their parents. We egg the big kids that go out to fuck with the younger kids. We like to keep it 15 years old and up, about the same age that I like my women.

This year didn't end up being as good as years past, like in 1996, when we egged our old high school gym teacher's daughter in the head. But it was better than sitting at home and givin' away candy to those little creeps. Nobody was home at my house. We put a big bucket out front filled with ice and beer and condoms with a note that said "only take one." Now that's "keeping it real."

Christmas is now upon us. I hate that fucking holiday. The only good thing is that I'll get to go "Grinching." You know, the sport where you divide up into two teams and see who can steal more Christmas decorations in an allotted amount of time. That's a sure way to make the little kids cry in the morning. Bah humbug.

This issue is all about keeping it real. In what other magazine on the planet will you find Popular's Tammy Lynn Michaels and spray-painted Australian road kill? In no other magazine is the answer. And nothing is better than that except maybe if Tammy was spray painting the road kill herself—na-ked. We're working on that.

I'm sorry to report that we have still not located ALF. We have been trying, as you all know, to locate this furry alien for quite some time now. But in this issue's six-page alien special you will find an exclusive ALF update. Who loves you? Currently, not your mother. But *While You Were Sleeping* does.

—*Roger Gastman, Editor in Chief*

Originally printed in WYWS Issue #12

Illustration by Linas Garsis
Photo by Roger Gastman

Blah, blah, introduction… Funny story about me, and how it relates to this issue, blah, blah, blah. Here it comes, get ready. Sit down on the couch with some junk food or stay seated on the crapper and continue to export the junk food already eaten. At this issue's birth, it was dubbed the "Virginity Issue." Guaranteed to be our most offensive and tasteless issue to date. Every article related to virginity in some way or another, and of course stories of young chicks losin' it. We even had wallet-sized *WYWS* get-out-of-jail-free cards for you, complete with the ages of consent for all U.S. states and territories, Canada and Mexico.

Surprise! It didn't work out as planned. Inside, you won't find that pocket guide, or half as many pictures of nipples, poo, blood, broken/unbroken hymen diagrams or girls that don't look a day over 18. Why, you ask? It's because magazine distributors are a collection of retards. While they have no problem accepting titles like *High Times* that promote drug use, and straight-up skin magazines like *Swank* and *Barely Legal*, they do have a problem with *WYWS*. Although we're a seasoned favorite to loyal readers, we are relatively new to the distributors, and boy, are they scared of us. They put their tails between their legs and wet the carpet in their offices. A recent letter from a large nationwide book chain stated the following:

"Sorry to say but XXXXX rejected *While You Were Sleeping* for the following reasons: animals having sex, underage children touching each other, nudity and article captions using the F word."

That's right, I'm busted. Bring on the vulgar police and write my ass a big fat ticket. I'm a repeat offender. Doctor, I have a problem. Please forward all my cars to the pervert ward, thank you. Illustrations of a teenage boy having sex with a dog were just too much to handle? Too bad, it was a true story that's still in the courts around here. I'll admit, the "red rocket" might have been over the line, but just a tiny bit. At the time, it sure as hell seemed fitting.

Stop fretting already. This is not your grandma's copy of *Reader's Digest*. While this issue of *WYWS* might be lacking a few of the above mentioned things, we haven't strayed far from our intentions. Inside, you will still read stories of pubic hair (Kevin Smith), domestic violence and drug abuse (NEWA), men in diapers (The Babies), ghetto Bar Mitzvahs (RZA), virginity (10-page virginity special), sex, sex with teachers, SPAM and so much more.

"What can I do to help the cause?" you all must be asking yourselves. "Should I start hoarding weapons, water and canned food to help *WYWS* with a world takeover? Should I beat up the magazine buyer at my local bookstore and/or newsstand that won't carry *WYWS*?" While that's not a bad start, the real answer is going to the newsstand and requesting *WYWS*. Tell them you must have it; that your existence depends on it. If they already carry *WYWS*, steal them all (we get paid either way), so they will have to order more next time.

Now everyone at once say thank you to Mr. and Mrs. Distributor. Because of them you had to read the above, instead of my own personal virgin stories. You will just have to wait for my *E! True Hollywood Story* to come out sometime next year, with a feature film to follow.

I'm out for your brain.

—Roger Gastman, Editor in Chief

Originally printed in WYWS Issue #14

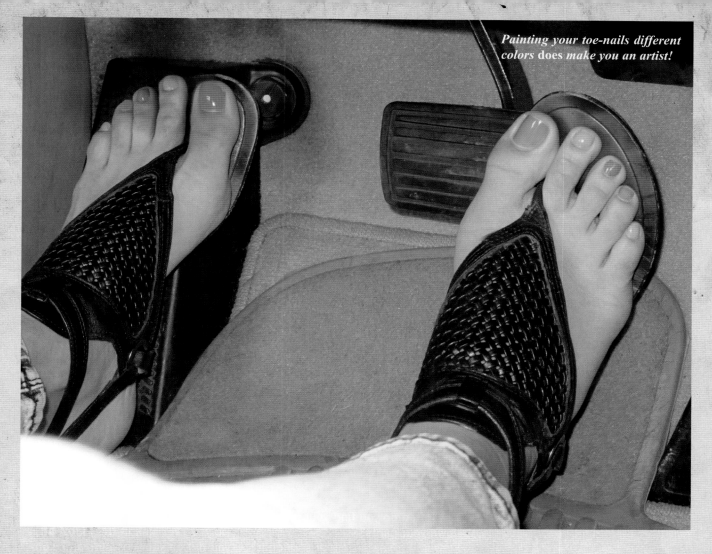

Painting your toe-nails different colors does make you an artist!

There's a good chance that you're concerned about our cover right now. If you're not talking about how awesome it is, you're probably pissed off. Either reaction is a sign that art is nearby. This shocking/amazing photo was taken in Florida, home of Disneyland, yet guaranteed to give Elmer Fudd (a Warner Brothers trademark) a big, fat chubby. The sugarcane was burning, and the residing rabbits made it no further than the cover of our summer art issue.

The art issue brings up an interesting question: Why does everyone think they're an artist or a critic? Burning candles in empty wine bottles and painting the molding a different color than the door doesn't make you an artist. It makes you a girl. Writing a paper that compares Picasso's blue period to Koons' asshole photography does not make you a qualified critic. It makes you a pervert. I bet you're the kind of punk who spent a grand on a camera, and thinks it makes you a pro fucking photographer, too. Aperture? What the fuck is that? I took a picture once (see it above). It was with a disposable camera and if that's not art, then I don't know what is.

I've taken art classes—from finger painting in kindergarten to typography and some other crap in college—and all I learned was that most teachers are failed artists themselves, and the gifted students have a "gift" to be annoying. These pages are full of real artists—artists you wish you could become, artists full of imagery and ideas you will steal and pass off as your own.

Artists are my friends. We love to mutually exploit one another. One day, one of these artists will make me so much money you will hate my guts even more than you already do. You'll see my house on *Cribs*, and it'll be the biggest, baddest motherfucker ever, full of cool shit from all my artist friends. I'll have a moat complete with a drawbridge, an army of midgets and a chef that makes the best goddamn rabbit dishes this side of the continental divide.

Who's the artist now, fool?

—*Roger Gastman*

Originally printed in WYWS Issue #19

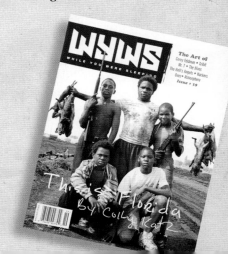

Roger Gastman **gets his clothes stained and his 6th grade dream comes true.**

What animal do you wish you could trade places with?
Flattus: A dog that doesn't get his balls clipped. Dogs get everything done for them. They just run all over the neighborhood fucking other dogs. They get fed and a place to stay.
Balsak: I already am an animal, so that's kind of a pointless question.
Flattus: He has got legs. You just can't see them right now.

Given the chance would you try human meat?
Flattus: No. I wouldn't put human parts in my mouth. Wait a minute. I'm out of character. Yes, I would.
Balsak: It depends on how it was served. I wouldn't slop some ketch-up on it and put it in a bun. If you put it in a nice sauce, definitely.

How often do you find yourself drunk?
Flattus: I don't drink. I was drunk one time when I was 14.
Balsak: I usually don't find myself when I'm drunk.

How heavy are those costumes?
Flattus: Really, really heavy, and I have more attachments on mine for bigger shows. It keeps getting heavier.
Balsak: Yeah, they're heavy.

How hot does it get in them?
Balsak: Hot! Especially when people forget to turn off the heat.

Groupies in the U.S. compared to Europe?
Flattus: Groupies, period. Wherever we can get them, please.
Balsak: I don't meet groupies. I meet nice young girls. And by young, I mean really, really young. We play chess.

How often do you find your hand down your pants?
Flattus: I'm always either scratching my balls or jerking off.
Balsak: Normally, if I want to fondle myself I take my pants off.

I was hooking up with my friends little 17-year-old sister. Do you see anything wrong with that?
Flattus: Absolutely not.
Balsak: Now that I know you are a brother, you will understand my perversion. I have this thing for under-age girls. It's kind of a weakness.

A friend of mine saw your show a few years ago and his clothes got stained. Can he forward you his cleaning bill?
Flattus: No, you can tell him to go suck it.

I first heard about you all when I was in sixth grade. You were on this kick that you were going to rule the world. How much progress have you made?
Flattus: Slim to none.
Balsak: Everything we try, we fail.

Where are you claiming to be from?
Flattus: Antarctica.

What's the age of consent there?
Flattus: I don't think you can get a boner in Antartica because it's so cold.
Balsak: I have the age of consent memorized for every state in the U.S. The youngest is Pennsylvania, which is 14.

Do you ever look in the mirror after you put on your costume and wonder what the hell are you doing?
Flattus: Costumes? What are you talking about?
Balsak: I constantly wonder what the hell I'm doing.

You wear costumes every day, so what the hell do you do on Halloween?
Balsak: We usually play a show.

Would you punch an alien?
Flattus: If he pissed me off. If he was cool, then we would bro out. I could probably kick an alien's ass. I don't care about that mind control bullshit.
Balsak: I wouldn't punch an alien because they are smaller than me.

Is Brittany Spears a piece of shit or what?
Flattus: I think she's a lot older than she says she is.
Balsak: She's not quite as hot anymore since she turned 18. She was way hotter when she was 17.

GWAR

"CRACK IS THE MOST EVIL THING BETWEEN SNAP, CRACKLE AND POP. HE PROBABLY WOULD KILL. STAY AWAY FROM HIM."

Crack kills: true or false?
Flattus: Crack is the most evil thing between Snap, Crackle and Pop. He probably would kill. Stay away from him.

Do you have a recipe you would like to share?
Balsak: You take water and put it in a pot. You put it over a fire or high heat and it will boil. It's hot water; it's how you make it.

That was a great episode of *90210* when Kelly became a cokehead and went to buy some coke and almost got raped—what do you think?
Balsak: I like the one where Brandon was dosed by his girlfriend. He was all into it, but the next day he broke up with her. What the fuck is up with that guy?

When are you going to be playing at the Peach Pit After Dark?
Flattus: Thursday.

This girl that was supposed to come with me chickened out at the last moment. Any message for her?
Flattus: Fuck her!
Balsak: Is she cute?

Real cute.
Balsak: What's her number?

You want to call her?
Balsak: Yeah.

[I pick up my cell phone, dial Anna's number and hand it to Balsak. He drills her about why she didn't come for more than five minutes. I don't think his sweet talking found a place in her heart.]

Flattus: Is she your girlfriend?

No, just a friend.
Flattus: You just want to fuck her?

No. Well, I guess I would.
Flattus: How old are you?

21.
Flattus: You're 21 and you have a magazine!

Is the South going to rise again?
Flattus: Sure.
Balsak: If it rose, it would be the North, wouldn't it?

Do you recycle?
Balsak: Only condoms.

Are you a No Limit soldier?
Balsak: I'm not sure what that means, but I would like to do the girl from No Doubt.

What would taste better: Kermit or Miss Piggy?
Balsak: I don't dig on swine, so I would go with Kermit.
Flattus: Well, Miss Piggy has a pussy. A big, bacon pussy.
Balsak: We talking sexually? You would eat out a pig?
Flattus: Yes.
Balsak: I would just snap the legs off Kermit and leave the dick alone. Fry them bitches up in some butter.

When are you guys all planning on calling if quits?
Flattus: Whenever there is nothing to make fun of anymore, which will probably be never.

Originally printed in WYWS Issue #7

—*Editor's note: I was so excited to interview Gwar. I remember getting the* Hell-O *tape in sixth grade and being blown away. I still bump it on my walkman. Seriously, Gwar is the shit, they kick ass. I fucking love Gwar.*

while you were
sleeping

GIANT
Interview by Roger Rock
Photos courtesy of GIANT

Give me the GIANT history.
I started writing in 1989 in Albuquerque. I just saw some guys painting in the middle of the afternoon in this ditch I was skating in. I thought it looked like fun. The next day I stole all of my dad's spray paint from the garage and did a piece in the same spot. I decided that I needed to start painting places people would see. We immediately started hitting freeways.

Living in San Francisco, do you eat a lot of Rice-A-Roni?
I don't think I've had it.

Do you consider yourself a nerd?
Yeah. I've always been the guy that was a schoolboy as a kid. I've always been kinda geeky.

Recall your first experience with porn. How old were you?
I must have been six years old. I had taken these magazines I had found somewhere and me and this little girl would go into a barn and look at the magazines and then pose ourselves in those positions.

Naked?
Yep. I wasn't doing anything—we were just playing. I didn't really start fooling around with girls until like freshman year in college. The first time I went down on a girl I was kinda shocked because I remembered the smell from when I was a little kid.

I laughed and told the girl what I was remembering. I must have been getting pretty loose when I was a little kid.

IT WAS JUST STRANGE TO SEE THE SAME PERSON COME IN AT 3 A.M. ON A TUESDAY TO WATCH PORN MOVIES AND JERK OFF ALL NIGHT.

So how did you end up working the nightshift in a porn store? Was it a lifelong fantasy?
I had just moved back from England. I had no money, my girlfriend kicked me out, and I had to pay the rent. I was just going through the paper. I think I made $7 an hour. I could take videos home but after the first week I was sick of it. At first it was kinda funny because there were regulars that would come in a few times a week. It was just strange to see the same person come in at 3 a.m. on a Tuesday to watch porn movies and jerk off all night. The psychological profile of some of those people is just amazing. I couldn't believe that these people would do this consistently. I would go to a porn shop once every other month to pick up something but I was never a regular.

Did you have to clean up the floors in the peep show rooms?
I never had to do that. There were two different groups of guys that came in twice a day and mopped shit out. I never really had to go back there.

It was pretty foul back there?
Yeah, I caught people blowing each other, drug deals, and other stupid stuff. There was a fistfight back there one night that I had to break up.

Did you parents know where you were working?
Totally. When I was looking for a job in college when I was still living at home, my mom was looking through the paper and saw an ad for an adult bookstore and told me I should apply there.

How do you feel about transsexuals?
I got no problem with anybody for any reason.

Have you ever had an experience with a transsexual?
No. I guess I would be open to it but I just haven't met the right transsexual yet.

You're one of those guys that likes stock caps—why?
No. That's a rumor. Before I started using caps I wondered how people got real clean lines so I made these gigantic cardboard stencils that were like four-feet long. I was in architecture school so I was trying to figure out how shit was getting done.

Would you consider yourself one of those hip-hop gangsta graff writers or as trailer trash?
I guess between the two I would have to go for the hip-hop gangster guy because I get all my clothes from hip-hop-related companies.

—Note from GIANT: Roger always asked the weirdest questions and I can't help but be honest. I don't think any of the stuff I said in that interview has come back to haunt me or anything. But I certainly don't think any other interview included as much frank discussion of human sexuality. In the end though, I think I would still answer those questions the same way.

Aren't they free?
Yeah, that's the thing. If I wasn't getting free gear, I would be wearing flannel shirts and jeans.

What do you consider good music?
I'm all about old heavy metal. I like some hip-hop, but not particularly rap music. I'm really into punk and always have been. I would like to go out to more punk shows. I'm really into jungle—all kinds of down tempo breakbeat shit.

Would you punch an alien?
I guess it would depend on the situation. If it was pissing me off, yeah. But I would probably be so scared I would piss my pants and not be able to do a goddamn thing.

What do you think about all the damn hippies in San Francisco?
Hippies are cool. They choose to live that way and I don't. They don't really bother me. They sleep in the park or in buses and don't really cause any problems and they got good bud.

Do you think Wilt Chamberlain really slept with all those women?
I don't know. Personally, I can't comprehend being that psyched to fuck constantly. I would much rather go paint or draw or drink a beer than fuck 24/7. There are only so many positions and so many girls. He must have just been a super horndog.

How do you feel about this statement: White Castle, the best food for the change in your pocket.
Yeah! I would probably go for that. I don't eat meat anymore but if I did and I was broke I would probably be hitting up White Castle.

Why don't you eat meat?
I just don't want to eat anything that I wouldn't kill myself. I'm all about fishing. Yanking a fish out of the fucking water and whacking his head on a rock and cooking him up. I got no problem with that. But killing pigs and cows and chickens—it's just not in me to do that.

Do you like fat chicks?
I like girls. If a certain girl is a little hefty but she is cool.

Heaviest girl you got down with?
I've never fucked a girl that had folds or anything.

What is the most perverted thing you have done?
I don't think I do a lot of perverted shit. I'm just down to push the limits of human sexuality. If you're not using what you have to the fullest potential you are missing out.

What skate companies have you worked for?
I worked for Think Skateboards for almost four years. Through working there I also did stuff for Adrenaline, Venture and a bunch of other companies. At a certain point I didn't really give a fuck about the job or the money and just left. I like to have my bills paid and be able to go out out to dinner once or twice a week. If I can have that, I'm chillin'.

What's up with your zine _Huffer_?
Just send me a 55-cent stamp.

What's up with other mediums?
I just try to learn as many mediums as I can. There are so many options. I don't get into painting with brushes on canvas. That doesn't really get my dick hard. I like doing stuff that is in the public. No matter what I'm fucking with, I want it to be on the street, forced on the public. It's the act of doing and forcing it on the public that is important to me.

Did you cry when you found out Ronnie Van Zant died?
No. I didn't even care. I'm sorry, I'm a heartless son of a bitch.

If you had 10 minutes alone with Jessica Hahn, what would you do?
I probably would want to take some pictures of her doing some stupid shit. I would see how far she would go, push her buttons. Dare her to do weird shit.

I'M JUST DOWN TO PUSH THE LIMITS OF HUMAN SEXUALITY.

Anal sex—any pointers?
Take it easy. If you are trying to convince your girlfriend to take it in the ass, it might not be a bad idea to let her know that you are down to do the same. It seems kinda fucked, but I'm down to have a girlfriend stick something in my ass. I've had all kinda of stuff in my ass. Like butt plugs of all different shapes and sizes and dildos and fingers and tongues and feet and whatever.

Do you have a hairy ass?
No, luckily I don't. If it does get a little out of hand, I'll have my girlfriend shave it. I shave everything and she does too.

You have all of your pubic hair shaved?
Yep, there's nothing like getting a blowjob with no pubic hair.

Can people purchase your pubic hair through mail?
No, I don't want to start getting into the pubic business. I have done my time selling perversion.

Do you dig lesbians?
I just dig girls in general. If they happen to be gay, whatever. I've actually had two or three girlfriends break up with me to be with girls. It is kinda weird to be in that situation.

If you could kill one cartoon character who would it be?
I would kill Bart Simpson. That would cause so much panic in the world. That would be so much fun to watch people shit their pants that I killed Bart Simpson. I think Bart kicks ass.

Ever have to go to the store to buy your girl tampons?
I don't think so.

Would that have embarrassed you?
No, I send them to the store to get enema kits.

Are you a breast man?
I'm a full-body man. Breasts to me don't weigh more than anything else. They are really low on the scale. I never really know what to do with them. What the hell do you do with them?

I smack them around.
I like doing that. There is definitely something to be said about the comedic aspect of fucking.

Do you ever just stop and smell the roses?
Oh yeah, all the time. What was it Ferris Bueller said? "Life moves pretty fast. If you don't stop and look around once in a while, you could miss it." I'm down with Ferris Bueller.

Have you ever stolen a car, beaten up a cop or done something really cool like that?
No, if I come across cops I pretty much am a total wuss and agree with them that I'm a total asshole and need to grow up. I don't want to go to jail. If I have to kiss some cops ass for five minutes so I can go home and eat dinner, I'll do it. Stealing cars and shit? No, I haven't really done anything buck wild.

What do you jock?
I don't really jock anybody. That would be me wishing to have their life. I am happy with the life I have. I look up to a type of person that keeps busy and has a lot of heart.

Anything else?
Nope, I'm pretty boring. What is it everyone says? Keep it real. I should say that.

Originally printed in WYWS Issue #4

PAT THE PARTY JERK

OFF THE MARKET?

by Trevor Michaels

—Editor's note: It was late one night, and we needed to fill space. Trevor Michaels was at my house getting drunk as usual, and slurred out the words, "Let me write something." I am proud to say that all of the stories in the "Pat the Party Jerk" columns are real things that happened to Trevor. Many times, we didn't even change the names to protect the victims. Trevor was an amazing person. We miss him. RIP.

If you want to hook up with your best friend's girl, or any girl who appears to be off the market, you must be willing to go to extremes in order to receive your ultimate desire. You will have to be a complete asshole, navigating a storm of deceit, treachery and lies.

First, remember that the girl probably isn't anything especially important to the guy. The only reason he spends all of his time with her, and not you (what a sell out), is because he likes the sexual acts and maybe because she is one the few girls he can hang out with that doesn't make him physically ill.

If you have a conscience that will inhibit you from accomplishing your goal, you shouldn't even attempt to hook up. Remember, you're just following your instincts to get some ass. It doesn't have to be a personal vendetta against the guy—if it is, it's even more motivation to destroy their relationship. However, if you are a normal guy full of lust and sexual desires, who really gives a shit as long as you get what you want.

Assuming that you are willing to commit to the effort, you must carefully pick a time and place and develop an intricate plan. Pick a night where you will be isolated with the boyfriend and girlfriend. First, you must dispose of the boyfriend without allowing the girl to uncover the plan or leave.

Here's my game plan to take the boyfriend out of the picture and get with his girl:

1. Get him shit-faced. Make him pass out early or spend the whole night with his head in the toilet. I like starting with 40 ounces, then moving to mixed drinks. You are going to have to drink with him, but by declaring him a pussy and questioning his manhood in front of his gal, he can easily be forced to drink much more than you. Once he is bombed, start him with the shots. Preferably using a king-size bottle, follow a similar fashion until he passes out or pukes all over himself. This will repulse his girl, allowing you to make your move.

2. The girl must be drunk also. Alcohol numbs her ability to make competent decisions. Be careful! You don't want her to pass out, or else you'll spend the night with your right hand. Using a combination of weak mixed drinks and beer, she will be involved with the drinking while consuming far less alcohol. If there is any chance she will just go to bed when her boyfriend is out cold, you might want to slip her some Vivarin or MAX Alerts to keep her nice and awake.

3. You must have some sort of game. After laying a strong foundation of kind gestures and remarks such as, "I like your shoes... and tits," start questioning the integrity of her boyfriend. Tell lies about him while making her feel comfortable with you as someone she can trust. Remember, if the situation is right, she can't second-guess anything you say because you two are alone.

4. Make your move. Be smooth and calm. Tell her numerous times that what you two are doing is all right (because it really is a good thing that you are getting a piece of ass).

5. GET OUT. You must leave before your friend or his girlfriend wakes up in the morning. I suggest taking off for a couple of days, checking in to see how the progress is coming.

On another note, if you want to increase your chances of hooking up at a party, I suggest bringing a watermelon full of grain alcohol. Girls won't realize the amount of alcohol in the melon, and will easily become susceptible to any type of game, no matter how bad it is.

DISCLAIMER: WYWS does not promote the consumption of alcohol by those of age or minors.

WARNING: Alcohol can cause you to make a complete ass out of yourself.

CAUTION: 190-proof grain alcohol is flammable.

Originally printed in WYWS Issue #4

Photo by Roger Gastman

I remember when Roger first started *WYWS*. It seemed like an outlandish thing for someone just out of high school to do. I kind of thought it was a phase. But this was the beginning of me realizing what a genius Roger was. I will never forget going into Tower Records and seeing *WYWS*. It was real and anyone could buy it; it was not just something for our friends to see month to month. Roger made a magazine out of something he was so passionate about. I became a namedropper of Roger Gastman. After all, it got me free stuff. At one point, I had a closet full of Pumas that were donated to Roger and *WYWS* T-shirts and sweatshirts.

I will also always remember my modeling debut in *WYWS*. I agreed to be the subject of a stalker (aka, I hung out in my kitchen while Roger took pictures of me from the bushes, which created a lot of explaining to do with the neighbors); I put on a baseball uniform even though I had, and still have, no clue how to play baseball, and even had a real modeling shoot with makeup and a super weird hairdo (a photo that my mom still cherishes). That was as wild and crazy as I got. I always told Roger I would be up for being in the magazine, but as long as I could still run for president one day.

It is a shame that *WYWS* isn't around anymore. *WYWS* was Roger's baby and should always be thought of that way.

—*Bethany*

I met Roger Gastman in Chicago at a book trade show in June 2000. He was in the next booth, Soft Skull, with a copy of his first book, *Free Agents*. He also had a magazine, *While You Were Sleeping*. It was looking good for both of us.

I had been a publicist. Or rather, I had just become one, a couple of months earlier. My job was to make connections, put together the perfect pair like Chuck Woolery on *Love Connection*. I showed Roger a book by Polly Borland called *The Babies*, photographs of adult infantilists (that is, men with a penchant for wearing diapers, being breast, bottle, and spoon fed, wearing little girl clothes—the whole bit). He was horrified.

It leaves a lasting impression, much like *WYWS*, which later published a couple of photographs by Borland—but no copy. That made me laugh. Cat got your tongue...

I was pleased. I had a wide range of disturbing books that looked beautiful in spreads in the magazine. In fact, I pitched Roger my dream: Me. I thought a large photograph in the next issue would look fabulous for him. Somehow, he always seemed to act like he didn't hear me.

See, I wasn't just a shameless self promoter, I was a ~*~ FAAAAN ~*~ and I wanted to be where the action was, in those pages, with all those distinct personalities that delight in the perverse, subversive and immature things in this world.

It was not to be, I never made the magazine, but I eventually got copies of them all, and held them captive on my bookshelves. Until that fateful day, I spilled iced coffee. I'm usually quite good, but sometimes I'm not. The magazines weren't destroyed but they were a little worse for wear, and that got me thinking...

My then-boyfriend was in Berlin, visiting family while I carved up every copy, turning it into a 40-page Christmas card. I sliced and diced several other magazines and even an old copy of *Where The Wild Things Are*. I paged through every issue of *WYWS*, finding the perfect photographs and best words for my man who loved ALF so much he had it in German on his hard drive. Another *Love Connection*!

And even though my boyfriend is now an ex, he still has that book 'cause it's amazing. I think. I had forgotten nearly all the spreads, so I had him unearth them for this essay. Cheers, Roger! Long live *WYWS*!

—*Miss Rosen*

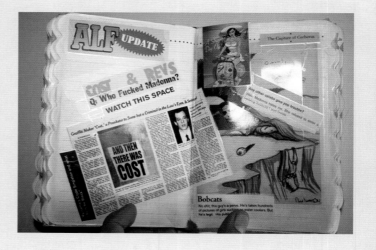

Photo by Carlos Batts

I saw issue 4 of *While You Were Sleeping* at Reptilian Records in Fells Point, Baltimore in 1998. I thought it was a pretty cool magazine, so I met with Roger in his home in Bethesda, Maryland. I liked Roger as a person and editor, and his enthusiasm and fun spirit made it a unique relationship. I thought graffiti was an interesting art form. I knew it was a subculture, but the magazine focused on the personalities and lifestyles involved in graffiti, street art and all things underground including films, galleries, books and people. I did a range of assignments for the magazine—covers, fashion editorials and live bands from issues 5 to 19. From the beginning, the magazine was an unstoppable force of art, ideas and ambition. I felt a part of something progressive. WYWS documented the street artist and underground culture in a whole new way not being covered by other media or magazines. I met a lot of great artists along the way and made some long lasting creative friendships.

—*Carlos Batts*

I've only had subscriptions to three magazines over the course of my lifetime: *Mad*, *National Geographic* and *While You Were Sleeping*. And as I write this, I realize just how much the third publication in that list resembles the bastard child of the other two. Juvenile, but educational. Raunchy, but timely. Lowbrow, but artful. *While You Were Sleeping* was a jambalaya of awesome.

Serial killers, rap music, fetish porn, graffiti, ALF and tattoos never blended together so smoothly. The photos ranged from gallery-quality portraits to restroom-quality Polaroids and the writing was Bukowski with just a touch of Ice-T. I ate up every issue and licked my plate clean.

Today, most of the hip kids on your block will flash their cred by talking about Jumbo's Clown Room or Kaiju Big Battel, but I read about that shit in *WYWS* before The White Stripes were signed to a major. (And I know that for a fact because I first learned about The White Stripes in issue 14.)

WYWS didn't try to be cool, it just was cool. It was for people with a dirty sense of humor and an even dirtier sense of adventure. It was counter-subculture. Or sub-counterculture. Either way, it was fucking rad, and I wish it was still around.

Yet, as magnificent as it was, I almost never run into anyone who knew of its existence, so who's buying this book anyway? Honestly, are there that many people out there who loved *WYWS* as much as I did? Roger and his fucking books… Have you seen his house? Are you seriously telling me he's paying the mortgage on that thing with a *WYWS* book? Whatever. You're probably holding part of a cocaine front in your hands right now.

—*Jeff Penalty*

Photo by John Preskitt

FUCK LIFE
by EXAKTO

These two words are probably muttered on a daily basis by anyone who's been in the game long enough to know that graff is first and foremost a lifestyle, and a risky one at that.

November, 1995: So I was chilling in my Boston apartment on a rainy Wednesday night, hooking up AREST's blackbook. This outline was coming off fresh. I mean these letters were ill. This was going to be it. I was going to rock this book, and when I was done, no one would ever open up this thing without seeing my piece and going, "Damn, that's some shit right there."

Knock knock.

Hmmm. "Yeah, come on in," I mumbled. All of the sudden, there I was staring up at about five detectives and a few cops in uniform. Immediately, I knew what was up. What had I bombed lately that would really piss them off? Well, I'd written on everything I could since day one. Oops. Oh well. I knew I was fucked. They took me into the living room and I just listened to them run their mouths.

So I was sitting there, and this lady cop named XXXX walked into the room holding up some stickers I had made about a month before. Oh, great. She held them up and she looked pretty pissed. They were the ones I made especially for her. In fact, they had such catchphrases written on them as "XXXX has perky boobs" and "XXXX has a smelly cooter." You see, this lady wasn't just some ordinary cop: She was the head of the transit system's vandal squad. She'd been doing this shit since way back in the day. This chick was famous and she knew it. She was so (un)popular that she was a on first-name basis with all the Boston writers.

She looked at this flick of a freight I painted with CLEAR and says to this other cop, "They painted this over in Cambridge at the blah blah blah…" and I wanted to say, "No, stupid, I rocked that freight in D.C.," but I just kept my mouth shut. All the cops were asking XXXX questions like this one dude who picked up a magazine off the table and looked at her as if to ask, "What is this?" "Headbanging," she coolly responded without even glancing in his direction. Hmmm, I never knew that the thing sitting on my coffee table could simply be referred to as "headbanging." Interesting.

The phone rang; I answered it. Holy shit, it was my man BRAKE. He says, "Yo, I found this fresh new piecing spot down by the…" "Cool, awesome. Well, I'm getting my house raided so let me hit you back when I get out of jail. Bye."

So at this point, I've been told about a dozen times how fucked I am. They put me in the back of a police van with all my paint, caps, flicks, videos, and all that jazz. Maybe I shouldn't have shot a bombing video in D.C. starring yours truly. Maybe I shouldn't have posed in front of that train I caught a tag on. Fuck it. Thinking about it was pretty pointless.

So I'm in the station. "We'll help you if you help us. Who's this guy? Who's that guy?" "Sorry detective, I can't help you out, buddy." That was it. They didn't even try after that. I was like, "No," and they were just like, "OK." $1,000 bail and I was only in the cell for a few hours.

At arraignment the next day, I had to hide in the elevator to talk to my lawyer because we were being hounded by reporters. "Did you do these tags? Why? Why!" The proceedings just never ended. The whole time I was sitting there, I was being taped from across the courtroom. I couldn't take it anymore and I looked straight at the camera,

EXAKTO

flashed them a big toothy smile, and waved like I was a celebrity on a float at some shitty parade. It was awesome, and they got every bit of it on tape. I was actually lucky enough to witness the whole thing in slow motion that night on the five o'clock news during my own special segment. It was on all the major networks except for CBS. They get props for having more important things to do.

I went back to my apartment and the phone started to ring. I was already radio material. I got calls from all local papers and even the Associated Press. There were even some creative phone calls thrown in the mix. "Hello? Is this the graffiti guy?" a mystery man asked. "Who's this?" I asked. Then there was a long pause and some slow breathing. After about five seconds, I hear a very soft, shaky voice reply, "One of your victims!" and then he hung up.

So to speed up the pace of this story, I was sentenced in January 1996 to serve six months of house arrest, pay restitution to each of my "victims," and perform 600 hours of community service. The most interesting part of this sentence was that I had to pay $50 a week for the privilege of being on house arrest, for a grand total of $1,300! So anyway, this sucked, but I knew I just had to stick it out. Now this is where the real confusing shit starts to happen. About halfway through my sentence, I started to see some imitation graff pop up in my neighborhood. Fake ALERT tags were all over the place. I didn't want to think it was going to happen to me, but soon enough fake EXAK-

CRIME

Police track copycat 'EXACTO'

Crime Stoppers tip ma lead cops to graffiti tagger

It has been more than two months since police seen the copycat "EXACTO" graffiti tag in Allston-Brighton, but investigators may be close to catching the person who was spray-painting the tag throughout the neighborhood this winter.

District 14 Community Service Officer Dan Daley said last week that the department's Crime Stoppers unit recently received a tip from a person who revealed the name of the tagger. Daley said the department has been unable to find the tagger, who is juvenile.

The "EXACTO" tag had been used to identify another graffiti tagger, who was arrested for his graffiti vandalism throughout the neighborhood, who is still serving his com-

TO tags were showing up all over the place. I asked everyone I knew what was up, but no one had a clue. It seemed like either someone was trying to get me even more fucked up, or some kid out there had a serious mental problem. Finally, some writers tipped me off that it was this local kid named XXXX. I called the kid up and he said it's some other kid and it ended up being this stupid endless cycle of shitty little fucks that were doing their best to play dumb. As far as I was concerned, every little fucking kid who wanted to meet me could go fuck themselves.

Time went on, and the situation got worse. This kid was bombing hard. He was even hitting up spots where I had been buffed with the same color paint. Every tag was a carbon copy of one of mine. I just sat back and hoped it would stop. I talked to my lawyer and we figured it would be a bad idea to tell the cops. In August of 1996, I got out of house arrest and moved my ass out of Allston. For those of you who aren't familiar with the Boston area, Allston is this shitty place filled with college kids, crusty punk rockers, old Irish drunks and a whole slew of ridiculous "community improvement" organizations. It sucks.

By the winter, this kid was going off. He had my hand down pretty well, and was even rocking fill-ins and trying to pull off pieces. Lucky for me, every writer I knew was out dissing his shit. It sucked because no one could tell the difference. I couldn't tell the difference sometimes.

One night, I went to Allston to watch a movie at my friend's place. I got a ride home after, and at the end of his block I saw an EXAKTO tag that hadn't been there before. We rolled down the main street and saw three kids walking around looking like writers look. We drove by and looked back to see one of the kids catch a tag on a mailbox. "Bust a U-turn!" I yelled, and we screeched over the other side of the street and headed back. By the time we got to that mailbox, the kids had dipped into some alley. I jumped out and looked at the mailbox. Surely enough, there was a fresh EXAKTO tag right there in front of my face. We drove around for about an hour, and we even reported it to the cops. I couldn't believe it—I never in my life would have thought that I'd be driving around looking for some kid writing EXAKTO and reporting vandalism in progress to the Boston Police.

After that incident, I sent letters to all the graff detectives and the City Councilor letting them know that I wasn't responsible for any of this new handiwork. I also agreed to do an article with a Boston newspaper hoping that this kid might see it. If he thought he was doing me a favor by putting up my name, maybe he'd stop. After I did the article, everything calmed down. I used my community service hours to buff this kid's tags and everyone else scribbled over them whenever they went bombing. At that point, people believed me and I stopped worrying about it. I pretty much thought it was over, although I still wondered what the fuck this kid could have been thinking. He probably did more damage than any other legitimate writer in Boston while he was active (that says a lot for this city's graff scene). He broke every rule in the book.

A couple weeks ago, I got a call from the police. They caught the kid in the act. He had white paint all over his hands, and when he saw the cops he threw his can into the bushes and ran. The cop seemed pretty calm. "The kid was only 15 years old, so there's not much that can happen to him." In the article that was just published, the cops couldn't release his name because he was a juvenile. The same cops that sent news cameras after me to make an example out of me, tried to get me thrown in jail, and even called my school to try to get me expelled won't make this kid's name public because he's a fucking juvenile.

Fuck life.

Originally printed in WYWS Issue #2

—Editor's note: I'm sorry to say that while EXAKTO rocked many nice walls after this, it was never the same for him. He was in too much trouble to do damage like he used to. Regardless, I learned a lot from this jerk. In related news, EXAKTO's wife posed for several cap ads in the magazine. Bet she regrets that now.

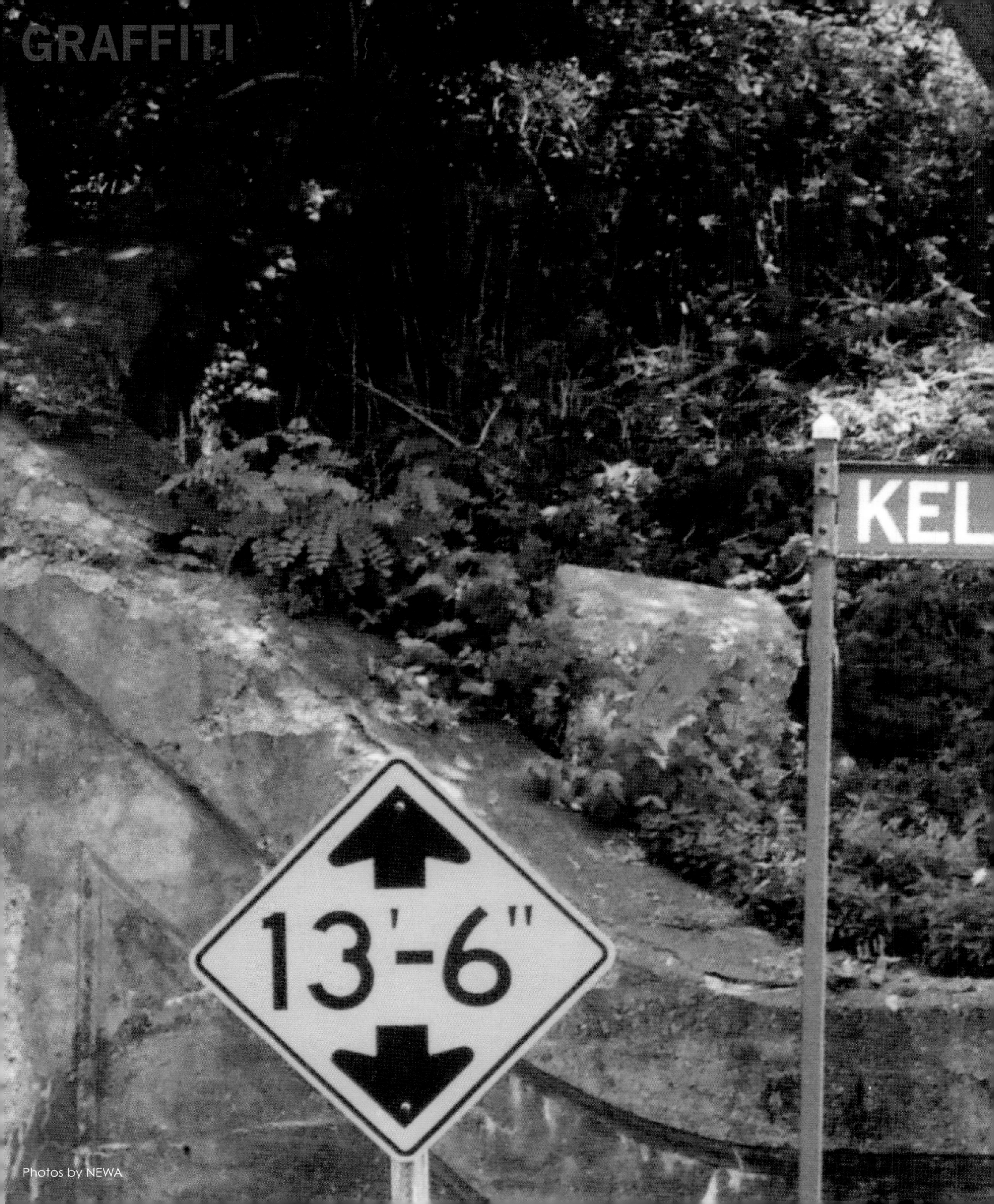

Photos by NEWA

ADD **MAYHEM** TO YOUR ADVERTISING

"CALL TOLL FREE" 1-800-NEWA-END

LAMAR

NEWA'S A Grrreat Source Of Protein

FROSTED FACES OF CUM

tony the tiger

GET SPRRRAYED!

VIACOM

DISCOVER THE SENIOR PROGRAMS AT MERIDIAN.

1-800-560-9990

LOOK HONEY, ITS NEWA RAV!!

Meridian Health System

BRICK HOSPITAL

JERSEY SHORE MEDICAL CENTER

POINT PLEASANT HOSPITAL

RIVERVIEW MEDICAL CENTER

5512 OUTDOOR SYSTEMS

norton

Cocoa Muffs

A WHITE SURPRISE BETWEEN YOUR BLACK THIGHS

NO SUGAR NO CREAM THATS THE BROAD IN MY DREAMS

11560

ON TAP

GATEWAY

White Newa

THE CAUCASIAN YOU CRAVE

482

GATEWAY

Trix

WP

839

CHESAPEAKE

"AND GOD SAID, BELIEVE IN ME OR YOUR COCKS SHALL FALL OFF"

NEWA 3:16   BOOK OF R.A.V.

AMERICA'S SWEETHEART CONFESSES "I RODE NEWA RAW"

OOPS, WE HIT IT AGAIN

LAMAR

PAT THE PARTY JERK

WHISKEY DICK
by Trevor Michaels

Usually striking after a long night with Jack, Jim, Johnny or Ol' Grandad, "Whiskey Dick" plagues horny guys across the world. Although the blissful effects of alcohol often give us the power to approach and land beautiful women, the consequences of a long night of drinking can lead to embarrassment and lack of productivity in the bedroom. Since alcohol is a necessary component of any true gentleman's social effort to lure girls to the bedroom, the simple solution of abandoning drinking is not plausible. This is what's known as a "paradox."

Men do not want to admit that anything associated with females has influence over their actions. So single men drink to excuse themselves from responsibility of the actions necessary to get laid, and married men drink so they won't be responsible for their aging wife's pleasure. But in a free man's quest, alcohol can leave his swinger helpless under the sheets. A liquor-limp schlong cannot be revived by blowjob, nor the gentle caressing of a moisturized hand.

I believe that all men deserve a second chance, and a third, fourth, fifth and sixth, but most females won't agree. Thus, if you find your manhandle unable to execute the game plan, follow these suggestions to ensure that you will not be haunted by failure and will secure a second chance for conquest.

1. If you are hung like a buffalo, you can try and penetrate using your limp penis. "Stuffing the softy" is a risky approach, as it does not guarantee you will be saved from embarrassment. The size of your partially inflated tool might not meet her expectations, and her subsequent gossip could be just as damaging to your manhood. The best use of this technique is to stuff it in for a minute of two, then stop and explain you feel you need to get to know her better. Displaying your sensitive side lays the groundwork for future relations.

2. Satisfying a girl without even taking your pants off is a talent that most men lack. If you are, however, one of the few technicians who can push the right buttons, this approach offers an easy olive branch to an engine unwilling to turn over. Yet because most men have been brainwashed by the faked orgasms and screams of previous hook-ups, this approach affords little security that the girl will be hailing your performance to others. Shielding one aspect of your sexual proficiency from embarrassment, you've opened the door to criticism of another part of your arsenal.

3. Rather than attempting to gain carnal knowledge, you could opt for a few hours of cuddling. If you can withstand your testosterone-based impulses, some snuggle-time could prove beneficial in the longrun, contradicting your reputation as a scum-

bag. Unless the girl wants to get some action at the moment, future sexual encounters can profit from Eskimo kisses and spooning.

4. Maintain you infallibility. Claim you have never had this problem before, so it must be her fault. This will often save face on your part and keep the girl quiet about the incident since she is as scared of embarrassment as you are.

5. If you find yourself unable to pitch a tent and have no interest in ever seeing the girl again, simply go to the bathroom and don't come back. Please make sure you are not in your own bedroom when you use this approach. The focus point for your disinterest becomes your dislike for the girl rather than your inability to perform. Additionally, this will continue your reputation as a dirtball.

In closing, please note that Whiskey Dick can be an indication that you and your bladder may "hit a dinger." If you do end up hosing down your partner, make sure to blame her for your dampness in the morning. As soon as you leave her presence, call your friends and hers and spread the news of her loss of control. Remember, you are never at fault.

Originally printed in WYWS Issue #16

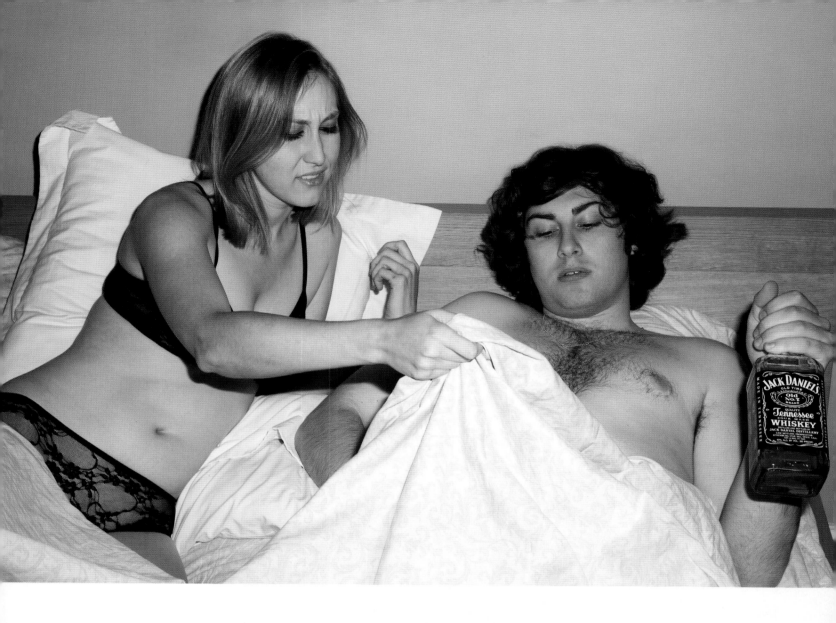

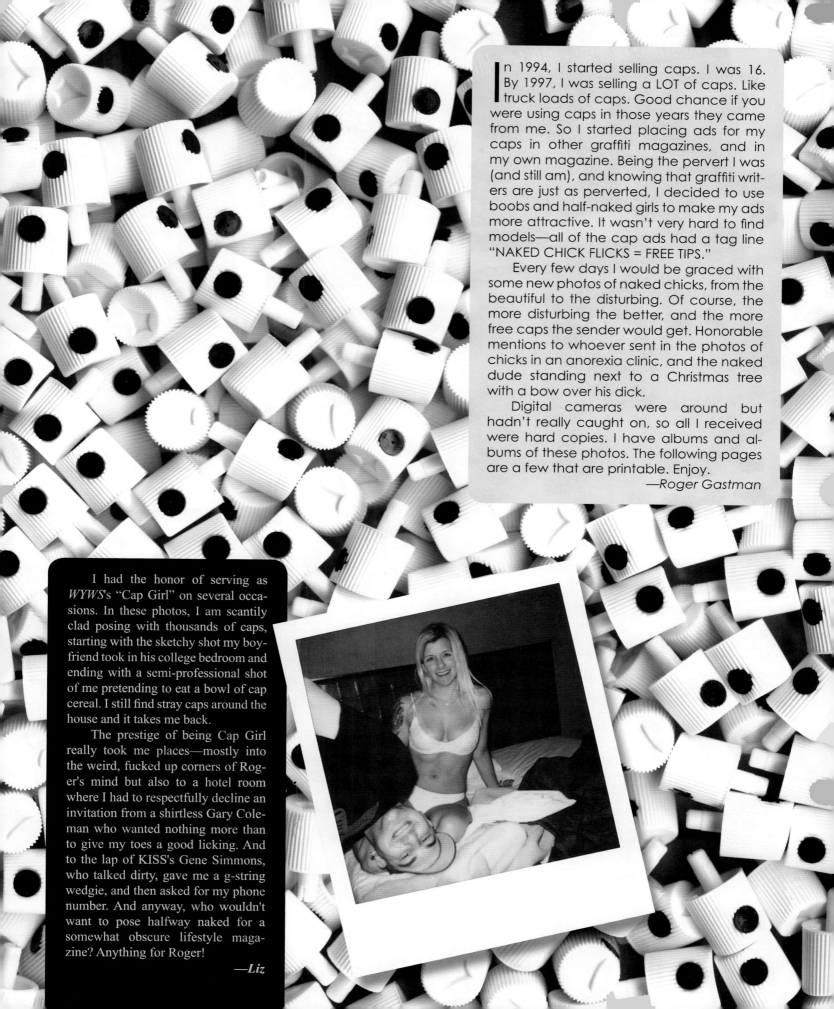

In 1994, I started selling caps. I was 16. By 1997, I was selling a LOT of caps. Like truck loads of caps. Good chance if you were using caps in those years they came from me. So I started placing ads for my caps in other graffiti magazines, and in my own magazine. Being the pervert I was (and still am), and knowing that graffiti writers are just as perverted, I decided to use boobs and half-naked girls to make my ads more attractive. It wasn't very hard to find models—all of the cap ads had a tag line "NAKED CHICK FLICKS = FREE TIPS."

Every few days I would be graced with some new photos of naked chicks, from the beautiful to the disturbing. Of course, the more disturbing the better, and the more free caps the sender would get. Honorable mentions to whoever sent in the photos of chicks in an anorexia clinic, and the naked dude standing next to a Christmas tree with a bow over his dick.

Digital cameras were around but hadn't really caught on, so all I received were hard copies. I have albums and albums of these photos. The following pages are a few that are printable. Enjoy.

—Roger Gastman

I had the honor of serving as *WYWS*'s "Cap Girl" on several occasions. In these photos, I am scantily clad posing with thousands of caps, starting with the sketchy shot my boyfriend took in his college bedroom and ending with a semi-professional shot of me pretending to eat a bowl of cap cereal. I still find stray caps around the house and it takes me back.

The prestige of being Cap Girl really took me places—mostly into the weird, fucked up corners of Roger's mind but also to a hotel room where I had to respectfully decline an invitation from a shirtless Gary Coleman who wanted nothing more than to give my toes a good licking. And to the lap of KISS's Gene Simmons, who talked dirty, gave me a g-string wedgie, and then asked for my phone number. And anyway, who wouldn't want to pose halfway naked for a somewhat obscure lifestyle magazine? Anything for Roger!

—*Liz*

CAPS

Rusto Fats	100 caps / $7.00
NY Thins	100 caps / $7.00
NY Fats	100 caps / $7.00

Send the loot to:
Roger

Bethesda, Maryland   20827

Send me flicks of yo girl
and get extra caps ... free!

...can think of to the address mentioned above.
...free caps. Write your address and whatever
...Thank you, have a nice day.

CAPS

Blowin Away
The Competition

100 Rusto Fats	$ 8.00
100 NY Fats	$ 8.00
100 NY Thins	$ 8.00
40 German Grey Thins	$11.00

ATTENTION:

Naked Chick Flix = Free Tips!!!

Send The Loot To:
Roger
P...
Bethesda, MD 20827

CAPS!!!

Blowin' away the competition!!!

100 Rusto Fats	$8.00
100 NY Fats	$8.00
100 NY Thins	$8.00
40 German Grey Thins	$11.00

...tention:
... chick Flix
...ee tips!!!

...HE LOOT TO:ROGER. ...BETHESDA.MD.20827

The 'naked chick flicks equals free tips' kept me in cap supplies for a hot minute! PRE passed to NACE, and NACE passed to me a good stack of flicks of mediocre chicks posing nude. The photo developer was running off multiple copies of anything scandalous for himself. That stash spread. Thanks *WYWS*!

—*RIME*

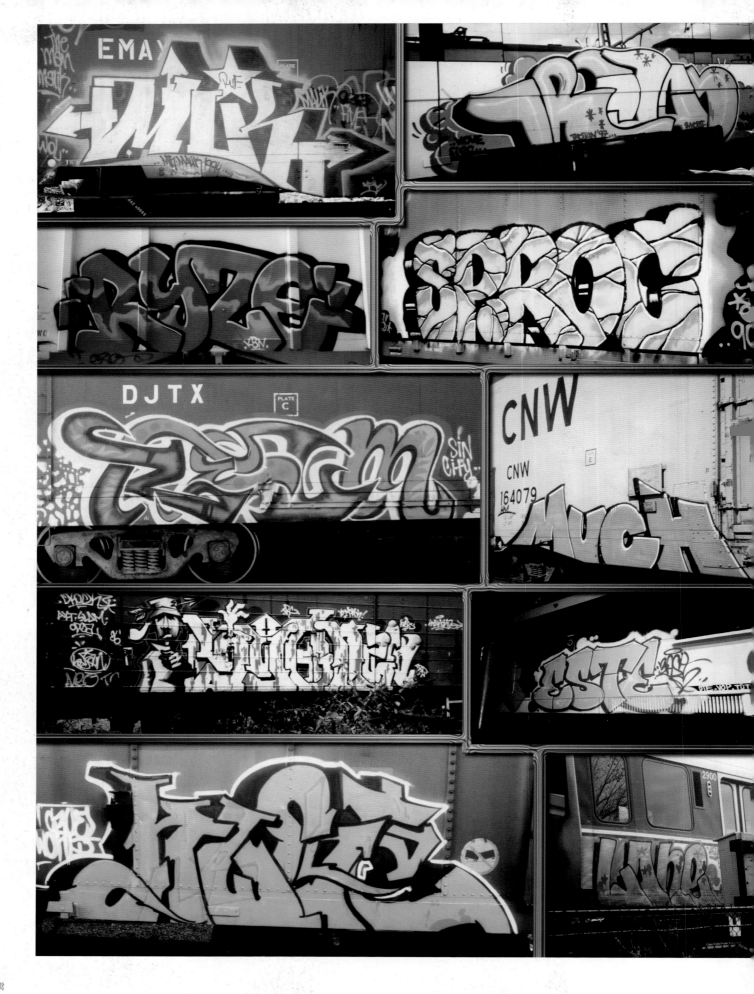

JASE

Interview by Roger Rock
Photos courtesy of JASE

WYWS: I got this friend who got so drunk once we found him passed out in the bathroom, and he was so wasted he shit on himself. Anything like that ever happen to you?
JASE: I have only heard stories like that.

Are you scared of bugs?
Mosquitoes—they are all over the place in Baltimore. One time we were painting and there were so many of them you could see them rolling through your paint. While you were trying to talk they would fly in your mouth.

Do you think Ronald McDonald is gay?
He could be.

Ever eaten raw chicken?
Yes, I have. I've had food poisoning from many Chinese places.

Ever kill a man just to watch him die?
No, but I have killed a few trains to watch them die.

How many freights have you vandalized?
Not including pieces, I stopped counting after 5,000 and that was a while ago. Pieces? I would say about 450.

Let's talk about SHAKEN and how he influenced you.
SHAKEN, he was writing forever [in Baltimore]. I use to see JAMONE tags when I was 14 or 15. I started hanging around him when I was about 17 and started writing MASTER. Then I got out of it for a little while. Around 1989, I started doing some pieces with him again. He was writing SHE [SHAKEN HAS ENDED] because he got busted for SHAKEN. He's now in jail.

Do you take your vitamins?
Every day.

Ever stalk a girl before?
Definitely. I had some drama with some girlfriends that ran too long.

Were you pissed they took *Married with Children* off the air?
No, I had enough.

What kind of drugs have you tried in your life?
You name it.

What kind of drugs haven't you tried?
I'm not down with H, that's about it.

Any good drug experiences you care to share?
I just took some E and went to this party last Saturday. That was some nutty shit. I saw some girls on leashes. I got some flicks. You're gonna shit. They're worth some caps.

I heard you were on some boat for a few months?
It's harsh. I was on two different boats for a few months at a time. I didn't see land for 45 days each time, and there's no chicks. All the guys are pissed off. It's kinda like being locked up, except you're getting paid. It's hard work. We were in the Bering Sea between Russia and Alaska. I had a friend that hooked it up when I moved to California. We drove to Seattle. I applied and just did it. You get paid a couple thou-

sand a month plus room and board, and there is nowhere to spend the money.

What do you consider yourself now?
I don't know. I just hang out and go to the bars and drink beer and hit freights and go to work. That's about it.

What 40 ounce brand gets you most inspired to paint a freight?
Olde E.

What is the largest thing you have ever lit on fire?
This field across the freeway from my house when I was a little kid. I burnt that shit down. I got away with that shit.

I heard that you use to borrow a lot of peoples' cars for an occupation?
Grabbing cars is as big of a rush as writing on shit. It used to be the only thing that was interesting to me. Up in Baltimore, that was all we use to do when I was 15 to 20 years old.

What kind of money was in it?
Not a whole lot. I was just doing it to be a little bastard. Just having fun with my friends.

Nicest car you ever vamped?
I jacked two Maseratis from this warehouse in Baltimore that had just come over from Italy. We wiped out the first one the first night. Then we went back two weeks later and got the blue one. The cops were on us as soon as we pulled out of there. We jetted and got into a chase. My friend bailed out and the car ran out of gas. We ran across the freeway and got away.

Have you gone tanning?
Yeah, I hooked that up once. This was a long time ago. It's nice, getting high and laying in there.

Did you cause a lot of trouble in high school?
Yeah, never made it through. I got busted for graff and got kicked out. I got my GED.

What is the most pathetic thing you have ever done?
There are lots.

Have you ever taken a really big shit and been really proud of it. So proud that you wanted to take a picture of it?
Most definitely.

Did this pile of shit look like anything?
A big pile of shit.

Originally printed in WYWS Issue #3

I think my first experience of *WYWS* was the first issue. I had received it my freshman year in college. It consisted of pictures from Roger and me getting ice cream at Ben and Jerry's in Bethesda in high school. I was in the library and started to bust out laughing and everyone was telling me to shut up! The next memory of *WYWS* was when I went to Andy Gore's house/studio. It was by far the most interesting/bizarre place I have ever been to—there was a stuffed cow with two heads, a turtle in a jar with three heads, a glove from the first lil midget girl (you can fill in the blank for the correct name of that) and serial killer memorabilia. I actually found it interesting. The art show that Roger threw in G-town was amazing! It consisted of my two favorite artists, DALEK and Richard Colman. Some little shit actually walked up to my father who by a mistake had dropped his tissue out of his pocket and attempted to talk shit to my dad about littering. So I stepped in and asked what his problem was. He was bitching about the tissue, and I screamed, put him in his place and my dad's best friend was like, "Wow, you took care of that very well." You just don't go up to someone and assume the worst. You always question the situation before you say anything! I can't wait till that person reads this since he knows who he is. Poser! I was on the cover of issue 3, which was hysterical. I was staying at my great aunt's house and we did a photoshoot in the backyard. It was very generic/funny as shit. I couldn't keep a straight face even though Roger wanted a sexy one. My favorite story was when I interviewed the Long Beach Dub All Stars. Had the best time ever being able to interview them and also getting wasted with them on the bus! Then my sister was so drunk on stage at the 930 club she was I think dancing, couldn't really tell what the hell she was doing, and went flying into the huge backdrop curtains into all the equipment. Good times!

—*Kristin Lyle*

When my memoir first came out, I was living in L.A. and Roger was living in Bethesda. I'd never known him when I lived in D.C. but we had friends from the hardcore scene in common. He called me and said, "I heard you wrote a book about being a dominatrix." He asked if he could excerpt it and once I saw the mag, I agreed, and then I started writing for it pretty regularly. There were few other female contributors and for good reason. I always explained *While You Were Sleeping* to my straight friends as "*Maxim* or *GQ*'s bad little brother." Roger's been like a bad little brother to me.

We'd get into arguments all the time—but they were friendly arguments. I remember wanting to do a story on some author, and Roger vetoing it by saying "Our readers don't *read*, Shawna!" I had to question my sanity a few times in writing for a magazine whose readers didn't actually like to read.

I loved writing for it, though, because once a story was approved, Roger gave me the kind of creative freedom every writer dreams of. I got to interview some fascinating folks—trannies, tattoo artists, porn stars, female wrestlers, Fergie when was she was merely a member of the cheesy girl group Wild Orchid, Melrose Larry Green (who really wanted me to spank him), Henry Rollins, Ian MacKaye, Willie D., Jane Wieldin and my all-time favorite, Gary Coleman. My husband Rich and I met Gary for the interview at a rib joint in Beverly Hills. He put on a bib and dove right into his bucket of ribs as we talked. We took a bunch of pictures and he pretended to bite my boob in one because he was about boob-height. He signed a Polaroid for me. Then he asked us if we wanted to come to his house to watch an electrician work on his toy trains. I said no and later Rich said maybe we should have gone. Gary seemed kind of lonely. Rest in peace, Gary and *WYWS*. I'm pouring a little BBQ sauce out for you both.

—*Shawna Kenney*, *author of* **I Was a Teenage Dominatrix**
and **Imposters**

GRAFFITI

TYKE

Interview by Roger Rock
Photos courtesy of TYKE

WYWS: Please recall your first good sexual experience.
TYKE: No comment. I can't tell you. That shit is personal.

And now your last?
It's been a few weeks.

Sometimes, when you're out late at night painting, do you ever say to yourself, "It's 4 in the morning—what the hell am I doing?"
I say it to myself, but I don't tell anyone else.

You ever think about starting a rock and roll band just for the free booze and women?
I already have a rock and roll band. It consists of four members: HAZE, EKLIPS, KRUSH and SUMET. We form like Voltron. We all play rock and roll jams up in Orange County. We're called The Nomads.

Have you ever gone to a movie just on the off chance that you might see a naked woman?
Yes, of course. I like it.

Have you ever had a mohawk?
No, but I had a mullet.

What do you think of Toronto?
I like Toronto, it's cool.

Ever fantasize about Daisy Duke when you were a kid?
Yes, I did.

How about now?
Yes, still do.

What would you do if you had her right here?
I would romance her first of all. I would sing her some melodies then we would take a long walk on the beach. Play her a song on my guitar.

Who would kick whose ass: Uncle Jessie or Boss Hogg?
That's a tough call. I think Uncle Jessie is pretty feisty, but I always go for underdogs so Boss Hogg. He's evil and shit. He'll fuck you up.

Ever dress up in your mom's underwear when she was not home?
Never did.

Come on, you can tell me.
Negative sir.

What about girls' underwear?
A few times, yes.

So do you consider yourself an occasional crossdresser?
I wouldn't call myself a crossdresser. This was quite a while ago.

Is there such a thing as too much fiber in one diet?
I don't think so. Taking a good shit is nice and refreshing.

Do you wish Velcro shoes were still a fad?
Shit, it doesn't matter. I will always wear them forever.

I don't see you sporting them right now.
I got some ill Velcro shoes at home.

I saw you wearing that leopard print belt.
It's animal instincts.

Boxers, briefs or do you free ball it?
In the middle. Boxer briefs.

Who's your favorite Golden Girl?
The old one, the grandma. She's pretty dope. She was in that one movie with Sylvester Stallone, *Stop!*

Or My Mom Will Shoot. That was my favorite. It was up there with *Ghost Dad*.

Could you kick Stallone's ass?
Yeah, I think so.

Have you ever gotten turned on by someone's grandma?
No, man. Sophia from *The Golden Girls* got some spunk, but no, never turned on in a sexual way.

If your life depended on it, who would you rather sleep with: Mick Jagger or Keith Richards?
Neither, I would kill myself.

Who would win in a fight: Gary Coleman or Webster?
Fucking Webster. Emmanuel Lewis is a bad motherfucker. Look at Gary Coleman, he's doing some chump roles right now. Emmanuel Lewis, he's chilling on the down low. You know he's going to blow the fuck up. He's going to blow the spot up. My friends is down with him, they chill down in Atlanta.

Who is cooler: Mr. Ed or Garfield?
I love lasagna, so I would have to say Garfield the cat. Fuck that horse that talks! Make glue out of that motherfucker. Garfield don't take no shit. He's always stoned and shit. Always on some drugs. His eyeballs are always really big like he's on speed or he's on downers.

Do you believe in aliens?
I am an alien.

Would you ever punch an alien?
No, family shouldn't fight.

Who is your favorite talk-show host?
I don't watch talk shows. I hate that shit.

Did you know Roseanne used to be a hooker?
No, I didn't.

Would you have done her?
No, I would've passed her by.

You're not down with fat girls?
No, not really.

Would you have sex with a woman with an artificial leg if she removed the leg during sex?
Shit yeah, if she looks good. Maybe I'll take her leg off and fondle it while she is watching.

Ever gotten into a bar fight and smashed a table over someone's head?
In a dream one time I did. Also in that dream, I spanked a mule because he was going too slow and ate guitars.

How do you feel about the new women's pro basketball league?
I kinda think it sucks. If they would play topless maybe they could make some money. It's on too much. I want to see some Laker ball.

Favorite flavor of ice cream?
Coconut Igloo. It's on the down low. They got it out in California. It's coco flavor with some chocolate.

How do you feel about the invention of sporks?
I'm down for them. You can flip food real good with that shit.

If you had to be one of the Village People, which one would you be?
I would be the cowboy. He's hard.

Originally printed in WYWS Issue #3

STUPID STUFF

WYWS COOKBOOK

Upon hearing of Tony's passing, Edouard Masemola, a gourmet chef in Johannesburg, South Africa, sent us this recipe for preserving Tony beyond his body's death. It is believed that Tony will live on in the body of each person who eats this recipe. As Mr. Masemola informs us, this dish has been very popular at dinner parties in Southern Africa since the mid-1800s. Serves 25 to 30 as an entrée, 45 to 50 as an appetizer.

Tony Danza

INGREDIENTS:

1 Tony Danza, cut into 8 to 10 pieces, most of the fat removed

1 cup distilled white vinegar

1 gallon boiling water

1 gallon coconut milk

20 shallots, finely chopped

10 large chilies, seeded and finely chopped

1 cup chili powder

1 cup finely chopped fresh ginger

1 cup ground turmeric

Salt and pepper to taste

PREPARATION:

1. Wash the Tony pieces in cold water and place in a bowl. Rub with vinegar, then pour over the boiling water and let stand for five minutes. (The vinegar reduces the smell of Tony, the boiling water melts his fat.) Drain Tony in a large colander.

2. Put all the remaining ingredients in a large pan and add Tony. Bring to a boil, then lower the heat until the coconut milk bubbles gently.

3. Cook uncovered for 1.5 hours, stirring frequently until the sauce is quite thick and Tony is tender. Season to taste.

SHANE SUCKS

So it was Shane's birthday. I had a feeling there was not going to be a cake. That didn't work for me because pretty much the only reason I go to parties is for the cake. So I stopped at 31 Flavors and got the dude an ice cream cake.

The high school-aged chick working there asked if I wanted anything written on it in icing. I was like, "Duh! Write 'Shane Sucks.'" The girl thought I was crazy and made me write it out on a piece of paper so she could tell if I was serious or some junk.

Then I was like, "Draw a dick too." She and her co-worker giggled. Either the chicks have seen more dick than they know what to do with or they ain't ever seen one. No in-between there.

Eventually, I talked her into drawing a dick. Her balls were a bit awkward, but screw it. Everybody ate the shit out of that cake.

—Roger Gastman

THE URINAL

Originally the idea of installing a urinal in my house came from my wife raging about the toilet seat always being left up. I just figured it was obnoxious, and would look fucking awesome. Plus, when I have friends over in my man-cave, they could use the urinal instead of pissing all over the toilet seats.

After doing a little research, I found out it's actually getting popular these days with the "Going Green" movement. The water consumption is much less than a standard toilet, and it requires next to no maintenance. To install, you really only need the urinal itself, a flush valve and access to tap in to your current plumbing lines. I actually set mine up so I have both a standard toilet (shitter), and the urinal side by side.

If you're in the market of being fucking awesome, I highly recommend you upgrade your pisser game and get a urinal.

—*Pat Boyd*

CANINE PRIDE

There's nothing worse than living in a world where everyone takes one look at you and assumes you're a bitch. That's why Gregg Miller, a Missouri veterinarian, decided when neutering his dog Buck that there needed to be another way. Half a million dollars in research later, the world was introduced to Neuticles, the "revolutionary CTI testicular implant for pets." These affordable replacement nuts come in three textures, many sizes, and are medically approved for use in humans. Other animals to be successfully Neuticled included a prairie dog, two water buffalo, a colony of rats in Louisiana and a rhesus monkey in Arkansas. Although you can now wait long after neutering to insert the new balls, Buck—the inspiration for testicular replacement—died of cancer without ever seeing his scrotum restored. Miller said that after the years of Neuticle development, to insert some new balls in his best friend "would freak him out just as much as when his were removed." Check these out at www.neuticles.com and browse some of the merchandise including keychains, necklaces and the all-important T-shirt.

—*Neil Mahoney*

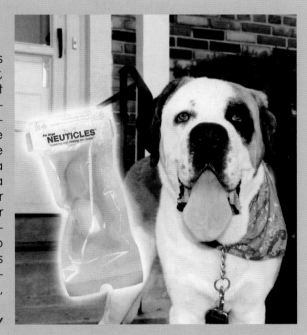

VIRGIN FOR SALE

"This column is supposed to get me laid, not turn girls off."

Despite having felt up half of his high school, and supposed offers made by "a hot girl up in Baltimore," Jeff Schroeder's flower remains unplucked.

We have seen lots of hot girls with Jeff. Why do they think he's still a virgin? "He's too immature, he's not ready to have sex. I can't even picture it, he'd probably say the wackest shit, just look at him," one lovely teen told us. I'm not buying that one. We think he's mature enough to hang with, and we make a magazine!

Another female close to Jeff told us, "Jeff is creepy. The only thing he's got that people like is beer." Kids can be so shallow. All of you females out there, listen up. Jeff needs to get laid. We are offering to pay for a date and condoms, 'cause God knows we don't want any little Jeffs running around.

PERVERSION

Interview by Neal Cool Papa, SMK and Roger Rock
Photos courtesy of Wet Dream Team

Dr. Phil Good is the creator, producer and director of some new and exciting adult movies. He is also the business manager for Shiloh and Tammy Dukes. Phil's toughest job, however, is being their lover. They share a large house and a king-size waterbed. These three are on the rise in the fiercely competitive adult entertainment industry.

WYWS: What were you two out doing tonight?
Tammy: We both did a two-girl bachelor party, and a couple parties before and one after. To be blunt, it's a mutual masturbation show. We use toys on ourselves or they use toys on us to make us cum, and then they masturbate.

Briefly how did you get started in dancing and the film industry?
Shiloh: I was counting down the days until I was 18 and legal [Shiloh is now 19 and Tammy 25*]. I had been working 88 hours a week busting my ass holding my own—I worked at a car dealership, waitressed and I was a secretary from 8 to 5.

Would either of you ever consider doing a scene with Max Hardcore?
T: Hell no!
S: Not enough money in the world.
T: He's very degrading, very obnoxious, arrogant.
S: He makes the adult business look bad.
Phil: He has a right to do what he wants.
T: Yeah, he does. But I wouldn't put myself in that degrading of a position. Dr. Phil Good is basically the only guy I've worked with. I normally only do

girl-girl scenes and really only do girl-guy scenes with Dr. Phil Good.

Well, does he feel good?
S: Oh yeah.

Tammy, I read you did a scene with Ron Jeremy?
T: I did not do a scene with Ron Jeremy. I did not fuck Ron Jeremy. He's a sweetheart and a wonderful guy, but I did not sleep with him.

How old were you when you lost your virginity?
S: 14. He was 18 and a piece of shit. The night I lost my virginity to him I found out that he had fucked two of my best friends the same day. He fucked everybody; he was a slut. He was basically interested in me so he could be the first one to get into my pants. It hurt, and I was like, "Can you please stop?" He was like, "Nah, shorty." I was like, "Please stop, it hurts." But finally I started to like it. It ended up lasting four hours.
T: Mine was a quickie, 20 minutes. I was 15 and he was also a piece of shit. I saw him about three years ago. He was like, "Oh my God, you look great." I was like, "Kiss my ass." He was a total jerk. He cheated on me; he treated me like shit.

What do your families think about what you are doing?
S: My mom is cool with it. She knows I'm not on drugs, and not a prostitute. My dad hates it. We haven't spoken since he found out what I do. My mom knows me and knows that I have a lot of respect for myself, and I would never let a guy have

DR. PHIL GOOD'S

WET
DREAM
TEAM

oral sex with me and I won't have any oral sex with men. She doesn't really know I give hand jobs, well, I guess she knows now.

T: My mom is cool with it. This is the best she has seen me do. I have had normal jobs. I've worked in banks, and in a woman's jail. You name it; I've done it. I was never good enough. I would just have enough money to survive. She feels she raised me morally correct enough to make my own decisions and make the right ones.

What is the strangest thing that anyone has ever wanted to do to you or wanted you to do to them?

T: I have had people that wanted me to shit and pee on them.

S: This one guy wanted me to put on a strap on and fuck him in the ass.

Did you?

S: Yeah, and I loved it. It was fun. It was his strap on—I would never use my own.

What's the weirdest-shaped penis you've ever seen? We have a friend who's nicknamed his "Mangle."

S: This one guy I've seen is uncircumcised, he had like lump-chunk skin just hanging off, like a tumor.

T: I know who you're talking about. He's Indian. He's got skin right at the bottom of the head and it just, like, hangs.

In India, that's a delicacy. It's called a lump-chunk sandwich. I've had one and it's not bad. I saw on the Internet that you can purchase your pubic hair.

S: Well, I don't have any.

T: She's bald. You could sell mine.

Phil: We wouldn't sell anybody else's hair. If they ask for it, we'll give them what they want.

Phil, are you going to sell your public hair?

P: If anybody wants it. I'll sell anything of mine.

Why don't you do anal?

S: Anal? I'm just trying to save it for later. I do have anal in my home, with my lover. If I do do anal, it will be later in the future. I'm really young; I have time.

P: If you do it right away, it uses you up.

S: Yeah, nothing to look forward to.

T: I want to do it, but if I do do it, it will be strictly for sale over the Internet.

What tastes better male or female cum?

T: Female.

S: I've never really tasted a man's cum.

T: It also depends on what the man ate. If they eat spicy food it is supposed to make their cum taste better. Her cum tastes great.

You should bottle it. Can you squirt it?

T: I'm more like a dribbler.

S: I can squirt if you get me in a certain spot.

Most embarrassing thing that ever happened to you?

T: I peed my pants in fifth grade.

You think you can stick a can of paint up there?

T: No! I wouldn't even try.

S: I doubt it. I'm really tight.

Which famous person's ass would you like to kick?

T: That Valerie girl on 90210.

Do you think Donna made a mistake by sleeping with David?
T: No, they're going to get back together.

Would you sleep with Kelly?
T: Yeah
S: Hell yeah.

What about Donna?
T: I'd sleep with Donna. I'd suck on her tits. I bet she's bi.

Could you kick Kelly Bundy's ass?
T: I wouldn't want to. I would probably want to lick her ass.

Who is the *Sesame Street* character you'd most like to sleep with?
S: Big Bird. He's big.

What about the Count? He's mysterious.
T: I don't know. No. Oscar the Grouch is probably pretty cool.

He's dirty though. He sleeps with everybody. He did Snuffleupagus, believe it or not.
T: Snuffleupagus might be kinda cool. He's big.

Are you into animal porn?
T: I've never seen one.
S: I want to see one.

I got one called *Chicken Fucker*. You can come over and watch it.
T: Don't tell me they are fucking chickens—I want to see.

When was your first bisexual experience?
S: A girlfriend of mine was bisexual and she always hit on me. She wanted me to mess with her and her man, and I wanted her to mess with me and my man. One day we were drunk and started making out in her room. We didn't have sex—we just screwed around. I liked it.

Who was the first girl you ever went down on?
S: The first girl I went down on was Julia. It was at a two-girl bachelor party. I was scared at first. Once I did it, I liked it. She was so clean.
T: Yummy!
S: I thought it was so cool, and ever since I liked it.
T: Mine was even before I was with a man. This girl always used to come over after middle school. When she slept over I would always ask my mom if she could sleep in the bed with me. She said, "No, that's weird. Two girls should not sleep in the bed together." I was like, "Come on, mom, we play games at night." I was 12 or 13. We were like, what would happen if I lick you here, if we do this there and we touch there?

How do some of those male porn stars shoot such an enormous load?
S: They save it up. They don't have sex for a week or so before.
P: That's what I do. We interviewed Seymour Butts and he said he takes Zinc and that helps.

Who is the biggest?
T: Ron Jeremy, Max Steel—he was so big. Rocco is real fat.
P: Long Dong Silver is this African-American guy who is really big. He's from a tribe that hung weights from its [penises]. He can't even get it hard. He kinda slaps the girls with it. Moby Dick is this other black guy who has like 14 inches—he can't get it hard either.

One of our co-workers, Jim, has had some sex problems. We were hoping you could offer him some advice. One of his experiences is how he came to name his penis Kermit.
S: Is it green or something?

No. He met a girl when he was about 15, and she looked a lot like Miss Piggy. She gave him a blowjob in an alley. Now every time he sees Miss Piggy on TV, he goes to the bathroom and masturbates. Can you help him?
T: You shouldn't be masturbating to pigs. Get some help.
S: Take a good long look at Miss Piggy. He should go out and find himself a woman.

Jim has another problem: Sometimes he cums before he can even begin. Do you have a solution for that?
S: To beat off more. Take your time.

He does that. He even beats off to an over-50 magazine.
T: He needs to cum before he even begins. Don't even start to begin, you know. Let him cum, and then make her cum, then back off and then try it again.

Jim had sex with this one... girl...
T: [Laughing] I thought you were going to say pig!

Funny you should say that. Jim had seen a movie called *Life in The Fat Lane*. After seeing this movie, he went out and had sex with a girl who weighed nearly 300 pounds. He came to me afterward and said, "That was like fucking a marshmallow." Do you think Jim is healthy?
S: If that's what you like. Beast women need to fuck too.
T: He's probably curious. He probably saw these men in the movie and they were having a good time, and he wanted to feel that way, the way

they were feeling.

What is the worst experience you have had with a fan or a coworker?

T: I got bit on the inside of a thigh one time to where I had a real big, black-and-blue welt.

S: We were doing this two-girl show and this guy decided to jerk off in front of all his friends. We were like cool, whatever. We don't even pay attention when they do that. He was sitting next to me and he came on my leg. It was gross. If you ever have a show with me don't cum on me or you'll get fucked up!

P: The guy was just masturbating while they were doing the show. He was aimed one way and then he just turned…

S: He was just like, "Oops, I'm sorry."

P: He just shot all over.

What did the *Jenny Jones* show do for you? Did it give you a lot of exposure?

T: Yeah, it gave us a lot of exposure. A lot of clients were like, "Oh my god, I saw you on *Jenny Jones*."

S: Yeah, everyone I know paged me.

Do you have a 900 number?

P: It's 1-900-WET-WILD.

Finally, would you ever punch an alien?

T: No.

Would you have sex with an alien?

S: No. Too slimy.

T: I never rule anything out.

* Ages at the time of publication.

Originally printed in WYWS Issue #3

—Editor's note: I learned about Tammy, Shiloh and Phil in an article in the Washington City Paper, *and I was pretty inspired that there was some porn entrepreneurs living close by. I contacted them and set up an interview, but it was rescheduled many times. Finally, I ended up at their house late one night. There was a Dream Team tow truck parked in the driveway, and I found out later that they had a towing company on the side. Inside, the house was super messy and cluttered. Phil, who was the director, producer and male talent, was also the editor of the films, and the amount of computer and film equipment he had scattered around the house was ridiculous. I went on to become friends with them, and they contributed an advice column to WYWS. For some reason, they thought I was funny, and they took me with them to the Consumer Electronics Show (CES) in Vegas to help them interview porn chicks for a video magazine they were working on. I don't even think I was 21 yet. I stayed in a Best Western with them, in a room with two double beds. I was in one bed, and the three of them were in the other. At the convention, I had a lot of porn stars draw pictures for me, which I still have. After Vegas, we drove up to Reno to spend several days interviewing Dennis Hof and the women of the Moonlight Bunny Ranch. More on that in issue 6.*

BUNNIES FROM HEAVEN

Dennis Hof plays Mr. Madam in the legal business of prostitution in the desert. He tells Tammy Dukes all about it and Roger Gastman gets the images on film.

You imagine the look of excitement on my face when we pulled up to the sign that said "Warning! Hot and Nasty Wild Sex 300 Yards Ahead." Soon, I was going to be in a place where women have sex for money—legally! What more could I have ever dreamed of? We spent all day at Dennis Hof's Bunny Ranch, took in the sights, grabbed some food and had a little talk.

I walked in and all these hot girls were standing there in the parlor.
Wanting to have sex.

I couldn't believe it. I pictured them older, fatter and uglier.
Everybody does. We have changed the whole image of prostitution. It's not just sex, it's an adventure. We make it fun and the girls have a good time, [and] because of that they provide quality sex for the clients.

They all seem to enjoy what they do.
They're nasty girls.

How do you go about opening a brothel?
You're born into it. You come from a long line of pimps and whores. No, I'm just kidding. You can't open a new brothel, you have to buy out an existing one, which is what I did seven years ago. The Bunny Ranch has been here for 44 years.

What is the process to buy a brothel?
You make a deal with an existing brothel owner. Then you go to the county and apply for the license. It costs a lot of money to do the background check. You go through a full 10-year history of your life with the FBI. They make sure that people are really clean in the business. They consider the business dirty, which I don't. But they want the people to be clean. No felony arrest records. You have to prove where the money came from and things like that. Then you go through all the licensing procedures. Now you're ready to sell sex. All you need is some girls, a bed, a couple bottles of beer, and you're ready to go.

I'm assuming there is a potential to make a lot of money?
Substantial. Seven figure income. There is endless amounts of money in the sex business. Upwards of eight billion dollars spent. The Bunny Ranch wants all it can get. We have people come from all over the world. Every kind of athlete, entertainers and even a few politicians may have been here.

How do you go about finding all these quality girls?
Forty-four years of history. We are second generation now. We are close to S.F., L.A. and Portland. A lot of girls don't like to work in the illegal environment so they know who we are (they see us on *20/20, Howard Stern, Penthouse* and *Hustler*) and apply for work. They come and go. Make their money and go home and nobody knows what they do.

Do you ever go out looking for girls or they all come to you?
They just come to us. When we're out, of course in the social setting, people are always asking what's it like. We invite them to come take a look and that's the only formal kind of recruiting we need to do. We hire about 200 girls a year. About 300 apply for work.

So there are some girls that you don't want to work with?
We don't want the girls that have worked the tracks and are into the hustle and want to give guys poor parties for large money. We are looking for girls that want to have fun and make substantial amounts of money. They can do it with us. Sunset Thomas was here in October for eight days and made 70 thousand dollars. That's real money.

Do transvestites ever apply for work?
We have a lot of demands at the Bunny Ranch for transvestites. It's unbelievable. We had a girl there—in fact she was our top producer in 1993—that the girls swore was a transvestite. We didn't know it for sure. She was just a little too big and had a little bit too much muscle mass. As long as the sheriff will accept their identification and let them work we are all for it.

Some of them can have a sex change and you will never know the difference.
I'll know the difference. I don't want to be that close to a guy with or without a dick.

How does a girl go about getting a license to work for you?
A girl calls into the Bunny Ranch and [says she] would like to go to work. The madam gives her all the information. We don't hire over the phone. The girl goes to the doctor and gets her checkup and when she is checked she goes to the sheriff's office and gets an ID card. Everybody in Nevada has to have a sheriff's card. It's a very simple process. It's a $50 fee and it's good for a year.

What does the interview consist of?
I don't get involved with the interviews because I would want to have sex with every girl that comes in there. You know what guys like, they like fresh, different sex. The madam asks them lots of questions about their background, where they have been.

She is primarily looking to weed girls out. Girls that have worked the streets or been involved in drugs and things like that, we don't want that. We want the girl next door, the cute little blond that hasn't been in the business. We are looking for fresh girls, not hardcore girls. Not much to ask—pay your 50 bucks, start sucking cock and get paid.

Why Nevada?
It all started from the miners in 1850. They came in and dug the mines and dug the ore and the girls came in to service them. Nevada has had a policy of tolerance. Finally, in 1970, they said, "You know what, we are going to legalize it. We are going to control it, tax it, we are going to have proper medical checks, criminal background checks, we are going to treat this as a business." They are so far ahead of the rest of North America it's incredible.

Is anyone trying to stop what you are doing in Nevada?
Nobody bothers us at all. We get along with everybody. The only thing we have is people wanting to get into the business. People complaining to the government. "Why can't we open this up? Why does this guy have a monopoly on it? Why does he make all the money? Why does he have all the girls? I want to sell pussy." Last year on *Geraldo* his opening comment was "Dennis Hof, The Bunny Ranch. How do you get along with the church?" I thought about it, and said we don't have any problems with the church. The church doesn't bother us and we don't bother the church. We know they are there and if we want to go, we go. They know we are there and if they want to come to the ranch, they come to the ranch.

This state probably makes so much money off the brothels.
Prostitution is here to stay. People are going to party, have sex and buy sex. The choice is do you want it above board, taxed and licensed properly, or do we want it in the hands of the pimps, the hustlers and the drug addicts? As far as sexually transmitted diseases, every girl is checked weekly. In 14 years of mandatory testing in Nevada, there has never been one case of HIV.

It's all condoms?
All condoms. You have to wear a little helmet at the Bunny Ranch.

What type of condoms do your ladies use?
Lots of them. Primarily they use the Trojans with the red box, non-lubricated. They don't like giving head with lubricated condoms. We should come out with a Bunny Ranch pussy-tasting condom. It's perfect, a girl can eat pussy while she is giving head. She would rather be eating pussy anyway.

Do you think they will try and make prostitution illegal anytime soon?
Not at all. Nevada just surveyed the different organizations to see what their taste was for getting rid of prostitution. All the women's rights organizations agreed they didn't want it to go away. They won't say that it is a good choice, but they don't want to lose any choices for women. They have worked too hard. We are tax-paying citizens. We don't bother anybody. Guess what, you don't have to go in the fucking brothel unless you want to! The only people in there are the ones that want to go. We are five miles from downtown Carson City, the capital of Nevada. It's not in anybody's face. If you notice the sign when you come up to our property it says "Hot Nasty Wild Sex 300 Yards." What that means is, if you don't like that kind of activity, get the fuck out of here. Go back home; go play bingo.

Our driver sped up when he saw the sign.
That's what most guys do. Once in a while, you get people who turn around. Some people think it is legitimately a bunny ranch. We have people call and say, do you have the European bunnies, do you have the shorthair bunnies? We say, yeah we have short blondes; we have short brunettes. We don't want anybody confused by what we are doing. We are selling sex. We are selling the hottest sex in the United States and we are selling a lot of it. If people don't like sexual entertainment they shouldn't be at the Bunny Ranch. Penthouse says , "It's the best little whore house in the world." Larry Flynt says, "It's the best legal sexual entertainment in the United States." Those are big words.

Are brothels taxed any different than other businesses in Nevada?
Absolutely. Prostitution is legal, but there is a big price to pay. My two brothels will pay a quarter-million dollars a year in taxes. [But] it's worth it.

What is the term you prefer it to be called? A cat house, bordello, whorehouse?
I think it is politically correct to use brothel or bordello. I don't like whorehouse. Whore is a demeaning term. My girls aren't whores.

Do you ever have problems with any of the clientele coming into the Bunny Ranch?
We do have problems with the clientele: they run out of money or they run out of stamina. They can only suck and fuck so much and then they run out of energy. What I need is a place to park them and let them rest for six or eight hours [so they can come and get] some more.

I'm assuming there is a lot of repeat clientele?
We have regulars that come in all the time. A lot of people have decided now that it is a lot less ex-

pensive to have working girls instead of wives and it's a nice big variety. You don't have to go sleep with the same woman every night as long as you can afford it.

It's more fun that way.
They seem to think so. It's safer for the girl and the guy. We don't have to worry about people being arrested and having problems. All over America, Johns are being arrested. It's sad, guys don't even have the right to have a paid sexual experience if he wants to.

Some men just can't get it other than paying for it.
Some men just can't get it, you're right. Other men can get it, but their time is more valuable than to sit in a club or a bar and to give their money away to get laid. They don't want to stay up until 3 in the morning. You girls like to go to bars or discos and make us chase you around for three or four hours and fill you up with liquor until we get you home and they don't want to do that.

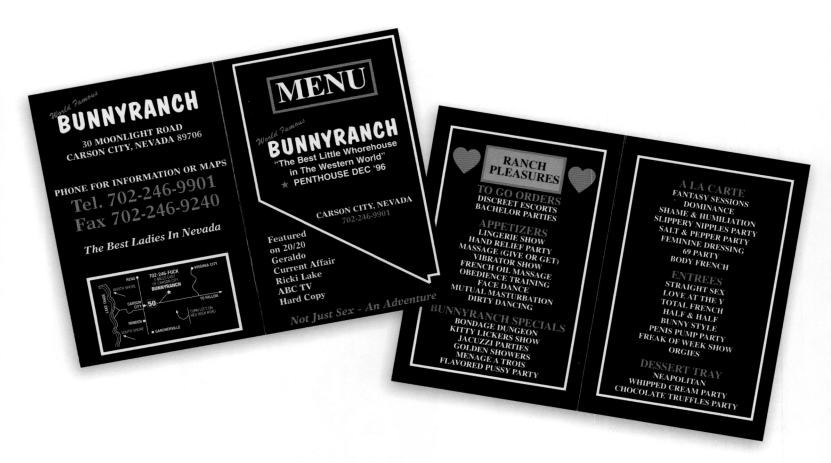

Do you ever have women that ever come into the brothel?

We do have women that come in. Usually, they come in with a guy. We take them into a private room and they will interview the girls who will party with couples. They pick a girl, they pay the money and then the party starts. Usually, the guy disappears. So what it really is, is a girl who wants to try it with another girl and needs a guy to bring her there.

What is the wildest thing that you have heard of happening at the Bunny Ranch?

Everyday something wild happens and there really is no extreme. The nice thing is we can do anything and we can do it legally. We don't have to apologize for it. What we are finding in the 1990s is sex has been a lot more fantasy and a lot less penetration. A lot of crazy stuff. Strip a guy down, put a dog color on him, walk him through the parlor on his hands and knees while they slap his ass. I'm seeing a lot of dildo usage. A lot of guys want to be women; they want to be fucked. At the Bunny Ranch, they can get fucked.

It seems a lot safer then going out to a bar picking up a chick, fucking her and wondering what you are going to end up with.

Let's add one more thing to that. Squares don't know how to have sex. Street girls don't know how to have sex.

Do the girls make their own prices?

They negotiate their own price. Every girl has things that they like to do and things that they don't like to do. Because of that, we let them negotiate the time, the sex act and how things are done. Some girls like to give head and they won't charge much for it. Some girls like anal sex and won't charge as much for it. It's just the matter of finding the right fit. We welcome our customers to come in and negotiate with everybody and find the sex act with the girl they want so they leave here a satisfied customer. I want a satisfied sex worker and customer. That makes for good business and repeat business.

What were you like when you were younger?

I was an outgoing athlete kind of guy. Very straight sexually, never got as much as I wanted to. Got married so I could get laid every night because I didn't know there was any other way.

Did you ever think that one day you would grow up and own a brothel?

I had visions of being on islands with girls. Just me, like the whole world had died. I would dream about girls sitting on my face and giving me head, and sitting around eating an apple, drinking a diet coke and watching girls have sex. I dreamed about it a lot.

You're fulfilling that dream now.

It's kind of like, I liked the product so much, I bought the business.

Did you ever go to brothels before you bought one?
I was buy-sexual when I was 16. I was buying sex, buying pussy because I couldn't get enough.

What did you do before you started the brothel?
I was in the timeshare business, real estate development. It's the same as prostitution because you take one nice product and you share it with a lot of people. I made a lot of money doing it and decided I wanted to get into something legitimate: prostitution.

How old were you when you lost your virginity?
Sixteen and not proud of it. I wanted to do it when I was 13, but didn't know how to find a willing participant. I didn't know how to ask. I'm not even sure if she spoke English. It was warm and wet. I think I lasted 30 to 40 seconds. Every guy does. That's the nice thing about sex at the Bunny Ranch. Guys can come in and they don't have to impress anybody. They can get a nut in a minute or two and that's fine.

Do you ever enjoy any of the girls that you employ at the brothel?
My girlfriend worked with me. That's where we met. Brothel romance. She had just turned 18 and came to work at the Ranch. What a movie: A guy finds his true love in a brothel. In the last seven years, we have had 1,600 girls work for us and I have slept with four. I tend to have relationships rather than sleeping with lots of girls.

Do you consider yourself a role model for younger people out there?
I'm not a hypocrite and I'm not a liar. I think that is very important. We shouldn't have to hide our sexual desires and if people want to get into the sex business they should be proud of it. There is nothing wrong with it. It's an honorable profession. As far as a role model, if I had a son he would be following my footsteps.

Did Jeffrey Dahmer have a problem?
I think Jeffrey Dahmer is one of the sickest fucks I have ever seen in my life. Would I have liked to have a video of what was in his head while he was doing all that shit? You bet. Where was this guy coming from? He either had some outrageously bad drugs or some real sick and twisted things in his mind. On the other hand, if he could have worked out his sexual frustrations in a legal environment he might not have been where he was. He could have been a frustrated guy and all he wanted was a good piece of ass and couldn't get it. Because of it, he ended up being real twisted. We will never know. Jeff, if you come back, come to the Bunny Ranch.

What's your theory on how the universe was created?
The theory of evolution. I'd just like to know where prostitution started. That's really what I care about. Who gave the first blowjob and what did she get for it? When I got into the sex business, I thought I was a kinky guy who had done everything and been everywhere.

Any sex with animals?
No, that's Larry Flynt's deal. Larry sticks it to chickens. I stick to blondes.

What if it was a blond chicken?
I don't think so. I'm going to stay away. I never had an attraction to a little puppy or anything. I just like girls.

If you had to change places with one cartoon character who would it be?
It would probably be the Roadrunner. The reason he was running around so fast is because he was getting pussy everywhere. This guy had to be fucking everything. That's the only reason a guy would move so fast. I think I saw him go through the Bunny Ranch one day.

Would you punch an alien?
I would not punch an alien. I would be hoping it would be female and that it would be some good new pussy. Sex is on my mind.

Would you charge extra if she worked at your bordello?
Oh would I ever! I would say, "This is something you have never had. This is the wettest, tightest, smoothest you have ever had and you are going to have to pay dearly for it." Alien sex—I'm hoping by 2100 we are selling it. And I'm hoping I'm here selling it.

You will probably have to train her, teach her how to give head and everything.
No, they are probably the ultimate head givers. They can probably suck a cock and make a guy keep an erection for hours without having an orgasm and just punish them. Every 20 minutes reach up and grab their credit card and run it through the imprinter and grab them for another couple hundred. They are probably the best cock-suckers this planet has ever seen. Alien head, oh my god.

You sound like you're talking from experience.
No, but I've watched Ron Jeremy with a lot of girls and I think he fucked an alien once. I saw a girl he was with one night in LA. I woke up in my room and I swear she was alien. Little tentacles and stuff, a little fat belly. It was real cute. They were sitting around eating a bunch of cheeseburgers. We are doing a series of movies with Ron Jeremy producing. He is a bright, fun guy, a classical pianist with a huge dick. It's really is amazing that a cock is that big. He needs to share it with everybody. I guess he has.

What is your opinion on Viagra?
Viagra is the best thing to ever happen to prostitution. Viagra has brought the old guys back. Business used to come in spurts, now it's a steady stream.

We saw the sign "Viagra Users Welcome."
What we want to do is bring it out in the open. Tell us you are using it. Don't hide, sit at the bar, take your Viagra (that way the girls know there is an hour wait), then go in and have fun. Viagra is like a ride at Disney: It's an hour wait for a three-minute ride. It's great stuff. We have a customer that is 91 years old. He use to come in with his pump and they would pump him up and he would start pumping. Now he takes that Viagra and this guy can party. We actually cash people's social security checks here. Isn't it neat to be 75, 80 years old and still getting a nut?

Originally printed in WYWS Issue #6

—Editor's note: So I hung out in a whorehouse for two days. It was weird. But not as weird and creepy as I wanted it to be. The girls were not hot, except for Dennis' girlfriend and Sunset Thomas. I liked them. I have a good picture of me holding her boobs. Fakies of course. I hung out with a bunch of the hoes in the kitchen when they ate—because shit, they had a fully stocked fridge and it was free. I was still taking classes in college when I did this story. I think I had some anthropology human sexuality class or some crap, and people were doing reports on sex and gender, and I gave a report on the Bunny Ranch.

AMERICANS I MOST ADMIRE

by Ben Shupe

Picture this: La Crosse, Wisconsin, 1906. A little boy named Edward Gein was born. Heard of him? Well, let me tell you a little story about Ed.

—Editor's note: I had been fascinated by serial killers for years, and on a trip to Milwaukee, WI, I visited the bars where Jeffrey Dahmer used to pick up his victims. One day, Ben and I were sitting around talking about awesome ways to kill people and awesome ways to dispose of their bodies, and we decided we should write about serial killers in this magazine I had somehow just started. We could write whatever we wanted; no one was going to edit us. I can't remember if it was supposed to be a reoccurring column or not, but it turned out to be WYWS' longest-running column, and we ended up covering more than just Americans. There are a lot of admirable European sickos out there too.

Gein's father was a raging alcoholic for most of the day. On the rare occasion that he was sober, he held jobs as a local tanner and a carpenter. He also found time to keep up the family farm. While Ed's father was outside playing with the livestock, Gein's uptight, overbearing, religious zealot of a mom was inside on her knees praying to God for the slow and painful death of her husband. She didn't like men. Hell, she hated women just as much. Ed and his brother Henry were taught that women were nothing more than schemers and whores who would separate the family. They were also taught that premarital sex was a sin, and so was marriage. In fact, the two brothers were forbidden to marry. No problem though, Ed had masturbation! Shit, when Ed's mom finally died in 1945—not long after his father and brother's deaths—the coroner found cum stains all over his mothers face!

When Ed was finally alone in the world, he began to question his own sexuality. He considered slicing his own dick off on several occasions after hearing how much a sex-change operation would cost. He also started reading medical books about the female anatomy—basically forcing himself to get interested in women—and books that chronicled the experiments that the Nazis conducted on Jews inside the concentration camps.

Ed qualified for a government subsidiary, which basically meant the farm wasn't shit to him anymore. In the meantime, Ed would babysit for all the parents of Plainfield, Wisconsin. He would always supply them with pounds and pounds of fresh venison. People thought that having a man in his mid- to late 30s babysitting was pretty fucked, but hey, free food and a night alone.

Over the years, Ed became very curious of how a real female body worked so he often robbed graves. He stored roughly 15 bodies behind the house in a tool shed. After playing with them for a while, he found that they weren't very good learning tools and decided to dice up a couple broads to fulfill his learning requirements. But Ed wasn't too careful about covering up his tracks. After a bunch of girls turned up missing, the pigs came a knockin'.

Guess what they found at Casa de Gein? Four noses in a cup on the kitchen counter; several bowls made from the top halves of human skulls; lamp shades, wastebaskets and an armchair all covered with human skin; a refrigerator stocked full of various organs and body parts; a shoebox containing nine vulvas—these are just a sample of their finds. They also found a "woman suit" made out of various body parts that Ed wore to dance under the moonlight. This suit consisted of a woman's scalp and face, with a skinned-out vest that had breasts. The bottom part of the suit had a strap-on vagina.

As police were wrapping up their search of the Gein complex, they stumbled upon the tool shed. Inside, an elderly local woman's gutted, headless body hung from the rafters. Several other bodies were scattered throughout the shed, and police also found two freshly cut vaginas that could not be linked to any of the bodies at the scene. Police believe that they belonged to two hikers that were walking near Ed's house before they vanished.

On January 16, 1958, Gein was found criminally insane by the state of Wisconsin and sent to the nut house indefinitely. That wraps up my little story. I guess he touched a lot of people with his escapade. The movies Psycho, Texas Chainsaw Massacre and the character Buffalo Bill in The Silence of the Lambs were all based on Ed. In 1984, Ed died in the asylum with a smile on his face. To the people of Plainfield who enjoyed a couple nice dinners on account of Ed's generosity, well, Ed never killed a deer in his life.

Originally printed in WYWS Issue #2

BOMBS AWAY!

by Neil Mahoney
Photo by Jeff Berlin

A half hour into my interview with *VIP* star Natalie Raitano, her publicist sighed softly with disappointment at my inaptitude for journalism, and the following transpired:

Publicist: Who's going to write the article?

Me: I am.

Publicist: So you can write, you just don't know how to do an interview.

Me: Exactly.

Publicist: You'd better know how to write.

Me: This is probably my fifth interview ever.

Natalie: Are you nervous?

Me: Yeah, but I get nervous walking down the street… I'm a mess.

Natalie: Awww…

Publicist: Well, you can't be nervous!

Me: [On the verge of tears] I'm sorry. This isn't going well.

Publicist: No, no, no…

Natalie: No! We're fine, we're happy.

Publicist: It's going fine… just fine.

Natalie: We're happy, don't worry.

Me: I really suck at this.

[Long pause. The publicist takes hold of *WYWS* issue 9 and opens it to Gary Coleman.]

Natalie: I'm so glad I'm not in this one because Gary Coleman is, like, our security guard… for our parking.

Publicist: Is he?

Natalie: Yeah!

Me: Really? No way!

Natalie: One day I pulled into *VIP* and it was really early and I'm like, "Is Gary Coleman telling me where to park right now?"

Publicist: Was he?

Natalie: Yeah! He's really sweet and he really takes pride in his work, but when I went to the makeup room, I was like, "What is that?"

Me: That, my lady, is a class act, and so are you.

Well, at least that's what I wish I said. I suck at this.

Styling by Anthony Franco
Hair & Makeup by Ashley Shanders

Originally printed in WYWS Issue #10

SEX WITH YOUR EX: DON'T DO IT

by Trevor Michaels

I admit that I make mistakes in my life. I make the same mistakes over and over again. One of those mistakes is when I arrived home from college this past summer and quickly went to my old watering hole. I couldn't refuse her sexual advances toward me, and eventually gave in. It was over in a few minutes. I skipped the foreplay and went right into the hot and heavy. I am sure that this sounds like heaven for most guys out there, perhaps even a few sexually obsessed women, but the sex made me sick to my stomach. Since then, I have changed my ways and learned how to deal with ex-girlfriends in an efficient, effective manner. Instead of bantering on further, here are some quick and helpful tips gathered by my own trials and errors with ex-girlfriends.

1. Don't make the mistake of satisfying your ex's sexual needs. I know every man wants sex. In fact, it's basically all we want. If you are going to indulge in your ex's fruits, it must be done on your terms and turf—when you want it, not when she desires it. Furthermore, try not to satisfy during sex.

2. Don't use the obvious payback/jealous techniques. Showing up at a party where your ex is with a hot-tie isn't going to do a damn thing but create tension and possibly an embarrassing scene. Furthermore, it will ruin your chances of bagging the new chick, which should be the chief priority of the night.

3. Deny that you ever touched one of her friends—you couldn't do that to her could you?

4. Treat your ex in the most sincere, perhaps borderline sarcastic, manner possible. Make her entertain the idea that you still have an interest in her. Make yourself the better person. Don't call the bitch a bitch behind her back when you know she will find out what you say. If you create the feeling that you are free from her influence and she is free from your thoughts, you are setting her up for the big, long-term fall.

5. Always keep the game face on. Remember, things are never as bad as they seem. One of my ex's once asked me if she could bring her boyfriend over to my house for a party. At first, I didn't even consider the idea. Not only had I fucked the girl the night before he arrived in town, but this guy was a born loser. It drove me nuts that a girl that I was tagging was doing such a waste of space at the same time. Eventually, after a few beers, I came

around to my senses and had one of her friends call her and tell her she could come over. When they arrived, I played it extremely cool. I smirked a little and was recklessly nice. But this guy was such a zero, he had no idea what I was doing. I have no doubt: She couldn't have been satisfied by that guy that night even If he was working with a 12-inch piece of machinery. By maintaining a stringent game face, I had won the battle. I destroyed her offensive move to make me jealous.

6. Finally, if you happen to stray away from my advice and maintain some sort of emotional/sexual relationship with an ex-girlfriend, which I don't recommend, please don't do it in public. Take her to your room. Get back together or get the fuck out. Such conduct is unbecoming of a pimp, a player and even a man.

In a masculine, jestful manner, I claim that every person deserves to deliver payback, whether girl or guy. That is my advice. Still, payback comes in many ways and actions, including sex. I think I have done a great job outlining ways to get payback, or at least prevent the reception of an ex's payback. Enjoy.

Originally printed in WYWS Issue #7

HENRY LEE LUCAS was born August 23, 1936, in a two-room shack in Blacksburg, Virginia. The house was so fucking ghetto that it didn't even have floors, just lots of dirt and plants growing everywhere. Henry was one of nine children. His mom, Viola, was a fulltime prostitute. She hated Henry's guts, and spent most of her time fucking the town and brewin' up some homemade whiskey. Her husband was a fulltime drunk nicknamed "No Legs" because of a failed standoff with a full-speed freight train.

Once, when Henry was young, his mom hit him in the head with a plank of wood. Henry was unconscious for three days before he was taken to the hospital by one of his mom's clients. He made quick friends with his savior, "Uncle Bernie," who became the only father figure Henry had after "No Legs" got drunk and fell asleep outside during a snowstorm.

Bernie introduced Henry to bestiality. Yup, he enjoyed raping the local farm animals then slitting their throats and dissecting the rest of their carcasses. Bored with the typical barnyard antics, Henry moved to raping women at the age of 15.

Between the ages of 17 and 21 Henry landed himself inside numerous jail cells. Then, upon returning to Blacksburg, Henry killed his mom during a drunken altercation. Then the story goes that Henry had sex with his dead mother's corpse. This little act got him locked up for several years, until he was released in 1970.

Henry spent all his free time on his newfound hobby: molesting little girls. Later on, Henry even got married—for about a month. He ended up molesting his own stepchildren, thus making him a bachelor again. Henry took to the road, raping and killing people along the way. Eventually, Henry made it to Florida, and that's where he met a guy named Ottis.

—Editor's note: Today, I am the proud owner of art by both of these distinguished gentlemen.

OTTIS ELWOOD TOOLE was born March 5, 1947, to the coolest Jacksonville, Florida, parents an aspiring serial killer could ever hope for. His drunk father departed Florida soon after his birth to walk the desert with his dog or some stupid shit like that. His mom, a bible thumpin' Jesus freak constantly dressed Ottis up in

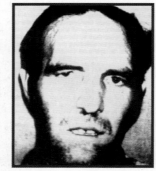

girlie panties and other sexy stuff. Confused, Ottis spent most of his time running away from home and burning down houses in Jacksonville.

Ottis somehow got his retarded self though the eighth grade—an IQ of 75 can only get you so far—and pursued a career of loitering in front of the local 7-Eleven. At the age of 14, he got his first taste of dookie-lovin' from a traveling salesman. Ottis freaked after it was over, and ran the guy down with his own car. He was in and out of jail for the next three years. At age 17, Ottis decide to find himself a woman and get hitched, but his raging homosexuality was too much for his new wife to bear. So the marriage was called off after three days. An eligible stud once again, Ottis toured the Midwest killing and consuming whatever crossed his path. A short while after Ottis returned to Florida, he met a man named Henry.

TOGETHER

Well, Henry and Ottis hit it off right away. That night, they went home with a couple of six packs and made love all night. Instant soul mates, the two worked various odd jobs but left constantly to "go kill people."

After having butchered, dismembered and eaten many human folk, the pair split after a short while. Henry went picking for mushrooms in central Pennsylvania, and Ottis went back to Florida. Ottis killed a bunch of little kids, nothing out of the ordinary for him.

Henry went back down to Florida to meet up with Ottis. Henry helped Ottis' niece and nephew, Becky and Frank Powell, escape from a local juvenile home. The four of them headed west toward California, killing random hitchhikers and anyone else fit for butchering along the way. All this excitement put Frank Powell in a mental institution for good.

The pigs came looking for Becky, so she and Henry sped toward Northern California to stay with relatives. Henry and Becky began to fight one night. Henry got a slap in the face. Becky got pieces of her body scattered across the Texas landscape. Henry got arrested a few days later in Mexico on handgun violations and was summoned back to Texas.

"I've done bad things," Henry whispered to a Texas guard. Over the next year and a half, Henry confessed to more than 500 murders. Numbers would skyrocket each day as he would disclose valuable information regarding the location of numerous missing persons and mass gravesites. Ottis was already in jail on arson charges so they had no problem finding him. Henry talked about his solo killings, the combined efforts of Ottis and himself, and so on. When they asked why only Ottis ate people, he responded, "I don't like barbeque sauce."

Originally printed in WYWS Issue #3

Missing Girl Found Dead; Police Search For Others

Woods Near UNF Campus

Sgt. Jim Suber, above center, coordinates search activities in the early morning fog off Beach Boulevard near where the body of 12-year-old Virginia Suzanne Holm was found during the night. At right, members of the Sheriff's Mounted Posse prepare to head into the dense woods near the campus of the University of North Florida in search of other possible graves.

by Ben Shupe

HENRY LEE LUCAS & OTTIS TOOLE

PITCH A TENT
by Trevor Michaels

As the Frat Pat toast goes, "To staying single, seeing double and sleeping triple." Unfortunately, three-somes involving busty blondes are hard to come by, but, lucky for you, a ménage a trois with your lady of choice and Mother Nature is only a matter of careful planning. Follow these tips and you will be backcountry shagging as sure as a bear shits in the woods.

1. Camping works best in couples. Get a friend, get a couple of cute girls and head to the wilderness, sort of. Find a campsite that has all the amenities of a Holiday Inn. The last thing girls really want to do is actually "rough it." Lakes and rivers are a plus, as this summer's bikinis will provide the necessary motivation to give 110 percent in your efforts to secure the nookie under the stars.

2. Forget everything you learned as a boy scout. Forget it all! Only scout leaders want to sleep with boy scouts—your lady wants romance. Don't seem more into camping itself than "pitching tents," and forget building anything with tree branches or starting a fire by rubbing a stick against a stone. Bring a lighter.

3. Bring booze (naturally) and the ingredients to make s'mores. There's nothing that puts a girl in the mood like melted marshmallow and chocolate smothered on a graham cracker crust. Rub some on her neck, and then lick it off. Slurrpppp!

4. By the time you get to the ghost stories, she should be snuggling next to you for warmth and safety (and s'mores). Break out the tickles and grab her strategically to increase the effectiveness of your bone-chilling tales. If you need help with material, visit www.stories.com for some hints. Make it scary!

5. Convince her to share a tent with you. Remind her that the wilderness is dangerous—not to mention all the psychos that you talked about in your ghost stories.

6. After you get her into your tent, start talking about how beautiful nature is and state your desire to become "one" with the wilderness. If s'mores + booze + ghost stories + pillow talk ≠ sleeping bag sex, then try this equation: her beauty + your beauty + nature's beauty = one time opportunity to go wild in the wild.

7. Lastly, bodily fluids are like delicious, genetically engineered honey. If you have any house pets, you know that animals have sex antennas and are drawn by instinct to the wild thing. So pack your contraceptives and anything else soiled in bodily fluids in a double-sealed zip-lock bag, and be on the alert for lions and tigers and bears.

Originally printed in WYWS Issue #19

VISIT TO LEGOLAND

by Shawna Kenney
Photos by Josh McQueen

Hey kids! Selene Luna went to Legoland and all she got was a lousy headache! For future reference, please keep the following fun facts in mind:

• **Grownups who like Legos are called AFOLs (Adult Fans of Legos).**

• **Selene is an adult fan of nail art, Barbie, Tan-in-a-can, Pamela Anderson, hot rods and all things sparkly.**

• **Selene is 3-feet-10-inches and weighs 63 pounds.**

• **Selene was in Madonna's "What it Feels Like For a Girl" video.**

• **Located in Carlsbad, California, Legoland is the first Lego theme park in the U.S. In the Village Theater part of the park, guests can be dazzled with amazing tricks every Tuesday by Scotty the Magician.**

• **Legoland also features miniature models of Washington D.C., New Orleans, New York, San Francisco and the California coastline.**

• **Selene thought it all sucked.**

Originally printed in WYWS Issue #18

SPICE GIRLS

by Peter Rosenberg
Illustration by Linas Garsys

On Sunday, June 21, the Spice Girls performed at the Nissan Pavilion, an amphitheater located about an hour from Washington, D.C. On most nights, this is just a normal amphitheater. However, on June 21, it was home to every pedophile in the metro area as well as me and my best friend Ben (we aren't pedophiles, in my opinion).

I actually feel bad for any pedophiles who did not know about the show. The reason I say that I feel bad for these clueless pedophiles is that they will never again have the opportunity to see that many scantily dressed 11-year-olds in one place at one time. And trust me, there were plenty of them. It was truly packed with the upper crust of the area. Until now, I didn't know that most elementary school children these days wore shirts showing major cleavage, but then again, they are from Virginia.

So, after getting lost in Hicksville, Virginia, we finally arrived at the spot midway through the show. I was a little shaken from our experiences with the insane white trash we had encountered on our way, but we pushed on. We arrived so late that the girls were already in-between sets.

We positioned ourselves perfectly so that we could have a good view of the stage and keep an eye on the rav-

ing pedophiles that were out in strong numbers. At one point toward the end of the show, Ben and I noticed a middle-aged man jumping up and down in the orchestra pit. Being the logical suburbanites that we are, we just assumed that some father was trying to show his kids how even in his old age he could get down and party. However, when the man walked by us covered in sweat and with no kids in sight, we knew we were dealing with a professional scumbag. This night was probably a dream for people like him who wait all their lives for a gathering of young girls dressed up in slutty outfits. Don't get me wrong, it's not just the pedophiles with which I have a problem. I place blame on the parents who encourage these children to be like and dress like the Spice Girls.

As the show went on, I started to dream. I began to imagine a female super group that looked more like the fans filling seats in this place. If you think the Spice Girls' British accents are sexy, wait till you hear the accent of some sexy Virginia trailer trash. The special powers that allow them to pronounce the word "the" as "duh" and look their best in cut-off jean shorts from Walmart is enough to keep up the image. I can just picture the Billboard charts now: "Trailer Spice's debut album featuring

the hit singles 'Mah, The Trailer's Leaking' and 'Dad Ate My Panties.'" Judging from the fanbase here at this show, those songs would shoot to number one immediately. All of a sudden, Trashy's family would have the best trailer in the park, and those Walmart shorts would be replaced by the illustrious designer Sears shorts. I know I shouldn't reinforce stereotypes, but before I stop, I think you all should know that the entire state of Virginia is currently overrun by poor, sloppy, drug-addicted white families who live off SPAM and wait their whole lives to star on Jerry Springer. I mean, I like sex with siblings as much as the next guy, but you've got to draw the line somewhere.

All in all, the trash, the pedophiles, and those sexy Brits made for a great night. After the show, I came home, locked the door, and danced to Spice Girls CDs for the rest of the night. But I couldn't stop thinking about those girls and their dreams of becoming the next Spice Girls. I just don't know if the world is ready for a pop star with a portable home and a toilet in the living room. Oh, but don't you worry Poor White Spice, your day will come.

Originally printed in WYWS Issue #4

AMERICANS I MOST ADMIRE

by Ben Shupe

Way back on May 19, 1870, in Washington, D.C., a true American hero took his first breath. **HAMILTON HOWARD FISH** had problems from day one. Half of his family had well-documented cases involving severe mental disorders, and when Hamilton was five years old he found himself in an orphanage. At the orphanage is where Albert could trace his earliest sadomasochistic tendencies. Here, he thoroughly enjoyed watching boys get whipped, spanked and paddled. He would even go out of the way to get spanked and paddled because he found the pain very arousing. A few years later, Hamilton decided to change his name to "Albert" after kids constantly teased him as "Ham and Eggs," and the fact that he pissed his bed every night for six years straight. By age 15, Albert decided to end his formal education early and go out and make a name for himself.

Albert drifted back and forth across the States, taking odd jobs as an interior decorator and a house painter. Albert soon married, but after their sixth and final child was born, his wife left town with her lover. Albert was left all alone with the kids, which was a big mistake.

Fish practiced coprophagia—the art of eating shit and drinking urine—both his own and that of his children. Albert would have his kids and their friends flog him on his ass with a homemade spiked paddle until his cheeks bled. Other practices included shoving pins underneath his fingernails, inserting sewing needles into his ass and genitals, shoving a thorny rose stem up his urethra and placing cotton balls soaked in rubbing alcohol up his anus then lighting them on fire.

After his fourth marriage had ended, Albert decided to pack up and take his bag of tricks out on the road where voices in his head told him to castrate little boys and sacrifice their penises to God. Albert claims that he has had his way with close to 400 boys in 23 states. In one attack, Fish said that he "put strips of bacon on each [butt] cheek and put it in the oven. When the meat was roasting for about a quarter of an hour, I poured a pint of water for gravy and put in the onions. In two hours, it was nice and brown. I never ate any turkey that tasted half as good as his sweet, fat little behind did. I ate every bit of the meat in about four days."

Sometime in 1928, Fish befriended the Budd family. Posing as "Mr. Howard," the elderly Fish invited their young daughter Grace, to a mythical birthday party that he was throwing. This was the last time the Budd's would ever see Grace.

Fish was compelled to gloat about his crimes, and mailed the Budd family this nice letter:

> "Dear Mrs. Budd… On Sunday June the 3, 1928 I called on you at 406 W 15 St. Brought you pot cheese—strawberries. We had lunch. Grace sat in my lap and kissed me. I made up my mind to eat her. On the pretense of taking her to a party. You said yes she could go. I took her to an empty house in Westchester I had already picked out. When we got there, I told her to remain outside. She picked wildflowers. I went upstairs and stripped all my clothes off. I knew if I did not I would get her blood on them. When all was ready I went to the window and called her. Then I hid in a closet until she was in the room. When she saw me all naked she began to cry and tried to run down the stairs. I grabbed her and she said she would tell her mamma. First I stripped her naked. How she did kick – bite and scratch. I choked her to death, then cut her in small pieces so I could take my meat to my rooms. Cook and eat it. How sweet and tender her little ass was roasted in the oven. It took me 9 days to eat her entire body. I did not fuck her tho [sic] I could of had I wished. She died a virgin."

Well, the genius used personalized stationary and letterhead, not to mention a real return address, so it wasn't too long before the police came looking for him. The 64-year-old Fish pleaded insanity but was found sane and shipped off to trial. Albert Fish was found guilty and got a date with the electric chair. Upon hearing the verdict in court, he stated, "What a thrill it will be to die in the electric chair! It will be the supreme thrill. It is the only one I haven't tried."

On January 16, 1936, Albert graciously helped the prison guards strap him into the chair. Due to the 29 pins still corroding in his crotch and ass, the chair blew a fuse and short-circuited. Right after the second jolt, a puff of blue cloud rose from the lifeless body. At 66, Fish was the oldest person to die in Sing Sing's electric chair. To this day, Albert Howard Fish continues to inspire a wave of perverts and pedophiles worldwide. Not to mention, giving a bunch of sick fucks like us some ammunition to open healed wounds and piss the rest of this sorry world off.

Originally printed in WYWS Issue #5

...TORIES

In the late 1990s, graffiti magazines were very important to the graffiti culture. The internet had not matured yet, and magazines were really the only way to know what was going on in graffiti in other cities. Magazines allowed city-to-city networking to happen all the way down to meeting other graffiti writers in the magazine aisle of Tower Records. As far as magazines went, Philadelphia and NYC had *On The Go*, Miami had *12 Oz. Prophet*, Ohio had *Scribble*, *Juxtapoz* did a great job covering San Francisco, and it seemed like each city had its own outlet for a national spotlight—except D.C. Roger Gastman stepped up and filled that void with *While You Were Sleeping*.

The D.C. graffiti scene wasn't that big and even though I didn't know Roger personally, I saw him at hardcore shows and knew CLEAR [Roger's graffiti name] had started a magazine and I was curious. I checked out the first issue and I realized immediately the potential for this magazine because the magazine was smart enough to focus not only on graffiti but also on the lifestyle surrounding it.

I liked *While You Were Sleeping* and I wanted to be a part of it, but I didn't have much to offer in the way of photography, articles, graphic design, etc., but I did have two things going for me: I was a part of the D.C. graffiti scene and had a strong background in video production. I worked for a production company that allowed me to come in on my free time and use their high-end Avid editing system to learn. I had a huge desire to make a graffiti video/documentary and was shooting lots of Super 8 film. I'm sure Roger would never remember this, but I had an AOL conversation with him in a graffiti chat room (it was the late 1990s!). His screen name was WYWSINFO, and I asked him what his video plans would be for the magazine. He told me they had just racked a camera and were going to be filming shortly. I felt a bit blown off, but I wished him luck and thought that would be the last of it.

Several months went by and I was working on my first music video for a hardcore band Better Than A Thousand. While finishing the video, the band showed up with Brian McTernan the singer of Battery. Brian was really impressed with the music video and told me he had a friend that was trying to make a video. He asked if he could pass on my number and I said sure. A few days later, I got a call on my answering machine at home from Roger, saying he was looking for help in making a *While You Were Sleeping* video. My roommate at the time and I listened to it and even joked about not returning the call, but in the end, I did.

So we met up, and bonded over our mutual love of The Misfits, vegan restaurants, D.C. graffiti and retarded video footage, and soon after started working on *While You Were Sleeping: Bedtime Stories*. We rounded up as many of our insane friends as possible and filmed them taking a crap from elevated heights, inciting people with mullets and other questionable acts. I pulled from some footage from my personal archives (mostly filmed during my very destructive teenage years), and we compiled some of the strangest video footage we could collect. (This was before *CKY*, *Jackass* and the massive amounts of retarded, disgusting and offensive video footage that you can now easily find on the internet.) And then *While You Were Sleeping: Bedtime Stories* was born.

We did all of the editing at my job during the night. I was always worried someone would stumble across it because I would have a lot of explaining to do and probably be fired. But we did it anyhow and Roger urged me to list the names of my employers in the credits, but I drew the line there. It's amazing we never got sued for all the music we ripped off. If you ever see this video, you'll never look at Britney Spears "Baby Baby" the same again. You'll also see that we liked Johnny Cash before it was cool. There is one questionable song in there that I defer to Roger about.

We talked about doing a sequel to the video and had filmed quite a bit for it, but it didn't work out. I'd like to say, "Fuck you," to the person who ruined the sequel and also I'd like to thank the other person, if you don't finde buit into that

movie, I'm sure we would have all been sent to prison. Anyhow, I'll save that story, and the story of Rocky Hightower, for another time.

It's hard to believe it's been 12 years since we made that video (which was released on VHS initially). I have gone on to do many more music videos while Roger has gone on to publish other magazines and books. We continue to our video ventures together with more prominent and mature films, but it all started with this *WYWS: Bedtime Stories*. To our surprise, *Bedtime Stories* keeps coming back and we keep hearing of it. The video has a strange cult following, and unless you own one, all that you'll ever see from it is a promo of it that I put on YouTube (which Twisted Sister filed a copyright violation against), and every so often someone writes to me begging for a copy or tells me a story of how they picked it up used at a Goodwill and how much they loved it. The video is long out of print and that's a good thing because the legend of this video is a much better story than the video itself.

To me, the most interesting thing about the video was that it mirrored the magazine perfectly, which going back to my first impression of the magazine was that it wasn't just graffiti but a documentation of the lives of the people who were doing graffiti. To the masses, *While You Were Sleeping* was a graffiti magazine turned lifestyle magazine, but to us it was the diary of our lives.

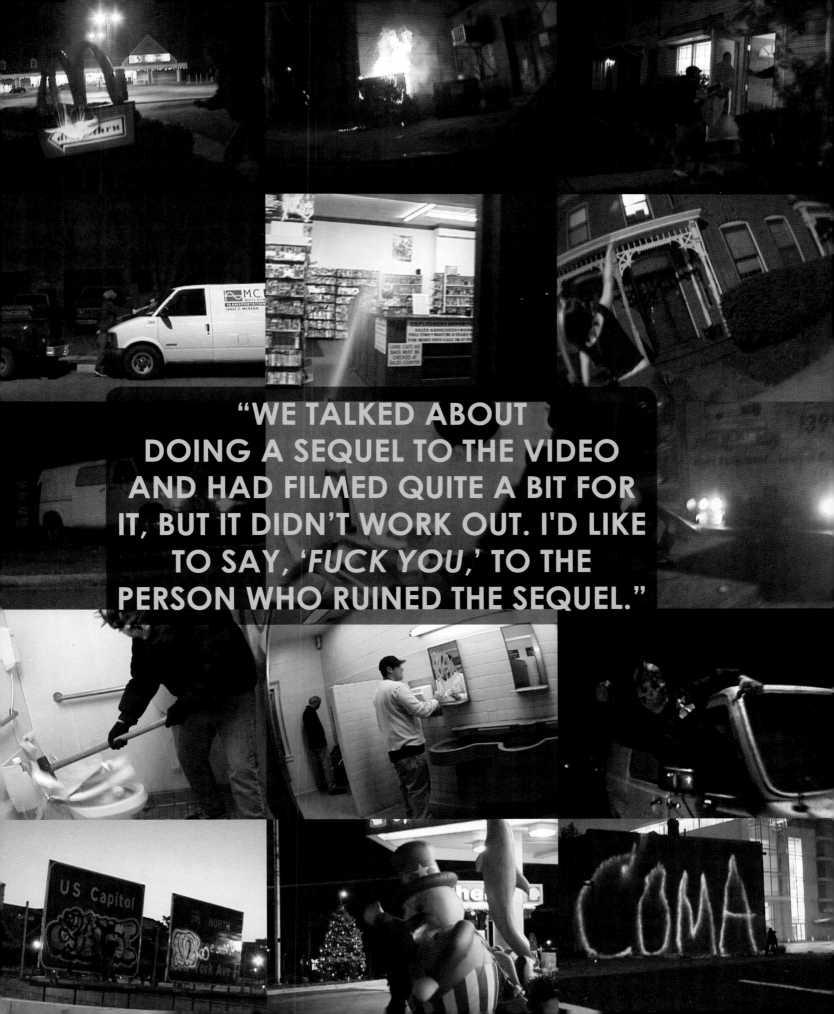

"WE TALKED ABOUT DOING A SEQUEL TO THE VIDEO AND HAD FILMED QUITE A BIT FOR IT, BUT IT DIDN'T WORK OUT. I'D LIKE TO SAY, 'FUCK YOU,' TO THE PERSON WHO RUINED THE SEQUEL."

BEDTIME STORIES PREMIERE

Photos by Michael Simon

I can't stand New York City. Most people love it; I hate it. I can't really give you a good reason why, either. So what better place to launch our video Bedtime Stories than the Big-fuckin' Apple? As it turned out, I was in for way more than I bargained for. The location was The Cooler. It is owned and operated by the biggest coked-up asshole I have ever met. This cocksucker didn't care that there was a line of people down the entire block for over three hours. At the end of the night when the police showed up and gave him several fat tickets, I had a smile on my face. Too bad they didn't ship him off to jail.

Despite the problems he gave us, the night was an overall success. We packed the freaking place. Prince Paul, Down Low from Boston, Carol C and Phon-X made sure the music kept flowing all night. I tried to get midget clowns but they wanted $350 an hour with a minimum of two hours. What a rip off. We got Majik instead. This guy kicked ass. He walked around the place for a few hours doing his tricks making people laugh. Who the hell needs midgets making animal balloons anyway?

If Majik wasn't enough, Shepard Fairey showed up all the way from San Diego to show us a little bit of his artwork and pass out more of his GIANT propaganda. Ricky Powell and ZEPHYR hooked up the slideshow that everyone seemed to enjoy. It was definitely an interesting night with two separate people passing out in front of me appearing to be dead only to jump back up and start dancing a few minutes later. They must have been smoking some weird shit.

I would like to give a special thanks to Base Brooklyn, Emagine, Spiwak, Rollercoaster, Guerillaone, Gabe Banner and Red Bull for helping make this event happen. An extra special thanks goes out to everyone that brought a marker with them and destroyed the club. Buffing the place the next day was fun, wish you could have been there.

Until next time,
The Guy in Charge

Originally printed in WYWS Issue #9

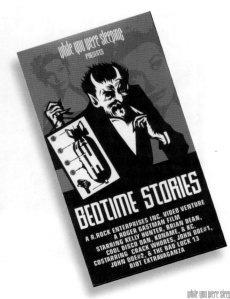

COOKING WITH PORN STARS

DEVINN LANE HEATS UP THE KITCHEN

by Jelly
Photos by Carlos Batts

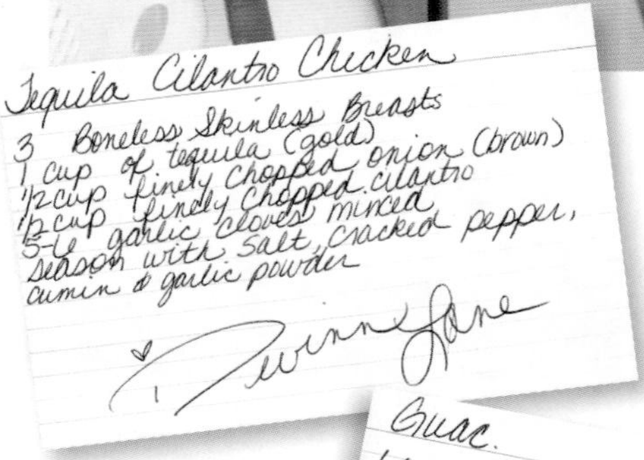

Tequila Cilantro Chicken
3 Boneless Skinless Breasts
1 cup of tequila (gold)
1/2 cup finely chopped onion (brown)
1/2 cup finely chopped cilantro
3-4 garlic cloves minced
season with salt, cracked pepper,
cumin & garlic powder
♥ *Devinn Lane*

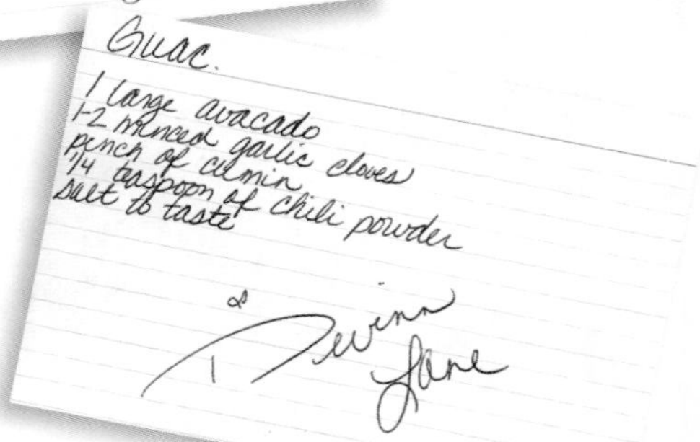

Guac.
1 large avacado
1-2 minced garlic cloves
pinch of cumin
1/4 teaspoon of chili powder
salt to taste
♥ *Devinn Lane*

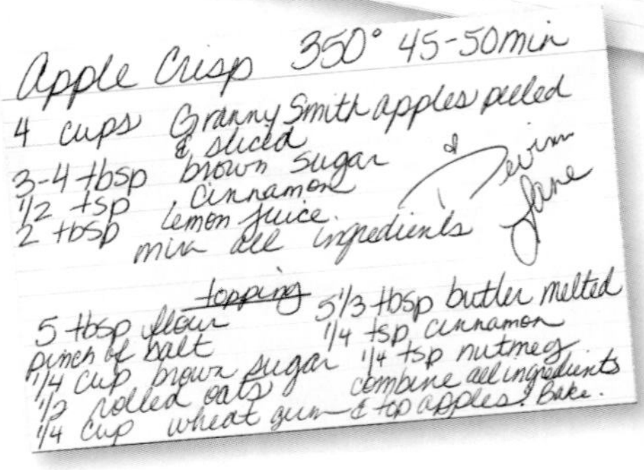

Apple Crisp 350° 45-50min
4 cups Granny Smith apples peeled
& sliced
3-4 tbsp brown sugar
1/2 tsp cinnamon
2 tbsp lemon juice
mix all ingredients ♥ *Devinn Lane*

topping
5 tbsp flour   5 1/3 tbsp butter melted
pinch of salt   1/4 tsp cinnamon
1/4 cup brown sugar   1/4 tsp nutmeg
1/2 rolled oats   combine all ingredients
1/4 cup wheat germ   & top apples & bake.

Your jelly-bellied journalist nearly swooned with gastrointestinal infatuation. Not only can Devinn Lane cook Apple Crisp like Martha Stewart, she's soft and curvy enough to be a latter-day Bettie Page. Not surprisingly, couples familiar with her award-winning work in Wicked flicks such as Beautiful/Nasty, No Man's Land #28 and Spellbound often approach her in public to propose three-way romps in the hay.

"Usually, it's the wife who really wants to have sex with me. I always tell them straight up that I don't have sex with anyone unless they have a test [for HIV], but I do entertain invitations. Occasionally, I accept."

I was so overwhelmed with the mental image of Devinn caressing another female form that I neglected to ask if she would permit yours truly the opportunity to worship her in the flesh. Fortunately, my local video store stocks plenty of Devinn titles, and such Devinn toys as "Devinn Lane's Oral Seduction," a reproduction of her mouth with a piercing through the tongue, like the real deal. Mmm, mouth watering, indeed.

Originally printed in WYWS Issue #17

TV GUIDANCE

There's an old song that says, "Breaking up is hard to do." While this nugget of wisdom is true, we need to remember that a girl sang this song, and she must have been referring to the behavior of her crazy-ass gender as the reason for difficult break ups. I've run the gamut of bad post break-up behavior, from groveling to attempted murder. But like everything else in my life, when the going gets tough, I turn to TV for answers. In its infinite wisdom, TV has spelled out for us a list of possible scenarios you can expect after a break up. Choose your path wisely.

—Ian Sattler

SCENARIO #1: YOU DECIDE TO DUMP A GIRL AFTER YOU NAIL HER.

As Seen On TV: Angel (the Vampire with a soul) lays pipe with Sarah Michelle Gellar, and then he turns evil and remembers how much fun life was running around killing people and having unprotected sex with multiple anonymous partners. He's just trying to have some relationship-free fun when Buffy shows up all pissed off and jams a sword into his face. Ouch.

TV Guide Says: If you break up with your girlfriend right after you have sex for the first time, she is likely to develop some sort of vendetta against you. They are at their most attached point right when they fist start giving it up. Your best bet is to have sex with her a few more times while you're out shopping for new blood. This way, you give her some time to get adjusted and jaded like all the other girls.

SCENARIO #2: YOU TRY AND MURDER YOUR EX.

As Seen On TV: Kimberly from *Melrose Place* is perhaps the worst ex-girlfriend of all time. So bad that Michael isn't too upset when he kills her in a car accident. He figures the BMW did all the talking for him about their relationship being over. He ditches the body and tries to move on. Unfortunately, Kimberly comes back from the dead. Kimberly tries to kill Michael several times, cons him into taking her back, kidnaps Jo's baby, tries to lobotomize Michael's friends, and actually blows up all of the Melrose Place building. Wow. That is one crazy bitch.

TV Guide Says: No matter how bad it gets, never try and kill your ex. Unless you are planning on doing a really, really good job to make sure she stays dead.

SCENARIO #3: YOU DECIDE THAT HAVING SEX ONE MORE TIME CAN'T HURT ANYBODY.

As Seen On TV: That Ross guy on *Friends* is as stupid as his pet monkey. So he dates hot-as-Ben-gay-down-your-pants Rachel and gets off the hook pretty light after they "were on a break." But then he makes two fatal mistakes. First, he remains "friends" with her. Then, he goes in for one last round of "Do you mind if I stick this inside of you?" with Rachel. And wouldn't you know it? Rachel gets knocked up and decides to keep the bastard. Poor misguided fool should have stayed away.

TV Guide Says: Staying "friends" with your ex will cost you big time at some point. Being "friends" is for guys who can't get it up.

SCENARIO #4: YOU NEVER COME TO YOUR SENSES AND BREAK THINGS OFF WITH HER.

As Seen On TV: Ever wonder what would happen if you decided to just tough things out and stay with your special lady? Corey from *Boy Meets World* was so confused by the fact that he gets to bang Topanga that he gets convinced that it's their destiny to be together. He holds on for dear life and ends up getting married at an early age.

TV Guide Says: Run while you can! Getting married is stupid at any age, but it's downright crazy for a young guy. Yeah, you can still keep mistresses, but unlike your ex-girlfriend, your ex-wife can take 50 percent of your money when you get caught.

SCENARIO #5: BREAKING UP IS GOING TO MAKE THINGS BETTER FOR YOU.

As Seen On TV: Kevin Arnold spends all of high school wrapped up in one sort of Winnie Cooper drama or another. She has to be the most frigid female lead of any TV show ever, but Kevin just adores her. And you know what? He gets nothing but strife in return. On the last episode of *The Wonder Years*, Kevin finally leaves Winnie behind. The disembodied voice of the adult Kevin that has been our guide throughout the show goes on to talk about how happy he was and how he went on to meet a better girl than Winnie and have a good life. Kevin Arnold was not tricked into marriage, he never tried to kill her, and he never went back for sex. He was a man and ended a dead-end relationship.

TV Guide Says: Good job, Kevin! You taught us all a lesson. All of us should remember Kevin Arnold and dump our girlfriends right this second.

Originally printed in WYWS Issue #16

GRAFFITI

ESPO
Interview by Roger Rock

—Editor's note: This was the first interview I ever did. I was 19 years old and I had absolutely no idea what I was doing or what to ask. I just knew I didn't want it to be a traditional interview. I had advertised in On the Go and had been a fan of the mag for years. It was one of the first graffiti mags that I knew about. My friend Gabe, a future WYWS contributor, worked at On the Go as an intern, and hooked up the interview with ESPO, who was one of the founding members of the magazine. ESPO never sent me any photos to run with the story, so I ran the only photo I had in my archives. Since then, my archives have gotten a little bit bigger.

Is Elvis still alive today?
Elvis is dead. But the cool thing about Elvis is I think he is reincarnated into people. I think his soul is still around, and I think he is just taking people over, moving from host form to host form. That's why all the Elvis appearances. He could take over your body and you could turn into Elvis. You might look the same when you look in the mirror, but when you're walking down the street people see you as the King.

What do you think Elvis would think of *On The Go*?
He would probably like *On The Go*, but he would probably be wondering why I wasn't writing about his music.

Would you give him an interview?
I would definitely give him an interview. He'd probably call me up and be on some shit like, "Yo, kid, why didn't you print my flicks in the last issue? You're fucking foul."

Would you please give me the history of *On The Go*?
We started it—me, MEEZ and SUROCK in 1988. It was a crummy little Xerox fanzine kind-of-thing. During the first five or six issues we experimented with a lot of different things and still managed to diss cops and diss the anti-graffiti network and get our point across. Sometime in 1992, MEEZ and SUROCK got into other things. A guy named DES came in and started designing the magazine and moving it toward a more professional appearance. I toned down a lot of the radical stuff that we were doing in the earlier issues and went on to

try and create a mass-market publication. Four-and-a-half years later, here we are now.

Where do you see all of this going?
Right now we are set up to be distributed on a wide scale. It would be great and a lot of people could be open to it or it could just sit on the stand. There's been a lot of questions about how far a publication like this could go. *Spray Can Art* has sold about 160-thousand copies. That's a considerable amount, but this is also after 13 or 14 years. At first glance you might not say that the market is big, but we feel that the hip-hop market is huge. If we can get people open on that, the sky is the limit. So we'll have to see. What we are really about is putting as much graffiti as possible in front of people who would never see it or care to see it, hopefully converting them a little bit towards how cool our cause is.

Was 90210 better before or after Brenda?
Definitely with Brenda. She had it going on.

You down with Vanilla Ice?
You know who I'm down with, this group called the White Boys. The White Boys were ill, man. They were three guys from New York, and they had songs like "This is Hardcore, is it Not?" They did this shit with the *Mission Impossible* theme called "On a Mission." Yeah, they were crazy hype. As a matter of fact, I gave UPSKI a copy of their record that I found in Chicago. I think he's learning from it even as we speak.

I heard that you prefer to use stock caps.
Yeah, stock caps are the shit. I mean, that was just some shit like when I started. That's what all the old heads used and the guys that taught me. SUR-OCK, who taught me a lot of shit, that's what he used. We would use fat caps for filling in and stock caps for everything else. It's a fucking hard way to paint. It's tough to fill in if all you have is stock caps. The trade off of it is that you get completely constant spray. Over time, you really learn to work with the pressure that's in the can. You never have to say, "Damn, I don't have caps. I can't go painting." You learn to take advantage of the fact that you have a guaranteed consistent line every time. I do a lot of tricks and techniques to pull a lot of very thin lines out of it. Nothing really fancy, nothing that couldn't be shown, nothing that I would have to hide from somebody if they came around and looked at what I was doing. They could probably just see it emerge and just do it themselves. If somebody were to hit me off with a couple caps when I was at a wall I would try and use them. I always tried to use testers caps. I just sucked at it. I didn't have the patience for it. Now you call them phantom caps…

We call them soft caps down here, but everybody calls them something different.
Well when the World Aerosol Art Congress gets together, we will figure out what to call these caps and pass it down. But in the meantime, stock caps are great. Those new Rusto red caps are incredible. They are comfortable; they fit my finger.

Do you have a favorite professional wrestler?
You can't really fuck with Hulk Hogan. My man is kind of the king. Of course, everybody under-stands the universal appeal of Andre the Giant. Not too much light is given to Sgt. Slaughter. I think Sgt. Slaughter had a lot of shit going on. I know there's a whole new generation of wres-tlers, but I'm just not up on them. The Iron Sheik, man. There was a time when wrestling took on our greatest fears and our biggest hopes. So you would have the Iron Sheik on one side and Sgt. Slaughter on the other. They need to have some shit now like the Infectious Disease on one side and the Doctor on the other side. Maybe Con-dom Man, just totally dressed in latex, dropping on people, just rubbing his ribs against people, just totally fucking them up.

IT'S GENERALLY NOT THE SURFACE THAT I PAINT THAT PISSES THEM OFF, BUT WHAT I PUT ON IT.

Is there any certain surface that you have painted that has really pissed people off?
It's generally not the surface that I paint that pisses them off, but what I put on it. You know that you have really painted a wall right and done some fucked up shit on it when they paint over it the next day. I've painted Klansmen on tattoo shops. They were on some shit like, "You can paint any-thing you want." I was painting the tattoo shop and I would hear these guys inside talking about how when black people come into get tattooed they would be on some shit like, "I'm sorry, we

can't tattoo you today. We don't have all our equipment ready. Perhaps you can come back next week." Then when the people left they would get on some shit like, "Fuck that, I'll never tattoo no nigger." I was in the middle of doing some dumb wizard so I just changed it to a Grand Imperial Wizard. These guys that owned the shop were on their way home. When they came back the next day the wall was totally on some Klu Klux Klan shit. It got painted over in like two hours.

You ever watched any midget porn?
I have not watched any midget porn. I'd be open if anybody would send me some tapes. There could be lots of free goodies in it for you. I'm a tall motherfucker, so I've got to say I've got a fascination for vertically challenged people.

If you could trade places with anyone who would it be?
Although at first glance Russell Simmons looks pretty appealing, I'd have to go with John Popper from Blues Traveler. That's the shit, man. You could be 400 pounds and you could still get laid. You get crazy cash, and you wear cool vests with harmonicas all over it. You couldn't ask for anything more.

Do you play the harmonica a lot?
No, but I do play the skin flute.

Who would take who out: Freddy or Jason?
I'd have to go with Freddy. He just had the one-liners. He had good wit. If it were just brute strength it would be an even match. Maybe if Jason had a few good mom jokes, but Freddy just came through.

I heard that you were abducted by space aliens that looked like ALF a few weeks ago and they took you to their planet and they made you teach the alien youth how to paint. Do you have any comment on that?
Ah, yes, as a matter of fact I do. I would like to thank my alien captors for not giving me an anal probe. I thought that was very respectful of them. The only message that I brought to them was not to do Vaughn Bodé characters.

What do you think about the freight movement?
Freights are dope. If anyone has pictures of the freights we painted in 1988, I'd love to see pictures of them. We got some freights going back in 1983. I got flicks of them. I don't think they are still around. Freights are definitely rolling; they are really getting buffed too. I think people who are just doing strictly freights could benefit to expand their vocabulary and paint other things because the dopest thing about painting freights is that if you have mastered the art of painting them you can paint anything. If you can paint on hot steel in the summertime, there is basically nothing you can't do. I would love to see those dudes take their expertise on the metal and flex it on the concrete.

Any last comments?
Yeah, this magazine shit is cool, man. But I'm still waiting for the *On The Go* rope link chain that I ordered so I can totally go out on the street and flex. Rope chains, that's where it's at in nine-seven. And Rustoluem. Don't waste your time with Krylon.

Originally printed in WYWS Issue #1

Photo by Lauren Gifford

WRONG WAY.

LAUREN GIFFORD'S STORY OF A GREYHOUND BUS DRIVER.

Bus stations are weird places. The bus patrons are trashy, the ticket sellers are downright mean, and the maintenance people seem to have only one correctly functioning limb. But what about the bus drivers? They never seem to weigh into the equation. No one ever wonders about them—until now. It takes a special someone to be a real Greyhound bus driver; all those long drives could drive the average person mad.

Greyhound's website lists the stringent criteria they look for in drivers: They must be able to read and write, and speak English. The website also says that they are always looking for drivers, however, when I emailed an inquiry to them, they were quick to tell me that they currently have enough drivers and are not accepting applications. There go my dreams; I guess I should stick with college. Or maybe I shouldn't have used the WYWS email account.

After researching this fascinating career on the internet, I wanted to get into the mind of a real-life Greyhound driver. I wanted to see what makes them tick. My friend Ilana and I went down to the Washington, D.C., bus station in search of a humble bus driver to question.

The first person I approached just so happened to be a bus driver. He was in his late 50s. He was wearing his official all-grey Greyhound outfit, his hair was cut close with a nice fade, and when he smiled I saw a shiny gold tooth in the front of his mouth. I asked him for a quick interview. Armed with several copies of WYWS, I was prepared to give him the spiel about how we are a young man's magazine interested in doing a short feature on bus drivers, however, before I got into that he told me that Greyhound has a policy against doing interviews of any sort. Quickly, I changed my plan of attack.

I gave him a cute smile and convinced him that I was writing a story about bus drivers for a class at college. I assured him his name or picture would not be used and the questioning began. John, as we'll call him, has been driving a Greyhound for two years and boy, has he seen a lot in that short time.

John opened our interview with a story about how he, "got up and kicked some fucker's ass," after the passenger threatened to kill him, all while driving the bus. Apparently, John pulled the bus over, broke the guy's nose, threw him off the bus, and continued on his route.

The fighting story was good, but I needed to know about more important things. I wanted to know all about sex on the bus. "I find used condoms on the bus all the time," John told me. "If I see someone doing it, I'll say something."

Then John took notice of my friend Ilana. "You're cute," he told her.

This interview was getting exciting. John began asking the questions: "Have you ever had a threesome?" "No." "Well, why don't we try it?"

He offered to take the two of us to New York, feed us "good food," put us up in a nice hotel, and "show us what a threesome is all about." This was very nice of our new friend John, but I told him we had to work in the morning, so his proposition would not be possible. "You ain't gonna wanna work when I get through with you honey," was his reply.

"I'll make you two feel real good," John continued. He told us that he had never had a threesome, but since we approached him he thought that we were outgoing and "crazy." "You gal's seem wild," he explained, "walking up to strangers and all." I reminded him that the purpose of this interview was to find out about his job, not to find a sex partner.

John realized that he wasn't going to get laid and soon the interview was over. Although I didn't find out exactly what a bus driver's job was like, I considered this interview a success.

Originally printed in WYWS Issue #11

HOGGING
by Trevor Michaels

The sad truth of dating is that you can't always land that hot, stinking babe you've been drooling over all summer. It just doesn't work out some of the time—well, most of the time. But you don't have to go home empty-handed. If you're willing to swallow your pride for just a few minutes, then your bed never has to be empty at 3 a.m.

Hogging, what we call this unglorious yet essential practice, is the only joy a lonely man gets after a failed night of hitting on the buxom beauties who torture us by wearing revealing clothes to show off their luscious bosoms yet allow us n'ary a touch. The only real task to hogging is getting some monster over to your place before your buzz wears off. Wait too long and you're bound to have second thoughts.

I myself have had numerous steamy bouts of love with young ladies who have different anatomical records in Guinness for one reason or another. Take Hildegaarde, for example. I was introduced to her at a party at her cousin's house on a night I couldn't land a hot chick for my life. But Hildegaarde and I were destined for each other this drunken night. I was enraptured by her voluminous belly, which hung over her tight size 42 jeans. I imagined myself stroking her thick ankles; I imagined my tongue spelunking in her cavernous bellybutton. I resorted to my standard hogging tactics: First, I expressed my satisfaction with her beauty by complimenting her lovely eyes. Then, I stole a flower out of the vase in the front yard and presented it to her with my most charming smile. For a hog, this is just about all it takes.

Needless to say, Hildegaarde couldn't resist my advances. I took her by the hand and led her to a dark—darkness is quite important—private room in the basement like a tugboat pulling an ocean liner out to sea. And that's just what it was like: going out to sea. I rode her waves for several minutes. I made the unfortunate mistake of smooching her bosoms, on which the bristly stubble that encircled her nipples felt more like my father's cheek than the fine paps of a succulent female. So, my young apprentices, let this be a lesson to you: Never try to make an Elle Macpherson out of a Hildegaarde. Leave your lips off her body and never, no never, kiss her lips—that's just an invitation for her to call you the next day.

There are many different types of hogs, not just minivans like Hildegaarde. I have personal experience with female versions of Lawrence Taylor, enchanting lasses who resemble Bilbo Baggins from The Hobbit or the troll from The Three Billy Goats Gruff, and a girl with one eye and a harelip. My point is that women come in all different shapes and sizes; some are descended from animals other than apes; some, in fact, will eventually evolve into apes. Regardless, they all fill a great need and come enthusiastically to our aid. It is a mutually fulfilling relationship; all animals on the farm have a purpose, and hogs that sleep in their own feces are no less important than the beautiful filly horses that are groomed impeccably by the stable hands. In fact, sometimes I even prefer to keep company with unassuming swine than to be repeatedly kicked by snooty thoroughbreds.

Originally printed in WYWS Issue #6

NOISE

NIKKI SIXX
Motley Crue's guitarist spills the beans.
Interview by Fat Rich
Photo courtesy of Motley Crue

Would you rather open up for Yanni or John Tesh?
I think John Tesh. He rocks harder.

Have you ever sucked milk from a cow's utter?
Do you mean from the moo line or from the oink-oink line?

From either.
From the oink-oink line back in the old days probably.

Who is the most fucked up Motley Crue fan you have ever laid eyes on?
Probably one of the guys in the front row with two teeth.

All those pentagrams and songs about the devil on your first record, did you guy's really believe all that or were you just starved for attention?
I have been looking for attention my whole life, but I am a complete and utter believer in Satan and Nazism as well as every other ism except Buddhism.

Back in the old days when you were experimenting with home pyrotechnics, I heard there was some burns to certain areas?
Consistently. I had this one pair of leather pants that were red and the crotch had kind of worn out and I didn't have money to fix them. When Vince would light me on fire the flames would lick up there and do damage.

So you burnt your testes sometimes?
I'd say I took a scorch or two.

At this point in time, how many power tools do you own and operate?
At this point, the only power tools I own are under the bed.

—Writer's note: This dude was the best. Personally, Iron Maiden was my shit but Roger hooked me up with a Bruce Dickenson interview and he was a complete tool. I remember muttering to myself during that interview that he was destroying the dreams of 16-year-old me. Anyway, NS told some cool stories about him being declared dead for like 10 minutes and jumping off bridges on acid. He seemed pretty relieved I was just asking him dumb shit. He recorded a voicemail message for me. He brings the sizzle to the Crue. I'd fuck him.

What jobs did you have before you were in the Crue?
Dishwasher, moved irrigation pipes, busboy, carpenter, sold drugs, sold illegal light bulbs, stole car stereos, delivered newspapers...

What are the pros and cons of raping and pillaging?
The cons would be no condoms, and the pros would be that you don't have to ask.

Would you rather have a peg leg or hook hand?
A hook hand so I could so I could hook people with it. Think of all the sexual things you could do with it.

Did you get beat up a lot when you where a kid?
I think I got laughed at a lot because I had silly haircuts. [Editor's note: This was his way of saying that, yes, he got his ass beat when he was a kid because he had stupid haircuts.]

What do you think of graffiti?
Graffiti I think is really fucking awesome.

How do feel about domestic violence?
I don't believe in it. I've never hit a woman. There has been a few that need to be hit.

Would you let a good-looking transvestite perform oral sex on you?
If I didn't know it was a transvestite, I guess I would.

If you went into a public restroom and there was a sign that read "insert your dick here" above a small hole would you do it?
Absolutely not. I'm a pessimist. I would fear the chomping teeth of a 6-year-old-boy.

Does your penis have a name?
Ego.

Have you ever lit your own farts on fire?
Hell yeah, dude! Everyone has.

I haven't.
You should try it.

How old where you when you lost your virginity?
Nine. To Bobby Bond's 13-year-old sister. It was Halloween night in a closet in my house. It was great. I asked her if she wanted to see my Jack o' Lantern lamp. She said, "Yeah." I said, "You have to go in the dark to see it."

Do girls flock to you because of your reputation?
Girls run to me because of my reputation.

Back when you first started, were the groupies real ugly and they progressed into better looking ones?
They're all pigs, aren't they?

Tell some groupie stories.
During the Shout at the Devil tour, this groupie took the whole band and we drew all over her body and there was [cum] all over her. She got out of the bus and was walking down the street and the cops were coming up the street at the same time. We thought we were all going to jail, but they didn't say anything. Then there was one time we were playing a festival. One of the guys in the band was getting a blowjob from some chick and shot it in her mouth. Then the girl left the bus and saw Ted Nugent. She ran up and gave him a big wet kiss. We were rolling around laughing. Ted blew Motley Crue by proxy.

NIKKI
SIXX

COOL AS ICE
Mr. Ice Ice Baby Himself
Interview by Roger Rock

Where the hell have you been the last six years and how did you sink to cold, cold baby? Why your sudden reappearance on the metal/thrash scene?
When I made my first record, I was opening for Ice-T, EPMD—all those people. My whole crowd was black. EMI said they were going to cross it over to the pop market. I said no way, I don't even listen to that shit and this is hip-hop. They were so sure of it they gave me a check for a 1.5 million right there to make me change my mind. I was three car payments behind on my 5.0, so it was like winning the lottery. I was 19 years old and I basically sold out. It had its pluses and it had its minuses. One of the pluses is it sold millions of records. One of the minuses is that it put me into this novelty-type category and cheesed me out. I let the money influence my direction. It led to a lot of depression. I had millions of dollars in the bank, a $600,000 Porsche in the garage, a million-dollar house with a million-dollar boat in the backyard, but all that I thought was making me happy brought me nothing. It was horrible at that time. I couldn't find any happiness. I had to eliminate the drugs and the whole crowd I was running with. Time and God helped me out a lot.

So where did you pick up your new style of music?
First of all, the reason why I changed to this style of music is because I have been through a lot of changes personally. When I'm delivering that, I have to have the intensity of the band to match it. There's no way you're going to do that with some kind of break-beat, sample, a drum machine or some shit like that. I was working with this band called Picking Scabs about three years in Miami...

Have you ever picked your own scabs?
That's a silly, silly fucking question— of course.

Did you eat them?
Hell fucking no! That's disgusting.

Back to the question...
It was a grunge band and we were trying to come up with some stuff. I got a call from Monty [a producer] and he hears that I'm out doing shows, and the shows are doing really well. He said, "Let's do a record." I actually turned him down. Then he started offering me more money. It was funny because it wasn't about the money. Because I'm not like all these other artists who spent all their money—financially, I'm set. I turned him down because the first record almost killed me. It led to a lot of depression. From 1991 to 1994, I was heavily on drugs—from coke to heroin and ecstasy. I wanted to escape reality permanently, so to speak. I got another phone call from Monty and he tells me this guy Ross Robinson wants to work with me. He said he produced Sepultura, Limp Bizkit and Korn. I was like, "Killer." He flew down to Miami and saw my motocross trophies laying around. He's a motocross racer himself, so we had a lot in common. We had a great vibe going. I flew to L.A. and we had the record finished in a month-and-a-half. We didn't expect the record to come out so dark. It's just the subjects I was tapping into contained a lot of anger and anxiety. I actually fainted one time in there. I was screaming so hard, I killed too many brain cells. I opened my eyes and it was still dark. I lost my balance and fell into the drum set.

What were the groupies like back in the day?
I have this one crazy story I'll tell you. It started at that Wembley Arena show. This chick was in the front row. She had nothing on except a trench coat. She was really beautiful and was flashing us. We saw her at the next show, and the next show again. Then we flew back to the U.S. for three shows before we went to Japan. She was at all those shows doing the same thing. I was on the airplane to Japan and I wake up halfway through the flight and I hear somebody screaming. It was the girl. She was like, "I gotta have him! He's my destiny." A couple friends of mine stood up out of their seats and basically tackled her there in the hallway. Everybody was freaking out. They thought the plane was crashing or something. They arrested her off the plane. I got to my hotel room, and the first night I get a knock on my door about 2 a.m. and somebody slid a satanic book underneath my door. It had a message to me in it. I was kind of tripping on that. I called my tour manager and told him about it. We didn't know who the fuck it was or what was going on. The next night, the same thing happened so we added some security guards. So she came up the fire escape and... the security guards caught her. It was the weirdest thing I have ever seen in my life. This chick was completely possessed. Her voice completely changed. She went down on her knees and started crying. She kept saying, "He's my destiny. I gotta have him." Then she would snap out of it and start crying saying "Oh my god, somebody help me!" Then she would get back into it. I didn't think anything like this existed. It was amazing.

VANILLA
ICE

"WE INHERITED THIS PLANET. WE TOOK IT OVER. WE KILLED THEM BECAUSE WE COULDN'T LIVE WITH THEM. IF YOU ASK ME, A TRUE EARTHLING IS A DINOSAUR. WE ARE FROM ANOTHER PLANET."

What do you think about graffiti?
I love it.

This is for a graffiti magazine.
Oh killer! I tag myself. I haven't much lately. I'm kind of getting old. But when I was younger for sure.

You said you saved most of your money from the first album. You had to blow some of it. What did you buy?
I went on a spending spree at first—boats and cars. They depreciate and you lose money on them. I've made great investments and ended up with a lot more than I ever thought I would. I'm set for my life, my wife's life and my daughter's life. It's good, but it's not what brings happiness.

What was it like hooking up with Madonna?
She came to a show of mine up in NYC. She hooked up with me backstage and made a move on me.

Madonna took advantage of you?
You could say that if you want. She came on to me, that's for sure. She just came up to me and started hugging me. I was like, wow!

I think Madonna would rip me apart. What's she really like?
She's alright. I don't even know if she knows who she is. She has so many characters in her you don't know which one she is going to wake up to the next day. She can be this sweet little girl or she can be this bitch or this man-like dude. She's very unpredictable.

Would you punch an alien?
Of course! All humans are aliens, I believe. I can kind of prove it. First of all, we were not here as humans anywhere during the whole dinosaur period. There's not one human bone fragment. Not even a Neanderthal man bone fragment found anywhere in the whole entire dinosaur period until they were extinct. So where the fuck did we come from? What I believe is that we came from another planet that had been around millions of millions of years. Look how far we have come in just 100 years. One hundred years ago, we didn't even have cars. Fifty years ago, we didn't have television. If we're traveling to the moon now, in another four million years we'll be able to go to the moon for lunch. We will have space stations built and be able to travel way beyond where we can travel right now.

If you check out what happened with the dinosaurs, there were five meteorites that hit the planet exactly at the same time. That killed off the dinosaurs and for about 15,000 to 20,000 years after that there was a cloud of dust around the earth that caused the ice age because of all the explosions and shit from the asteroids. That killed everything living. We inherited this planet. We took it over. We killed them because we couldn't live with them. If you ask me, a true earthling is a dinosaur. We are from another planet.

What is the strangest thing you have ever been asked to autograph?
Someone's toe.

Did you?
No way, dude! I'm not going to do that. Probably get some athlete's foot all over me or some shit.

Originally printed in WYWS Issue #6

—Editor's note: I have watched the movie Cool As Ice hundreds of times. It is amazing.

STUPID STUFF

Congrats to the *WYWS* women's summer season soccer team! They kicked a record 5-4-1, with only two team members refusing to wear the jersey and one incident of "sucker-punching" an opposing team's mid-fielder. Go She-Devils!

THE POPCORN TRICK
Illustrated by Linas Garsas

"I somehow created the worldwide phenomena of 'vodka eyeballing' by doing a step-by-step how-to in WYWS, not sure what issue, and then touring the Midwest partying at colleges and giving away WYWS swag and mags, and doing eyeball shots. It took 10 years to reach critical mass, and now has its own Wikipedia page, describing the practice. My bad." —**Chachi**

DO NOT TRY THIS AT HOME

1. Press lip of bottle to eye.
2. Tilt it back.
3. Flush eye with alcohol.
4. Feel the burn.
5. Catch a short-lived but wicked buzz.

Aloha, Mahalo!

While on traveling holiday, contributing contributor Richard "Oatsie" Colman had a reminder of his days spent in the tropical paradise of Covington, KY, stitched into his ass cheek. Graffiti pimp SAGENT provided the needlework, while Roger Gastman provided the therapeutic, pain-relieving massages and ointments all the way back to D.C.

FUGGIN' EUROS

```
HELLO...
WE WOULD LIKE TO KNOW IF WHILE YOU WERE SLEEPING CAN MAKES AN INTERVIEW TO
AN ITALIAN HARDCORE NEW SCHOOL GROUP CALLED F.U.G.
IF YOU CAN,
WRITE TO:
```

WHILE YOU WERE SLEEPING
P.o. bo█████
Bethesda, MD 20827
U.S.A

Poste Italiane
filatelia
UN GUSTO NUOVO PER
UNA PASSIONE ANTICA
ITALIA 2400

File Edit View Message Format Tools Window ⑄ Hel

🖃 f.u.g. interview

Send Now   Send Later   Save as Draft   🖉 Add Attachments   Signature

From: WYWS (Rev. Neil Mahoney)
To: @ ██████████
Cc:
Bcc:
Subject: f.u.g. interview
Attachments: *none*

Default Font ▾ Text Size ▾ **B** *I* U T ≡ ≡ ≡ ⋮≡ ⋮≡

```
HELLO...
WE WOULD LIKE TO INTERVIEW AN ITALIAN HARDCORE GROUP CALLED F.U.G.
WE LOVE TO GO WORLDWIDE WITH OUR CONTENT.

HOW OLD ARE YOU?

WHO IS IN THE BAND, AND WHAT INSTRUMENTS DO THEY PLAY?

WHAT POP R&B FEMALE VOCALIST DO YOU PREFER?

DOES YOUR ITALIAN ICE GO "BLING BLING?"

I LIKE SAMBUCA. IT TASTES LIKE FUNNY LICORICE.

WHAT NOISE DO YOU MAKE AT GIRLS WHEN THEY PASS YOU ON THE STREET?

DO THEY PLAY ITALIAN HARDCORE IN IBIZA?

DO YOU GO TO FOAM PARTIES?

WRITE YOUR OWN QUESTION, AND ANSWER IT IN THE SPACE BELOW:


PLEASE RESPOND IMMEDIATELY AND EMAIL A PICTURE TOO.

THANK YOU
```

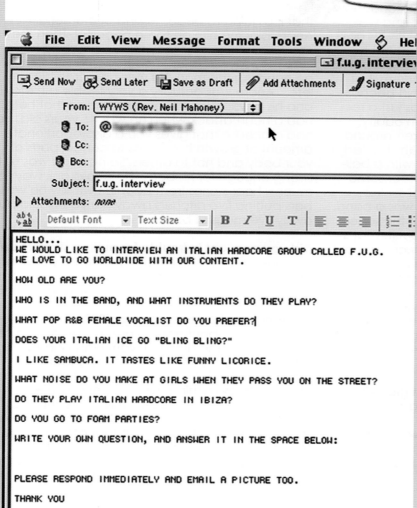

SHEPARD FAIREY
Obey the Posse
Interview by Roger Gastman
Photos courtesy of Shepard Fairey

"The Andre the Giant sticker attempts to stimulate curiosity and bring people to question both the sticker and their relationship with their surroundings."

—Excerpt from the Giant Manifesto

Why Andre the Giant?
I saw his picture in the newspaper and saw it as something that I could use to show my friends how to cut a stencil. I was just amused by it and we decided to make it our inside joke that it was going to be the new cool skate posse. It makes fun of the popular culture, but it is a popular-culture phenomenon. It makes fun of consumerism, but then I encourage people to buy a T-shirt because it funds me making more stickers. It was just a really funny, memorable picture. He is an oddity. This was around 1989. We put the stickers around town. I thought it would just be a joke that lasted a few weeks. I made the original sticker with a ball-point pen and a photocopy machine. For some reason, people kept asking where that sticker came from. They wanted to know if it was a band, a cult or what. I was even in the line at the supermarket and heard people talking about it. That's when the plan started to unfold. The more you put out there, the more people are going to think it means something important. It was just something funny to do. The local indie paper had a contest that anyone who writes in and says what the Andre the Giant sticker campaign was really about would win tickets to a show. This was going on in Providence, Rhode Island. I had a few friends who were doing it for me in their cities.

You don't have a sick fascination with giants?
Not at all. It's just the power of propaganda.

Did Andre know about this when he was alive?
I don't know if he did. He lived in Seattle and North Carolina. It wasn't at the level it's at now when he died.

Have you ever talked to anyone in the wrestling community about the stickers?
I get a lot of funny emails to my site. They think that it is going to be some kind of memorial to Andre placing him on some pedestal. Then they see it's my thing and they think it's making fun of him. They say, "This site is disgraceful. You should be honoring the man. He was an incredible athlete." Andre was actually a very feeble athlete and his physical condition was so bad that he had a heart attack when he was 46 years old. He had a disease that gives you a disproportionate amount of growth hormones to certain parts of your body and not to others. So his heart was not strong enough for his body. He also drank way too much. I hear stories from people that say he was in bars putting five pitchers away like you would put away five mugs of beer.

Did you ever get in trouble for putting stickers up?
I've been arrested five times, mostly for stenciling or pasting. All art-related crimes other than shooting bottle rockets at my neighbors when I was 12.

So what you do is based on graffiti?
To me, it's all about getting as much exposure as possible. With the stickers I want high-visibility. As far as pasting, I kind of use the same technique that REVS and COST were using. I'm trying to go higher with everything using extension poles. I want the scale of it to be so impressive that no one thinks that it is just one person doing it. There are always going to be things that only run for a few days, but if it's a really prime spot it doesn't matter. When I go to New York, I'll try to get higher up windows that will run for a long time. There

OBEY
GIANT

are so many people that you are competing for space with. Because I mass-produce my stuff, I can afford to send out a greater volume of stuff, whereas in traditional graffiti it's very discouraging to go out and spend all this time hitting a spot when it gets cleaned in a few days. I consider the artwork preparing the printed piece. Can-skills graffiti amazes me, but it's just not my approach. All I do with spray paint is stencil.

If you had four bottles of urine what would you do with them?
Probably pour them on the bums that keep pissing next to my car.

How big do you think Andre's penis was?
I would assume that he was a little bigger than average, maybe eight inches or so. I doubt his dick got the benefit of the growth hormones.

Have you ever been in a circle jerk?
No, but now I do feel open enough about my sexuality to discuss masturbation. It took years. I can admit it. I think daily is healthy. It relieves stress.

Use any special tools?
I'm a switch hitter. I think that is a skill.

Would you rather kiss a guy with or without a mustache?
If you're going to kiss a guy you might as well go all the way. I want a leather vest; I want it all.

Where did you grow up?
Charleston, South Carolina, and I lived in Providence for eight years.

I heard there are a lot of sluts in Charleston.
There are a few.

What do you think of amputees?
I feel bad for them. I have never seen a female amputee. I have only seen dudes with hooks and stuff instead of hands. The first thing I thought was, damn, they probably don't get laid and they can't masturbate.

How do you feel about my favorite subject, pornography?
I like pornos. It's visual stimulation. I'm into that.

What's the strangest place that you have done it?
Probably on one of the screenprinting tables at the RISD studio. A security guard walked in and the only thing keeping him from seeing my girlfriend and I was a thin drying rack. One time, I was having sex with my girlfriend in the car right outside of an art opening. They were showing the video, and my friends came out to tell me and walked up to the car and there was my girlfriend on my lap. I hadn't seen her in a few days. It was obvious what was going on, and the windows were all fogged up.

How about some more stories like that.
This should be about art. [Sex] is art. Being creative about that sort of thing is definitely artistic. I've done it in the mall garage, in the car during the middle of the day with people walking to their cars left and right.

Want to talk shit about anyone?
People that diss you just because they are jealous of your fame, that's wack. There is plenty of room on the streets. Get into it for the right reasons. If you're a gangbanger with a spray can, why don't you just go out and kill other gangbangers with a gun instead? Do what you should be doing. Don't become a graffiti artist.

Originally printed in WYWS Issue #4

—Editor's note: This interview started off a very long relationship between WYWS and Shepard Fairey. He went on to re-design our logo, designed the box cover for the Bedtime Stories *film, and made many WYWS stickers and other ephemera. Years later, Shepard and I would go on to found* Swindle, *an arts and culture magazine that was a little more serious than WYWS.*

PAT THE PARTY JERK

DATING WHORES
by Trevor Michaels

I should have never hooked up with the girl. I knew better. Not only had she just recently broken up with one of my friends, but she also had made the rounds with a few more. My instincts and mind told me, "No," but my piece was telling me, "Yes." As we all know, I take my advice from between the legs, so off to my bedroom I led.

My first mistake was that I made it more than a simple hook-up. I took her out to breakfast the next morning. As the weeks followed, my judgment became obstructed as she flaunted her tight little ass in front of my face. I kept on telling myself that I couldn't get involved with this girl, but somehow my usual bedtime routine was switched from watching porn to hooking up with this girl (and no, I wasn't fucking her, I would have been in more shit if I had been).

This girl was a flirtatious vixen, but my concerns were appeased by her gentle strokes along my back and her constant reassurance that I was the only guy she wanted to go home with. I should have limited this little fling to the amount of time it takes me to get off (about 30 seconds). My friends had told me she was psycho, in fact, some of them were the ones who made her that way. But I liked her, especially after she told me that she would "fucking kill" me if I was lying when she asked me if I was fucking another girl.

The weeks passed, my anxiety did not end, and I still didn't believe her feelings to be sincere. This girl carried a lot of baggage. Not to mention there were numerous rumors floating my way. The pussy wasn't getting much better and I could feel the inevitable confrontation approaching. Being the good guy that I am, I got drunk one night and decided to question her loyalty. After telling her that I was sad that my house only had three floors, because throwing her out my window wouldn't really hurt her and therefore it was a waste of time, I went for the kill.

Was it the right decision? I don't know. I had misplaced my crystal ball the night before while I was blacked out. Here is the point: Never get involved with a girl who has tons of baggage and/or numerous rumors floating around about her. For every rumor that is false, one is true. Here are some ways to spot the girls that should be one-nighters rather than long-termers.

1. The night before she shows an interest in you, you observed her grabbing another guy's cock.

2. When you point her out, your friend says, "Yeah, I know her."

3. She is constantly checking her messages to see who has called her. In reality, she is checking to see who her next appointment is.

4. During pillow talk, she vents about her most recent boyfriend.

5. Your friend from another school has heard about her.

6. She has posed in *While You Were Sleeping*.

7. You can't remember where you have seen her before, but then it comes to you: It was the other night at a friend's house when you were watching a video he took of him fucking some girl.

Originally printed in WYWS Issue #10

GUMBALL CHALLENGE
by Deanna Guzman
Photos by Dan Monick

It was a typical day at the office. Roger's eyeballing this jar of gumballs we had sitting on the counter. So what does Roger want to do? "Let's see how many gumballs could fit in your mouth." "Fuck it, I'm down."

So here I go. One at a time, every little gumball strategically stuffed in a free corner in my mouth. Did I mention Roger had a few visitors in the office? So here I am with a gang of gumballs in my mouth trying not to let any of them slip down my throat—I do not want the Heimlich performed on my ass. So this group of his friends are starting to cheer me on and, boom, my mouth is full to the brim with 56 colorful gumballs!

I'm tilting my head back to keep them from falling out and to keep my drool, which turned black from all the different colors of gumballs, from splattering all over my desk. After a few photos were taken and my mouth could no longer stay strong, I spit all the gumballs in a glass and my mouth tasted like I just poured high-fructose corn syrup all up in there, but in a good way. I made a little rainbow on a paper towel with the saliva-drenched gumballs by rolling them around and everyone was kind of confused but it looked pretty like unicorn sky, so fuck it.

EDMUND EMIL KEMPER III
by Ben Shupe

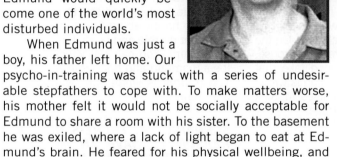

If you couldn't get an erection, would you pick up hitchhiking teens and dissect them? You would if your name was **EDMUND EMIL KEMPER III**. Born in the mid-1950s in San Francisco, Edmund would quickly become one of the world's most disturbed individuals.

When Edmund was just a boy, his father left home. Our psycho-in-training was stuck with a series of undesirable stepfathers to cope with. To make matters worse, his mother felt it would not be socially acceptable for Edmund to share a room with his sister. To the basement he was exiled, where a lack of light began to eat at Edmund's brain. He feared for his physical wellbeing, and begged to go live with his father.

However, Edmund found no solace in his father and stepmother. They quickly grew tired of his company. Perhaps it was the way he tortured and killed small animals that set them off. So pops shipped Edmund off to his unsuspecting grandparents' house. It was there, with the .22 rifle his loving grandfather gave him, that Edmund's hunting really took off. What should he do with his new toy? Why not blow the heads off both his grandmother and his grandfather? "I just wondered how it would feel to shoot grandma," Edmund said later.

The judge didn't have to take off his glasses to realize this kid was bonkers, and he was sent off to Atascadero State Hospital for treatment. Edmund adapted well to the environment. Hell, it was going to be his home for the next five years. He made some friends there, but an overwhelming majority of these friends happened to be older men who were in for serial rape

A wonderful aspect of the United States juvenile justice system is that unless tried as an adult you can only be incarcerated until you turn 21. What more could a young man want for his 21st birthday than to be released from a loony bin? I'm not sure where the doctors thought his insanity had gone, but I'm not sure that they cared either way.

Edmund landed a job as a laborer for the Division of Highways, and saved enough money to purchase a car that appeared to be an unmarked police vehicle. It was this vehicle that spawned his most devious plots. He removed the antenna and rigged the passenger door so it could not be opened from the inside. He filled the inside with radios and turned the trunk into the bat cave. Items of note included knives, guns, plastic sheets to wrap bodies in, as well as a blanket. In no time at all, his ride was ready to cruise.

Edmund fixed his sights on the beautiful hitchhiking ladies of the 1970s. Mary Ann Pesce and Anita Luchese were the first to take their last ride. The two quickly found themselves gutted and mauled in Edmund's trunk. He drove their bodies around the city for a while before taking them to his apartment. With cloak-and-dagger tactics he snuck the two women into his evil dwelling. Chop. Chop. Anita lost her head, and Edmund dissected Mary Ann, then tidied up by throwing the heads in a nearby ravine and burying the bodies.

The months went by as fast as the bodies could get in and out of the trunk. This psychotic mastermind baffled police; they didn't have a single lead. Good old mom was still itching and complaining when Edmund finally decided that he lived with her tyranny for long enough. He went right over to her apartment and in pure Edmund fashion removed the witch's head. After all, it was the woman's fault he could not maintain an erection after all those years of being stuck in the basement and verbal abuse. To turn the investigation away from himself, Edmund happily decided to do away with his mother's best friend using the same technique. After he killed her, he quickly undressed the woman and laid her naked corpse on the bed. I'm sure your sick minds can figure out what he did next.

Edmund left the scene in a stolen car fleeing the place he once called home. A few minutes later, he pulled over and decided to call the police and inform them of all the brutal murders he had committed. In total, Edmund confessed to eight slayings, although he is suspected of several more. Edmund even led the police to where he had buried some of the bodies. Last we heard of Edmund, he was doing well and residing at Folsom State Prison. A few of the heads still remain missing.

Originally printed in WYWS Issue #7

TV GUIDANCE

You should always avoid buying an imitation, no matter how good it looks. Generic drugs? Mexican Rolex? Fruit Rings cereal? No, thank you! TV has taught me all about the horrible things that can go wrong when a fake is introduced to the mix. I now know life's problems are too complex to be solved by slapping a goatee on them or spelling their names backwards. In a pinch, using a fake can be tempting, but the all-knowing TV shows us that the road to hell is paved with imitations of good intentions.

—Ian Sattler

Originally printed in WYWS Issue #18

SCENARIO #1: THE FAKE YOU USE IS SHODDY AND EASILY DETECTED, THUS CAUSING YOUR PLANS TO FAIL.

As Seen On TV: In the classic episode of *Star Trek* "Mirror Mirror," a transporter accident hurls Captain Kirk, Uhura, Scotty and McCoy into an alternate reality, where things are decidedly different. For one, Sulu keeps trying to kill Kirk and bang Uhura. Spock is also sporting a decidedly illogical goatee. So obvious are these fakes that Kirk immediately figures out they are not his real crew and smashed their scheme to destroy a peace-loving planet.

TV Guide Says: The "evil" Enterprise crew is so whacked out that they don't even come close to selling their story. Sulu especially doesn't seem right, running around all crazy, sweating, with no shirt on like some sort of space crackhead. On the other hand, while on the real Enterprise, the "evil" Kirk is such a good fake that the crew doesn't notice anything is wrong when he starts humping nurses in Sick Bay and urinating on the Bridge.

SCENARIO #2: PEOPLE MAY PREFER THE FAKE OVER THE ORIGINAL.

As Seen On TV: On the very last episode of *Small Wonder*, we witness the return of Vanessa, Vicki the Robot's evil twin. Vanessa locks Vicki in her cabinet and poses as her during the Lawsons' trip to Hollywood. Vanessa, who acts like Vicki on roofies, makes a ton of friends and entertains the family with her more outgoing personality. She also blows her brother, Jamie.

TV Guide Says: Vanessa was so popular when she first appeared in the episode, "The Bad Seed," that producers considered giving her a spin-off show, Too Good to be True. In fact, Vanessa's party girl image was so much more interesting than Vicki's stiff robot act that fans of the show were chomping at the bit for an all-Vanessa vehicle. One fan site states this desire eloquently when it says, "Vanessa's dominating the very last Small Wonder episode was more like a cruel tease of what could've been." Indeed.

SCENARIO #3: SOMETIMES A FAKE CAN BE SO GOOD THAT EVEN YOU FORGET IT'S NOT REAL.

As Seen On TV: Boy oh boy, do they love evil twins on *Buffy the Vampire Slayer*. From Willow's leather-clad, lesbo vampire doppelganger to the physical manifestation of Xander's personality traits, *Buffy* viewers must think that everybody has an evil twin running around. Spike really hits a home run when he has a villain build him an exact robot version of Buffy for him to have sex with. That's right. Sex. With a robot. Hmmm… Anyway, Spike starts to think of the robo-Buffy as being as good as the real thing, causing him to slip up and let the real Buffy find out about his sex toy.

TV Guide Says: Needless to say, Buffy isn't too happy about Spike turning out her robot double and beats the holy crap out of him. You can tell your girlfriend it's a diamond and not cubic zirconium. The trouble is when you believe it's a real diamond.

SCENARIO #4: THERE'S NO GOOD REASON TO HAVE AN IMPOSTOR OF SOMETHING THAT IS SHITTY TO BEGIN WITH.

As Seen On TV: Oh, how we all yearn for the classic days of TGIF. If the Sitcom Garden of Eden ever had a mascot, it was Steve Urkel from *Family Matters*. And we all know how much we hate mascots. Urkel tainted each TGI Friday extravaganza with his nerd routine and inability to get laid. Realizing that an Urkel revamping was needed, the show produced his twin, Stefan, who was like a cross between Urkel and R&B sensation Gerald Levert. Stefan kept returning for more and more episodes, his low voice and Ghetto Romeo vibe only serving to remind us on how painful Urkel was to begin with.

TV Guide Says: Would you buy a fake Geo Metro? Neither would I. So why the fuck would anybody want an Urkel impostor? When you look back on the wondrous TGIF lineup, the only time you should ever be happy that there were clones of anything is when thinking of the Olsen Twins or the tits on Suzanne Somers.

SHORTS

VARSITY BLUES

Story and Photo by Andrew Black

I remember walking out of the double doors of my high school on my last day and promising myself to never, ever, ever walk back through those doors again. Well, last week I broke that promise. What could possibly have brought me back to my old, affluent, suburban stompin' ground? If you're thinking, "It's got to be either money or girls," then you're half right. The sweet young girls of my old high school's Pom-Pom Squad were going to the Montgomery County Pom-Pom Competition and needed some drummers for the squad to march in and out of the gymnasium, and I guess that's where I came in. I hesitated and thought to myself, "You're not in high school anymore, and shouldn't be doing this," but when I thought of how happy making the Poms Squad would make my friends and I, I couldn't resist the offer. I found myself strolling to Poms practice through those big high school doors one more time.

Maybe it's because I'm not in high school anymore, but it was really strange seeing all of these girls, some who weren't even fully developed. They were in that awkward freshman phase: braces, zits, straight hips, and non-existent curves, which should have filled out those tight-ass Pom uniforms.

Before the competition started, Poms from all schools were in the lobby pushing out their chests, smiling with their immaculate painted faces, sticking out their asses, and arching their backs for every photo opportunity that came along from every stereotypical soccer-mom. So, while I remind myself that these supple little things are still in high school, I know that it is only a matter of time before they get sent off to college, stop being daddy's little girl, and they start being someone else's little girl. Sorry, dads of America, but the truth hurts. Some of these girls know what's up, though. They're the type of high schooler who dates 25-year-old guys, has the body every other girl that age dreams of, and has a fake ID to hit the bars and clubs with her older sister when she's home from college. But I digress, let's return to the competition.

The whole time, still kind of embarrassed, I was sitting there with a camera, a pedophile playing shutterbug. I snapped away at girls of all shapes and sizes (the big girls are the fun ones to watch) from all over Montgomery County (one of the 10 richest counties in the USA) as they danced, gyrated, shook their hips, and kicked their legs up to a eclectic mix of songs ranging from Blink 182's latest hit to Ozzy Ozborne's "Crazy Train" to Kiss' "I Want to Rock and Roll All Night." I'm pretty sure I heard a Scorpion song too, you know, the one about rocking you like a hurricane (that one was priceless, right?), and you better believe that every high school had a little bit of Fatboy Slim in the mix. So while I was checking it out, now, with the funk-soul brother, I caught my friend staring at one of these young Pom's derrieres. However, he caught me looking, too, so we had a quick talk about how we would have to look out for each other in the Big House.

I sat through about eight different routines from eight different high schools before the girls from my old high school took the floor. Now, I don't know what makes a pom-pom routine stand out from the others, but these girls looked pretty good out there and managed to get first place. Tears and celebration ensued, and then it was off to the victory party. I contemplated taking my friends, but then I thought about those stock footage nature films of lions ripping antelopes to shreds, and concluded that it would be best if I rolled to the party solo. The moral of this story is don't let the WYWS staff near large groups of underage girls unless you want something bad to happen. The other moral is that high school Pom competitions are weird fucking events.

Originally printed in WYWS Issue #11

THE WALK OF SHAME

by Trevor Michaels

I heard this story the other day at a concert, and I feel that all of you would benefit from its message. And besides, it's about a great subject: college women. In college, two things are clear. College guys are horny assholes just looking for tail, and college women are horny bitches just looking for dick. Anyway, the story goes like this.

A freshman girl sits in her room one night soon after arriving on campus. A frat guy knocks on her door. "Hey babe. Do you, uh, maybe want to go to a party with me?" At this crucial moment, the chick thinks, "I am at college. My parents aren't here to tell me what to do. I am free and independent now. I am going to the party."

So she goes to the frat party with this guy and they're hanging out. One of his friends comes over and has something in her hand. Her date grasps the object and a lighter, and starts sucking from the top of it. A rumbling, bubbling noise reaches her ears. She asks him what it is, and he asks her if she wants a hit from the bong. So she's thinking, "I am in college. I am free and independent to do what I want. I am taking a hit." So she starts pulling hits, and eventually she has a nice buzz. She's feeling pretty good by now.

Next, the boy cracks open a brew and offers her one. So she thinks, "I am a college woman. I can have a beer if I want one." Crack! Crack!

Crack! Crack! Crack! Crack! She downs six or seven beers and now she's feeling great. She's loving the party and talking to everyone.

Toward the end of the night, the boy asks her if she wants to go back to his room. So she thinks, "I am in college. No rules. No curfew. I can go home with a guy if I want." So they go back to her room and start hooking up. It gets hotter and hotter. So she thinks, "I am in college now. I can fuck this guy if I want." So she decides to do it.

The next morning she wakes up confused. She rolls over in bed, looks over and jumps up in fright. She is now on the floor, praying, "Please God, tell me I didn't do that. Please say I didn't!" But she knows she did. She quickly dresses and starts her walk across campus to the freshman dorms. It's about noon. As she struts across campus in the same clothes she had on last night, everyone knows who she is from the party the night before. Tons of people wave and say, "Hi." And of course, they know that she is wearing the same clothes from the night before and they know where she has been since then.

That is the essence of the "Walk of Shame." Anyway, back at the dorm the news has also spread. Everyone's talking about how she didn't come home and where she slept. Her roommate wants details.

Here is the point of the story. I want to have a daughter. And when she goes to school I am sure that stuff like this is going to happen. But I will tell her this: If she wants to go home with a guy and fuck him, that is her decision. But she better take him back to her place. Fuck him. And then kick his ass out and make him walk home.

Here are some pointers to get laid and not have to suffer from the "Walk of Shame."

1. Why not just fuck at the party? Bathrooms, closets and parking lots all make great spots.
2. Tell her or him that you have a huge waterbed that vibrates.
3. For girls, tell the guy you have pizza back at your place. For guys, tell the girl that you have last week's Felicity and Dawson's Creek on tape.
4. Just start walking toward your place. Human nature dictates that your partner must follow.
5. Tell your date you only live two minutes away even if it is more like an hour.

Good luck.

Originally printed in WYWS Issue #8

GRAFFITI

EVER

Interview by Roger Rock
Photos courtesy of EVER

—EVER note: I remember this being a lot funnier. I think this is a perfect example of why it is a bad idea for teenagers to interview teenagers. This interview is like if a bad high school photo could talk. We did have a lot of fun then though. I love you, Roger.

Would you do the deed with a 12-year-old boy?
If he was wearing a wig.

What maturity level do you consider yourself to be?
About seven. I still like Transformers.

What is the most violent thing you have ever done?
I dragged a kid out of his house and beat him up on his front lawn while a girl and two boys watched. He was being a dick. I had been good friends with him before.

What is your record for jerking off in one day?
I would say about 13.

When was this?
You know, every now and then I have been known to pull a marathon.

When you go to the beach do you wear a Speedo?
I wish. I can't pack one of those things.

Ever had the Vanilla Ice haircut?
No, man. Around his time, I had more of a mullet—you know, long in the back, short in the front.

What do you think of ping-pong as a professional sport?
I think ping-pong is fucking awesome and I'll tear anyone apart who dares to take me to the table.

If you had to be one, which member of the New Kids on the Block would you be?
Is there any fucking question? Donnie. He gots the coolest moves, the coolest hair and pulls the most chicks.

Would you have sex with your cousin?
Depends on how much I had to drink that night. I might.

Do you fantasize about midgets?
I fantasize about midget men watching me. As for midget women, I fantasize about actually fucking them.

Let me get this straight, you want midget men to watch you have sex?
That would be pretty cool.

You were telling me about a dream you just had where your brother busted you doing it on a rooftop?
Oh my god! My brother busted me. It was like this: I'm going real good, we're talking some serious John Holmes-style porno shit. I had been drinking all day, drinking all night, I'm crazy at this point. I'm going real good, in deep. She was moaning, I was moaning. The next thing I know, my brother comes around the corner. He sees my pants down around my ankles. I made eye contact with him and I probably looked like a deer in headlights.

So you didn't try to keep working it?
I tried to.

NEVER
SAY
EVER?

Your brother didn't join in?
He joins in, right. I got him from behind. He has her from behind. There's this midget there and the midget is wearing this weird clown suit and sunglasses. I have never seen sunglasses like them in my life. The midget is loving it. The next thing I know, the fucking midget shoots off. Then she goes, then my brother goes, then me, I showered all of them.

Favorite drinking partner and why?
Myself. I like my own company.

What actress gave you your first boner?
Wonder Woman.

What is the largest thing you have ever stolen?
A car. It's a long story. OK, I'm lying. I never stole a car—I stole a house.

Do you snore?
A little bit. I fart a lot in my sleep. I can smell real bad.

What's the worst sexual experience that you can remember happening while you were actually having sex?
I thought I broke my dick once. You know when you're on the bottom and they are facing the other way and you get moving pretty hard. I heard a crack and it felt like something broke.

When is the last time you got kicked in the balls?
Two weeks ago.

Have you ever considered defecating on a girl?
A few times, but that's pretty rude. I think about it when I masturbate. I don't really think I would have the balls to do it.

Who do you miss more: John Belushi or John Candy?
Candy. He was way fatter.

If you were reincarnated as an animal what animal would it be?
A monkey. They get the most.

What are you drinking right now?
Bush.

What are you going to be eating later?
Bush.

Are you pissed stonewashed jeans are not the fad?
With or without holes in the knees?

Would you date Lisa Simpson?
No way. She's smarter than me.

Would you do her?
Yeah, I would.

She's in fourth grade.
That's OK.

What is the most unnatural thing you have ever swallowed?
A bolt. I did it for five bucks in eighth grade. I don't think it's come out.

Most girls you have slept with in a 24-hour period?
One.

Do you know karate?
No, but I know ca-razy.

Most money you have ever given to a homeless person?
Ten dollars. He had a good act going and I bought him beer. He was the Black Elvis.

What about when the homeless guy gave you money?
I don't know what you're talking about.

Tell me.
No.

Yes.
I gave him a blowjob.

You want me to print that or do you want to tell me the truth?
Print it.

Have you ever picked your nose and wondered what it would taste like?
I still do. It tastes pretty good. After painting, I get the snow-cone boogers.

Do you hear voices in your head?
Sometimes. They say, "Stop doing graffiti."

Why are you so dirty?
I'm a genius; I don't have time for hygiene.

Why do you hate graffiti writers so much?
Because they are all a bunch of fucks. They have no lives and need to move out of their parents' basements.

When you fell 40 feet and landed on your head, did that change your life?
I don't know.

How many years did you spend in high school?
Six.

Any fond memories of those six years?
A lot of chicks. A lot of drugs. A lot of beer. Drinking beer. Studying for tests drinking beer. Failing a lot of tests. Hanging out in the principal's office. Drinking beer. Going to parties. Drinking beer. Basically drinking beer.

What have you done with yourself in the last year-and-a-half since graduating high school?
Pretty much drink beer.

Your favorite kind of beer?
Whatever is the cheapest.

Why don't you wear underwear?
It chafes. I like to hang.

How many times a week do you get drunk?
About seven days a week.

Do you like cowboy hats?
They fit real nice. They make you look like a man. The chicks dig them. The boots are pretty hot with a zipper on the side. No zipper on the vest though.

I heard you like the movie *Shakes the Clown*?
It's the best. It's the *Citizen Kane* of drunken clown movies.

Have you ever tried shit?
No. Almost. Well, maybe when I was little. Cat shit.

Remember how your brother hurt his neck back in seventh grade?
He was going down on a real beast of a girl. She wrapped her legs around his neck, and all it took was one quick jerk and he ended up with two nights in the hospital and three weeks in a neck brace.

—Editor's note: EVER was my graffiti partner, and someone I got into a lot of trouble with. EVER would go on to contribute to almost every issue of WYWS, including a feature in which he got a pregnant hula girl tattooed on his ass cheek.

Originally printed in WYWS Issue #4

COOKING WITH PORN STARS

JESSICA DRAKE AND MONIQUE MAKE JELLY SOME RICE KRISPY TREATS
by Jelly
Photo by Carlos Batts

Normally, jolly ol' Jelly travels to a porn star's crib to enjoy the decadent delights prepared by their delicate digits. But in this case, Sin City's Jessica Drake, star of such skin flix as Trick Baby and Modern Love, wanted to make a house call to WYWS' own Jabba the Hut to stir up a batch of sticky-icky Rice Krispy squares.

"I brought along my friend Monique," the athletic blonde beauty said as she slid out of her black SUV. "And look, I made some fudge!"

Jelly loved eatin' Jessica's fudge, and her friend Monique was so fine that it'd take a team of N.Y. firefighters to pull his head out from between her golden thighs. But alas, time was limited, and those big-assed boxes of Rice Krispies were ready and waiting.

A cute pink apron was produced for the petite Monique, whose pert buttocks poked out the open back. Barefoot, she tiptoed next to Jessica, the soles of her feet squishing into the thick, gooey white cream that had dripped all over the linoleum.

"This is yummy," cooed Monique. "Feed me one of the squares, sweetie."

Alas, ol' Jelly didn't get to participate in this all-girl cooking session, but he did get to watch. Oh, and Jessica left him her panties as a souvenir. Ah, doesn't life smell grand?

Originally printed in WYWS Issue #18

jessica drake does Rice Krispies!
- 3 tbsp. butter
- 4 cups mini marshmallows or jd.
- 1 7oz jar of marshmallow creme
- 6 cups rice krispies

Melt butter & marshmallows in large saucepan on low heat. add rice krispies, stir until well coated using a buttered spatula or your hand, press mixture into a 13x9x2 pan coated in cooking spray. Cool, then cut into squares, then share with a friend!!

enjoy!.. jessica drake

TV GUIDANCE

TV teaches us so much about real life—everything from how to live with four other elderly women in a Florida retirement complex to sharing custody of a child when both you and your buddy banged the girl's mom. Most importantly, however, the talking box has showed us how to lose our virginity. Here now is a look at the top five cherry-popping "Very Special Episodes" in television history, and what they taught us.

—Ian Sattler

1. *BEVERLY HILLS 90210*, EPISODE 207, "GRADUATION DAY"

Synopsis: "Donna Martin Graduates!" was the battle cry. But after the smoke cleared, the question remained, "When will this girl graduate to womanhood, dude?" Producers answered quickly. On graduation day, Donna seals the deal with rapper David Silver. While her experience was not as raunchy as Brenda and Dylan's hotel fling during Spring Dance, Donna's loss of innocence was more significant. The pristine daughter of real-life TV mogul and the only prude among a cast of jezebels, she nails a guy who cheated on her. That's awesome.

Message: Even if your dad's the boss, it still takes longer to get laid when you're ugly.

Originally printed in WYWS Issue #14

2. *MARRIED WITH CHILDREN*, EPISODE 190, "DIAL 'B' FOR VIRGIN"

Synopsis: Never in TV history has a character more deserved sex than Bud Bundy. After thousands of painful near misses and sharing a house with a hot slut of a sister, we all felt Bud's pain. Here, he finally gets sexed-up by his cousin's fiancé. Unfortunately, nobody believes Bud because the chick is so smoking.

Message: Keep hope alive, every troll has his day.

3. *DAWSON'S CREEK*, EPISODE 414, "A WINTER'S TALE"

Synopsis: The girl-next-door caves in to the village idiot. On a ski trip, Pacey hooks up a fresh ski lodge for the sexual coup de gras of 1990s dramedy. An experienced cocksman, Pacey guilts Joey into the sack by telling her she'll always wish her first time was with Dawson.

Message: Make sure everyone knows you nailed your English teacher because experience pays.

4. *THE WONDER YEARS*, EPISODE 88, "CARNAL KNOWLEDGE"

Synopsis: Gangly geek Paul has sex while Kevin and the nerd herd go to a dirty movie. After a chance encounter with a family friend, Paul finds out how buddies will turn on you when you get some tail. But rather than get some follow-up action, Paul wastes hist time arguing with Kevin as his girl boards a plane, never to be seen again.

Message: Don't waste your time on local girls, out-of-towners don't know you're a loser.

5. *FACT OF LIFE*, EPISODE 201, "THE FIRST TIME"

Synopsis: Natalie (the fat one) gives it up to her heavy metal boyfriend, Snake. They aired an "adult content" warning, giving the episode the show's highest rating in its nine-year run. FYI, Blair (the hot one) was first pegged to do the deed. But due to the actress's "ideological problems" with premarital sex, she refused to even be in the episode.

Message: If you are nice to fat girls, they'll put out.

ASHES

by Ian Sattler
Photos by Roger Gastman

In the early 1990s, being around Ashes was like having a soundtrack for your every high school experience. If you were driving around D.C. looking for a party that you never found, you were probably listening to them in your car. If you were watching your friends getting busted for graffiti, they were probably wearing an Ashes shirt. If you were late for a show because none of your friends drove, you were probably late for an Ashes show. If you were proud of the scene you hung out in, it was probably the D.C. scene they played. If you wondered how a bunch a high school kids could play such engaging music, you were, well, I think I've made my point.

Ashes gave every hardcore, straightedge, emo core or whatever-the-fuck-you-want-to-call-them kid in D.C. something to do. Ashes went out, played shows, recorded CDs and made a name for themselves. For a lot of people, this was the first time they had proof that this type of shit could be done, and that helped get them up and out doing their own stuff.

Today, those people are still doing all kinds of stuff, including making the magazine you're holding in your hands and writing the words you're reading right now. It is be-

cause of this that they will always hold a special place in my heart and the hearts of many others. It sounds like I'm writing a eulogy for them, but with this new disc out people who have never heard them before will start to find out how good they really were. On the other hand, they did force me to eat Denny's and get food poisoning. I also missed a lot of their shows because I was selling

merchandise for them. On second thought, the reason so many kids started doing stuff because of Ashes is that the band worked their friends like fucking dogs. Small dogs.

In all seriousness, when I was talking to Roger (the brains and balls behind WYWS), we both agreed that the times we spent with our friends in Ashes not only exposed us to situations and people who we would

draw on to become who we are today, but also made for some pretty stupid stories.

Ashes had been on tour in Indianapolis and Ohio for the better part of five days. Most of the shows had been with Shelter and 108, and there were tons of kids at all the shows. This was near the end of a summer that had seen us go to the West Coast and back, in addition to all over the East Coast. It was fucking hot, and I was sick of sleeping on some stranger's floor. We had two different cars with us in the days before we could rent a van, one of which was my brand-new Eagle Talon TSi. Matt [the drummer], Jack [the bass player] and I started to bitch about having to sleep on the floor. The three of us decided to start the 10-hour drive back from D.C. that night.

This is the part where we totally lost our minds. Despite the fact that Jack had jinxed the trip by getting a speeding ticket at every possible moment (three in the first two days), and despite very strong disapproval from Brian [the guitar player] and Elena [the singer], we decided to go. I should point out that Roger was the only one who thought it was a good idea for us to go. This was fueled by his desire to be able to

claim a couch at the house with the rest of us out of the way.

I interrupt this story for a Zack Morris, Saved By The Bell-style timeout. A couple months ago, I found the soundboard tape from the Ashes set that night. During the song "Burns So Deep," a fight breaks out in the crowd over some meatheads playing with a football. On the tape, you can hear kids yelling, and then Brian gets on the mic and tells the kids that this isn't what shows are about, and how they should take it somewhere else. He was absolutely right, and he managed to quiet everything down until some other kid got on the mic and said, "Yeah, you assholes! Hardcore is not about fighting! Now stop that shit before me and my friends kick your ass!" I guess everybody that night was out of their minds.

After hearing several more pleas not to go, we left for D.C. very pleased with ourselves for avoiding a horrible sleeping situation. Things went fine until about 7 in the morning. I was riding shotgun, Matt was in the back, and Jack was driving. This arrangement was a real shame, because I was the only one awake in the car.

Jack proceeded to speed up to 90 mph as he dozed off. The car hooked the side of the road, did two 360 turns so that we were going backwards down the road, then a 180 that flipped the car onto its left side into a ditch, where we skidded for about 150 feet. We got out of the car with the aid of some truckers and a pair of Vietnam vets. (We know they were vets because they told

> FARSIDE
> ENDPOINT
> FUNCTION
> ASHES
> SUNSPRING
>
> SUNDAY AUGUST 8th AT "CLUB BINGO" (the american legion hall) IN WESTMINSTER. 14582 BEACH BLVD. LOCATED BETWEEN BOLSA AND HAZARD STREETS. FOR INFO CALL (714) 846-0DIG 6pm
>
> WEDNESDAY AUG 4th
>
> TUESDAY AUGUST 10th
> BLACKSPOT
> DRIFT AGAIN
> ASHES
> ENTITY
> DARKROOM
>
> X CHORUSX
> MEAN SEASON
> FUNCTION
> ASHES
> SCARECROW

Matt he would have made a good "tunnel rat" in the war.)

To make a long story less long, we eventually made it home intact. Nobody was hurt, which was a miracle. We all should have died. After telling this story for the millionth time (it always impresses the chicks that I survived a fiery death trap while I was on tour with Winger), I find it really amusing that the first

thing we all did when we got home that night was go to a show.

As I find myself about to graduate from college, I realize that it was a lot harder to get by without any sort of soundtrack like the one Ashes provided me with during my high school times. I wish this disc had come out sooner, it would have made college a lot more fun. Maybe it will help with that "adult life" thing I'm supposed to start in a few months.

—*Writer's note: Oh god, I'm gonna be just as sappy as Roger. This was the first written piece I ever had published. My affiliation with Ashes and WYWS had a lot in common in that they both gave me a lot clarity and purpose at a time when I would have been at risk of becoming something insane like a meth dealer or a police officer. These are the lifetime friends and experiences that are so vital and awesome that they almost seem like hitting the lottery when you look back on them. And I love* Saved by the Bell, *but I'll always hate that reference in this piece. I didn't know that story about Elena crying at the gangbang though. That is some classic WYWS shit right there.*

PERVERSION

HOUSTON DOES...EVERYBODY

Interview by Roger Rock & 2TONE
Photo courtesy of Houston

Who are you and what do you plan to undertake February 6, 1999?
Let me go look in the mirror! Houston is an adult porn star. I started when I was 18 doing men's magazines. I did Penthouse, Cherry—pretty much all of them. I plan to beat Jasmin St. Claire's record and take over the title for the world's biggest gangbang.

Any hostility between you and Jasmin?
There isn't from me, but I have heard things from her. She is just realizing that it is time for her to step down.

How many do you plan to do?
500!

If each guy has a minute, that will be over eight hours.
It will be a while. They will be in groups and each have a few strokes.

Any training?
[Laughing] Squats, deep knee bends.

How about somebody beats your pussy up with a wiffle ball bat?
No, I'm sure I'll have a lot of ice packs.

Are you allowed bathroom breaks?
I'm sure.

Do you get paid by the guy?
I get paid a lump sum.

Why not Pay-Per-View?
I think they are trying to get Pay-Per-View, and that's why it got pushed back.

Your mom is in the other room, what does she think about all of this?
I don't even think she knows. She's very supportive.

I got this idea for a gangbang. It's a gangbang with gangsters. So it's like a gang bang gangbang. You have rival gangs and they have a gang truce in you. It would make you the unifying factor.
You might want to talk to Metro.

Any special plans for number 500?
Howard Stern is picking out the first person. I did his show a month a go and we're letting him choose. The spot goes to the worst story, the biggest loser.

What was your first sexual experience?
Sixth grade. There wasn't insertion or anything. We were kind of messing around and he kind of came on my chest. He was this really cute guy who was my boyfriend.

He busted a nut in sixth grade! That is amazing. I hope my son has that physical prowess. Were you a bad girl in high school?
I was a good girl. I was a good student and got straight As, but on the other hand, I was hanging out and partying and having sex.

Were you popular with the boys?
Very. I was most likely to marry five times. I was pretty talked about. Girls were jealous because their boyfriends wanted to go out with me.

Did you have sex with more than one guy at once in high school?
Yes. I did it on a boat and we liked it so much we did it again.

What if a leprechaun wanted to enter the gangbang?
As long as he has a current DNA HIV test.

If the gangbang were to have a theme song, what would it be? I'm thinking "Eye of the Tiger." You have to have something inspirational.
That is kind of far from what we are thinking about.

You were just in jail?
I got a DWI a year ago and I was just paying my dues. It was my second one. It really made me appreciate what I have and who I am.

Do you think your pussy will have calluses afterward? I still think you should have some kind of training, like letting an amateur boxer use your pussy as his punching bag.
I have no idea what to expect. I just want everyone to have a good time.

Originally printed in WYWS Issue #5

THE HOUSTON 500

RON JEREMY

Interview by Roger Rock, Fat Rich, and Richard Colman
Photo courtesy of Ron Jeremy

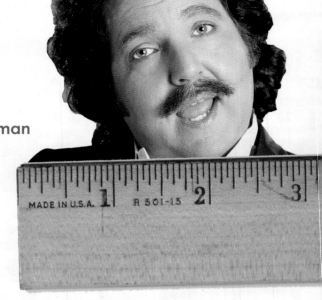

Do you think the Incredible Hulk has a bigger penis than you?
No, because usually guys that are into bodybuilding have very small penises. That's why they go into bodybuilding in the first place.

From one stud to another, do you ever cry yourself to sleep at night?
Why? There are times that I might get sad because there is nothing romantic in my life. That's one thing you miss being in porno. It's hard to have a relationship because no one will take you seriously. It's like Sam Kinison used to say, "Well honey, I really enjoyed having breakfast with you but now I gotta go fuck somebody. I'll see you Thursday." How many girlfriends want to hear that? It gets lonely once in a while.

Have you ever had your heart broken?
We all have. It's hard to be in porn for that reason. I love it for every other reason.

How do you feel about blood and sex?
They don't match. If a girl is having her period, I'll still give her head because you don't eat on the inside you eat on the outside.

How did you first discover that your penis was larger than normal?
My ex-girlfriend told me that it was larger than normal and that her girlfriends would get a kick out of it when she would tell them my size. It was junior year in high school. I asked my dad if it was unusual if a guy could kiss his own penis and he said, "It certainly is, son." Then I wound up making money on it years later. I sucked my dick in a couple of films. Eddie Murphy did a routine about it.

Have you ever stuck anything in your ass?
No! I haven't had a prostate exam since I was in my teens, and I'm now 45. My dad tells me I'm going to have to have one. I'm nervous about it—nothing has been up my ass.

Since you're in pornos and you get all these chicks, what do you do for kicks?
Get chicks some more, read Shakespeare, go to concerts. I have a normal social life. I go out a lot.

Where did you go to college?
Queens College BA and Queens College masters.

How many hot dogs could you eat in 60 seconds?
If I'm really hungry, more than I would want to because I would be burping and shitting the rest of the night. I really could probably devour more than most people. If someone wanted to pay me for that type on contest, I would do great. Just for the hell of it, I would not do it because of the after effects. I would be lighting up my farts with candles.

Does your penis have a name?
Herman. I like that name. I'm more like a teddy bear than what you would call a sex symbol. Lord knows I haven't been a sex symbol since 20 years ago. I went from *Playgirl* magazine to *Field & Stream*. The thing is, I went from working out in the gym to working out at the buffet. When you say something cutesy girls like it. If I say something like, "Come here honey, and suck on my cock," it doesn't work for me. It works for maybe Rocco or Peter North. So I say, "Why don't you come over here and kiss my Herman?" It's less threatening.

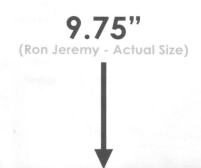

9.75"
(Ron Jeremy - Actual Size)

All-you-can-fuck or all-you-can-eat?
That's a tough damn choice. Can't answer that one.

What's your favorite food?
Basically anything except Limberger cheese and blue cheese.

What do you think of shit and sex?
It doesn't go. We have all done anal scenes when you yank it out you hear this little pop and there's a little bit of shit on your penis. It happens. Some girls get very embarrassed and some guys make girls feel bad. You don't want to do that. You just cover it and run to the bathroom and wash it off.

According to Genghis Kahn, what do you do when you have 17 rapists and one girl?
They get cannibalist? You either share or they do each other.

You cut holes in them.
I though I was kinky until I met you three guys. I'm so straight, you know. I do these movies, I give a little head, I fuck, I roll over and I burp and I watch HBO and sleep till spring. I really am a rather boring guy. You guys are way kinkier than I will ever be.

How many women do you think it has been?
Including your mom, I've had 1,500 women in films. Probably a couple thousand.

Didn't you do a movie where you had sex in a pot of baked beans?
Yes. I also did a movie where I had sex in a pot of spaghetti. I recently did a film where I'm rolling around in grapes making wine.

You look just like my friend Todd.
Does he have a big penis also?

I don't think so. What do you think of Jesus Christ?
I feel like all Jews feel that Jesus Christ is probably a hell of a nice guy, a great carpenter and had a lot of special powers.

If you were an alarm clock, how would you wake me up?
I would probably piss on you.

Would you punch an alien?
I believe in making friends.

Do you have any patented moves?
The back massage, the kiss on the back of the neck giving the girl goose bumps then rubbing her rear end and playing with her boobs. Then within five minutes I'm doing anal.

Is it hard having the most beautiful eyes in the industry?
I'm going to kiss you right where you stand you sexy bastard. I do have nice eyes, nice teeth and a decent penis. A lot of other features can go.

What does your cum taste like?
Debi Diamond said in an interview once that mine is actually not bad. I don't eat a lot of spicy foods. You are what you eat. I was told by a lot of girls that for a fat, chunky little bastard my cum tastes fine. You get some of these guys that have this chunky stuff and you look at it and you just want to hurl.

—EVER note: That place was a hellhole. Strip clubs in general make me uncomfortable, and we had to wait around this one for what seemed like forever. I can't remember a time before this when I had been more uneasy. I couldn't get out of there fast enough. Ron was very nice and fun to talk to though. He was a good guy and a real sport for putting up with us.

Originally printed in WYWS Issue #4

The VIPER ROOM
WHILE YOU WERE
SLEEPING PARTY
DIVINE STYLER
TEENAGE FRAMES

divine styler

danny boy

Everybody loves a good party. Especially when you're on the guest list plus one. There is no telling who the hell they'll show up with—a fine young piece of meat, your sister, hell if there's nobody to bring, maybe the bum who is sitting outside the club begging for money will do.

So with the help of my sponsors (Red Bull, KIK Wear, Fila, Spiewak and Black Flys), promoter Eddie Donaldson (GuerillaOne.com) and I threw a party at the Viper Room in sunny, star-studded Los Angeles, October 12, 1999 to celebrate the release of issue 7.

My crew flew in from all over the country for the event. I lured them there with promises of a crazy party with lots of girls, good music, and an endless supply of free drink tickets. They evidently took advantage of the latter, and their memories of the party are just one big blur.

While they were sleeping, the Teenage Frames, a bunch of punk rockers from Chicago, tore up the stage followed by L.A.'s own hip-hop headliner Divine Styler who was joined by Danny Boy (ex House of Pain), and DJs Daz and Dina. Shepard Fairey was busy passing out his trademark "Andre The Giant Has A Posse" stickers and posters. Equally popular were the special event T-shirts printed up by Fila. We tried to make sure no one walked away empty-handed but some of the Viper Room staff members were consumed by greed.

Overall, the party was a huge success. Thanks to all those who helped us wreak havoc. Luckily, we escaped the long weekend with just a few minor moving violations. Until next time…

—*Roger Gastman*
Editor in chief

This article first appeared in WYWS issue #8.

STRIP CLUB ETIQUETTE
by Trevor Michaels

Strip clubs are one of the last places on earth where manliness exists in its purest form. Where else can we drink while watching live naked chicks dance within inches of our faces? But they are also places of danger that can cost us black eyes, bloody noses or, even worse, a semester's tuition. Hopefully, by conducting yourself as outlined below, you will leave strip clubs with only a shit-eating grin. In my research, I enlisted Tinker Bell, a dancer at a popular D.C. club.

BUDGET
A strip club is like a restaurant— don't go it you can't afford it. Although they aim to create fantasy worlds, strip clubs have one similarity to the real world: No one works for free. Strippers depend on tips to make a living. Thus, you need to tip and make the dancers believe your pockets are full in order to get the attention you desire.

If you're running on a budget, Tinker Bell recommends bringing a wad of dollar bills wrapped with a few twenties. "Tip slowly and selectively, and when a girl sits down next to you, buy her a drink." But, she adds, "Drinks for dancers are sometimes three to four times the normal club price. At some clubs, we get half of what we get the guy to spend. If a girl keeps hustling you for drinks, it is a good idea to politely ask the bartender how much drinks cost.

SEATING
When you enter a club, be aware that where you choose to sit has a bearing on how much money you are expected to spend. If you take a seat at the main stage, you are expected to drop some coin. If you don't meet your expected quota, chances are the girls will shy away from you and direct their efforts toward whoever's flashing the chunkiest wad of money. As Tinker Bell tells it: "Never sit center stage. Find a seat where you are easily accessible. A place where the girls can find you and join you for a drink." The dancer, who has made upwards of $1,500 in one night, also recommends, "Never sit in the dark corners of the club because it makes us think you are jerking off or touching yourself."

LAP DANCES
If a dancer comes up to you and asks, "Want a dance?" She means, "Want to give me a lot of money?" After a few beers, I've been known to purchase a few of these private shows and have realized that, unlike 'Nam, there are rules of engagement. Specifically, don't touch. Tinker Bell reccommends "putting your hands behind your back and avoid thrusting your groin into the girl." Even though the dances can cost from $20 to $500, Tinks says that guys must always tip extra since the club takes 50 percent of the fee. Finally, avoid getting multiple dances in a row, "Unless you want girls to think you are a perv."

GETTING A DATE
"Every time a girl sits down with a guy, he will ask her out. But you guys don't realize that most of the girls are married with kids," explains Tinks. Besides bragging rights, why would you want to date a stripper?

For those who have no common sense and still wish to date a stripper, "you must be funny and have a real conversation with the girl," Tinks explains. "Save your staring for when you are on stage and talk to her a few times before you hit on her or ask her out." If you do get a date, Tinks advises to "take her to a really nice place" because, after all, the girl is a stripper and has lots of class.

Originally printed in WYWS Issue #18

Mardi Gras

Story and photos by Roger Gastman

—Note from Pat: I went to LSU, and started out majoring in political science and later changed it to business, but I think I was only taking one class at the time toward my major, Spanish I, which I was already fluent in. I was also taking Chicken Judging and Poultry Science. You pretty much went out and you felt chickens' breasts and you'd rate them whether they were in good shape, bad shape or rejects, and then you'd take an egg and you'd spin it in front of the light to see if it had a yolk and see if it was acceptable to make it into the store. I don't think they used any of the shit I judged for any groceries, which is good.

Don't ask me how I did it, but somehow I managed to get myself on a 7:20 a.m. flight bound for New Orleans with a short layover in Shittsburg, though you may know it as Pittsburgh. Mardi Gras, here I come. Of course, I couldn't help but notice all of the fine-looking women in the airport. Knowing that they would never see me again, I thought perhaps one wouldn't mind slipping into a bathroom stall for a little romance. However, that's an entirely different article that the staff of WYWS is currently working on.

Once in Pittsburgh, I made my way to the bathroom to wash the sleep out of my eyes. The noises that I heard the businessmen making from the stalls were phenomenal. I hoped that one day I would be able to make those noises, and wondered if women made those noises in their bathrooms too. I considered waiting for one of the men to come out of a stall so I could ask him to teach me how to make those noises—kind of like that old Asian guy in Revenge of The Nerds teaching Booger how to burp—but I had to catch my flight.

When I arrived in New Orleans, my friend Pat met me at the gate. The large grin on his face could only mean one thing: He was already shitfaced. He explained that he had gotten to the airport about an hour early, so, with nothing better to do, he sat at the bar. We headed off to LSU, where Pat had a class today and one Friday morning he needed to go to. After we got there, we ended up going to Poultry Science. Yes, the study of chickens. In this class, you study eggs and learn how to grade them, as well as decide what makes up a good chicken. You get college credit hours for this.

The liquor store was the next stop. Tonight, Pat's fra-

PAT

What makes up a good chicken?
Pat: No yellow in the plumage. It has to have a nice vent.

Have you ever seen chickens having sex?
Pat: Not in my day, I wish I had. I tried to fuck one once.
Hudson: I whacked off thinking about one once.

How many eggs have you fucked up and dropped?
Pat: A few. I'm pretty good about handling my eggs. I take pride in my eggs. The teacher doesn't like it when you break them.

How many kinds of chickens are there?
Hudson: Numerous. Peacock, Rudolf Hen, Gray Goose…

What's next semester, guys? Turkey class?
Pat: We were thinking about Football Coaching, Construction Management, Golf—if it's not to early in the morning—Rodeo, and there's a few others we are looking into.

ternity—whose symbol was a coffin—was having a party with the "slut" sorority and I was promised a good time. This was no normal fraternity house that I had ventured in before. All of these lads were pure lunatics and their choice of music was superb. None of that dance top-40 crap, strictly country and heavy metal. Animal House is alive and well in Baton Rouge. The sun set with me painting flames on Hudson's pick-up truck while Quiet Riot's "Cum on Feel the Noize" blared out of the house over and over again. Everyone was excited to get some "bangtail" and party.

In the meantime, I was then introduced to Elvin, the man that cleans up the messes these fellows make. What a shit talkin' mess of a motherfucker. Next, I was introduced to Russ, a man who was not afraid to pay for what he wants. Russ came complete with plaid pants and a tattoo of Hank Williams holding a bottle of Jack Daniels on his arm. The party had finally begun.

Pat displayed excellent drunk-driving skills on our way to Bogies, a local bar. Only once, when we almost ran straight into a pickup truck, did I feel that my life was in danger. Mad props. Once we were at Bogies, Dennis, another one of Pat's animal friends, decided the speaker would be a great place to take a piss. Laughing hysterically, he told me the story of how Pat had drained his while waiting in line at the bar to get another drink. This brought a whole new meaning to the words "drunken slob." I bumped into Pat waiting in line for the bathroom a few hours later and asked him why he didn't just piss in the sink. I was informed that the sink was too high and if he pissed in it, pee would splash back all over himself. Why didn't I think of that?

SORORITY GIRL ONE

How old were you when you got fucked the first time?
Sixteen.

What do you remember from that?
I was in a car.

Are you good in the kitchen?
Yes.

Do you play with yourself?
I'm... I'm just going to say no. Wait, why am I answering these questions?

What's the thing you have done that has made you feel most like a dirty slut?
I'm not answering that!

Are you a moaner?
No, a breather.

Have you ever had someone give you the shocker?
I'm leaving—no.

Have you ever given someone the shocker?
No.

Do ribbed condoms feel different than regular condoms?
No.

What do you aspire to do with your life?
I have no idea.

What turns you on?
Fuck this. I'm not doing this—oh my god! You're taping this!

GIRL TWO

What do you think of foreign people?
I like everybody.

How old were you when you got fucked for the first time?
I'm not answering that.

Are you good in the kitchen?
Hell yes.

Sexual fantasy?
I'm not answering that.

Do you play with yourself?
This is not for a magazine! This is all about sex!

GIRL THREE

How old were you when you got fucked for the first time?
I haven't had sex.

Do you play with yourself since you have never had sex?
No.

What do you think of graffiti?
It's cool.

Would you like a guy better if he painted a graffiti piece for you?
Maybe.

Would you pose topless for my magazine out of the kindness of your heart?
No! I sure as hell wouldn't. My mom raised me good.

Did you want your daddy to buy you a horse when you were a little girl?
I have a horse.

Do you ride your horse a lot and perhaps that's the reason you haven't had sex?
No.

Why haven't you had sex?
I'm waiting until I get married.

Has a finger ever entered your vaginal hole?
You're trying to sound all scientific on me now.

Has a finger been in your fucking cunt? Yes or no?
Oh my god!

Bra size?
They're small.

How old were you when they started to come in?
I didn't write it down on the calendar or anything.

Do you give blowjobs?
No.

If you did, would you spit or swallow?
Definitely spit. That's disgusting.

I was tired as shit. I had been awake for over 24 hours now.

On the way home, I was sober as hell kicking myself for never learning to drive stick while Pat drove home totally obliterated. Back at the house—and surprisingly still in one piece—I found out that I was not going to get to sleep for a long time. It was time to break things. Who needed four sinks in the bathroom? Three would do! I watched as one poor, helpless sink was ripped from the wall. Next, Pat found a new friend, Mr. Crowbar. He and Mr. Crowbar got along great. They both enjoyed causing senseless damage. I watched Pat re-decorate the hallway and several doors with new, strategically placed holes. Back in the bathroom a few minutes later, Pat decided that the jar of Kool-Aid would look much better outside. Out the closed, second-floor window it went. Following the jar of Kool-Aid, was a hammer, screwdriver, trash cans, bottles and an empty keg. This sent shattered glass all over the floor. Each time a window broke, I was reminded that it was a $59 fine and I didn't see anything. Well Pat, if my calculations are right, your bill is about $250.

We found some helpless sorority girls, and decided to question them. Most girls were afraid to venture into Pat's room to even sit down—who knew what evil danger lurked behind his doors—but these four girls were champions. One girl labeled me the "dirty magazine boy" and called me that for the rest of my stay.

I finally got a few hours of sleep and woke up the next morning around 11 to AC/DC's "Highway to Hell." We took showers and ate a little. Pat kicked me out of his room for a few minutes so he could play some cock and ball games before we left. The rodeo was in town and I wanted to go, but there was no time for that. It was off to New Orleans and Mardi Gras. First, we stopped at the beer store so we would have something to drink for the ride.

As we entered New Orleans, the large sign on the highway read "Welcome to New Orleans, Thou Shall Not Kill." We went straight to Justin's apartment to drop off our stuff and then headed to a parade. I wanted to see some girls flash their tits for beads. The parade was crazy. People love beads. They will do anything for beads. Why? I will never understand and no one could answer that question.

RUSS

Tell us about your night.
I passed out on a toilet with the door open while taking a shit. Then I vomited in my pants while pulling them up. Next, I chased a fat young lady around threatening to stick a chimichanga up her ass. Well, not that fat, I'd fuck her without a thought. I passed out naked next to my friend who pissed on himself. My friend Alex took a paper plate with ketchup all over it and shoved it under my cock and balls and wrote "bon appétit" on it. The girl I threatened slept across from me.

Did you piss on her?
I was in no position to piss on anyone.

Except yourself?
No, my friend next to me took care of that for me.

When is the last time you got some ass?
That was at the Oriental Spa in New Orleans where they massaged me and then I asked the masseuse to perform sucky-sucky on me because I had no idea she spoke English. She said, "You want blowjob?" It was good. She didn't swallow, but I spooged all over my chest and didn't have to wear a condom.

Did she look good?
No! She was a fat mama-san.

How much was it?
A hundred dollars. I woke up the next morning and had to go and do drills for the military. I called my Sarge and told him it was impossible for me to show up. I told him it had something to do with bourbon and oriental prostitutes. He understood.

they were pretty ugly. When the next float came around I threw them back. I guess I kinda threw them a little too hard and knocked some guy on the float upside his head. He was not too happy and started pegging beads in my general area. Before the parade ended, I spoke with a few more lovely sorority girls and a middle-aged man.

After the parade, away to a party we went. This house was nice. Everyone was eating some crap called jambalaya. I think it looked pretty gross. It's rice with sausage and who-the-hell-knows what else. Boy, do they eat some weird food down South. Pat, Justin and I were all sitting around at a table when Pat felt the urge to tackle Justin and his chair for no reason. It had been nearly 24 hours since Pat had broken anything so I use this for justification. At least it was only the chair that broke. We hit a few bars with no exciting incidents to report before we went to sleep and Pat had another night of championship drunk driving notched under his belt.

The next morning, Pat went off to get drunk before I woke up, and then he was headed to some fancy ball. I headed toward the shower when Justin's girlfriend Kelly warned me that it was real small and I should be careful if I do any other extra activities in there. The shower was cold so there would be none of that this morning. We spent the afternoon in front of the TV, watching epi-

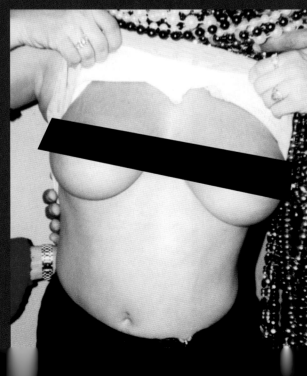

ELVIN

How old are you?
'Bout 35.

Are you in a gang?
I used to be in the Crips, but I got out. I'm a one-man gang. I got some Catbook at home and I'm gonna get me some more.

What's a "Catbook"?
It's naked woman with pussy all hanging out. Big tits. I like big tits. I was playing with big tits before I come here. I see a big tit women coming up here and I had to stop 'n' play. I don't like big women though. I like slim women.

Ever shot a man?
Yeah. I shot him 'bout four, five times. He was messing with my people. I did eight years for it. It's rough. You don't want to be there in that kind of position. You got the Crips; you got the Bloods. Gimme my five dollars, this ain't going in no magazine. I got to go clean up.

When you were in jail did you get fucked in the ass?
Nope.

You have a girlfriend?
Yeah, but that don't mean nothing. With the five dollars I'm gonna go out buy a woman a drink and get me a little cat. Everybody got a woman, but everybody like to fuck too.

How many women you got?
I got 10. I slept with about 20. Pussy is a drug.

Let's talk about women.
[Face lights up] You want to talk about cat? You can get all kinds of cat if you have enough money. Lion cat, fat cat—all kinds. I tap 'em on their ass and eat their puss. It's good. But I ain't gonna eat ass and ain't ever gonna try to eat ass. I had mine eat once. I didn't like it. I hate that shit.

Most women you have slept with at one time?
About 10.

You had enough dick to go around?
I had enough to go all around. You go to a bar and you buy them a drink. If I buy them that drink I wanna fuck. Then, boom! I turned them around and hit that ass.

You fuck them in the ass?
No, I don't fuck 'em in da ass. You can turn a woman around and still go in their puss, not in their asshole. I fucked 'em all behind the building. You know I wouldn't care where. They line up to fuck me. If they got my money and my drink I will do it to them. Now give me five dollars. [Noticing a few pennies on the floor] Oh, that's mine. Floor dirty. I'm gonna sweep the floor [leans over and picks up the change]. Floor clean.

sode after episode of Diff'rent Strokes and Happy Days.

Shortly before night fell, I found my way down to the French Quarter. The streets were packed with maniac after maniac. It is safe to say that I was the only sober person in the state of Louisiana. The streets were slippery from spilled beer and they were covered in trash. I had never in my life imagined a disaster like this. There was not one person that didn't have a drink in their hand. If you went into a store, the people that worked there were drunk. Walking down Bourbon Street, I stopped to talk with someone I knew. I looked down and saw someone pissing right next to me. I looked up and saw someone on the balcony flashing their tits.

If you have beads you can see tits. Groups of drunk, horny men surround women and chant "show us your tits" until they do. Once the men have seen the flash of tits, they give the women beads. I saw this one chick lift up her skirt and pull down her underwear revealing her behind to a group of scum. They were way too happy. I was way too disgusted with the amount of cottage cheese that I just witnessed. Was that vegan?

People were passed out all over the place and piles of puke and mile-long lines for bathrooms were common. The girls were hot and the guys were trash. Being brave and venturing into the gay quarter, I witnessed a few drag queens that put Roseanne to shame. These women—I mean men—were big! I

made my escape. A few minutes later, a drunken man approached me and asked to buy my hat. He offered to trade me his sweatshirt for it. I told him that it was a gift and I could not get rid of it. The man tried and tried to bargain with me. I offered him an interview. He said he would only do it for the hat.

We left him begging to purchase my hat to find an even more trashed punk rocker trying to play Frisbee with us. This quickly grew old and we left. People were using the most pathetic pickup lines I had ever heard and they were working: "You are the most gorgeous girl at the bar and it takes a real unique person to get me down on my knees"—you get the idea. And this was all coming from some redneck motherfucker who escorted the girl to his trailer parked illegally on the street. What class.

It was time to once again go to sleep. But first, I had to watch TV, and I was in luck: Stallone's old movie Cobra was on. "You're the disease and I'm the cure..." Pat woke us up the next morning banging on something. He said the ball he went to the night before was great. Hell, there was an open bar, how couldn't he like it? While people were on stage throwing beads, a 60-year-old was supposedly grabbing at Pat's crotch. He said that Jerry Springer, Ian Ziering and some other famous people were there. Chicago and Kool & The Gang also played. Now I was jealous.

We headed off to a block party. On the way there, we passed a graveyard. I was scared. In New Orleans, since it is so far under sea level, they bury people above ground. My stomach turned. The party was held by four neighbors whose houses faced a park around back. The band was kicking, and I think Pat summed up the best way to describe them: the black version of Santana. Everybody was at this party—old people, married people, little kids—and they were all trashed. I swear I saw a 2-year-old with beer in his bottle. Once again, it was safe to say that I was the only sober one in attendance.

I overheard Hudson's dad asking him about the ball he had attended the night before with Pat. He wanted to know if his date had big tits and if they were nice. Hudson told his father that his date hated him, he ditched her, made an ass of himself, serenaded some lesbians, and that his date's father of-

RANDOM GUY

How old are you?
Thirty-seven.

What do you do for a living?
Some people accuse me of practicing law.

What do you think of your boss?
I am my own boss. I love him; he's a great guy.

What brings you out here?
My children.

How much have you had to drink today?
Not enough.

How many times have you been drunk in the last week?
None.

What do you think about the stuff in this magazine?
This is artwork.

Could you do it?
Not as well.

When was the last fight you got in?
When I was 16.

Did you kick his ass?
He is no longer in the world we live in.

What's your favorite kind of beer?
Cold.

Your feeling toward legal prostitution?
Too expensive.

How much money would you pay to have sex with her?
More than I could afford.

Have you ever taken a shit in public?
Not that I recall.

What does ass taste like?
I'm not competent to answer.

Would you make a good president?
Probably not because my little head says more things than my big head.

Would you consider yourself having a large penis?
Large enough.

How many women do you think that you have slept with?
I can't count that high.

About how much do you think the heaviest one weighed?
A lot less than me—except for one.

The last time you jerked off was?
I'll skip that question.

What were you thinking about while you were doing it?
I better not answer that one either.

Last time you had sex?
What time is it?

Are you going to get some tonight?
It's looking pretty good.

Ever looked at two animals fucking and wonder what it must feel like for that male animal?
Where's my daughter? [Making sure she could not hear him] Yes.

Do you consider yourself a redneck?
No.

Do you own a pick-up truck?
I have a Cadillac.

Do you think that I'm just a smart-ass kid?
I don't know about the smart part.

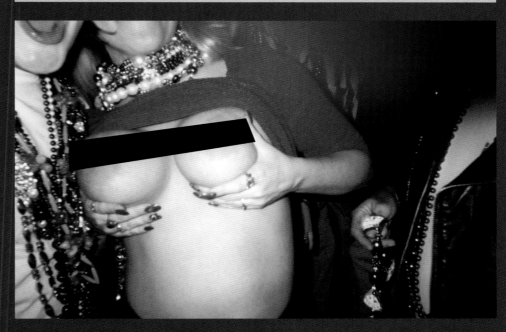

HUDSON

Would you consider yourself having a large penis?
I'm in the middle, nothing too big, nothing too small.

The last time you jerked off was?
It's been awhile, probably two days ago.

What were you thinking about while you were doing it?
Probably some bitches I saw the night before.

Most people you have ever had sex with at one time?
Just one. I'm just a regular Joe.

Do you own a pick-up truck?
Yes.

Does it have a gun rack?
No, but I wish it did. I just got some guy to paint flames on the sides.

Are you a redneck?
No, but I like rednecks. I listen to a lot of country music and I might sound like one sometimes, but I don't consider myself a redneck.

How do you pick up chicks?
Not too well.

Are you going to get some tonight?
I hope so. I'm going to give it all I got. I got a POA for this Mardi Gras holiday, but it got shot down because the girls I had planned on didn't come to town. So now I gotta to go meet some new pussy. If I want to get laid I know who to talk to, but those people are not in town. I still think I have a good chance.

Have you ever paid for sex?
Yeah, I have. I've been around town, you know. It was worth it. Definitely well-spent money.

About how much do you think the heaviest one weighed?
Holy shit! I have slept with some fat bitches in my day. Big, way bigger than me. I weigh 240. God damn it! Are you printing this shit?

fered him $20 to leave. Hudson's father walked away a proud man.

Back at Justin's, we ate dinner and listened to Pat philosophize about the amount of calories in Zoo Animal Crackers since they were each shaped different. "The bird cracker is clearly bigger than the dog cracker, and I don't know why the hell the dog is even in here. I have never seen a dog in a goddamn zoo." For some reason, this really bothered Pat. He ate the last cracker, which happened to be a dog, and when asked what it tasted like, he responded, "Chicken."

We headed off to another parade, where there were more people going nuts for plastic beads. This parade was much better than the two previous ones. There were huge floats shaped like King Kong, Lady Kong, Baby Kong, an alligator, and a giant lobster complete with a giant boiling pot of water at the rear. When we got back to the car, there was "crap" all over Pat's door handle. It turned out that the "crap" was mace, and it got in Pat's eyes. Oh well, it didn't matter because Pat liked it. It reminded me of the night before when Pat was complaining that tendonitis in his elbow was driving him crazy. After he finished complaining, he proceeded to bang his elbow on the steering wheel. Why? I cannot answer that.

We went off to some classy apartment building for a party. It took the mom about 10 minutes to kick all of us out. On the way back to Justin's, a truck of high school kids pulled up beside us and they started talking to us. Once these kids realized the back of our truck was packed with girls, they insisted to be introduced. Hudson was quick to point out that they all had small penises and the girls we were with had no interest in meeting them because of it. The high school children looked sad, even somewhat frightened. Hudson laughed and played his toy trumpet. Hudson screamed for Pat to speed up and catch the bangtail in the car ahead. "Hudson, you moron," Pat said, "that's a guy." Hudson did not care, and continued to play his trumpet.

Back at Justin's, I enjoyed myself in front of the TV, eating breadsticks with garlic butter sauce. I flipped through the channels for a while, hoping to find some tits or Springer, but nothing was on. I got up at 6:30 the next morning to catch my flight home so I could get to class and further my education. I had only made it to the French Quarter once and was not even staying for the wildest day, Fat Tuesday, which is the day all the lunatics dress up and all hell breaks loose. I had seen enough. My stomach was full.

I have learned many things from my Mardi Gras experience. I have learned that the South is a true adventure. I have learned how fabulous the girls are. Oh yes, the girls—so fine, so young, so firm, so drunk and so vulnerable. The term "Southern belle" does hold true. I have learned that mosquitoes bigger than my head do exist and that Animal House is still alive and kicking. I learned that during Pat's fraternity hazing, one kid tried to fuck a goat. When he started to gain penetration someone pulled him off. Most of all, I have learned that if you weren't there, you suck. You missed the biggest, drunkenest party of your life and you should already be planning how you are going to get there next year.

Originally printed in WYWS Issue #4

JAY TURNS 21
Story and photos by Roger Gastman

I'm sure you remember Pat, the maniac drunk from last issue's Mardi Gras article. Since my last visit, he has moved into an apartment complex that is more like one big party complete with a kegerator in the backyard. The grounds are decorated with beer cans, plastic cups and broken bottles—a landscape that we would soon contribute to. Our starting lineup for the weekend included myself, Pat, Jay, *WYWS* staff writer Trevor Michaels, Justin, his lovely girlfriend Kelly, and his older brother Mackie. We were also stalked along the way by Allison, Pat's neighbor and wife-to-be, if she has her way. We all had one mission, to celebrate everybody's favorite Asian's birthday. His name is Kuanchai. Ever since third grade everybody has called him Jay (why I don't know). But it was his 21st birthday weekend and we weren't so sure he was going to live through it...

TIME TO DRINK. After watching a great fight in a parking lot, we headed back to the apartment to party on. I guess the neighbors who had a keg thrown through their window several weeks before weren't so happy and called the cops. Being the genius he is, Pat started arguing with the cops saying that he didn't do anything. The cops didn't see it that way and Pat ended up getting a ticket for interfering with police business that he properly signed, "Bull Shit."

Trevor, having many years of training, instantly ran at the sight of the men in uniform. Leave it to him to find the only hill and stumble head first into the dirtiest swamp/creek I have ever seen. Trevor, now known as Swamp Boy, cleaned himself off and quickly continued to drink. Later, someone from the neighboring apartments got busy with a paintball gun and shot up most of the cars in the parking lot.

FRIDAY morning rolled around a few hours later with a wakeup call from the landlord. Surprisingly, he said that the previous evening had been strike number two and that maybe Pat and his roommate should find another place to live because he didn't want to cramp their style. So what happened Friday night? Why a party of course. The police arrived and everybody stumbled inside. The police left as quickly as they had come. The stroke of midnight meant it was officially Saturday, and officially Jay's birthday.

Jay wanted to get a head start on the 21 shots he would need to take to prove his manhood. He downed quite a few before everybody passed out around 4 a.m. With Allison snuggled up next to Pat that meant we had an apartment with beds to sleep in. We knew she had to be good for something.

SATURDAY was game day and that meant we needed to get up early to start drinking. We were on the bar stools by 9:30 a.m. downing screwdrivers. Jay worked some more on his shots and we went back to get showered before the party. Justin's mom met us at Pat's house. On her way to the car someone stopped her and asked, "Are you the mother of the boys because they are out of control!" She shrugged it off. It was nothing she hadn't heard before.

By noon, the day party had begun and Pat's parents and little brother, Charlie, had joined us. Allison ran up to greet them like they were her own family. Funny thing was, they had no idea who the hell she was. They played it off pretty well. Maybe Pat had just forgotten to mention her, or it could be that he had no interest in her. Jay drank and drank but nothing fazed him. We had made a bet previously on who would do the dumbest thing. Jay's money was on Charlie, the kid who, when asked

21
SHOTS TO
MANHOOD

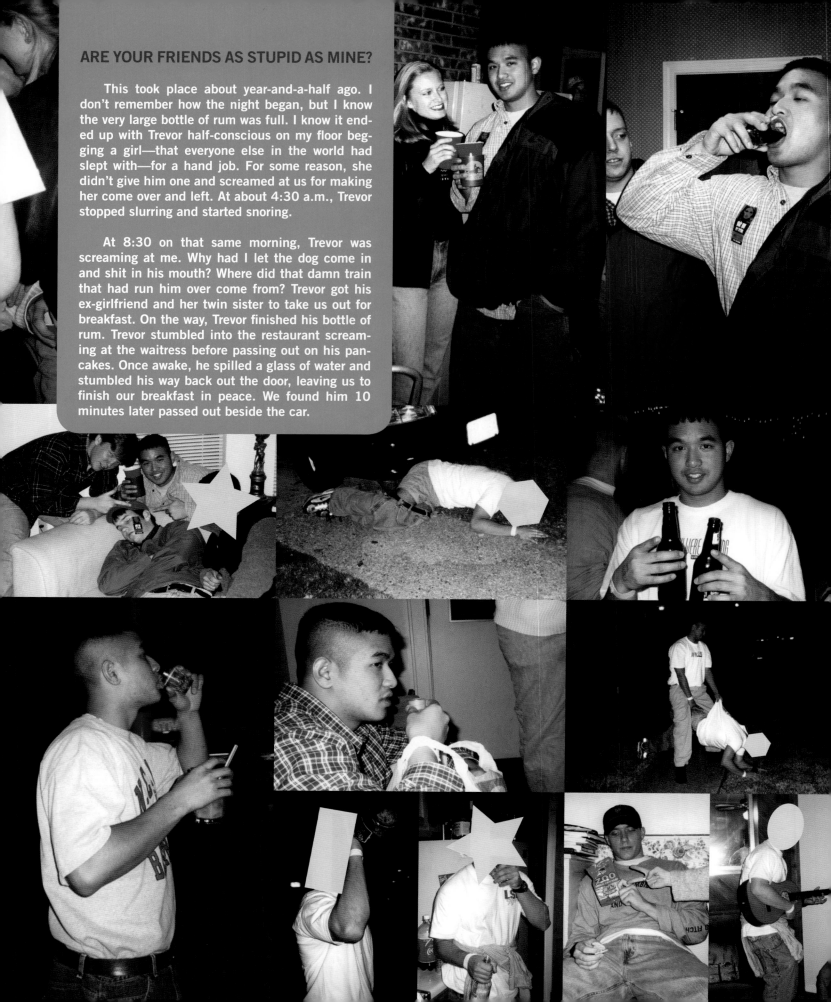

ARE YOUR FRIENDS AS STUPID AS MINE?

This took place about year-and-a-half ago. I don't remember how the night began, but I know the very large bottle of rum was full. I know it ended up with Trevor half-conscious on my floor begging a girl—that everyone else in the world had slept with—for a hand job. For some reason, she didn't give him one and screamed at us for making her come over and left. At about 4:30 a.m., Trevor stopped slurring and started snoring.

At 8:30 on that same morning, Trevor was screaming at me. Why had I let the dog come in and shit in his mouth? Where did that damn train that had run him over come from? Trevor got his ex-girlfriend and her twin sister to take us out for breakfast. On the way, Trevor finished his bottle of rum. Trevor stumbled into the restaurant screaming at the waitress before passing out on his pancakes. Once awake, he spilled a glass of water and stumbled his way back out the door, leaving us to finish our breakfast in peace. We found him 10 minutes later passed out beside the car.

how he would like his chicken cooked, said "rare." My money was on Trevor. There was no way that the Party Jerk would let me down. By the game's end, Jay had sobered up and Trevor was fascinated with his new free T-shirt that he had already spilled nacho cheese on. In my eight years knowing him, I don't think he has ever finished a meal without some of it landing on him.

Upstairs in the fraternity house, Jay was working on his shots as a party raged below. Trevor was working on some girls, telling them he wanted them to pose for the magazine. Somehow, I didn't think that line would ever work but it looked like he wouldn't be sleeping alone. Charlie puked all over somebody's leg and fell flat on his face while hitting beer cans with golf clubs. Pat's destruction was at a record all-time low. He only turned over one table and broke one radio. I don't know how many shots Jay was on before we ran out of booze but he was pretty damn close to 21.

Around midnight the cops showed up for about the fourth time that night. That was our cue to leave and head for the bars. Justin, Kelly and Charlie decided to be lightweights and go back to the apartment and get some sleep. Pat was in fine form, cock-blocking Trevor from the girl he had picked up. Trevor sucked it up. He was used to it: In high school, I made a game out of getting on every girl he liked. (I might add that I did a pretty good job at it.)

We had been at the bar for about a half hour when Kelly charged in wearing her pajamas screaming for us to come back now. We filed out of the bar into the waiting car. Charlie had gotten himself into a fight and four people jumped him. For a 16-year-old Charlie is a pretty big kid and handled his own. It didn't hurt that Justin threw one of them across the courtyard and dropped another. Pat ran through the apartment complex screaming at everyone and asking them if they tried to fight his brother. Nobody knew what the hell he was talking about. The guilty party had obviously left.

Frustrated, Pat stood in the middle of the road stopping cars and asking them if they knew who tried to fight his brother. If the car refused to stop he simply kicked a few dents in it as it passed by. Pat quickly calmed down after the police came by for the third night in a row. Then he quickly disappeared to his bedroom to hump the girl Trevor had been hitting on. What are friends for? Mackie and Trevor pulled a disappearing act and went back to the bar. Everyone we came in contact with kept asking us why all of us "Marylanders" were so fucking crazy. Maybe it's our water.

Jay and I went to pick Trevor and Mackie up from the bar. "I got some!" Trevor was babbling as the crowded bar let out. The young lady might have looked like a prom queen with beer goggles on, but she was sickening in real life. Unfortunately, the girl Mackie picked up ended up being someone's little sister and was escorted home in tears. Jay started drinking Ghetto Juice, and a lot of it.

The party was still raging and we quickly rejoined it. Trevor was in true form and didn't disappoint me. He could barely stand and went shot for shot with a bunch of 17-year-olds, then his pants fell down and he couldn't figure out how to pull them back up. I have never seen anyone act so stupid in my whole life.

Jay definitely celebrated his 21st birthday in style, even though his stupid friends tried to steal the limelight. He drank more than anyone but refused to get *that* drunk, where his face turns bright red and he tries to fight cars. Regardless, Jay is now 21 and didn't even need a trip to the hospital to get his stomach pumped like we were all hoping.

I'll leave you to ponder Charlie's question from breakfast on Sunday. "Why is stuff made out of glass? It just breaks. Can't we just use plastic for everything?"

HAPPY BIRTHDAY, JAY!

—Note from Jay: I don't remember all that much about that weekend. I remember being put in a car and Justin making me drink a whiskey and water early as fuck in the morning. The worst part about drinking that early is Roger's non-drinking ass picking out the coolest-looking bottle for my first shot of the day—Bombay Sapphire. I knew at that point I was fucked.

—Note from Pat: Jay ended up trying to get on the stage because he thought the bathroom was behind the band, and he ended up knocking over the band's entire setup. He'd been to the bathroom three times already, but for some reason he thought it was behind the band the fourth time. When we got back to the house, the police were giving out noise violations, even though we weren't there. I wasn't that happy about that, so I signed the ticket "Bullshit." I think I got in trouble for that one too. Trevor was about to enlist somewhere, and that's when the cops came for the noise violation. He tried to run out and he thought he was running in the woods, but it was like five feet of woods and then a 10-foot drop down into a nasty, sewage pond. He came crawling out of that looking like Swamp Thing and smelling so bad. I don't think Jay will go back to New Orleans willingly ever again.

Originally printed in WYWS Issue #5

LITERATURE

Soleil Moon Frye (handwritten signature)

INTERVIEW Danny Masterson
PHOTOS Patrick Hoelck

Face it, you were raised by television. Most likely, you wore two different colored Chuck Taylors and called your best friend Cheri because you wanted to be *Punky Brewster*. We still do.

With a successful post-childhood-stardom career, a healthy marriage to a handsome lad, and a surprising lack of any felony drug convictions, Soleil Moon Frye continues her charmed life as part of the WB's *Sabrina, the Teenage Witch* and does whatever her creative heart desires.

Childhood friend and good sport Danny Masterson of *That '70s Show* agreed to ask (some of) the questions we wrote for her.

Did your parents steal all your *Punky* money?
No, I had the best family ever. I'm so fortunate. My mom was a single mom raising us. She worked so hard for us and made sure that she saved it so we could go off to college. I came from a single mom who raised us with such heart and soul. It was all about giving, sharing, working and coming home and roller skating... and going to New York to stay with you. Do you remember that?

You were always trying to get me in bed naked. You were pissed because I wouldn't let you sleep with me on the top bunk.
I wanted to crawl up in that bed with you.

I got to tell everyone that you had a racecar bed when you were a little girl. And you didn't used to wear underwear.
I hated underwear. They are too constricting. I never understood. They're too tight.

You know Winona Ryder just stole a whole bunch of crap from Saks Fifth Avenue. I heard you were with her.
Who steals from Saks? I like Winona a lot, but that's so sad.

I do too, and she's really hot.
When I was younger my friend Tori and I stole something from San Francisco. We didn't steal anything for ourselves, we stole it for our parents. My mom made us drive seven hours all the way back to San Francisco to return it.

SOLEIL
MOONFRYE

Damn, that will teach you to steal. Who kisses better, boys or girls?
Well, I love boys...

Tell us about the girls! How many girls have you made out with?
I've made out with one. I had to kiss Sean Young in this movie I did.

With tongue?
She put tongue in there.

Did you put tongue back in her mouth?
Stop it!

What's the best concert you've been to?
AC/DC was pretty damn cool. My mom took my brother and I. I was like four or five years old. It just stands out in my mind because there were crazy people with their faces painted and people going nuts.

What did kids tease you about?
I got teased about everything. I got teased about the fact that I came from this crazy family, this extended family with godbrothers and godparents.

Gypsies?
No, they weren't gypsies. They were more political activists and really strong-willed artists.

Black Panthers?
No, they lived in Topanga. And I used to get teased about my crazy family and that my name was Soleil. I always got asked if my father was Frank Zappa. They all thought that Ahmet and Moon, all of us were related.

Did you ever meet Gary Coleman?
I worked with Gary Coleman on Diff'rent Strokes. I played a boy. I played Danny Cooksie, his best guy friend, and one day my cap comes off and he figures out I was a girl and he didn't want to be my friend anymore. It was great, it was superb acting.

Do you like this magazine we're doing this for?
I love the magazine.

Is it your favorite?
Definitely my favorite. You know what I love? It's no holds barred, and I love the graffiti art and... it's just dope. It's awesome.

What's the hardest part about going from child star to adult star?
I've been really blessed. I love acting, I love writing, I love all elements of art. I always had things to back me up. I've been blessed to continue working. I'm having a blast doing the show I'm doing now.

Originally printed in WYWS Issue #17

—Note from Tim Conlon: Right in the beginning of issue four, I have a piece, a KFC piece that was done in Baltimore in 1997. It is a freight spot underneath a bridge where bodies would be buried with hookers and all that type of stuff. One of the times when we went to paint there, there were no trains, so we were like, Let's just do pieces on the wall, and I did this piece because there were always boxes of KFC and 40s on the ground out there. So the issue came out in 1998, but there was a lot of controversy in Baltimore about this, because the piece was censored. There's a big drainage hole in the wall, and that was the spot that I was stuck painting, and I was like, How am I gonna use this giant hole? So I just painted this giant face around the hole, and I painted blood around it like the colonel had been shot in the forehead, but in the magazine the hole was Photoshopped out. Everybody was like, Why did he censor it? So it was controversial. I think I'm the only one that's been censored in WYWS.

while you were sleeping

GENE SIMMONS
by Liz Gawel
Photo courtesy of Liz Gawel

Gene Simmons is a curiosity. A 6-foot Jew who dresses up in platform boots, glittery clothing and makeup, he's rumored to have had thousands of sexual liaisons documented via Polaroid camera. After spending only a few seconds with Gene, I realized why. The man with the 6-inch tongue wasted no time shaking my hand, and then pushing my head toward his dick. He tried this a few times before he succeeded in shoving my face into his crotch. I was unsure of what to do, so I just reached around and squeezed his butt a few times. When he finally let my head back up, I got on with the interview.

What is your favorite KISS toy?
The newest one that someone has approached me about is the "Gene Simmons Tounge Vibrator."

So that's a prototype based off of your tounge?
I haven't done it yet, but we will find out together what it's going to be. I have a feeling that the batteries are going to be a problem.

What's the worst toy?
The least profitable one.

Your favorite food on a regular basis?
Pussy.

I like pussy too. Are fake boobs better?
Fake boobs are OK, real boobs are OK, as long as the operative word is "mine."

And they look good.
They don't have to look good, they just have to be in my mouth.

Swinging around in your face.
And poking my eyeballs with their nipples. And when you are taking your clothes off, it's good to have some place to hang your shirt. That's very important.

Did you ever get acne from the makeup?
No, because the makeup is oil-based.

[Gene lifts up my shirt and pinches my nipples.]

These are very good puppies.

I'm flushed.
What is her name?

Who?
The girls.

There's more than one?
No, it's the whole region down there
When I get through, it will have a name.

Will you take a Polaroid of it too?
Usually not. I prefer the entire female form. Body parts are impersonal and not sexy. I think sexiness for a woman starts with the face and goes down. Not just body parts.

Strangest thing you have ever been asked to autograph?
A baby.

Best hangover cure?
I have never been drunk.

Really?
What's sad about your comment is that everyone has been drunk. It's just a personal choice. Everyone has the right to jump off a building or drink and smell like a pig and not remember what they did and have their member not work. By the way, those people work for me, "The Drunkards."

I heard a rumor that you are an incredible typist.
I am. I used to be a Kelly Girl.

[Gene gets behind me and makes thrusting movements at my butt, ending with a wedgie. Luckily, a photographer who was in tow shoots several pictures.]

Getting back to the typist.
Well, Kelly Services is a temporary typing service of big corporations in New York. They hire people who just come in and login information for people. I was a Dictaphone typist, which means you have the headphones, so you have to be about 90 words a minute.

Best non-kosher food?

[Gene kisses my cheek.]

That would be me. Favorite *shiksa*?
The next one.

What do you sing in the shower?
Rub-a-dub-a-dub.

Not "I feel pretty…"
No, I'm not delusional that way.

Your favorite summertime activity?
Boo-boo-boo-boo-boom-boom-boom-boom. It makes people happy and come together. It seems to me the more fucking there is the less fighting there is. The more holding each other the less fights. Why can't we all just get along and start fucking?

Gene thought he had me. I mean, how can a girl resist that kind of talk? He asked me for my phone number saying, "We could really have some fun together." But as of press time, he still has not called. Look out for Gene's new magazine *Tongue* and his venture with Dragonfly clothing.

Originally printed in WYWS Issue #18

PROJECT PAT
by Jeff Schroeder
Photo by Carlos Batts

I ain't 'flageing no more. Nope, not me. Project Pat showed me the ropes. I'm a certified gorilla pimp. I moved to Memphis and bought a shake-junk. All type of fine broads up in there—and you know my hos got to be stout. Don't bring yo' ducks up in my joint 'cause I will not hesitate to call the holice. Better yet, I might just break out my yawk. Feel me?

Probably not, seeing as you coudln't understand a thing I said. Don't worry, if you read on, you'll learn how to front like you're a Memphis pimp too.

I want to go down to Memphis and fake like I'm a pimp. How do I do that?
For one thing, people from the South, and especially Memphis, wear a lot of gold teeth in their mouth. I'm gonna tell you this: A lot of people wasn't wearing gold in their mouth until they seen Master P and 8 Ball. So you see, Master P is from New Orleans. Only three cities I've known, when I was growing up, that wore golds in their mouths was Memphis, New Orleans and Miami.

So that's imperative?
Well, you got to have gold teeth, that's just part of today. Now you look on TV and everyone got golds in their mouth. But I promise you back in the day it was not like that. Memphis, New Orleans and Miami had the only guys wearing 10 to 12 golds in their mouth. Memphis always been on golds. So what you got to do is get you about six golds—at least! That's a six pack. You can get the full pack, which is 12, but you probably don't want to do all that.

How you need to come off, since you coming out of Maryland, you trying to fit in, you should get six on the bottom.

I know you're a pimp, do you have any advice for me? I'm 17 and I'm still a virgin.
I mean you just got to get around them hos that are fast. You got to get out and get about. We call it steppin' out and get about. And when you get about you'll come across something. OK, I'm gonna tell you what we say down here. You got to get your jewelry and toolery in order. And your toolery is your car. Now you got to get that joint cleaned up and you got to have on some nice threads. Now your jewelry is your golds in your mouth and your diamonds. And once you have your jewelry and your toolery in order, oh man! You'll be like a magnet.

Alright, so I got my jewelry and toolery in order and I'm chilling at this club and I see this fine ass broad with a big ass...
Bigg ass, yum.

Huge. What is the first thing I say to her?
OK, what your best bet out is, you got to see what's up with her first. You got to see if she's looking your way, what she's looking at. What's she into, you know what I'm saying? Then you could compliment about her outfit, but I wouldn't say nothing about her ass, nope, that's what she might be expecting, like, "I know he's going to say something about my ass." And you reverse that.

So what if I'm white and I'm trying to get with a big black girl?
Oh man, they are going to love you, man. They going to think you got some money. They going to think you a player off the top. Oh man, you going to be in.

I'm coming this weekend, man.
You crazy.

Toward the end of the interview, Pat fell asleep.

PROJECT PAT MEMPHIS GLOSSARY
Poser: We call it 'flageing. Like camouflage.
Cops: The folks, the pigs, the holice.
Big Ass: Stout. In Memphis, skinny girls get no attention at all.
Gun: A yawk or a tone.
Ugly Girl: Duck.
Strip Club: Shake-junks.
Gorilla Pimp: The only person a gorilla pimp is weak to is his momma.

Originally printed in WYWS Issue #18

—Writer's Note: Out of all the shit interviews I conducted and misquoted, this one was the most memorable for me. Mainly because Project Pat literally nodded off after about 45 minutes of my ramblings and borderline racist line of questioning. Although most people struggle to stay awake while I'm talking in general, this was, without a doubt, a drug-induced narcoleptic fit. Sizzurp, oxy and/or heroine. He fell asleep and started snoring really fucking loud. It was all on tape. I remember seeing the copy after it went to print and being furious with Neil Mahoney [the editor] because he just slipped it in at the end there. "Toward the end of the interview Project Pat fell asleep." He downplayed the hell out of it. I thought he was undermining the pure genius I captured in the interview. It is only now I realize Neil was protecting me from Dirty South rapper retribution. Neil, if you're reading this: thank you.

GRAFFITI

2TONE

Interview by Roger Gastman
Photos courtesy of 2TONE

Are you down with Cross Colors?
Let me tell you something about Cross Colors—I'm still wearing them. I went to the factory and just came out with grips of shit because I know the guy that started it. Cross Colors are in my heart. I believe in their motto: "Clothing For Uncoordinated Niggas."

Do you consider playing the lottery a form of employment?
For some people. I play. I live in a Mexican neighborhood and lotto is hardcore there. They line up at the liquor store.

What Golden Girl do you want?
I'm not into them. They're kind of old and I don't like white chicks. I'll fuck the wrinkles on their face. I like deaf chicks. You can spit game to them and you don't have to say real shit, you just say "hfty-dgnh jktdfgufss sskgyg." I got the sign language shit going on. When you play with their pussies they think you're talking to them.

What would you do to freak people out in a crowded elevator?
What I always do—fart. I'm not playing. I will blow major biscuits. I just let shit go!

Run into any vampires recently?
I'm doing this film about a Crip. He's out trying to do his dirt, trying to get paid. Homeboy is chilling and serving fools and this bat bites him. To make a long story short, he becomes undead and I'm going to call it *Interview With a Vamp Potna*.

Who do you admire more: necrophiliacs or pedophiles?
Necrophiliacs. I don't admire pedophiles because you can't joke about that stuff unless it's sex with young animals. In a way I'm making a necrophiliac movie [*Interview With a Vamp Potna*]. He's running around fucking a bunch of undead bitches. He's going to be doing some vampire bitch and she's going to bite into a bottle of Old E and suck it out with her fangs. They are going to be wearing the red-and-green Cross Colors capes. Some sprung-ass vamp potnas flying around.

Back to the sex with small animals...
That's how a lot of STDs got brought to humans. Fools were fucking sheep. You got to go for it. I bang stuffed animals. I straight molest them. I like a nice stuffed lion. You can get behind that motherfucker and grab it's mane and be like pow, pow, pow! I feel like I'm Tarzan. When I was in high school, this fool I know and his dad went to Tijuana. His dad got drunk and something happened where he fucked a donkey. Homeboy said that when he pulled his dick out it was covered in black shit. We were like damn your dad is a sick motherfucker.

What is the craziest magazine you have ever pleasured yourself to?
I can't jerk off to magazines, only to videos. How are you going to jerk off and hold the magazine and turn the pages with one hand? It's impossible. I think about bitches in my imagination, crazy shit that could never happen. Like fucking girls and their friends at the same time and going in the other room and doing their mom.

Do you think that midgets should be stuck in the zoo for the whole world to admire?
I think we should all own midgets. When I make some cash I'm going to have a dwarf and I'm going to come home and beat the shit out of him. Like, "You little punk-ass dwarf. I had a hard ass day." I would make them carry my drinks, and put him out in the yard when he was bad.

Would your dwarf wear Cross Colors?
Hell yes! Customized nylon Cross Colors warm-up suits. When they weren't working I'll keep them jogging in place because I want my midgets fit. I want my midgets to be able to bench like 240. Buff-ass midgets. You can always chin check a midget with your knee, like boom! There's this midget on the boardwalk [in Venice Beach] who looks like Bushwick Bill. Instead of an arm, he has a tentacle. He dances and bumps and grinds with his boombox and gets paid.

How do you feel about midget tossing?
I think it's dope. Everybody has to get paid. I don't think I could throw a midget that far, probably only like four feet. I like to throw GKAE around. I got a GKAE story! On the record, I saved GKAE's life; I brought him back. This is years ago, when he was trying to get down with us. He came over and he had a bottle of Southern Comfort. We were like, go ahead and down it. He took the bottle to the head. He passed out and we tagged on him so much he looked like Motor Yard. We were going over each other to get space. We started doing throwups and outlines—we were getting beef over space on GKAE's chest. We were having battles on his ass. He overdosed on alcohol and started choking on his vomit. Nobody wanted to deal with it. I was like, I can't let him die in my house. If he died, I would have taken his ass to the beach. I love the guy but I'm not going to jail. He was choking to death, and I remember sticking my fingers down his throat and pulling out puke and my homeboy giving him the Heimlich.

Do you have any emotional problems now?
Yeah, I see a shrink like three times a week. It's expensive.

You wear your Cross Colors there?
No, I can't. I have to be real. Cross Colors are for when I'm straight flossing and dipping in my Nissan.

Where did the name 2TONE come from?
This dude FADE gave it to me. You know how you go through like 40 names when you first start writing? He said, "You should write 2TONE because you're mixed." I'm not looking at it like it means anything. It's just my letters.

Who do you relate with more, your white side or your black side?
I go back and forth. I'm schizophrenic. I'll be surfing one day and gangbanging the next.

Do you relate with Shorty the Pimp?
Short Dog did this chick's mom where I used to live. That was her claim to fame.

Did she wear a hair net?
Hell no, but she had some Cross Colors thongs on.

Would you punch an alien?
No, that fool would probably mess me up. I could start an international crisis like "2TONE destroyed the world" and that's how I would go down in history. I could see some fools blasting an alien if it landed in the hood, like "Fuck this punk-ass alien flying saucer, dog!"

Anything else you want to add?
I love ass!

Originally printed in WYWS Issue #5

BUS & CHUNK
Interview by Roger Gastman
Photos courtesy of BUS & CHUNK

Tell me about where you used to live?
BUS: With this ghetto girl from North Hollywood. Her mom had a beard and used to take me racking and bombing.

Was her mom in a gang?
BUS: She was "La Loca."

Did she know you were doing her daughter?
BUS: She didn't much care. She walked in a couple of times and shrugged it off. Her taking me painting was cool because then I could get all the spots by myself. It didn't look too obvious because it was just a guy with some old fat lady.

How much did she weigh?
BUS: Probably about 300 pounds.

What did she keep in the refrigerator?
BUS: At all times there were about six pints of Ben & Jerry's ice cream. She would eat one pint a day. Then she moved on to the half gallons and sometimes she would eat a whole one a day. She liked those Hot Pockets pizza things and Taco Bell. She smoked a lot of weed everyday.

Did she have any relationships with men?
BUS: She was talking about this one guy when she was younger. They were living together and she came home one day and everything was gone. The guy robbed all her shit.

How thick was her beard?
BUS: Pretty hefty. It was an unspoken thing. Everybody knew she had a beard, but no one ever mentioned it.

What is the story about the lady that lived upstairs from you?
BUS: She had all these kids. I guess she would get somebody to watch her kids and all the guys from the building would go up there and she would suck all there dicks.

What other crazy shit went on in that apartment building?
BUS: There were these projects next door and people would get shot all the time. One was totally crazy. You heard five or six shots, then you heard this horn for five minutes. Somebody had just got blasted and their head was leaning on the horn.

Tell me about fat chicks?
CHUNK: I love fat chicks, like 250, 300 pounds.
BUS: You would have loved my ex-girlfriend's mom.

Where did the name CHUNK come from?
CHUNK: Because I'm fat. I'm 200 pounds and I'm only 5-foot-5.

What is better about fat chicks?
CHUNK: They are just fat. Nobody wants them. You don't have to worry about somebody stealing you're chick because she's fat. They're always down to go eat because they're never watching their weight.
BUS: We were at the Dragonfly one night. CHUNK went up to this fat girl and said, "You know what? I'm fat, you're fat, let's go get some Del Taco."
CHUNK: It didn't work. She was pissed.

What do you do for a living?
CHUNK: I sleep all day. By the time I wake up, all the stores are closed so I don't even have time to rack anymore. I'm kind of unemployed right now. I'm a retired racker.

What kind of stuff have you stolen?
CHUNK: I've stolen some weird shit—camcorders, whatever I can get my clammy hands on. I got an

electric door lock with a remote control. My room is like a safe.

Have you ever eaten anyone's cat?
CHUNK: I have two, and if they keep pissing on my stuff or shitting in my room, I'm going to eat them.

ALF ate cats.
CHUNK: FATE thinks he's ALF. He always goes, "Here kitty, kitty, kitty."

Have you ever bitten the head off of a live fish?
BUS: When I was six, my dad took me fishing. He told me that in order to be a man you have to bite the head off of the first fish you ever catch. I ended up catching this two-pound Bass. It took like 45 minutes because I could barely get my mouth around that thing it was so big. It kept slipping out of my hands.

Would you punch an alien?
CHUNK: If I just saw an alien standing around I wouldn't go up and punch him.

If he probed your cousin?
CHUNK: Then I would be forced to punch him. I would put him in a headlock.

What if he gave you the reverse headlock?
CHUNK: I would try to bite him or something like BUS did to the fish.
BUS: I've punched an alien. When I was 11, I was on vacation with the folks in New Mexico. We were driving and I fell asleep. When I woke up things changed, there were all these weird-looking dudes. They were trying to stick things in my butt. I punched one in the eye and it popped and this orange stuff came out.

Were you circumcised?
BUS: I didn't get circumcised until I was seven. My parents figured on just leaving it on there. I was fooling around in the garage and I got my foreskin caught on a nail and it tore a big chunk out of it. When they went to fix it, they said they were just going to have to circumcise me because I was a real careless kid and I used to get my foreskin stuck on things. One time my mom slammed my foreskin in the car door.

Did you ever shit in the bathtub by accident?
BUS: Once when I was eight, I was taking a bath with my brother. I had to shit really bad, and I figured I could just sneak it out. So I went ahead and the log floated up to the top. My brother was 11 and he's kind of stupid. He thought it was the soap and started washing himself with my shit. My parents got all pissed off.

Originally printed in WYWS Issue #5

Photos by TOOMER

I met Roger years ago. He went to a bar mitzvah that me and my homie were pretending to be valets at. We knew Jews had money, so we beat up the attendants and were taking off with the cars. Roger drove up, and when I got in his car, I noticed he had a bunch of pictures of graffiti in there. I was like, "Hey, homes, you write?" He was like, "Huh?" I was like, "I write graffiti too." Then he gave me his card, and it said *While You Were Sleeping* on it.

Later on, I was broke as fuck, and I called him up because, like I said, I knew Jews had money. We started talking and somehow we got on the subject of Mexican wrestling masks and midgets. I told him I go to Tijuana all the time, and he should roll up and I would be his tour guide.

So he came to L.A. and we took him to Tijuana. He had a whole list of things he wanted to see—masks, donkey shows, midget wrestlers, piñatas—and we went out and found it. We tried to trick him into having sex with a transvestite prostitute, but it didn't work. So anyways, we ate some good tacos on the street and painted a lot of graffiti. On the way back, I actually put drugs in his car and smuggled them back over, and he never knew about it. Well, he does now.

Through that trip, I came to tolerate Roger and I actually learned a lot from him. Roger was the stupidest motherfucker alive and through the dumb shit he used to do, it made me change up my attitude toward life and graffiti. Where I grew up, in South Central Los Angeles, graffiti was taken real seriously. People were getting killed over graffiti. When I met him, I was more serious too, and he showed me another side of graffiti I didn't get to experience in the hood. It made graffiti fun for me, and also made me more creative because it got me to look outside the box. So for that, I have to thank Roger and *WYWS*.

—*TOOMER*

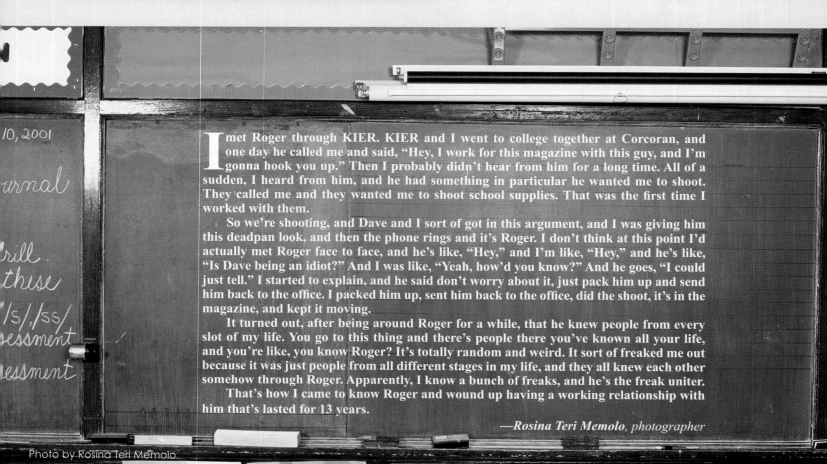

I met Roger through KIER. KIER and I went to college together at Corcoran, and one day he called me and said, "Hey, I work for this magazine with this guy, and I'm gonna hook you up." Then I probably didn't hear from him for a long time. All of a sudden, I heard from him, and he had something in particular he wanted me to shoot. They called me and they wanted me to shoot school supplies. That was the first time I worked with them.

So we're shooting, and Dave and I sort of got in this argument, and I was giving him this deadpan look, and then the phone rings and it's Roger. I don't think at this point I'd actually met Roger face to face, and he's like, "Hey," and I'm like, "Hey," and he's like, "Is Dave being an idiot?" And I was like, "Yeah, how'd you know?" And he goes, "I could just tell." I started to explain, and he said don't worry about it, just pack him up and send him back to the office. I packed him up, sent him back to the office, did the shoot, it's in the magazine, and kept it moving.

It turned out, after being around Roger for a while, that he knew people from every slot of my life. You go to this thing and there's people there you've known all your life, and you're like, you know Roger? It's totally random and weird. It sort of freaked me out because it was just people from all different stages in my life, and they all knew each other somehow through Roger. Apparently, I know a bunch of freaks, and he's the freak uniter.

That's how I came to know Roger and wound up having a working relationship with him that's lasted for 13 years.

—*Rosina Teri Memolo*, *photographer*

Photo by Rosina Teri Memolo

WYWS was a lesson in trial and error. We just sat down, and made everything work. It wasn't easy and it wasn't cheap—you couldn't email, there wasn't any server you could use, CD burners were rare and fetched retarded prices. Zip discs were the affordable solution. Dealing with distribution people like Tower, learning about getting a barcode so certain retailers would take them—it was all trial and error.

I remember from issue to issue, we would go to newsstands when other magazine came out, and we'd look at that and say what can we do, what can we bite from them, what can we keep original, look at design styles, look at what to do and how to keep things going. Carlos Batts got in touch with them after a couple of issues, and they started doing fashion, and trying to get better photography for it. It was definitely a grassroots, ground-up, DIY punk thing that just kind of morphed into this monster. It went basically from a fanzine to a full-fledged pop-culture magazine. It was awesome.

It was a chance for us to validate what we were into, and not just validate it to our peers, but validate it to the rest of the world, and it was completely on our own terms.

No one knew how to market it. I remember selling it at shows in San Francisco and stuff. Then there was the Warp Tour scandal. It was like issue 4 or 5, and we had Gabe Banner and a couple of other people handing out issues at the Warp Tour in Indiana or Iowa or somewhere. Apparently, they gave it to some kid whose mother was offended, and the local news did a giant story on how people were handing out porn at this concert event, and there were even people protesting. After that episode, no one was able to hand out merchandise. We were stoked we made the news, though.

I was amazed at the amount of random swag that people started throwing—random boxes of stickers would show up, T-shirts. Kids in the suburbs just going, Oh shit, free clothes! I remember I went to promote the magazine at this festival up in New Jersey, and it was when JNCOs were still big, they were one of the big advertisers on the back page, and they started handing me free sneakers and ridiculous shit. It was surreal just to see the growth of it.

It made perfect sense. We were a bunch of delinquents. It was just focused on paper as opposed to running around breaking shit. It reminded me of a story in a zine I read that basically told how to saltwater soda machines. It was basically where you make this super concentrated saltwater solution, like you spray it into the coin slot of old soda machines, and it would make all the money and soda come out. What we did was the same kind of delinquency, but like focused and not vengeful and not trying to fuck over anyone. We were just showing kids that you can go out and cause havoc.

—Linas

ALISHA KLASS

Interview by Roger Gastman and Fat Rich

KLASS DISMISSED

When I first called Alisha to set up this interview, I caught her in the bathtub. She told me she had just finished shaving her ass and that she would call me back. We spoke a few days later about all kinds of things, except I forgot to get advice on how to shave an ass without cutting yourself.

How did you hook up Seymore Butts?
I had a male roommate who was a huge Seymore Butts fan and had all the movies. I started watching them when I was by myself and started masturbating a lot. I just got really caught up in it. I had seen a couple of other adult films before that with an ex-boyfriend, they were girl-on-girl with fake screaming. I didn't understand what the point of watching them was. Seymore has totally changed my opinion on that. Basically, it's just real people having real fun and having real sex. I decided to write Seymore a letter, and it turned out that he only lived three miles away. He called and came over, and we met. He started fucking my ass, and that was it.

What was your first experience with anal sex?
That would be with an ex-boyfriend of mine. I probably only had anal sex with him five times. The only orgasm I remember with him was when he was in my ass and his fingers were in my pussy, and I had a vibrator on my clit. I just remember it was such a great orgasm. Now I prefer anal sex over vaginal. Now Seymore just sticks it right in my ass. "No pussy, just ass," that's what we say around here.

Photo courtesy of Alisha Klass

The first time you had anal sex did you have to be talked into it?
The biggest fear is that there is going to be poopy coming out. I was more worried about feeling embarrassed than the pain. I didn't know what to expect.

Ever had any "poopy" problems?
Yesterday, we had a little bit of poopy come out of my ass. For the most part, it rarely happens, because I do my enema, and I really clean myself out. I do it everyday on myself.

Do you wear underwear?
I haven't worn underwear for a couple of years. I hate wearing it. What is the point of wearing something you have to keep pulling out of your ass? If I get a little bit of cream on my pants, oh well, they have to be washed anyways. I wear summer dresses all the time and it feels really good. When I get out of the car the valet parker always sees my pussy. I like that stuff.

What is the largest thing you have ever had in your ass?
Besides my fist? I've had my whole hand. I'm doing a series called "Klassterbation." I went to the grocery store and got this huge, huge squash. I haven't tried it yet, but that will be the biggest thing I've ever had in my ass.

Have you ever had a dream about riding around on a unicorn naked?
Can I have the unicorn tusk up my ass?

That would hurt, tusks are pretty sharp.
No we could put some cotton at the end of it, it will be like a big q-tip.

How did you first discover that you could squirt?
For the past couple of years, I always felt like I had to urinate when I was having sex. Squirting is female ejaculation. When you put pressure on the g-spot, there is vaginal fluid that builds inside the g-spot, and it is released through the urethra. When Seymore puts that pressure—whether it's in my ass or in my pussy—I cum and squirt. I'm the first girl who only needs anal stimulation to squirt. Now it is so incredible. In this new movie, I squirted so much that we were soaked! It shoots out like a water hose. I don't know where it comes from.

Ever thought about bottling it and selling it to your fans?
Wow! If I could catch it. I should squirt it in a ziplock bag, and pour it into a bottle. "Squirt Juice."

How importantly do you value anal sex in the relationship? Do you think it is a must?
In my relationship, it would be a must now.

Throughout America?
I don't think it is a must, I just think people are missing out on some really great experiences. I love vaginal sex, but the reason I don't really care too much for it is because, when I have an orgasm in my ass—we'll call it an assgasm—it is just so incredible and so much more intense. It goes through your anus, through your vagina, and out your clit. Yesterday I screamed my head off. It is so amazing. It takes everything out of you, then you pass out and go to sleep.

What cartoon character would you most like to sleep with?
Charlie Brown, because I would just like to teach him everything. I would like to teach him to suck ass well so he could suck ass well his whole life. That's important, you know. Sex education!

What is your story of the three little pigs?
The first little pig only liked to get her pussy ate. So she laid down on her back, and Alisha laid down and ate her pussy. That was all she would take, she was missing out. The second little pig loved to have Alisha's tongue up his ass. When Alisha went to put the tongue up his ass he screamed so much, that he wanted more so Alisha got to put her two little fingers in the second pig's ass. She poked, and she licked, and she sucked until the second little pig came so, so well. The third little pig really wanted to fuck Alisha's ass. He had never fucked a tushy before. Just before he got to put his dick in Alisha's ass, he passed out and fucked it all up. The end.

What did Alisha do?
Alisha masturbated because she was pissed and still wanted to cum. Have you ever felt a women cum on your face?

Not like you would.
I think I almost broke Seymore's face yesterday. When I'm cumming, I just push his face so hard on my pussy. He is just so good at everything he does. I don't think I could ever marry another man.

Any mainstream projects that you are working on?
I'm basically the first girl to continue doing adult while still doing mainstream. That is my goal. I have done 90210, three episodes of *Melrose Place*, and I was on *Howard Stern*. He doesn't want me back on his show. I said things to him like, "Howard, you are all talk, why don't you come over here and lick my ass?" I have four commercials running—two for ESPN, and I just did a Virgin Cola commercial as myself, Alisha Klass, porn star.

What do you think of graffiti?
I think that it is disgusting and not right. I was driving down the 405 on Saturday and there were these really nice murals, and now they are all graffited. It disrupts what other people have already created.

Is there anything anal that you fantasize about doing that you haven't done?
I would like to do another double penetration. I've only done one in my life. I want to fuck somebody who is really going to open my ass up. That's coming in style now, the gaping asshole.

Originally printed in WYWS Issue #5

—Editor's note: I'm still in awe of many of Alisha's answers. During the interview, it was hard to stay on track because I just kept thinking about squash. Much later on, there was some controversy over Alisha's ability to squirt. Some said it wasn't female ejaculation at all, but that she was just peeing as she came. Either way, Alisha gets an A for effort. Klass is dismissed.

PLAYERHATERS

"Pimping ain't easy, but it's necessary."

I don't know which of the three wise men said this, but I know he was right. I know because as I embarked on my second curatorial experiment, the comparisons to pimping were easily made. Like many a pimp, I must put up a good front in order to keep the respect of my stable, I must show the clientele that they need what I have, and I must do everything necessary to keep my "game" true. Somehow, I did with my first venture in the gallery world: *Free Agents: A History of Washington, D.C., Graffiti,* which is the only reason the nice people at MOCA gave me the chance to have my *Playerhaters* strut the track once again for the people of D.C.

Playerhaters opened in Washington, D.C., on, October 19 to a full house.

Playerhaters stars Shepard Fairey, Ron English, Dalek and Richard Colman. All four artists have been featured on the fine pages of *WYWS*. Art openings are usually really gay, but we had three kegs, five cases of champagne (the kind with the photocopy label), crates and crates of Red Bull to mix with vodka, and many cases of beer to chase. That lasted our art dilettantes until 10 p.m. Those that did not black out made their way to East Coast Clothing's mixer at a club called State of The Union, where boys and girls danced together.

Those who arose and walked the next day were lucky enough to see the four artists of *Playerhaters*—along with many other well-known graffiti artists—paint a wall in Dupont Circle. D.C.'s finest made an appearance and tried to bust the party. After almost an hour of sitting in the hot seat, the law couldn't find anything in the rulebooks to keep us down.

Since you probably missed its running in D.C. be sure to check out the next stop on the tour at the Upper Playground Gallery in San Francisco, which opens December 13. Lots of art and booze to make it go down easier.

Thanks to the Starwood, Mario and especially Clark & Felicity at MOCA D.C.

—**Roger Gastman**
Editor in chief

This article first appeared in WYWS issue 16.

RON ENGLISH • SHEPARD FAIREY
DALEK • RICHARD COLMAN

Playerhaters

Dont Hate the Game—Hate the Player

Opening Reception Friday October 19th 6-10pm
Gallery Hours: Wednesday- Saturday 1-6pm or by Appointment
Show Runs Through November 30th

Music By Dirty Hands

MOCA DC
1054 31st st. NW Washington D.C. 20007
202.342.6230
COMPLIMENTARY DRINKS

BRONX FREIGHT KILLERS
MONE & *SIEN 5*
Interview by Fat Rich
Photos courtesy of MONE & SIEN5

Tell me about your craziest friend and what makes him so crazy?
MONE: My craziest friend sat at home and carved his girlfriend's name all the way from the middle of his chest down his arms. Then she came from work and found blood all over. He ruined a brand new couch that she had. He never had sex with her but he ran up her cable bill going in and watching the porn channel. He used to try and beat cops up and they would always wind up beating his ass. His claim to fame is that he beat Marilyn Manson up in Florida.

What do you think of Marilyn Manson?
MONE: He's fake. Hanson is more satanic than Marilyn Manson. I love Hanson. They are gods to me and I look up to them.
SIEN 5: My craziest friend had this family of wild kids living across from him. Normally you would call the cops. He doesn't do that. He comes outside with a machine gun and shoots it up in the air and tells everybody to shut the fuck up.

Do you own a machine gun?
SIEN 5: Not anymore. They have passed through my hands.

So you are an arms dealer?
SIEN 5: Not really. I've been known to sell a lot of things.

I need a bazooka.
SIEN 5: I could talk to somebody for you.

What's up with Ginger Spice?
MONE: I was so mad she left. She looked good in *Playboy*.
SIEN 5: If they were all deaf and mute, they would be super fine chicks.

I saw in one of your pieces it said, "SIEN 5, sex fiend." Tell me about that.
SIEN 5: This isn't the forum for it. It's a graffiti magazine.

How many freights?
SIEN 5: I started painting them in 1991, and I've done over 300 pieces and god knows how many throw ups.
MONE: I started doing freights in 1992, 1993. I've done over 100 pieces.

Do you think Jeffrey Dahmer had a problem?
SIEN 5: No, not really. He liked eating human beings, and he got to do that.

Ever kill anybody?
MONE: Not yet.
SIEN 5: I've come close to almost trying to.

Did Elmer Fudd ever get laid?
SIEN 5: I think he was banging Bugs Bunny.

What do you listen to as far as music?
MONE: Death Metal.

Were you ever in any bands?
MONE: Yes, Incantation and Mortician.

Do you think Shaggy touched Scooby?
MONE: No, I think he had his eye on Daphne.
SIEN 5: Shaggy was trying to get with the chick with the glasses.

What's the craziest shit that you have seen in the tunnels?
MONE: There's weird people down there. Naked crackhead bums.

Do you check them out?
MONE: Naked crackhead chicks aren't my style.
SIEN 5: There used to be this guy down here and he would jog and then stop all of a sudden and take off all his clothes and start doing jumping jacks under the bridge.

Did Wilma and Betty get it on while Fred and Barney were at work?
SIEN 5: I think Wilma and Dino were doing it.

Tell me a little bit about Bodé? I notice you rock his characters a lot.
SIEN 5: Bode was a very interesting man. He was really the first one to break through with weird cartoons of futuristic, pornographic and past and present bullshit. From what I understand—this is the rumor—this guy died an unnatural death. He used to jerk off and tie a belt around his neck and choke himself as he was cumming. When you cum and pass out that is supposed to be the ultimate high. So once you pass out you let go of the belt and you can breath again. This time the belt didn't loosen and he died. So he died with his dick in his hand.

What jobs have you held?
MONE: I've been a stripper. That was what I use to do on the DL. I used to take pornographic pictures of myself and sell them to magazines and on the Internet.
SIEN 5: You name it, I've done it.

ALF ate cats. Have you all ever tried cat?
MONE: I sacrificed a cat. When I was young I was stupid, and we thought we were into Satanism. My friend held the front paws and I held the back and we just pulled it real hard and snapped it in half. I also poured gasoline on a dead dog and lit it on fire and then when the fire went out I took the skull off and took it home and melted a candle in it. I still got it.
SIEN 5: Man, he's crazy. I'm sure that I've eaten cat and dog because I eat Chinese in New York.
MONE: I ate cat once in Colombia. It tasted good, then I found out what it was and I couldn't finish it.

—Writer's note: The graff interviews were always the best because these dudes would get so bummed. Here they are psyched that a graff mag wanted to interview them, thinking it was going to be somewhat serious and what does Roger do? Get's me, some dude who doesn't do, care, or on a lot of levels understand graff to interview them. Most people seemed cool with it but you could see the disappointment sometimes. I remember he had me interview REVOLT, kinda a big deal writer (you think) and at one point I implied he got a BJ from a dude or something. He was pretty pissed. I remember meeting him a few weeks later and he was not too siked on me. Kinda genius of Roger. I mean, if you had some graff head do these things it would be total ball-hugger style.

Originally printed in WYWS Issue #5

Satan

by MR. Shane Jessup

First off, how do you want to be addressed for this interview?
Well, I've taken on many names over the years, but I'd like to go back to the manifestation I held in heaven, which was Earl.

Why did you agree to do this interview?
I'm sure every one of your readers has heard some of the negative publicity that has been aimed to discredit my public image. Nothing but pure mudslinging from God's PR people. After a thousand or so-odd years of trying to silently work around this, my people and I have decided to start a positive publicity campaign. I've met with countless lawyers and public relations reps, trying to soften up my image to the people. Your magazine seems to hold the same target group we would like to reach.

You've been portrayed in a lot of movies and films, which seemed to portray you the way the real Satan would like to be portrayed.
Please, call me Earl.

Sorry. How would "Earl" like to be portrayed?
There's been countless movies about me that I liked. The Exorcist, for example. The Prophecy, The Omen, Seventh Sign—they were all entertaining. That delightful Rowan Atkinson [Mr.Bean] had a pretty funny representation of me. But I would have to say that The Devil's Advocate was the closest. Not that I would want that piss-ant Keanu Reeves to be my son—his only good roll was the first Bill and Ted's—it's just that they portrayed my business side. I've always had my hand in the business world, but I'm not always the luckiest when it comes down to it.

What bad decisions are you referring to? Give us some examples.
I've always been interested in the music business, and I've invested in quite a few artists' careers. I've also tried producing and some songwriting. But that's more of a hobby.

Why the music business?
It's the easiest way to reach a large mass of my target group, the 15 to 25-year-olds. They tend to be the biggest music buyers. I also work closely with television producers.

Back to examples.
Some of my more recent ventures: I co-wrote tracks one, six and seven on the Hanson debut album. Those guys would bring a smile to anyone's face. I helped produce the Backstreet Boys, and had a big part in Ginger leaving the Spice Girls. I've got big plans for her in the near future. I helped Aaron Spelling achieve his greatness ever since The Love Boat's first season. Mama's Family, One Day at a Time and Welcome Back Kotter were some of my other ventures. I helped write some scripts for Three's Company, Alice and Sanford and Son. I also worked closely with Geraldo and Vanilla Ice.

You're the cause of "Ice, Ice Baby?"
No, no, no. I was responsible for his comeback. I got in around the time of that Cool As Ice movie. I figured the dreadlocked, hardcore image would shoot him back to the top. Go figure.

Any more examples you would like to share?
There's countless other endeavors. Those are just the ones I'm comfortable releasing to the public. My most fortunate business investments actually happen to be laundromats. Everyone gets dirty, which keeps the loot rolling in.

Is Hell really that bad of a place?
We're not going to refer to it as "Hell" anymore as part of the positive image campaign. It will now be referred to as the "House of Eternal Flames." We actually are in the final stages of remodeling. We've added new escalators, better security, and the stench of death and burning flesh has been replaced with a strawberry-scented air freshener.

If you could sexually please any one of the cast members of *The Facts of Life*, who would it be?
Blaire. And I have.

Really?
And Tutti.

Anyone else we should know about?
Natalie and Ms. Garrett. That's it. I can't tell you anymore. Do you want to hear a secret that I've never told anyone?

Sure, give us an exclusive.
Back during a very rough period in my existence, I decided to play the field while I was staying out in Los Angeles. I entered the fifth bar of the night, when guess who I see in the corner booth? It was none other than John F. Kennedy himself. He was having drinks with Marilyn Monroe! She was a knockout! So, I walk over and introduce myself. John was pleased to finally meet me, and Marilyn was eyeing me the whole night. Anyways, to make a long story short, John asks me to take Marilyn home and we end up taking Quaaludes and fucking for almost two days straight! Those were the days. Nobody was worried about venereal diseases and all that. That's why I made them.

If you could choose any one special female to reign with you for eternity in Hell...
The House of the Eternal Flames.

Whatever, who would it be?
That's a hard question. I've had many relationships and quite a few females I've had my eyes on for some time. Right now, I would have to say Carmen Electra. I've got her calendar hanging in my office. Sometimes, I just stare at it and daydream about us being together. I stop when I realize I'm licking myself.

So what are "Earl's" plans for the future?
I'm going to continue to press forward with my campaign to soften my public image. I'm touring through rural America first, going door-to-door and introducing myself. I just finished filming a pilot for a sitcom that I'm trying to sell to the WB Network. It involves me and three orphan boys that just can't stay out of trouble. It's guaranteed laughs for the whole family. I'm considering running for mayor of Toledo, Ohio. Recently, I underwent some cosmetic surgery to make myself a little less intimidating to the public. It just seems that every time I do something big, Americans fuck it up somehow—bombing foreign countries, your leaders getting knobbers from fat chicks, etc. I might give this whole Clinton thing a while to "blow" over before I really push my new image.

Originally printed in WYWS Issue #5

STUPID STUFF

STREET PICKLES

I love pickles—not all kinds, but most kinds. They really hook up a sandwich or burger. The sweet ones are extra tight and, since the pickle companies wised up a bunch of years back and started making *big* sliced ones for sandwiches, I have liked pickles even more.

I am not a pickle snob; I don't need high-end pickles. I am happy with a regular store brand or Vlasic. Vlasic knows how to pickle a damn cucumber!

So, you an imagine how upset I was, when I was driving down the freeway and saw pickle after pickle getting run over by cars! The humanity!

– Roger Gastman

BIG GUY'S TRACK SUITS

The Big Guy has always really fancied the tracksuit and has been a connoisseur for light years. I really don't own a shitload of them, but believe me, the ones I'm holding get heavy rotation especially when my boy the dun is out. The all-white Nike really has to be my go-to tracksuit—he has been with me for a while and he's real nice in the pocket. You can dress him down and play the street or dress him up and hit the local watering hole with confidence! I really advise anybody not having one hanging in their closet to make a solid investment and cop one at your earliest convenience!

– The Big Guy

Mary-Kate &Ashley Update

On June 13, Mary-Kate and Ashley Olsen—the adopted sisters of the editorial staff of *WYWS*—turned 14, and we would like to wish them a happy belated birthday. We sent them dandelions picked from in front of the *WYWS* funhouse and some friendship bracelets each of us wove especially for them.

Don't forget to clear your calendar for June 13, 2005 because not only is that the twins' 18th birthday, but *WYWS* is going to blow the entire year's budget showering our darlings with everything that their little heart's desire at the most extravagant gala in the history of galas.

As most everyone knows by now, Mary-Kate and Ashley have started their own magazine. At the *WYWS* headquarters, we had to buy four different subscriptions because no one was willing to share (especially Roger, who recently took his fanaticism to the next level by lovingly feeding and bathing his new Mary-Kate and Ashley dolls—all I can say is, "Pajama Parties Rule!").

In a recent development, we have retained the services of two major investment banks to help complete our proposal to merge *WYWS* with Mary-Kate and Ashley's magazine. We think our demographic of 18 to 32-year-old males meshes fabulously well with their demographic of 10-17 year-old females. To show your support for our venture, send a letter (a nice one) to:

Mary-Kate and Ashley Olsen
c/o Dualstar Publications
2121 Waukegan Road, Suite 120
Bannockburn, IL 60015

Be sure to check back every issue to find out what's new with Mary-Kate and Ashley!

– *Rob Robdowski*

MK&A

Way to go girls—you're getting the hang of it! For those of you who are so stuck in last season, our girls Mary-Kate and Ashley followed up their blockbuster debut issue with an even glossier glossy.

This time around, they address some very important topics, including one tremendously moving dialogue on how to stop school shootings. Conclusion: It's going to take more than just words to make our schools safe—you must take inspired action and open the lines of communication.

Getting a little silly, the twins also challenged the boys from O-Town to make a Fruit Loop necklace. Did O-Town come through? They did. If only all your accessories stayed crunchy in milk!

Think that just because you're a girl you can't get an internship? Try telling that to Mary-Kate and Ashley! As they explain, girls can get internships if they don't take no for an answer. So, girls, by next issue, I want each and every one of you to have an internship! *WYWS* is currently accepting applications.

In related news, on his routine Saturday stroll through the San Diego Zoo, contributing writer Ian Sattler found some angels among the animals. The Olsen twins love caged beasts, so it was no surprise they took to Ian like moths to a flame.

MK&A

This just in: Mary-Kate and Ashley are taking the magazine world by storm, and no one out there should even think of trying to stop them. In issue 3, the twins go all the way to India to bring their readers a little Eastern philosophy, not to mention some hot tips on how to get outfitted in a really awesome sari. (Believe it or not, it takes 30 minutes just to get the darn things on!)

Sisqo makes an appearance to offer a little dating advice in response to readers' letters. Ever wonder why a boy would try to annoy you if he likes you? Sisqo says, "He's trying to get your attention. If someone is stealing your pencil and running away, go ahead and think, 'They definitely like me.'"

Not a straight-A student? Not anymore, now that the girls have published the definitive guide to studying effectively. You probably didn't know that getting high grades is less about how smart you are and more about how efficiently you study. With a little proactivity, you too can learn that reading really is fun-damental.

We always knew Jeff Timmons of 98 Degrees was a kung-fu expert, but we never knew that he was so totally buff. Mary-Kate and Ashley turn up the heat to something more like 198 degrees with their pictures of Timmons shadow boxing topless amid shooting columns of flames. This one is *definitely* going on the wall.

LET THE VEHICLE BE YOUR TOILET

by Patrick Kennedy

As any real driver knows, you can do just about anything in a car, and that includes high-speed urinating. However, it can be a risky endeavor, and the difficulty level only mounts with inclement weather, heavy traffic, direct sunlight and serious velocity. But those variables also bring out a spirit of adventure! Americans love a dare, and this is one surefire way to play Evel Knievel on the open highway—or at the McDonalds drive-thru. Exhibitionist or death rider, the choice is yours.

So let's take you through this step by step, and give you a few cautionary tips for the road. Example: You've had about eight cups of coffee and you're flying down the highway, late to work, barely able to focus on that solid yellow line and, damn, you've gotta go, there's just no question about it. You're either gonna soak your pants and seat or stop the car and piss out the car door. Now let's examine those two possibilities: If you show up to work with a nice urine ring around the crotch and leg of your pants, the boss is gonna send you packing in no time, and if you jump out of the car right then and there, Officer Friendly might cite you for indecent exposure, and maybe even haul your ass off to jail. Take that risk if you wish, but I've got a better, more exciting, more empowering alternative: Do it in the car.

Grab a bottle from the passenger seat or the floor, unscrew the cap and place the bottle between your legs, as if you were holding it to drink. Put the cap up on the dash, and make damn sure you don't drop it, because the cap will obviously become of vital importance in a little while. Take off the seat belt.

Your three cardinal rules once you've passed the point of no return? Keep your eyes on the road, don't swerve, and for chrissakes, maintain composure! Also, it's best to practice this part on a straightaway, because from here on out, you'll be steering with your knees. Undo that button and unzip your pants with one hand. You've done it in a panicked sexual rush many times, so this should be a cakewalk. Raise your ass about four or five inches off the seat, and with a quick flip, take out your dick. Next, yank it downward, so you are aiming roughly toward the accelerator.

At this point, you are nearly ready to piss. There's one final step before the waterfall can begin—and this is a difficult maneuver, much like a midair jetplane refueling—grab the bottle and line up the opening with your pee-hole. Make absolutely certain that the hole is staring at the bottom of the bottle, because if it is slanted upwards, or kissing the rim, you're going to have a massive fuel leak, and therefore, trouble. Here's the easy part: piss. Just do it, let it fly, fill that bottle like a man. The choice of container is up to you, but as you can see, I have rated various items on the market for their efficiency, volume and comfort.

So now you're done pissing, you've made it this far, but you're still cradling 16 ounces of unsealed urine in your lap at 70 mph. Obviously, it's a recipe for disaster, and one false move might bring you right back to showing up with urine all over your pants. The first thing you need to do is grab that cap from the dash and screw it back on. Put the bottle on the passenger seat and slowly, methodically zip up, snap, re-velcro, button and buckle yourself back to normal.

What to do with the piss? Ah, that little debacle. Actually, you have many options. If you're twisted enough, chug it. Most likely, you're not, and you'll just have to find an alternate means of disposal. Check the rearview mirror, and make sure that the nearest car is at least a football field behind you, roll down the window, unscrew the cap, hold it out the window with the mouth of the bottle aimed behind you, and jettison the contents. Most of it is gonna splatter the side of your car, but so what? Unless you're a pretty boy worried about the paint and fresh wax on his customized Jetta, you won't give a fuck, and you've completed the process.

Although I'm a skilled professional, I've definitely had some bad experiences with this. Many months ago, I was en route to a tattoo convention in Miami. It was about 4 a.m., definitely piss time, but why waste those five minutes at a rest area? All I had was the smaller Gatorade bottle variety, which I'd already filled about halfway many hours before, but neglected to empty. I had the head in the bottle and I was going for it. It felt great, and very relieving, when suddenly I felt something very warm and wet. It was a massive overflow. It was a mess, with many, many hours left to go until I would reach the tropical climes of Miami. So take that as a word to the wise. Follow all of the steps, and you're halfway there. Now just add your own style and variations. Perhaps you like throwing your urine on pedestrians or other vehicles. Do as you like, just keep it off of me.

HAND HELD URINALS:

32-ounce Gatorade: Naturally, the finest portable toilet made, and a tasty pre-urine drink. I prefer Lemon-Ice. You will feel like you are in better shape and a little healthier, peeing into this one. Consider the wide mouth of the bottle, and the roominess inside. Plus, it's plastic, so you can throw it around without worrying about it shattering upon impact. Truly, the perfect vessel.

20-ounce Gatorade: Again, the mouth on this one is pretty good, although not as spacious and user friendly as its 32-ounce brother. Still, it's a fine tool. Just watch the overflow.

Sobe bottle: Smooth contours, long neck, pretty good mouth. Deep. Sound sexual? It is. Enjoy.

20-ounce soda: Well, with any soda container of this size, you're stuck with a tiny mouth. You have to be extra careful when lining up the hole. You can fuck up like that, and suffer messy results, but it'll do in a pinch.

Coke can: Potentially disastrous, just think of what a horrid slice that aluminum rim could make on the head of your dick. Very little room to fill. A last-minute option.

Bags: At the end of your rope with no bottles in sight, you may want to try out a plastic bag, just make sure there aren't any visible holes. Fill it up, toss it out the window. Fuck it.

Fast food cups: These work quite well, and everyone has one of them laying around the floor in the back. Perfect if you are waiting in your girlfriend's car while she is using the ATM machine. If you empty discreetly, she'll never know, plus you are cleaning out her car! What a gentleman!

Anything under 8 ounces: It can be done with a little patience and hard work. Fill to the line, stem the flow, pour out the window, refill, repeat process until you are done. You are now a genius, a knight of the round table, move on to Calculus II.

Originally printed in WYWS Issue #6

WYWS was pretty ridiculous but ground-breaking in its own right. It was the first mag, that I remember, that was rooted in graffiti but ended up branching off into some of the most ludicrous subjects and probably ended up influencing an entire generation of writers and artists—although maybe not for the best.

—*KC Ortiz*

While You Were Sleeping is seared into my brain. It captured a moment in time and was the definitive source for documenting and celebrating the culture of the time. I still draw on old issues for inspiration.

—*Craig*, *former president,* **GOOD Magazine**

WYWS feels like forever ago, but two things stick out in my mind:

1. Roger and *WYWS* introduced me to *Bum Fights*. I walked into the office one day and he opened up the *Bum Fights* video he had just gotten. That shit was crazy.

2. Most importantly, my time with *WYWS* introduced me to this new group of artists and style of art coming largely from graffiti artists. Contemporary, urban, lowbrow, new-brow—whatever the hell it's dubbed, it's badass. *WYWS* really seemed cutting edge in pushing it so hard. More than I even knew and appreciated at the time.

—*Bensonn Anspach*

The minute I started reading *WYWS*, I knew I was liable for even possessing a copy. I also knew that I needed to know the people behind it. And now, unfortunately, I do.

—*WISE*

WYWS was a ticket to see and do a lot of things I never would have with my other everyday friends, and it was my hallpass to act like a total asshole.

—*Patrick Boyd*

Remember when you came to visit, after I'd gotten out of jail, and I was trying not to paint, but you wanted to paint? Then you went to bed and GAME and I went and did a piece, while *you* were sleeping. That was hilarious.

—*Mario Desa*

You guys are like the Beatles of graffiti.

—*SHAKEN*

While You Were Sleeping was a zine for the heathens. Nothing was sacred and nothing was off limits. It was a complete document on the debauchery and downfalls of the human race. I had this nasty, raw footage of a tranny crackhead blowing this troll of a homeless drunk in the Tenderloin of San Francisco and *WYWS* was happy to use it. That was some of the more mild content put out by Roger. It was a testament to complete social disorder in paper form. I still can't believe they sold it at stores.

—*SABER*

Was it around long enough to do a best of?

—*Fat Nick, Scribble Jam*

Thanks *WYWS*, for being a major contributor to my juvenile delinquency.

—*PBC*

I never missed an episode of *WYWS*! That George! What a character!

—*Todd B.*

Fun times, Roger brought fun times. I learn a lot from Roger still. We are only a few days apart in age. He is a really solid dude. We don't talk like we used to, but he always keeps you in mind. I think that's the best thing I learned from him, always hook up your friends when you can.

—*Frich*

FRAT STORIES
Story and photo by Pat Boyd

This is the true story of Pledge Hazing at a university in the Deep South, as reported by Vince Muller, class of 2000.

The first night I realized what I had gotten myself into was a night called Sizzle, where they build a pit about 20-by-20 and fill it up with hot sauce and oil and make you and all your pledge brothers wrestle in it. The first couple minutes don't seem that bad but then it starts to set in and burn. You can't see for the next 35 minutes or so. Your balls start hurting. You can't jerk off for about three days. You don't even want to touch your dick. The clothes you're wearing are ruined. Your whole body just feels like its getting cooked.

TWO PLEDGES GONE, 20 REMAINED.

The rest of us figured it couldn't get much worse, so we stuck around. The second (big) thing was something like a Chinese rack, which is a position in which you have your hands locked behind your neck. You're up on your elbows and your toes and they just constantly kick you in the ribs and the elbows. It goes on for about 45 minutes.

SIXTEEN PLEDGES LEFT.

Then there was the brick on the dick thing. They tie a brick to your dick with a rope and they put you on the roof of the house. If the string's not long enough for the brick to hit the ground when they drop it, your dick is coming off. There were a lot of small mental things they have you do like walk on glass blindfolded—you're walking on potato chips.

FIFTEEN PLEDGES LEFT.

In the middle of the semester they had the Ride. You choose the brother who has been the biggest dickhead to you and you take him for 12 hours and beat the shit out of him, making him do whatever he made you do, or more. We came late that night on purpose. All 15 of us had our faces painted like in the movie Dead Presidents. We grabbed our victim, put a sheet on his head and took him to a field in the middle of nowhere. It was a party; we brought a keg. Most of the time, he was in the Chinese rack position getting hot sauce thrown in his eyes, pissed on, kicked and paddled. The next morning, we left him in a thong and cheetah top with a check for 25 cents so he could make a phone call.

THE INITIATION.

You come back in early January knowing you're entering the worst part. They have you play these stupid games. One is called Cotton Picking, where you sit across from each other and tear each other's leg hair out and put it in your mouth. Or they'll play Tennis, where two guys lie on top of each other and two guys next to them. Another guy is the ball and each active member has a paddle and they smack you in the ass. You have to dive over the four guys without touching them. By this time, people had pneumonia so it really sucked. The first night of the final hell week, they take you one by one and they strap you up to this machine with baby jumper cables attached to your nuts. Then they ask you questions that don't have correct answers like "What's my favorite color?" After every question, you feel a gunshot right in your sack. Eventually, after five questions, you pass out. You wake up in a coffin, buried with a tube coming down into it pouring alcohol or water into your face. Some people freak out but I was relieved that there was nobody fucking with me anymore. That's the first night.

At the end of the week, there's the whole goat ceremony. You don't know what's coming. You are up alone in a room, but for the first time you aren't getting beat. You have these duct-taped goggles on so you can't see. One by one, they take you downstairs and the goat is in front of you. There is a bunch of porno all over the tables. They tell you, "Go ahead, here is some petroleum jelly and a condom. Fuck the goat!" Most people couldn't get hard so they'll usually mount you on the goat and say a little thing and take you back upstairs. I think only one person got penetration, which is sick.

Originally printed in WYWS Issue #15

—Editor's note: Vince became a fully fledged active member of his fraternity and, after five years, he was eventually asked to leave due to excessive hazing, including taking a pledge's brand new sports car and crashing it at 60 mph into a parked Pathfinder, telling the unfortunate freshman as he walked away, "Call your insurance company."

PERVERSION

SIZE DOES MATTER
by Gabe Banner
Photo courtesy of Smalley Pauley

At 6-foot-4, 300 pounds, Smalley Pauley is a pretty big guy in a lot of ways. Sadly enough, dick-size is not one of them. Growing up having a smaller than average penis can be hard, but for Pauley, small doesn't even begin to describe it. "My penis size is zero to six inches," says Smally Pauley, winner of the World's Smallest Penis Contest on the *Howard Stern Show* last April. "It's like a turtle in a shell, basically. It goes inside my body. It never hurts me, it's like fold up luggage."

THE DISCOVERY

"I knew my penis was small when I was 9 years old. Guys were going to urinals and standing three feet away and I was flush with it. There were guys who had their hands by their sides while they were peeing, and I'm holding my penis with two fingers. It wasn't that traumatic because when I got aroused I had a six-inch cock. I said fuck, I can work with this, basically. I just had to deal with the aftermath of being small. So every time I had sex with a woman, I was aroused ahead of time. I performed and I did a really good job. It was just the aftermath that they had to do a double take [when they saw] I was hung like an infant."

THE CONTEST

In April of 1998, *The Howard Stern Show* held a World's Smallest Penis Contest. Pauley called in and ended up naked in the studio along with about 30 other contestants. "There was a black guy there and I thought if a black guy thinks he's got a small dick, I've got no chance. So we're all totally nude in the studio, and it went down from 18 to three. And I was the winner, but the guy who sponsored the trip allowed all three of us to go, which was cool." Pauley has made the best of a bad situation. Winning a contest for having the world's smallest penis doesn't sound that great, but it has proven to be one of the best things to ever happen to Pauley. Since winning the trip to Mexico, he has enjoyed a celebrity status of sorts, getting to meet and fuck famous porn stars he had watched as a kid, hosting the Adult Video Awards and getting to direct his own films for Pleasure Productions. Pauley told me stories about banging chicks for like an hour and a half, so he must be doin' OK for himself.

RENAISSANCE MAN

Pauley's worked all kinds of jobs around New York City since the age of 13. "I'm a jack of all trades," says Pauley. "I'm a bricklayer, a mover,

—Writer's note: I already knew from our phone call that this guy might be a little hectic, but for some reason we decided to do the interview at this spot Zen Palate, a vegetarian restaurant in Union Square where I went all the time. From the minute we sit down, I realize this was a mistake. It's crowded, and he starts talking about his dick—which was sort of the point of the interview—ridiculously loud. He had just been on Howard Stern and was really proud of his title as World's Smallest Penis. He did not care what the family next to us had to say about it. I still can't believe we weren't asked to leave, but some people got up and bounced. Needless to say, I kept that one short.

I was in a rock band, I was a singer—I did everything." And now, he can add porn star and director to the list. We were pretty surprised to learn that, growing up in Brooklyn, Pauley even did a little graf for a while in the early 1980s too. "I used to write back in the day, like 1983, 1984. I wrote ROOK. There was a comic book character called Rook from Epic Comics way back in the day, and he was like a Western time traveler and I just liked the name, you know? I used to go bombing up in Harlem and at the train tracks down on 36th Street in Brooklyn. I used to write with the old guys—FUTURA 2000, AME and guys like that. Back in the day it was tighter. I wasn't good so they helped me do a lot of my stuff. Then the anti-graffiti trains came and that killed everything."

Pauley's 32 years old now and he's been a NYC bus driver for about seven years. "I'm like a god at my depot now. All these guys are married with kids, so their lives are basically over. They're living vicariously through me." You can guess a NYC bus driver would have a story or two, so we had to ask. "I got sex a couple of times on a bus. It's happening still, like right now, you know? It was chicks like bus groupies, you know? It's sick, man, it's like if you get a chick in that first seat and you start rappin' and shit." So what kind of game are you gonna kick to that honey in the first seat? "It's just, you know, it's just you. You gotta be you, man. If you're shy and shit, you ain't goin' nowhere 'cause that shit don't work. You gotta have a mouth. You'd think girls would be repulsed by the porn stuff. Really, you'd think girls would be like turned off, that you did that and you're naked and you got a video, but it's just the opposite. It's unbelievable, man."

OPPORTUNITY KNOCKS

Pauley's life has definitely taken an unexpected change, but he's ready for it. "To be honest with you, I want to go mainstream. I think I'm made for television or movies. I think I got the personality for it and I could really pull it off. I related to Belushi and Farley and all these guys, 'cause I was heavy, but these guys, I mean, I've gotten high and done what I had to do, but man, you know, you've gotta learn to grow up from it. There's more to life than all that bullshit."

Originally printed in WYWS Issue #6

SMALLEY
PAULEY

CAN-B-
LOANS
PAWNBROKER

CAN-B-L
PAWNBROKER

ONE WAY

STEVENSON

kryptocentricks

A DATE WITH BIZ MARKIE
Story and Photo by Pat Boyd

—Writer's note: We were supposed to interview Biz Markie before the show, but he was late as shit, so we had to wait till afterwards. We wore camouflage, backwards hats, and looked like two little Eminems. Some of the hood rat girls were hilarious. I probably had my ass grabbed 25 times. By the time we actually interviewed him, we were so drunk, all he did was laugh at every question we asked him. I don't think he was happy about two shitfaced white kids interviewing him.

I think the story came out pretty funny. Redbull had just come out, and while I was writing the story, I drank four or five cans because we wanted to see what the effects were when you were drunk. I wrote that story super fucked up. It was kinda like that theory in school: If you're studying drunk, you should take your test drunk, so we were shitcanned when we interviewed him, so it would probably be better if we were shitcanned when we wrote the story.

Recently, our trusty editor Roger, sent Justine and me to interview Biz Markie. On the off chance that you don't remember me, I'm the asshole that appeared in issues 4 and 5 breaking stuff. At first, the idea was very appealing, since I used to laugh at all the fucking skirts who jocked that song "But You Say He's Just a Friend." After accepting the offer without hesitation, we were informed by Roger that the concert was being held at Republic Gardens in Northeast D.C. In case you're not familiar with the area, it's a very relaxed and laidback atmosphere—if you're from Compton. But even before we could tell Roger we weren't going anymore, he questioned our manhood, and we went (Dumb Idea #1).

Our plan to stay alive was simple: just try to fit in. we went to a surplus store and bought every article of camouflage clothing that we could find (Dumb Idea #2). Roger called down to the club to find out what time Biz was going on and he informed us that there was a dress code that stated: No tennis shoes, jeans, hats, loud clothing or camo. Next time I go hunting I'll have a brand new outfit to wear.

Two hours before the show started, Justine and I decide it was time for some coldbeer (I swear it's one word). After knocking out a case ($12.00), we had grown from 6-foot, 200-pound men to 6-foot-8, 300-pound men, and we were ready for the show.

Once we got inside, we headed straight for the corner of the bar, kind of away from the crowd. The bartender was definitely bangtail, so to kill two birds with one stone we tried to get in good with her. When we ordered our drinks, we told her why we were at the show and asked her to pose for a picture that we would put in the magazine (Dumb Idea #3). We ordered our first round and tipped the shit out of her, only to have her shift be over two minutes later (bar tab: $90.00).

A few beers later, we decided it was time to nut it up. We started to mingle. Yeah, we looked like two Tic Tacs in a box of Milk Duds, but it seemed to be appealing to the women who were at the show. "Damn, y'all cute for white boys," seemed to be the phrase most frequently used that night. This motley crew of girls slipped us their numbered and scared the shit out of us until we agreed we'd call (priceless).

By 1 a.m., asking me even a simple question like my name would have gotten an amusing response, and all the money in my wallet had been stolen by the bartender. It was obviously time to approach "The Biz" (Dumb Idea #4). We walked into to the DJ booth and told Biz why we were there. He was actually happy to have us hang out with him, or at least it seemed that way. We attempted to talk to him a little but my words were slurring and his answers were brief. I did, however, learn that he's possibly doing a remake of a popular Frank Sinatra song on his new album that will "come out when it comes out," and still lacks a title.

After the club cleared out we finally got an opportunity to ask Biz some real questions like: "Would you punch an alien?" I thought his face said it all but his response contradicted it: "Nah, I chill with aliens." After thus revealing his secret fetish for aliens, he then started talking about his temporary diaper-wearing obsession (he claimed off the record that it had nothing to do with an uncontrollable bladder problem). Then we got talking about an armored truck getting robbed at the Albee Square Mall, and how the suspect was described as a big man wearing a diaper. (Biz swears it wasn't him.)

If you've been wondering about the rumors that Ricky Martin is gay, Biz cleared them up: "Nah, that's my man from Menudo." My final question for Biz was a yes or no question using one of my favorite theories: "Soccer is a sport for third world countries that can't afford football equipment." Though his answer was not a direct yes, the fact that I got him to admit that football was superior to soccer was enough for me. Justine and I left the show feeling that our mission was complete. Besides being broke and having almost nothing we could use for an interview, we also had a phone number, pool-party invite, brand new set of camo and a long drive home.

[Pat Boyd writes freelance for WYWS and spends most of his time getting drunk, starting fights and lifting weights. He believes soccer is for pussies and "coldbeer" is one word.]

Originally printed in WYWS Issue #7

BIZ
MARKIE

WHAT A FUCKING HOAR

by Hilary Hoar
Photo courtesy of Hilary Hoar

Growing up with the last name "Hoar" was never easy. When I was really young, I didn't know that my last name, which is pronounced "whore," would end up being such a constant source of amusement to everyone. Teachers would either laugh when calling my name in roll call, or else just ignore it, as if I didn't have a last name at all.

By about 7th grade age, kids had started to make fun of my name. For the first time they—and I—understood what a whore actually was. Thirteen is a difficult age: you are growing up, you look awkward, you are sensitive about your appearance, etc. For me, on top of all that, I came with a ready-made insult of a name. People didn't even need to try to make fun of me—my last name said it all.

Then in 8th grade, my biggest last-name nightmare came true. The most popular girl in middle school had just broken up with her high school boyfriend. We all worshiped him because he was so hot, and sucked up to her because she had somehow got him to date her. Then she heard me gossiping to another friend that I was happy he had dumped her. (I was just jealous of her and didn't realize she could hear me talking about her in the bathroom.) So that day at lunch she got even.

We were walking up to drop off our trays and she yelled, "I bet Tom dumped me for that whore!" and pointed straight at me. Practically the entire cafeteria began to chant, "Whore, whore, whore," while pounding on the tables and throwing their plastic utensils at me until I ran away crying. Even though it wasn't true, it was one of those incidents that made me really happy to graduate into high school and forget about the whole thing.

Now that I'm in college, whore jokes don't really bother me anymore. My big brother's friends call me "Little Hoar," and try to give me a hard time about it, but I blow it off. The times when it does get to me is with little stuff, like leaving reservations at restaurants of hair salons.

Recently, a friend of mine called a hotel in NYC where I was staying with my mother over Christmas break. She called the front desk and asked whether the Hoars had checked in. At first the hotel operator almost hung up on her, thinking it was a childish prank. Finally, she asked for the Hoar party's first name, and she gave her my mother's name. The thing is, my mom's first name is Gay, making her full married name Gay Hoar. This can cause serious problems.

This past winter, an ex-friend of mine bitched me out via email because her ex-boyfriend had asked me to his fraternity's winter formal. At the time, I had a boyfriend that I had been dating for a year. Plus, the ex-friend's boyfriend was a good friend of mine, so it really wasn't weird that he would take me as a friend to his formal. However, since he had asked me while he was drunk, she assumed that it was only because I had pressured him. She sent me this cute little email:

Hoar (sp.)

I write firstly to enlighten you about the origins of last names. In the olden days, one's last name was assigned according to his/her profession. For example, "Millman" would translate to "man who worked on mills." The rest, I trust, that a smart girl like you can figure out for herself. You are a desperate, insecure, social-climbing cunt that manipulated the good intentions of a drunk "friend" who did not recognize that you were a back-stabbing, makeup crazed, scantily dressed bimbo.

Despite all the makeup, Hilary, your true ugliness shines through, and those of us who are unfortunate enough to know you feel complete disgust. We both know the kind of person you are, and that said, I never want to hear about or from you ever, as anything you could say means as little to me as you do.

I hope you die,
Sara

Even though this letter was completely uncalled for, it wasn't surprising to me that she used my last name as a way to insult me. Hoar has always been a joke, and now I am completely used to it. For Christmas a couple of years ago, my Grandma Hoar even gave me an old western silver dollar coin that one side looks normal, but on the other says "Good for One Screw, Madame Ruth's Whore House." It is practically a family heirloom.

When I get married, I am going to keep my name and pass it down to my daughter. I think that having the last name Hoar has only made me stronger. Most every girl gets called a whore or slut sometime in her life, so it might as well be for a legitimate reason, right? Ultimately, my advice is either to be one or be born one. I was born a fucking Hoar and I'm proud of it.

[Hilary Hoar is our least promiscuous freelance writer.]

Originally printed in WYWS Issue #7

TATTOO YOU

by Josh Slater

Illustration by Linas Garsys

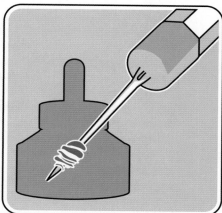

Got nothing to do tonight? If you pack the stones, you could greet the evening a Richie Cuningham and end it ala Henry Rollins. I'm talking about the age-old practice of self-tattooing. Some people shun it as a jailhouse activity, but I think it's the only way to get in touch with your creativity while producing what the squares call, "permanent disfiguration."

THE SUPPLIES

- Some clean (sterile) sewing needles
- A foot of thread
- Black Indian ink (I prefer Winsor & Newton ink, but if you're desperate break open a pen)
- One thin marker

PREP WORK

1. Pick a record or movie to play in the background while you get busy. Music that'll get the adrenaline going: Slayer, AC/DC or the MC5. If you choose a film, go with a motivational comedy. My suggestion would be Teen Wolf, Goonies or anything else with a fat sidekick. For surrealism, try Decline of the Western Civilization, Part I, where you can watch John Doe of X tattoo himself the same way you're about to.

2. Take your needle and thread it. Continually wrap the thread around the top of the needle until it's the size of a pea. This is your grip when you start the poking and also soaks up excess ink.

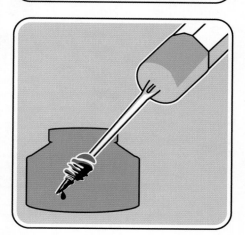

FUN TIME

1. For body location, I'm a big fan of the lower calf or right above the knee, since you can (almost) sit comfortably and get to work without twisting yourself into some yoga position. Know your limits and choose a simple design like a heart, skull, "mom," or something that will look good, even if it doesn't. I tattooed a heart with an arrow through it and a happy face on my kneecap, a tribute to Ozzy, who did the same.

2. Now that we're set with image and location, lightly outline the picture on your skin. This is the guide you'll follow.

3. Dip the needle in the ink, and start poking your skin, deep enough to get below the first layers of dermis. A good technique is to poke under the skin and kind of flick the needle. Remember, this shouldn't hurt that bad; carving yourself like G.G. Allin means you're going too deep.

4. Now each time you poke, you'll create a small dot, and to make an outline you'll have to go over the same spot many times. This is where the film or music comes into play—making sure you get ink under your outline can be tedious.

Good luck! Let us know how it goes!

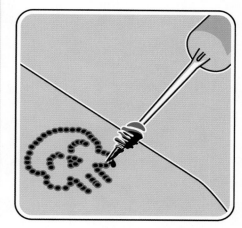

Originally printed in WYWS Issue #19

JANINE
Interview by Chri$ Nieratko
Photos by Carlos Batts

Ever since I got into the art of enjoying porn, there has been one beautiful blonde that has avoided me. I'd see her in the magazines, hear her on TV, and she even turned up briefly in Howard Stern's movie, *Private Parts*. But when it came to fuck films I couldn't find her, so I called Vivid Video a while back. Vivid is easily the world's largest producer of adult films, pulling in over $50 million in revenue each year.

I talked to my man Brian Gross over there, and was like, "Yo, who's that girl?" He told me her name was Janine, and aside from making dirty movies she is in *Club* magazine every month, she just made an MTV video with Blink 182 and she is on their album cover as well as having her image on a Birdhouse skateboard and is in Birdhouse's new skate video. "Yeah, that's all good, baby, but I need to see her bent over the hood of a 1969 El Camino getting her butt hole filled with man juice." And that's when he told me, Janine doesn't do dudes, at least not in movies (except for one of her and Motley Crue's Vince Neil). That goes against everything I believed a porn star should be. What is she, a lesbian? "It's not like that," Brian told me. "She just chooses not to do it." It kind of upset me for a while, like what, she's too good to get it on on-camera? Then I took another look at her. She's gorgeous.

If I have to fast forward through a bunch of boring lapper scenes to check her out, so be it. She's worth it. Janine is an exception to the rule and an exceptional woman. But as for the rest of you, y'all better bend over and spread 'em like God and Larry Flynt intended. Damn it.

Do you worry about your 8-year-old son finding out about what you do for a living?
No, I don't worry. He knows to a certain extent right now of what I do. He knows a lot of the mainstream stuff. He knows I have my image on a skateboard, the Blink 182 stuff, other music videos, bikini mags and stuff like that he's fine with. He knows that I go on the road and perform as a dancer. There's times when I take him and we go costume shopping together. I'm slowly introducing him to what exactly I do. We have had a few talks and he has asked if I go topless, and what am I gonna do, lie to him? I tell him how I feel, that it is for adults and some people are OK with it and for others it's not their cup of tea. He asked me if it's illegal and I said, "No," and he said, "Well, then it's OK." I stress that it's not for kids and it's something I choose to do and I like doing it. We have really good communication. As long as it is something that I want to do then I would hope that he would respect that when he gets older.

Children can be pretty cruel. Do you think he is tough enough to handle the abuse that might come his way?
Again, I'm not going to lie, I am scared if and when something happens, but I'm pretty sure he is going to be faced with it and I will be there to talk to him. He can ask me anything he wants to and I don't BS him. It's kind of touchy, you have to explain this stuff in a way he's going to understand. It has happened a little bit. I have a 12-year-old nephew who went to school one day and, sure enough, one of his friends was teasing him. Apparently, a father had gone to see my show and he's such an ignorant parent, he then tells his kid that he saw me at a strip club and so it gets back to my nephew. I talked to him, my sister talked to him, and he does know a little bit more than my son knows and we're all OK with it. We know it's something that people might have a problem with, but my family is close and we have unconditional love. I'm not ashamed of it. I go do my work and I come home and be a good mother and do all the things a mother should do normally. That's all I'm concerned about.

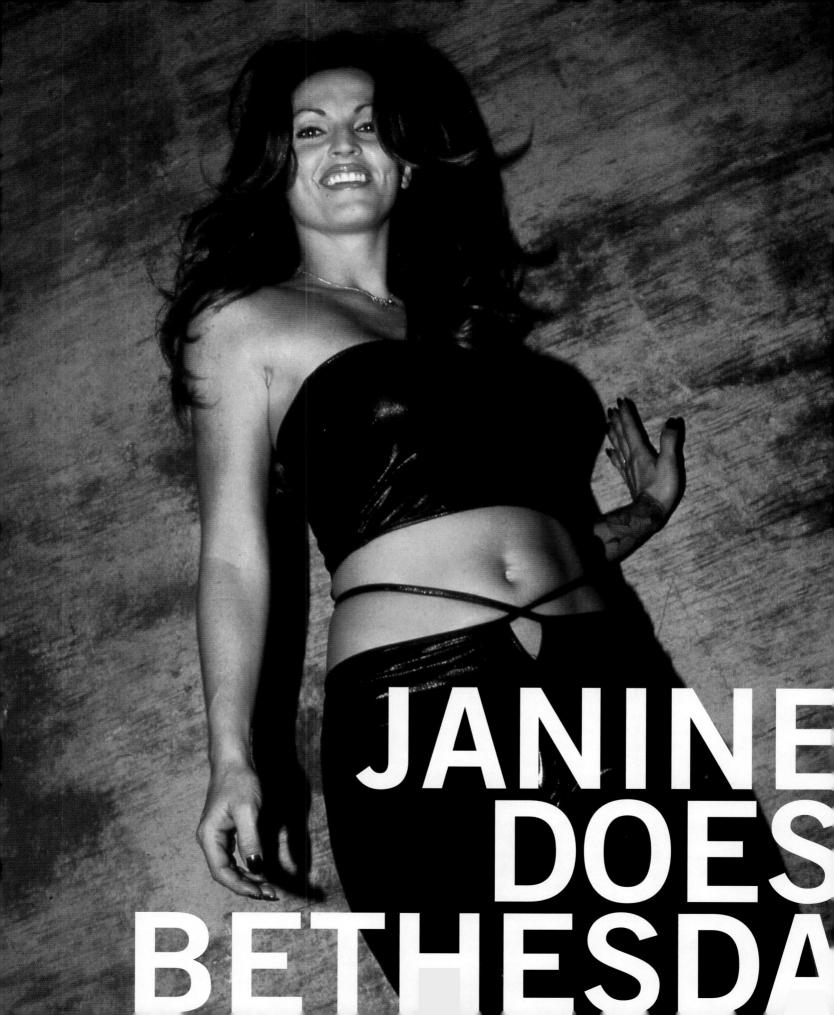

JANINE
DOES
BETHESDA

Aside from being on the bottom of a Birdhouse skateboard, you appeared in the Birdhouse film The End. What did you think of those guys? Did you think they were nerds?
Oh, no, they're great. Jeremy Klein and Heath Kirchart, Tony Hawk—all those guys, they're my son's superheroes. In fact, Jeremy and Heath agreed to come over for a surprise at his 8th birthday party. I told them if they could do that for my son, I'd mow their lawns, wash their cars and do their laundry.

How about Howard Stern off the air? What is he like?
I think his bark is much worse than its bite. When he's not on the air, he's very cool. He loves and adores his wife and I think all the crap he talks is all for the show.

Are you still dating Ricki Rachtman?
I am, and it's going on about two-and-a-half years. Me being in the adult industry really puts a strain on our relationship and there have been many times when we didn't think we would be able to tough it out. I think the secret is communication. I allow him to be a part of everything I do, I don't hide anything. If he wants to go on the road with me or go to my movies, he can partake in anything I do.

So there's no chance of a Janine/Rachtman skin flick anytime soon?
I have my own home collection. No, I learned my lesson. Every time I do that he has a real firm grip on the tapes, so I don't think that will be happening again anytime soon.

How exactly did that Vince Neil tape surface?
This is the crappy thing about it: five, six years ago I was dating him a little bit and we had a mutual friend, and the three of us decided to go to Hawaii. We were just playing around like billions of people do every day and we put some stuff on film. It was supposed to be for our personal enjoyment but unfortunately when the vacation was over, he hung onto the tape. And I never thought twice about it. We drifted apart and I find out five years later that this footage has surfaced. IEG had a copy and they offered to sell it to me, but come on, I know that's not the only copy and I can't go running scared trying to buy all these copies. So they said we can sue, but that it would still get out on the Internet. Or I could let Vivid take control and put it out properly. And that's what I did and they gave me a big chunk of change and so my kid's college is covered. I think the really shitty part about it is Vince going on the air saying he had

nothing to do with it, that it must have been me who put it out and how he didn't get a dime. He's lying through his teeth.

Will there ever be a day when you do a scene with a male and do some full-on penetration?
I really don't have anything against it. So many people misunderstand why I don't work with men on screen. I've been called a dick-hater and dyke-lover and chicken-shit and told get out of the business—all kinds of hate mail. It's kind of funny because I just think, if you don't like it, watch somebody else. They think that it's a direct insult to them that I'm not giving it up. When I went into this industry, it took me about seven months to agree to do it and I think it's necessary for girls to take the time to figure out what they can handle and what they're not going to be able to handle years down the road. By me doing women-only, it turns it into this fun slumber party. The girls giggle, we have a couple drinks and it's really fun. But anytime that I've had intimate contact with a man, there were emotions involved and I don't know how I would be able to handle it emotionally if I was to go and have this incredible sex scene with a guy and just walk away. Personally, I would feel a little empty. That's how I feel. There might come a day where I think that might be fun, my views on it might change and I'll go for it. I love watching it. I'll be there with my pompoms when my best friends are doing a DP, but me personally, I couldn't do it.

I understand men toss off to your movies but does it skeez you out to know dudes are out there putting their dicks in plastic molds of your pussy?
It's a little odd. A few years ago, they had to make the whole casting of the mold by putting papier-mâché all over my crotch. They had actually made a mold of my face. They put a big dildo in my mouth and surrounded my whole face and head with this mold stuff and I was breathing through a straw in my nose. It was weird. My ears and eyes were covered, my mouth was stuffed with a dildo and I panicked. So they ripped it off immediately and I don't know what ever happened with that. But yeah, looking at a realistic vagina, which looks exactly like my cookie, it's odd.

Do you like to watch the pooping videos?
I have no desire whatsoever to explore that. I'm all for golden showers, but the shit I'll leave in the litter box.

What about the videos where people roll them- selves up in aluminum foil and go out in the sun and then they get blow jobs while they sweat to death?
I never saw that. You'd probably pass out. I've heard one fetish thing which is odd, its called stomping and crushing where a guy lays down and he has bugs on him and he has a well-en- dowed women crush bugs on his chest.

I just saw this one where this guy lays on his stom- ach, with his cock and balls out between his legs, and this woman in heels just kicks and stomps on and pulverizes his whole privates.
I don't see how that has to do with crushing bugs on you but I'm sure there's a market for every- thing. I'm real comfortable in the market that I'm in. I save the freaky stuff for my home.

Tell me, Janine, for skinny boys who are into graf- fiti and skateboarding and aren't well endowed, what's a good way to get in to pornography?
For guys, it's tough. I really don't know. If a guy knows a girl in the industry, that would be the way to do it: get in the door through the girl. If you are on your own, that's tough. You can try your hand at your own amateur videos. There's a big market for amateurs. If you're not well endowed then you really have to work on a technique or something that will set you apart from all the rest.

What If you were a ninja?
A ninja?

Yeah, so you could do flips in the air and land inside the girl very softly.
I think that could work a couple of times, but I would imagine that the novelty would wear off. For porn, I think you might need more of a tech- nique sexually. You got to be either good orally or you have to be able to make the girl see God or something.

So juggling wouldn't really apply?
No. You might as well go on the Gong Show or something. You have to be good sexually.

You don't think juggling and having sex at the same time is worthy of something?
Well, that is a talent. I've never seen it done. It might work.

Do you think graffiti is a waste of paint?
Not necessarily. If you're doing it for the right reasons, using it as an art form. The gang stuff isn't even worth commenting on, it's stupid. Go do that in your bedroom. There have been times when

I've seen some really cool stuff. I think people should ask first, don't just go and damage some- one's property. If it looks good and you're doing something decorative and art oriented, go for it.

I have one last question. Guess what?
What?

Chicken Butt!
Oh my God! You must have talked to my son, you know why?

Chicken thigh?
Oh, damn. You got me!

You're damn right I did. And that'll be how we'll end it—me getting you.
I'm a big loser.

Yes, you are.

Originally printed in WYWS Issue #7

One of my first jobs straight out of high school was running a graffiti mail order business out of the local skate shop that we all hung out at and painted the side of. Pretty awesome job for a young kid that was obsessed with painting and skating. It was also one of the only places to buy spraypaint tips in the whole Bay Area. We sold thousands of them. Seriously. Boxes and boxes of those stupid things went out the door weekly. My first task on my first day at the job was to call and introduce myself to our tip supplier. That, unfortunately, was a young Roger Gastman.

Over the next couple of years, Roger and I became pretty good friends, he launched *While You Were Sleeping* shortly after we met and we released *Phantom Magazine* right around the same time so we were dealing with the same people across the country, sharing flicks and I ended up doing some interviews and articles for *WYWS*. Eventually, Roger put me in his END crew.

Years later, I found myself living in Boston. I was working from home so I had the free time when Roger asked me to come down to Bethesda and lay out issue 12 since he was "in-between" designers. It was miserable. Roger never stopped working and wouldn't let me. When I was able to eat, it was delivery and I ate over the computer. Staying at his house with his housemates was pretty much walking into a living, drinking, barely breathing issue of the magazine. I ended up sleeping on a futon mattress on the floor of the laundry room to get the little sleep I could. The bookcase full of porn VHS tapes and Harley were the only things that kept me sane that trip. Regardless of that, I found myself back down in Bethesda a month-or-so later to work on Roger's first book, *Free Agents: A History of Washington, D.C., Graffiti*. We had no clue what we were doing but we did it. Roger has been pretty good at just making it work. Flash-forward a couple of years and back in California, I was working on *Mike Giant: Manifestations* with him, eventually finishing it up when I relocated to Brooklyn.

Knowing Roger so long has gotten me in to some interesting predicaments over the years. I was involved in a 3 car high speed chase through downtown St. Louis. I've witnessed grown men dressed in cow suits walk through a high school prom and dance with the attendees. I've watched people puking up milk in the middle of the street after attempting to chug a gallon in less than 2 minutes. I slept in a meth dealer's garage in Los Angeles who thought it would be a good idea to get high himself so he wouldn't miss his court appearance in the morning. I filmed gangsters discussing removing rival's eyeballs from their sockets as nonchalantly as explaining what they ate for brunch last Sunday with the misses. I could keep going, but I'm not sure what the statute of limitations is in most states.

Now I'm 34 and find myself in this god-awful lime green office in Los Angeles working for Roger fulltime. Even though the location has changed, some things haven't. The pay still sucks and if Roger had his way, I would never stop working or leave the office. Besides that, we've been able to put out some pretty cool books and throw some cool events in my couple of years here at R. Rock and I somehow haven't physically assaulted him (yet).

Someone asked me the other day how a group of individuals that were all loosely connected went on to do some pretty amazing things as designers, artists, photographers and writers. One reason came pretty quickly, we all had Roger in common and he always looked out for opportunities for us and took us along on his endeavors. It will eventually be the death of him, but that 17-year-old I called back in the day to order tips from hasn't stopped working since (except to eat) and a lot of us owe him for that hard work. *WYWS* was the first physical thing you could hold as a result of that and I hate to say it, but I'm still proud of him for it. Congratulations on this piece of shit… can I get a raise now?

—*Shane Jessup*

Illustration by **UPSO**

While I haven't touched a spraycan since college, graffiti is always on my mind. When I first discovered *WYWS* magazine, I was fresh out of college and obsessed with becoming a professional illustrator.

I would send out cold call packages of flyers and drawings I had made to every magazine I found on the newsstand, and Roger Gastman was the first person to write me back.

Roger "commissioned" me to do an illustration on dry-humping. I was so excited to finally get a piece of my work printed, but somewhat mortified about the subject matter. I was convinced Roger was only fucking with me, seeing if I would actually do it. And I did it.

A year or so later through my art zine *Faesthetic*, I was given the opportunity to help curate a big art show for 55Dsl in NY. It was 2002, I lived in Toledo, Ohio, and didn't know the first thing about the NYC art scene. 55Dsl was like, "Yo, call this dude Roger Gastman up!" and I was like, "Yo! I love that guy!"

So I called up Roger, and he proceeded to give me email and phone contacts for some of my absolute favorite graffiti artists. With his blackbook, I was able to call CYCLE on the phone!

The art show ended up being a smash hit, in large part to Roger's help. Six months or so later I ended up in L.A. to help 55Dsl with a tradeshow booth. Roger was also out in L.A. at the time and we met for dinner. It was at this dinner that Roger told me how stupid I was for publishing an art magazine.

He was getting jaded at this point, having to spend more time hustling ad sales than hustling graffiti and street whores. This was still a year or so before *WYWS* folded, but you could already tell he was done with the BS. He wanted to keep it real, but things were out of his hand.

Over the past 10 years, I've had some great opportunities to work with Roger, and have always taken his fatherly advice to heart. I've always looked up to him, and all of his accomplishments. In another life, if I had the balls, I would have moved out to L.A. like him, started multiple magazines like him, and banged a million women like him. Only recently did I find out that we are the same fucking age. I almost killed myself when I realized how much more he's done in this short amount of time we've both been on the planet.

So to recap:
- Roger was the first person to respond to my desperate cold call emails.
- Roger was the first person to publish me.
- Roger helped me curate my first art show.
- Roger was the first person to tell me publishing a magazine was a bad idea, and he was absolutely right.

—*UPSO*

WARNING
THIS AREA IS
NOW PATROLED
& MONITORED
ANY PERSON SPRAY
PAINTING OR MARKING
ON THIS PROPERTY
WILL BE
ARRESTED & FINED

FACES OF DEERTH, OUR U.S. TOUR
by Neilrock
Photos by Neilrock and Toddomatic

I had just finished four months of interning in the bowels of Hollywood for my final college semester, and it was time to get the hell out of Dodge. My folks flew my best buddy Todd out from Boston to make the cross-country trek with me, my father's rationale being that it would be much more difficult for some tweaking trucker to dress me up like a girl and butt-fuck me at a rest area if there was someone else in the car. I packed my car to the gills with all my shit, leaving Todd with a small section of the backseat to store his gear, and took off for LAX to pick him up.

The key to a good road trip is a good mission—you know, one of the separate agendas that make those mind-numbing drives a little more exciting. We'd planned on pulling the old steal someone's lawn jockey and take pictures of it all over the country, and send the pictures to the victim's house with threatening random letters, but of course, Todd failed to come through with a stolen jockey. After that, we were left with the adventure of checking out all the "World's Largest Stuff," we came across, documenting road kill coast to coast, and drinkin' the fool fuel. We armed ourselves with eight rolls of film, two cameras, two Johnny Cash anthologies (an absolute must for any serious road tripper), shoddy directions from the Internet, a brand new flask and a quart of rye for starters (you don't think anyone could handle a drive like that sober, do you?).

I entered the airport to pick Todd up, flask in pocket. The crack security guards detained me for 10 minutes and frisked me twice before deciding that making me drink whatever was in the flask was sufficient precaution, and then let me into the terminal. Todd and I left quickly to fetch a tasty lunch before the four-and-half hour drive to our first scheduled stop: **VEGAS.**

OBJECTS IN MIRROR ARE CLOSER THAN THEY APPEAR

A
ONE-NIGHT
STAND WITH
AMERICA

A JOURNEY OF 3,000 MILES BEGINS WITH A SINGLE STEP

As we stepped from the bright L.A. sunlight into the darkened showroom of Spice Lady (N. Cahuenga, Hollywood), I was disappointed to notice that we'd missed the buffet. We met our obese friend Brendan there, and sat down to delicious Greek salads while ugly, fully-dressed Hispanic women did the "cabbage patch" on a floor that reminded me of Saturday Night Fever.

The worst thing about being in a strip club at 2 in the afternoon was that the asshole DJ was screaming and yelling like it was primetime. Truth be told, there were three of us in a booth eating, one drunk dude playing video memory (the kind that shows you an old wooly centerfold when you win), and two hundred empty chairs. That was it. Fucking jackass.

WORLD'S LARGEST LETDOWNS

Part of the allure of any good road trip is the promise of seeing the unusual and amazing. Shit like the Grand Canyon, Mount Rushmore, and Wall Drug become checkpoints along the journey. Sometimes, examining a two-ton ball of twine lives up to its hype—sometimes. There's about 60 miles or so between the last bit of civilization in California (Baker) and the Nevada border known as Death Valley. As if the last gas station in California needed any more advertising than that, it also happens to be the home of the World's Largest Thermometer. Needless to say, we were fucking pumped. Who'd have thought that a couple of kids from Cape Cod would grow up and one day, against all odds, see the World's Largest Thermometer? So, after a grilled cheese at the Bun Boy (I-15 Baker, CA) we strolled over to get a look at the beast. To our supreme dismay, the piece of shit is a digital thermometer. It's total bullshit. I could go into a 7-Eleven and buy a digital thermometer, glue it to my dick and call it the World's Largest Thermometer. I was all geared up for a towering tube of deadly mercury swaying menacingly in the evening winds of Death Valley. It sucked, it was a letdown, and it was 75 degrees.

Not to be outdone, Nevada had more disappointments for weary travelers. Once you pass a sign that says "Entering Nevada" on Interstate 15, you come over this hill and lo and behold, a brilliant light shines out amongst the darkness of the desert. Vegas. The promise of free booze, blackjack, hookers and all that other immoral and illicit shit was making us dizzy with happiness. When we'd reached the light, Todd spit out the window with disgust because it was just a single, lonely casino. This happened several more times before we reached the actual City of Sin. They sprinkle these toy casinos along the interstate like Hansel and Gretel's breadcrumbs so that everyone can find their way from L.A. to Vegas: one shithole to another.

HOW TO BURN MONEY WITHOUT FIRE

As we penetrated the Las Vegas city limits at a rate of 115 mph (oh, you thought I was kidding about how badass the Cutlass is?), our faith in the devil was restored. The strip is truly a spectacle. From 15 miles away it glows like a pregnant whore. And like that whore, it will fuck you, and fuck you and fuck you, because there isn't a damn thing you can do to her that hasn't already been done.

On the strip, we cranked Thin Lizzy and stared in awe of just how much we'd underestimated the insanity of the place. On the left side of the street at Treasure Island, a bunch of fruits in pirate gear were yelling and sinking some boat as part of the new "family entertainment" offered among the flood of grown-up fun.

We checked into a Days Inn (4155 South Roval Lane) with a coupon we picked up at the Bun Boy, and got ready to pillage and plunder. The concierge had asked us if we wanted two beds or one, which is weird, because most people usually know me for a while before calling me a homo. Anyways, we knocked back some rye and headed out to win money, drink for free and get some tail.

The Flamingo was the casino that Bugsy Siegel started, and as far as I know, it was one of the originals. Todd and I punched the ATM and sat down to play some blackjack. After 15 minutes, the first drinks came: bourbon and ginger ale for me, and a sissy gin and tonic for my accomplice. Todd tipped the cutie with two chips to make sure they kept coming.

An hour later I had been scolded three times for cursing, and 100 times for touching my chips after they'd been put down. Todd squirted lime juice all over the deck and was smugly enjoying the fact that he was $70 ahead of where he started, while I was down a fiver. Ten minutes later, I was up to $65 and Todd whittled his cash down to $30 and gotten comped a pack of smokes, so we split with our winnings and went to check out the skirts over at Caesar's.

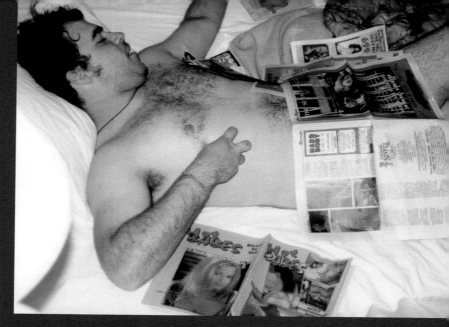

The bar at Caesar's Palace (3570 Las Vegas Blvd., across the street from the Flamingo) was called Cleo's Barge. The waitresses wear these gold Madonna-wear things that push their breasts up through the roof, and their hair is in these cone shaped things with long braided ponytails shooting out of the top. Our waitress was blonde and hot as all hell, so I spent all my money on booze so she would keep leaning over and talking to us. There wasn't much good looking strange-wool in there, mostly fat conventioneers and the kind of forest animal that takes much, much more moonshine than even Vegas can offer for the thought to cross your mind. I guess it was an off night, but the band did play Prince's "1999."

At 3 a.m., we left Caesar's and walked around a bit, picking up the free newspapers and marveling at the fact that there were 100-year-old ladies still working those one-armed bandits. We stopped at Bourbon Street for a final nightcap, mostly because they were still serving at 3:30 and cocktails were 75 cents. I was so depressed by the desperados at the bar that I demanded that we take our horrible tasting drinks in shitty plastic cups to go. I got no argument from Todd or the bartender, who was busy playing Keno.

I ended up dumping most of my cocktail on the welcome mat back at the hotel. By now it was 4 in the morning—7 if you factor in the jet lag for Todd. Check out time was noon.

IT'S A BEAUTIFUL MORNING

Hours later, we woke and I almost puked. Waking up seven hours later would have been a much more disgusting and awful task if I hadn't been for the World's Largest Collection Of Free Pornography we had in our room. We grabbed catalogs from all the escort agencies and strippers. These things are hardcore, completely nude layouts that rival upscale stroke publications like Barely Legal or While You Were Sleeping.

We didn't have any time to fuck around though, so we headed straight from checkout to the World's Largest Gift Shop (further down Las Vegas Blvd.) to grab ourselves some souvenirs to complement the matchbooks and napkins we'd salvaged from the night before. I got a slutty Las Vegas T-shirt, a mesh hat that says "Stolen from Mabel's Whorehouse," and a dancing hula girl for my dashboard.

From there, we made a b-line for the Sahara (2535 Las Vegas Blvd., South), which promised the biggest buffet on the strip for $3.99. To get to the buffet, you have to walk through about a mile of slot machines and other games, where you can win a Dodge Viper or a Harley. After the casino, there is a 200-yard long windowless hallway that twists and turns, but just beyond the end of it lies the precious Sahara Buffet and Conga Showroom, where for just $3.99 you can get an all-you-can-eat buffet that's worth $3.99.

PUT ON YOUR DEER GOGGLES

The highway out of Vegas is straight, flat and the speed limit is 85. In Arizona and the beginnings of Utah, it gets curvy on the mountain roads but then it straightens out again. We had nothing to do but kick off our shoes, set the cruise control on 95 and enjoy the scenery. After about four hours of this, the scenery was a little bit less than interesting, and highway hypnosis was quickly taking over.

Then, a good bit inside Utah we saw what we wanted: our first road kill. Todd got so excited he almost killed us trying to pull over. She was a young deer I think, a few days dead, as we guessed from the maggots that were crawling in her eyes and the fact that most of her guts had been eaten out through a gaping hole in her side.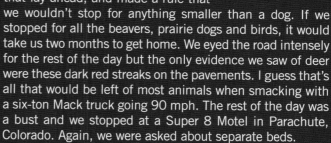

We were excited for the carnage that lay ahead, and made a rule that we wouldn't stop for anything smaller than a dog. If we stopped for all the beavers, prairie dogs and birds, it would take us two months to get home. We eyed the road intensely for the rest of the day but the only evidence we saw of deer were these dark red streaks on the pavements. I guess that's all that would be left of most animals when smacking with a six-ton Mack truck going 90 mph. The rest of the day was a bust and we stopped at a Super 8 Motel in Parachute, Colorado. Again, we were asked about separate beds.

The rest of Parachute consists of a post office, a gas station and The Outlaw Café. There you can eat breakfast anytime and listen to the hillbilly cook talk about how he wants to "fuck me black girl" because he "ain't no racist," all while he cooks your omelet. By far, the best features of the café are the John Wayne black velvet paintings, and the fact that you can pick yourself up a mixtape called Hot and Heavy (the greatest mix in the world). Included on this crucial compilation: Blue Oyster Cult, Rick Derringer, Molly Hatchet, Mountain, Suicidal Tendencies and The Edgar Winter Group. It is my new prized possession.

ROCKY MOUNTAINS HIGH

The next day in Colorado, we climbed up to 11,000-feet above sea level and threw snowballs at a rest area. Our ears were popping and the roads were treacherous.

A few hours later, we noticed signs for Golden, Colorado. It sounds familiar because it is the home of the Coors Brewing Company (300 12th Street, Golden, CO 1.800.443.8242). Because of our sense of civic responsibility, we stopped in for a tour and were surprised to find out that along with being the producer of some of America's finest banquet beer, it is also the world's largest producer of aluminum cans. The real reason we stopped is because you get to sample free suds on the tours.

After the 30-minute tour where we sipped a cold one straight from the vat, we retired to the visitor's lounge where we had a choice of Blue Moon, Zima, Killian's Irish Red, Coors, Coors Light and some other one I had surprisingly never heard of. Before we had a chance to order, we were hustled into completing a survey about our drinking habits. This survey turned out to be our ticket into becoming Certified Coors Beers Tasters. As it turned out, Hot Toddy and I drink enough for Coors to consider us experts. Then it was back to the lounge for our three complementary brewery fresh ones. So, that's five drinks in an hour-and-a-half. That would get most folks tipsy, but what we didn't realize is that being 9,000-feet above sea level affect one's tolerance. What I'm sayin' is, we was hammered. After the gift shop, we dragged our drunken asses to lunch in an attempt to regain our faculties.

NEBRASKA STINKS

We drove late into the night and far into Nebraska. We wanted to go out on the town and raise some hell cornhusker-style, but it was another couple of hours to Lincoln, so we were going to have to settle for something smaller. In a teeny town called Brady, we asked a girl at the gas station what the closest big town was. She said, "Lexington, but it stinks."

It really did stink. It was the worst smell I have ever encountered, like a rotting asshole sandwich with hot mayo. The stench came from a slaughterhouse three miles from the highway and was so powerful that we were gagging and stuffing our own turds up our noses to get some relief. As if it couldn't get worse, we got pulled over. Covert officer 41 took offense at our rate of speed so he stopped and searched us. He made us wait outside while he searched our bags, every single film container, the ashtrays and he even turned on the car and sniffed the vents. Then he opened he trunk and asked me what was in the big bag, so I say, "plastic coat hangers, magnets, silverware, an alarm clock and all my pens and markers." He had a dog give the Cutlass a once-over and after not finding a damn thing he decided to come right out with it and ask us if we had any "recreational Cannabis." "No, sorry," I replied. Seeing that he wasn't going to run us Yankees out of town, Officer Friendly had to let us go on our way.

That night we stayed at Fairfield Inn (121 3rd Ave, Kearney, NE) and polished off our rye before heading out to a bar that I can't remember the name of. It was one of those moments when you walk in the room and the record scratches and there's crickets in the background. There were four toothless dudes at the bar, a 15-year-old kid playing Ms. Pac-Man and a fat-ass bartender. They sold six packs over the counter, but we opted for a couple of drafts. Annoyed by the silence, I decided to play "Love Hurts" on the jukebox and left immediately afterwards.

HOORAY FOR IOWA

There wasn't anything worth a damn in Iowa except the World's Largest Truck Stop (off Interstate 80—you can't miss the fucker) and a nearly dismembered deer. It, too, was covered in flies and had been snacked upon in the belly area. As you can see, the back leg bone was sticking out, and when I touched it, it was so squishy my nipples got hard as quarters.

THERE ARE SOME PEOPLE YOU NEVER WANT TO BUY EXPLOSIVES FROM

We stayed with friends in the South Side of Chicago. Besides seeing lots of pretty women crying in public, the World's Largest Furrier and America's Largest Housing Project (or so I was told), the whole day was pretty uneventful. Around 9 that night we left for Toledo, Ohio.

From Toledo we headed towards Syracuse, which would be our final stop before our glorious and righteous return to Boss-town. We figured that all the kooky kids would be blowing off steam from their final exams and that the time was right for conspicuous consumption and devious destruction.

Right at the boarder of Ohio and Pennsylvania, there was this giant fireworks and martial arts supply joint. We ran in there trying to nab some M-80s to bomb the suburbs with, but inside all they had were $50 butterfly knives, sparklers and smoke bombs. When we started to look like we were going to leave without buying anything, the man behind the counter turned to us and said, "If you guys are looking for something more powerful, and have out-of-state ID, I can show you some pre-mo shit in the back room." More disturbing than his use of "pre-mo" was the fact that when he turned we noticed that he was missing half of his arm, presumably a result of an experiment with his own "pre-mo shit." I mean, the sight of that stump was enough to make me afraid of a bang snap. No thanks.

FUCKING CANUCKS

We dodged rush-hour traffic in Buffalo by taking a detour to Niagara Falls (Canada). We walked over the border, had a picnic and Todd went over the falls in a barrel, but when the duty-free liquor sales girl told me I couldn't buy that much sauce without a car, we went shithouse. We told the border guard his country was for pussies and once we were safe inside U.S. territory, hawked loogies into that demon nation. Leave it to Canada to not allow the purchase of alcohol unless you're behind the wheel.

Upstate New York can really be a drag, but we found a juicy little guy mid-afternoon who must have been struck early that morning because nothing had gnawed on him yet. I figured I'd pour a little out for my fallen street soldier. If live deer are your thing, head out to the highway at dawn or dusk, because that's when they're

out prancing about the grassy knolls along the asphalt. Be sure to bring a camera, because not all of them will be prancing for long.

This would be our last volunteer for the photo essay, although there were a bunch of dead Bambis that we didn't stop for. Sometimes it is just too damned treacherous to stop the Cutlass when it is slashing up the highway.

I DIDN'T GO TO COLLEGE

At the fine institution of higher learning that Todd and I attend in Boston, 60 percent of the male students are raging queens. Our college experience wasn't exactly the wet T-shirt toga party we'd been promised all our lives. We thought it only existed on MTV. Then we rolled into Syracuse.

After checking into the school-run Best Western, which was the first place to automatically give us separate beds without asking, we asked the concierge where the hot spots were. To our delight, Tuesday was Ladies Night at Roman's Tavern (Franklin Square, Syracuse, NY.) Fuck yeah. However, it got off to a bad start immediately. A completely hammered girl at the door told me that we were going to love it in there, because there was a ton of drunken girls, or boys. Strike one.

Ladies night was being sponsored by HOT 107.9, which apparently plays the "most hit music," which wouldn't be so bad, right? Wrong. This DJ had a headset microphone, was wearing spandex shorts and jumping around, doing splits and talking the kind of shit that can boil a man's blood. Strike two. Nevertheless, he was whipping all the girlies into frenzy. I had no idea what was going on. To my left, five girls were in a "Blowjob Shot Competition," drinking shots with whipped cream on top with no hands, and to my right, three DHL deliverymen were grinding on this drunken chick in a pink mini dress

to the classic rock vibes of Meatloaf. As I was taking this all in, I felt a woman's hand in my pocket, which usually would be a good thing, but this piece of garbage was trying to put the rough down on my wallet. Just as I was about to punch her in the fucking face, I remembered I was a guest here and the gigantic Syracuse basketball team might have considered such a gesture rude.

Labatt's Blue was a dollar; rail shots were two. Strike three. Most folks get friendlier as they become polluted, but I become sarcastic and ugly. By last call, we were outside and too drunk to find our way home.

We eventually got back to the hotel and I strode into the lobby with a huge sack of mustard pretzels that Todd and I were chewing up and spitting on the walls. We invaded our room and I began delivering the rock star treatment. I stripped the beds, flipped over furniture and continued to spit up pretzels as I stripped naked. Meanwhile, Todd set up the camera atop the TV as he had in everyplace we stayed and in doing so captured the essence of drunkenness. We ordered a porno movie and fell asleep before we could figure out how to get it to come up on the screen.

I re-awoke hours later and we checked out of what was left of the hotel room. That was it, our last night on the road and we were paying for it with some kick-ass hangovers. Then the brakes failed and I paid $130 to get them fixed. It gave us time to recuperate and notice how inbred Syracuse townies look.

SIX DAYS, 3,228 MILES, ONE HELL OF A TRIP

What is the beauty of the road? Imagine yourself taking a premium piece of foreign exchange student ass, who ships back to Afghanistan the next day, back to your pad for a textbook one-night stand. You freak, fold, smack, twist, tickle, squeeze, pinch, and honk for as long as you want, and finish up with a rat-nasty, Dutch-oven fart. The beauty is that you never worry about seeing her again. She doesn't speak a word of English, so she can't spread the word of your nasty freakmania alter ego and noxious fumes to anyone else. The road, she is a beautiful lady who tells no tales.

The road can be a bitch, my friend, but it is the only way to go. So go. Bullshit your way into cheap hotel rooms (AAA and student discounts are good and they never ask for proof). Go eat strange food and see the ugliest freak show people you've ever had nightmares about at truck stops like the Kum 'n Go in Iowa or Truck Haven in Utah. Leave your zone of safety, get out of your shithole apartment and manufacture adventure. The road is open to all your sick perverted thoughts. Especially those ones about dead animals.

Originally printed in WYWS Issue #7

THE DONNAS

Interview by Roger Rock and Fat Rich
Photo courtesy of The Donnas

Four young girls named Donna are verbally abused by Fat Rich and Roger Gastman—so what else is new?

How old are you?
20.

Do you still live at home?
Yeah.

What have you ever done that you would never want your parents to find out about?
Is this interview going to be all about sex?

No.
I've done a lot of things I wouldn't want my parents to find out about. Although my mom is pretty cool, and I think if I told her anything she'd be cool about it. She lets me do about anything I want.

Anything you want?
Not anything I want.

Would you punch an alien?
You mean if I met one? No.

Why?
Because why would I punch it if it wasn't doing anything to me?

What if it looked at you funny?
If it looked at me funny I would probably say, "What the fuck?" But I don't think I'd punch it.

Girls don't like me and neither do Canadians, but I have this huge crush on this girl who is half Canadian. What should I do?
Why don't Canadians like you?

I don't know.
Did you write these questions all by yourself?

Yes!
Do Canadians really not like you?

They really don't. Every Canadian I have met doesn't like me and I have no idea why.
And you like a girl who is half-Canadian? Just go for it. She should like you for who you are.

The other girl I like is 18 and is what you might call difficult. Do you have any pointers?
You shouldn't be defensive; you should be more open to things.

That's your advice to me?
Yes.

Do you think you could reenact any of the scenes from *Dirty Dancing*?
Right now? You mean the dancing scenes? If there was a guy here I would want to do it with, I guess I could.

Did you all graduate high school?
Yes. We were all planning on going to college but we decided to take some time off to do the band.

Which colleges did you get into?
I got into Berkeley, ULCA, NYU and Sarah Lawrence.

Jesus Christ!
What, you think that is cool?

I didn't get into any colleges. What did you get on your SATs?
1200 or something like that.

1200! It's no wonder you got into all those schools.
It's not as high as it should have been, or as some other people I know.

Do you drink a lot?
Sometimes.

Do you have any drunken stories you would like to recall?
This is one of the things I didn't want my mom to find out about, I guess, although she did and she didn't really care. One time my brother went out of town and I said I would feed his cat, so I had a big party at his house. I guess this is something I don't want him to find out about because I told him there were like three or four people there when there was really a lot more. We were all really drunk and dancing on the tables to KISS. Then this one guy got really mad and put a hole in the wall with his head. Then someone broke the stove while trying to make some food, but the most fucked up thing was that we lost the cat. Somehow it had escaped outside to this alley where you can't get to it. They guy who put his head through the wall was Bret's boyfriend at the time and the whole night he just kept screaming at her, saying, "I love you, you bitch!"

We've got some famous Donnas from history, would you like to comment on them? Donna Summer?
I think she is really cool and I like her music a lot.

What about Donna Martin?
From 90210? Every show she will wear a low-cut top, and her breasts, it is just

kind of scary, 'cause they are so stretched and shit. That kind of worries me a little bit. It's funny, because my name is Tori and her name in real life is Tori, so everyone thinks we named our band because of that. I swear to God we never made the connection until someone brought it up about a year ago.

Remember when Donna from *90210* got addicted to painkillers? That was a pretty cool episode, wasn't it?
Yeah. Wasn't that after she had sex? She just went totally crazy after that.

What about Madonna?
She's cool. I think we all really liked her when we were young. I wanted her album when I was in kindergarten but my dad wouldn't let me get it. All my friends had it and I was really jealous.

Quit trying to look at my questions!
You guys are crazy!

What type of guys do you get? They're all geeks, aren't they?
We get a lot of geeks. We also get those guys who are just obsessed with girl bands. They'll be like, "Oh my God, a girl band!" We definitely need a lot more hot guys at our shows.

Do you ever just pick guys out of the crowd and invite them backstage and stuff?
We've never done that yet, 'cause there aren't enough hot guys that come see us. It is really depressing.

Don't you have a roadie that scouts for guys and stuff?
First of all, we don't have a roadie and that's depressing too. We always talk about how we want more hot guys at our shows. We just don't attract hot guys, I guess. Don't you want to know anything about my band?

Wait, you have a band?
Yeah!

What are they called?
The Donnas!

Do you have a record or something?
It just came out last month.

You mean you play live and stuff?
Are you joking?

Originally printed in WYWS Issue #7

—Editor's note: I was pretty excited about doing this interview. I thought a couple of the chicks were hot. I knew they liked to get trashed, so I thought it would be fun to really fuck with them. And I really liked the fact they were in the movie Jawbreaker *and they cover shitty/awesome metal songs on each album.*

—Note from Fat Rich: I went into this thinking the guitarist was the hottest, and left having a stiffy for the drummer. She looked much better in person. She was always the beat-looking one on the covers. These chicks were pretty cool, kind of fun and laidback. I did my usual playing dumb act. At the end, when we do the whole "Wait you're in a band?" schtick, they actually fell for it. So I guess you could say I am either an excellent bullshitter or they are dumb broads. Let's play Kill, Marry, Screw with the Donnas. Def kill the ugly bass player. Not because she is tubby and busted, but because if I remember she didn't do the interview or if she did she didn't say shit. Marry the drummer. She impressed me with her wit. See, dudes aren't shallow we take personality into account (she also looked

while you
were sleeping...

...GIRLS AND GRAFFITI

while you
were sleeping...

...PURE PERVERSION

while you
were sleeping...

...WE WERE BOMBING

while you
were sleeping

...FAMILY VALUES!

I PITY
THE FOOL

WYWS
WHILE YOU WERE SLEEPING

...GIRLS AND GRAFFITI

while you
were sleeping

while you
were sleeping

...AMERICAN DREAM!

while you
were sleeping

...MOMMA TRIED!

"OK, so when I was at the tender age of 16, I put a WYWS sticker on my car (and by my car I mean my parents car that I was allowed to use). My mom asked me one day if the sticker was the sign of the devil, and she was worried I was exploring satanic things. Close, mom."

—Amanda B.

WHILE YOU WERE SLEEPING
LIVE THE LIFE

THE SAN FRANCISCO BAY
GUARDIAN

WHO, WHAT, WHEN, WHERE, WHY?

TWO HOUR
DIAGONAL
PARKING
9AM-9PM

MY FRIEND JOE:
HE'S A REPO MAN
by No Credit in Issue

I don't know about you, but even after 12 years of public education and four years of college, I'm qualified to do very little. The fact is, I'm not going to save anyone's life, I'm not going to play for the NBA, and I'm not going to invent anything useful for mankind. Chances are, neither are you.

So, if you're one of the many normal people out there who just wants a rewarding job that doesn't require you to spend all day in a boring office, then you may want to consider a career in automobile repossession. A few days ago, I sat down with Joe Marquez, a Baltimore-based repo man, to learn a little more about this exciting growth industry.

How did you get started in the repo business?
I used to work for a locksmith. He would always forget to pay me at the end of the week, and he was just a real pain in the ass. One night, I decided to break into his car and drive it to one of the worst sections in Baltimore and leave it there. I thought it was pretty funny. It's not like I really stole his car or anything. The next morning, the police showed up at my door. Apparently, there was a video camera in the parking lot that caught me taking the car. While the cop was putting me in handcuffs, he told me that I should get into the repo business because I was able to steal the car so fast and not mess anything up. I think he was joking, but I took him seriously. After a few months in jail I went right to work for the company I'm with now.

Is it more dangerous being in jail or repossessing cars?
Jail. No doubt.

What's the craziest thing that ever happened to you at work?
There was one time I had to go over by the University of Maryland. The car was parked right outside some frat house. When I went up to the car, I noticed it was moving a bit. I looked in and saw that two people were in the back having sex. I was like, "Oh damn!" So I just watched them for a minute, went out for some food, and came back about an hour later. They were gone, so I took the car. I just put a towel down first. The car smelled like someone was just doing it.

Was the girl hot?
She was real hot. I'm sure her dad would have been real proud.

What would you be doing if you weren't repossessing cars?
I'd probably be doing something stupid like selling drugs. Actually, I'd probably just be working for another locksmith. After one time in jail, I'm not going back.

What was the scariest job you ever had?
About three weeks ago when I had a job down off North Avenue in Baltimore. It was a sweet new Lexus. The guy hadn't had it that long. I got in, cut the alarm and started to drive off. The next thing I know, I hear two gunshots, the back window is blown out, and there's blood running down my face.

Did you get shot or was it just the glass?
I got shot, but the bullet only grazed the side of my head. I didn't even need stitches. But at the time, I didn't know that. I called 911 and passed out. The next thing I know, I'm in the emergency room. I thought for sure I was going to die.

Have you gone back out since then?
I was back out the next night. You can't let that stuff get to you. If you do, you won't last.

What advice do you have for those who want to get into this line of work?
Don't get into it unless you have to. It's not a bad job, but people don't like you. People shoot at you and get their dogs to chase you. I had one guy throw a firecracker at me. I nearly shit myself. I thought for sure I was shot.

Are there any rules for repo men?
You can't fuck with the cars. Don't mess them up. Don't smoke in them. Don't eat in them. Don't fuck in them. Basically, just get it back to the lot and move on.

What should someone do if their car is getting repossessed?
Pray it's not me taking your car. I'll take it and there won't be anything you can do.

Any last words?
Make your car payments.

Originally printed in WYWS Issue #8

E-CHAIN THE PSYCHO

Interview by Roger Rock & Fat Rich
Photo by Roger Gastman

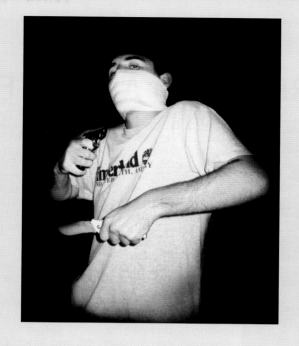

Often I ask people if they have ever stabbed anyone. So far, nobody has been cool enough to have done so—until now.

What's you're name?
E-Chain. Vitamin E. Some people call me Edward Scissor hands.

How did you get that name?
Stabbing fools for a living.

How old were you when you first decided to stab someone?
I was about 14 or 15. I was at my friend's birthday party. He was one of those kids that likes to show off. He was making fun of me, and we got into it. He hit me with a pan out of the sink, so I stabbed him in the collarbone area, and the hand, because he tried catching the knife. He was a little salty for a little while, then we became friends again. The next was a few years later. I was in the elevator with this big fat dude, and he started some shit because I bumped into his girlfriend. She was fat. I don't like fat people. I used to work in fast food restaurants and [fat people] would come in and order so much nasty food. I spit in people's food. Anyway, we got in a fight. I stabbed him in the eye with a punch knife. He got rushed to the hospital. I spent some time in jail.

Did anyone try to make you their bitch in jail?
No, they didn't. I wish they would have. There was this guy there that I thought was fine as shit. He had these cornrows. He was so bubbles. One day, I was watching him eat his brownie at lunch, and that made me want him to come to my cell and do me using blood as lubrication.

The third person you stabbed?
That was a few weeks after I got out of jail. It was more of a slashing with a box cutter. It kinda counts. The fight started because the guy was peeing in our alley. The fourth person was on Martin Luther King Boulevard. This dude grabbed a friend of mine's ass. I started talking shit and got surrounded by about 30 dudes. I stabbed him and ran. I was on the news. I don't think he died. If he had, I wouldn't have cared at the time, but right now I probably would. He would never be able to fuck again if he was dead. About a month ago, at the Tribe Called Quest [concert], I committed my most recent stabbing and the most brutal. I stabbed this guy about six times in the chest and the back with a four-inch knife. He got carried out with an oxygen tank. I was yelling, "Fuck your mother," while I was stabbing him.

Tell me about your new friend, booze?
I just started drinking about a month ago. I was a straightedge warrior, and now I'm a fucking lush. The other night I was drunk and tried to stab a girl. She was kinda cute.

Do you regret not stabbing her?
Yes, I wish the bitch died. She beat us at pool.

Anything else?
Yeah, my first girlfriend, right before I lost my virginity, she had her panties on and I chased her around my house with a BB gun and shot her in the ass. I was mean as shit to her and thought it was funny.

Would you have sex with a 12-year-old right now?
Yes, I would. I got a blowjob from a 15-year-old not too long ago. That's not bad—four years difference.

So if you were 14 and she was 10, that would be OK?
No problem at all. If I was six, I would be straight up hanging out at the hospital.

—Writer's note: What can I say about E-Chain? He was straight up fucking crazy. He slept with a machine gun. He stabbed some crazy White Power skinhead dude in a bar like four blocks from our house. He thought the dude saw him run into the house (our house) so me and my other roommate moved our beds away from the windows in case the house was going to get shot up. Aside from stuff like this though, he was a cool dude and actually really kinda sweet. He does scare me though. He's like that pitbull that is all loving but you can just tell at any minute that fucker will bite your hand off. I think he lived in Peru for a bit? It's funny how normal stuff like this seemed and how posing with a gun to your head and knife to your throat seemed like no big deal at the time.

Originally printed in WYWS Issue #5

STUPID STUFF

FIRED FROM A BONG FACTORY by Gordan Downs

In the Spring of 2001, a friend asked if I wanted to attend the "CTA" trade show in Las Vegas. "What the hell does CTA stand for?" I asked. "Contemporary Tobacco Accessories." A bong trade show? A stoner's heaven of glass and plastic chambers? Count me in.

A week later I found myself back in San Diego with a job drilling bong holes for Smoking Joe. Outside Smoking Joe's unit were two strip clubs and an ornery moving company; inside a drill press, several buckets of water, shelves of glass vases imported from China, and a ghetto-ass stereo with one working speaker. The entire staff consisted of Smoking Joe, a 30-year-old Deadhead, and Maurice, a 23-year-old S.D. native. The Brother and The Hippie made bongs all day, alternately listening to Phish and Bone Thugs-n-Harmony. Standing behind the bong drill all day wasn't the greatest feeling, but as soon as I grasped the concept of "This isn't a real job," I became content to be known as the "Mad Drilla."

Two months in, Smoking Joe got me high. Maurice soon followed, dubbing me an Honorary Brother due to my extensive knowledge of the music of Ralph Tresvant. None of us would hang out after work, but it was a pleasant work environment and allowed me to pursue a career in journalism.

Before long, I began sliding home during lunch breaks to conduct phone interviews, and with another computer added to the "office," I was able to check email much more frequently. This—in my opinion—led to my downfall and eventual dismissal.

However, Smoking Joe disagreed.

Ten Reasons I Was Fired From a Bong Factory:

10. **Got caught stealing merchandise instead of making bongs.**
9. **Got caught placing drug orders on the phone instead of making bongs.**
8. **Got caught receiving drugs instead of making bongs.**
7. **Got caught not sharing drugs while making bongs.**
6. **Got (repeatedly) caught coming in to work all fucked up.**
5. **Got caught calling the bosses' music "hippie-pussy-bullshit."**
4. **Got caught answering the phone, "Smoking Joe will give your dog a hand job!"**
3. **Got caught checking my email instead of making bongs.**
2. **Got caught "not caring about the quality of product you are sending out to the stores."**
1. **Klonopin!**

HIRED TO CARRY AROUND PEE by J. Bernstein

I'd always ignored ads proclaiming "$Research Volunteers Needed, Will Pay$" But that was before I lost my job and started stealing my roommate's change.

For several months after that, I rented myself to science. I got $50 to receive a hormone injection for my (conveniently brand new) obsessive compulsiveness, and another $50 for a hearing test. I underwent three CAT scans at $75 a blast. For an even C-note, electrodes were attached to my brain as I identified flashing squares, but the big payday came when I earned $150 for filling a jug.

"Do you drink much water?" the experimenter asked. "Some people need two jugs." I would not—carrying one jug of piss was funny, but two would be depressing. "Shame" had long since left my vocabulary.

For years, I'd appreciated my tinkle solidly hitting toilet water before diminishing to a trickle, drip, and then quiet satisfaction. My stream thudding against the slowly warming, shit-brown plastic jug just wasn't the same. I decided to pack up and venture from Queens into piss-friendly Manhattan.

With my urine sloshing, I hit Times Square. I rode the Toys 'R Us ferris wheel and harassed obese tourists. When I visited Virgin Records to listen to the new Jill Scott, my jug rode a crowded escalator. I jostled some fanny packs at a sidewalk taping of *People's Court*, and at Macy's, an impressed saleswoman showed me where construction workers urinate into water bottles. We even rode the subway twice!

The next day, as I handed in my jug and rolled up my sleeve, in walked the same doctor who injected me with the hormones for OCD.

"It's good to see you again, Josh."

I smiled, closed my eyes, and waited for her to tap back into my bottomless veins.

How to Get Paid Doing This Kind of Thing (Working the Medical Testing Circuit):

1. Date a Medical Professional – Doctors and nurses know all the good studies. Seduce a lonely M.D. and she could be your sugar-mama and medical pimp.

2. Scope Out Schools – Oodles of intrepid grad students have secured grants allowing them to pay you to test their hypothesis. Head to a college research department (psychology, medical, etc.) and peruse bulletin boards for cash bonanzas.

3. Lie – Say a study's requirement is a healthy intranasal drug addiction and you've never even snorted a pixie stick. The remedy? Lie. Tell the researchers you can't get enough of that Colombian goddess. Like life, the worst outcome is rejection.

4. Disregard Your Body – You can make loot getting zapped by CAT scans, but rent money will only come from enrolling in three-week experimental-drug studies at suspicious labs.

5. Read Alternative Weeklies – Your local free rag, while laden with left-wing rhetoric and porn ads, contains a wealth of contacts. Skip "SMOKE POT, GET PAID!!!" and head to "RESEARCH VOLUNTEERS NEEDED."

Originally printed in WYWS Issue #20

COOKING WITH PORN STARS

JENNA, INC.
by Jelly
Photo by ?

Marxism, schmarxism. So Karl said he was keen on workers owning the means of production, but what would the Bonedaddy of Communism have thought of uber-porno chick Jenna Jameson? After all, Jenna owns the means of production—in her case, that fabulously enhanced 32DD-22-33 finger-lickin' frame.

But Jenna's no lumpen prole. Rather, as the highest-paid performer in the adult biz, she preaches capitalism with every moan and groan, every thrust and squirt.

"People have no idea how hard I've worked to make it to this point," Ms. XXX tells ol' Jelly. "Fame didn't happen overnight."

Jenna works hard for the money, so hard. But today she's taking a break from filming on the set of her new series, Peach, to show Jelly how to make Kool-Aid pops. We're in a house that looks like Jed Clampett's crib with a buncha ladies finer than Ellie May runnin' around nekkid for a softcore, all-girl shoot.

Wait a sec, did someone say softcore? That's against Jelly's religion.

"Tell me about it," pouts Jenna, sucking on a cherry-red Kool-Aid cube. "How do you think I feel with all these hot chicks and no real sex? What a bummer!"

Sticky-sweet juice runs down Jenna's cheeks and all over her pink bikini-clad bod. There's the intoxicating odor of candy-coated cooze in the air, and Jelly's forced to walk funny. Jenna says her favorite cavity-causers are Pixy Stix and Pop Rocks. "Do they still make Pop Rocks?" Jenna wonders. Jelly's tempted to make his own right in front of Jenna, flashing his capitalist tool. He thinks of Karl and the moment passes. Communism kills boners, comrades.

Originally printed in WYWS Issue #21

A FOUR-MONTH PENIS POLISH WITH WAX: I WORKED FOR RICHARD SIMMONS

by ████████████

Illustration by Richard Colman

When everything you do and everything around you is so far from what you ever thought your life would be about, you stop noticing the weirdness. From here it takes some serious bumps in the road to disrupt your sleep at the wheel and remind you what you are doing and where you are going. When I worked for the Richard Simmons show, DreamMaker, I got in such a zone that all the pink-velvet happenings around me seemed totally normal. As I look back on the absurdity of that job, I sometimes have trouble remembering why I ever quit. But not that much trouble.

First of all—because I know you're wondering—I did not have sex with Richard Simmons and, as far as I know, neither has anyone else. What I do know is he has a pink house. It looks like the Gone With the Wind house except it's pink stucco. I know that he collects dolls. I know he wanted a white microphone so he would look like Shirley Bassey. I know there was a buff 60 year-old man with a San Francisco moustache that went everywhere with him. I know that I can estimate that of the 13-or-so men with creative influence over the show, maybe two were heterosexual. That's all I have

to say about that, so you can form any and all opinions you find necessary from there.

As far as "Big Dick" goes, the first time I went to Richard Simmons' house was to retrieve his 4-foot-by-5-foot photorealistic painting of him and his six Dalmatians. As we walked up the staircase, I commented that there was no banister. There were just different sized white balls mounted on triangles. He explained that the building inspector had required a banister, but after he left, Dickey quickly had had it torn out because in his words, "I just wanted the balls." Then he squeezed my arm. I found that exchange so creepy that it sort of haunts me. I sort of feel like I've been molested.

DreamMaker had aimed to promote hope and charity, as an alternative to the negativity of daytime shows like Jerry Springer, Sally Jesse Raphael and Richard Bey. To do this, they needed a crack staff of dedicated and hardworking television professionals whose credits read like an attendance sheet at the morgue for creative brains (Keenan Ivory Wayans Show, Howie Mandel Show and Vibe TV).

The show was hypocritical to the bone. Despite the fact that the show

was meant to help the "husky," there were several candidates who were deemed too fat to be on TV. Other times, when guests weren't crying in their pre-interview (which was taped), the kind and loving staffers were instructed that irrelevant and painful issues were to be brought up until they did. You see, crying gets ratings.

One time, a kid wrote in saying that he was a flop with chicks and wanted to some help picking up on the babes. (Here is step number one, Casanova: STOP WRITING LETTERS TO RICHARD SIMMONS.) So Dick's partner-in-crime Jerry Penacoli ambushed this kid at his crib and dragged him to this retarded country western bar at Universal Studios where the crew did tequila shooters and our letter-writing boy blunder sucked back a couple of longnecks. While lover-boy sat at the bar, Jerry fed him lines through a hidden earpiece and, miraculously, after a few botched attempts, he got a number. What he didn't know was that the whole thing was a set up, and all the chicks he talked to were actresses. I waited afterward to see his reaction when they told him, but they didn't, and this kid was played for a sucker on national TV.

Another contributing factor was that I was tired of fetching Cali Faux Rnia health food for the idiots behind that show. They always complained about the tasty junk-food-vittles we had lying around, but when I bought fruit and wholesome, overpriced yuppie treats, they'd lay about until they were moldy and gross. So instead of using their shopping list, other production assistants and I whipped up a list of our own favorite gourmet fare: sausage, egg and cheese breakfast biscuits, Jolly Ranchers, corn dogs, microwavable meatball sandwiches, pretzels stuffed with cheese, chicken quesadillas, Yoo-Hoo, and my favorite of the bunch, those pop tart things that were full of eggs, cheese and sausage.

In keeping with the overall hypocrisy, the fruit always spoiled and this stuff disappeared out of the kitchen like a fart in a hurricane. While I love eating junk, and know that it is going to kill me, it is my theory that the laughs I had watching two gay guys talk about gay guy stuff while eating corn dogs will replace the years lost to the triglycerides and cholesterol.

I learned a few things about the business of television production while I worked there but I mostly learned about my own personal preferences in behavior. What I learned is that if you are a mutt, let everyone know. If you see someone fall down the stairs, stop giggling and laugh like you mean it. Don't try to be an angel when you are really a punk. In the end, DreamMaker was two hundred pounds of menstrual clot, dressed in a silk vest. Holier than thou, yet as full of shit as Springer could ever be in his wettest of dreams. Jerry Springer, however, has the courtesy and respect for his audience to admit it.

THE FINAL STRAWS/TOP FIVE REASONS FOR QUITTING:
1. I wasn't allowed any of the free drinks at Universal Studios.
2. I couldn't justify working for a sleazy talk show when there was so much opportunity around, especially when I didn't get any free drinks.
3. Richard always touched my arm and gave me this creepy look, especially the times when I was wearing a wire and trying to catch him saying something bad.
4. I got a job at Troma Entertainment, and within a week, I was up at the Playboy Mansion shooting Toxic Avenger IV, and swimming in the Playmate broth of the grotto in nothing but my Munsingwear.
5. I always quit and never get fired. If you are fired, you are a victim, and portrayed weak in your life's story. Quitters are the aggressive warriors who always win, and always seem cooler in the end, and if I have dedicated my life to one thing, it is to be as cool as possible, at all times.

ADDENDUM

If you intend on using this blurb as the basis for legal action in any sense, I am telling you right now not to bother. I will immediately say that I made the whole thing up, but until then, it is 100 percent true.

—Editor's note: The author requested anonymity, and indemnity from prosecution, but had this to say, "Thank God no one who could read ever bought this magazine when it was originally published, or a lot of people would still think I'm an idiot."

Originally printed in WYWS Issue #9

CHRI$ NIERATKO WANTS TO KNOW IF GLENN DANZIG IS A GODDAMN SON-OF-A-BITCH!

I've never been much of a fan of Glenn Danzig, the solo artist. Actually, that song "Mother" he did a few years ago was as painful to me as getting a vasectomy by a doctor with a fork and a spoon without any anesthesia. But Glenn Danzig, lead singer for Samhaim or the Misfits, that's a whole 'nother story. Back then, his hair was shorter, he was more pissed off and his songs made me want to fight. When I found out I was interviewing Mr. Danzig, I was hoping that I would get to interview the other guy, the ex-lead singer of the Misfits. But that's impossible, 'cause he's dead. Instead, I got the "Mother" guy.

Are you originally from Lodi, NJ?
Yeah, I grew up in Lodi. I also grew up in Revere Beach in Boston and in Manhattan.

What is it they got out there?
Sluts.

Yeah, but what's that place where they teach nuns to be nuns?
Felician Community College.

That's the hot spot, huh?
I don't think so.

You got this new album out. Is there anything you wanna tell me about it?
What do you wanna know about it?

What do you wanna tell me about it? It's your record.
It's a fucking awesome record. I love it. It's pretty dark; it's pretty aggressive. I don't know what else to say.

Whatever happened with Hollywood? You lost a record in there.
Oh fuck, we were three weeks into our deal when Roy Disney found out we were signed to his label. One of the reasons I went there is they also offered me my own label, and no one was going to screw with me. My old lawyer left a long time ago to run Hollywood and got totally screwed over. But everyone assured us that it was different, and I met with a bunch of people they hired who I

knew, so I thought it was going to be a pretty good situation. It was the biggest load of bullshit. Roy Disney pulled the plug on us. He saw this "Tower Pulse" cartoon where I was shaking hands with someone, Mickey Mouse had 666 on his head, there were upside down crosses, and people were on rides burning. People started sending emails and faxes and calling to protest that we were on the label. It was a very fucked up situation. Long story short, we finally got out of there, got a settlement and started recording Danzig 6:66.

Where are the best groupies?
I think girls that come out to the show are pretty much the same everywhere.

How about the different eras: Misfits, Samhain, Danzig?
Clearly Samhain and Danzig had the better girls. There weren't many girls on the Misfits tour.

Have any good groupie stories you'd like to share?
I don't like calling them groupies, they're female fans. I'm sure there are groupies out there but I don't think for the most part that the girls who come to our show are actually groupies.

You ever have a stalker?
You always have stalkers. There are so many, it just becomes normal after a while.

Do you think it's weird that the Misfits are still touring?
Yep.

You'd never go see the show, would you?
No, not the Misfits. I think it would have more credibility if they never did a band before it, and if Jerry called it the "Jerry Only Band" because there are no original members in it except for him. The singer and songwriter is not in the band. It just lacks any kind of credibility whatsoever except let's make some money off this and beat it into the ground.

You're a pretty burly guy. You think you could kick that new singer's ass?
You know what... only time will tell.

Jerry said you can only have your head up your ass so long and he thinks that the two of you will work together again.
It'll never happen. If anyone's got his head up his ass, it's him. I'm not the one out on the road calling something the Misfits that's not, OK? So, let's get real about it.

Are you, in your personal life, actually Satanic?
I would say certain aspects of me are, yeah.

You don't go to Satanic church do you?
No. I don't believe in churches.

What do you like to do to relax?
Punch shit, watch videos, maybe hang out with some friends, just kick back.

Hey, you live over by Los Feliz...
Hey, I'd rather you not talk about where I live, motherfucker. I got enough people coming by my house going, "Glenn! Mother!"

But you live in a regular suburban house?
Yeah, I don't live in no mansion or nothing like that, just a regular house.

Your house isn't painted black with tombstones around it or nothing like that?
No, it's not painted black. You know how hot that would be in California, man? You might as well put some hotdogs in there and have a roast.

How about the inside? Painted black, no?
No, the inside's got some stone, like castle rock, and all basics, no colors.

How about the basement—a personal bondage dungeon or anything like that?
It's pretty fucked up.

Originally printed in WYWS Issue #8

GLENN
DANZIG

PAT THE PARTY JERK

PREGNANCY PREVENTION
by Trevor Michaels

While I was losing my virginity, the condom broke. Instead of calling my friends on the phone to brag, my frightened girlfriend and I took a cab at 3 a.m. to a 24-hour drugstore to buy spermicide. I was only 14, and here I was helping my girlfriend rub spermicidal jelly in her vagina. But I thought I was about to become a father if I didn't work fast. Lucky for me (and for my prospective kid), my girlfriend wasn't pregnant (and I don't think our drastic measures helped too much). I only wish someone had warned me beforehand of the dangers of sex and how to prevent premature fatherhood. So I'm going to use this section of "Pat the Party Jerk" to do a bit of community service by telling you how to prevent knocking up your lover in the first place. This isn't an article on how to abort kids—I don't want the Christian Coalition coming after me when you punch your girlfriend in the stomach and throw her down the stairs. No, prevention is the best medicine (your ferocious hormones will never let you abstain), and here are six quick tips on how to keep your little swimmers under control:

Prevention Tip #1: Make love to her when it's "that time of the month"
Popularly known as earning your "red wings," doing a girl on her period is just like doing her at any other time of the month except that afterward your penis smells like copper for a few days and you walk away bloody like a baby at a bris. If you turn the lights off, you probably won't even notice. If you leave the lights on, you'll soon learn why they call it a "hatchet wound."

Prevention Tip #2: Try door number two
This is a more popular alternative than you might imagine. Pick up a copy of the Kama Sutra and you'll soon discover that people the world over are shooting the moon and have been for eons. Heck, anal sex is a practice as old as the moon itself. Get her all liquored up and pick up a bottle of KY, and before you know it, you'll be fearlessly ramming it home just like your ancestors did.

Prevention Tip #3: Get yourself a post-menopausal girlfriend
If you happen to meet a motherly type and she starts complaining of hot flashes, you've got yourself a keeper. In this game, being over the hill is a good thing, and these women will cream at the notion of getting railed by your young, juicy pole. Remember, you're a goddamn rock star to them. (See WYWS issue 9 for my highly useful tips on how to pick up older women.)

Prevention Tip #4: Make love to transexuals
The difference between making whoopee with a "natural" woman and a transexual is the same as the difference between butter and margarine: "I Can't Believe It's Not Pussy!" is what you'll be screaming after a long night in her nasty sty. Your swimmers will hit a dead end, and you and yours will be carefree in the throes of romance without any troublesome, whining children.

Prevention Tip #5: Make love to sheep
Clem Clem, a veteran shepherd and itinerant preacher from Casper, Wyoming, insists, "During the Creation, God ran out of sheep wombs so he snatched up all the extra lady-wombs and fitted them sheep with 'em. If you look close, ain't no difference." Except for the much-disputed pickled fetus that remains preserved in a jar for display in R. Robdowski's Parade of Freaks in Atlanta, Georgia, there are no documented cases of man-sheep cross-breeding. Therefore, I highly recommend that you make love to more sheep and fewer women in order to prevent unwanted pregnancies.

Prevention Tip #6: Get a vasectomy
Over the past five years, vasectomies have become quite the rage among young men in America. So much so that Procter & Gamble recently announced plans to release a home vasectomy kit in the winter of 2000. By the year 2005, it is estimated that 18 percent of all men under age 25 will have had their tubes snipped, and with P&G's new product, the number could be twice that. I strongly urge any and all of you to take advantage of this wonderful advancement in home medicine.

So there you are, six quick-and-easy methods to avoid the burden of unwanted children. Six ways to maintain your high level of sexuality without any whining children pushing their way into your life. If you do happen to impregnate a girl, remember these three words: Deny, deny, deny. Take it from me, Big Trevor.

Originally printed in WYWS Issue #11

GABE BANNER ESCAPES FROM TROMAVILLE, USA, AND LIVES TO TELL THE STORY

Photos courtesy of Troma Studios

While some film studios play the role of the edgy independent, we all know the real deal to be Troma Studios, the original purveyors of the sick and twisted films that truly embody the While You Were Sleeping manifesto of "If you piss off enough people, you are doing something right."

Since 1974, Troma Studios, the independent film production company created by film genius Lloyd Kaufman, has brought to the screen images of exploding heads and mutant penis monsters in an industry where such blatant disregard for the MPAA ratings is rare. Lloyd has often been criticized for his (over)use of violent and sexual imagery, but these bare-breasted babes, crushed skulls and mutants are precisely what makes Troma the great filmmaking juggernaut that it is today, separating it from the herd.

Lloyd Kaufman and his partner Michael Herz are responsible for 25 years of Tromatic cinema, yielding almost 30 "true" Troma films directed by Kaufman himself, and countless others purchased from other sources. Among Troma's most well-known and well-loved films are The Toxic Avenger (1982), Class of Nuke 'Em High (1986), Surf Nazis Must Die (1987) and Cannibal! The Musical (1996), directed by Trey Parker and starring Matt Stone of South Park fame). And who could forget our favorite, Fat Guy Goes Nutzoid (1986), a film about two brothers who befriend a crazy fat man. The humor, of course, lies in the fact that this man is very, very fat.

The essence of the Troma movie, for those of you unfortunate enough to have missed out on these classic films, is in the minor—and major—flaws seen throughout. As Lloyd explains it, these movies are works of art with the seams showing, drawing the viewer into the process by allowing them to see how the movie was made. However, it is pretty evident that this is just how movies look when you don't have a whole lot of money to put into them.

Troma is the very pinnacle of filmmaking on a tight budget. Starting with only $300 in the bank, Lloyd and Michael have done amazing things with virtually no money in comparison to what other studios will spend on a movie. Today's average independent film will cost close to a million dollars whereas Troma's movies often cost less than $500,000 and are undoubtedly more fun.

Their latest project, Citizen Toxie (the new Toxic Avenger movie, duh), will have the largest budget to date and will feature more crushed heads and fake blood than ever before! Using raw hamburger, Karo Syrup blood, Bromo-Seltzer and Ultraslime, Troma's special effects team has created a new standard for violent death scenes on a budget.

With a penchant for overdoing the gore and full frontal nudity factors, Troma's films have a very tongue-in-cheek nature about them. The films are full of horrifying images, but they fit more snugly into the comedy genre than the horror genre. When Lloyd and Michael first set out to do a horror movie in 1983, tentatively titled Health Club Horror, they realized almost immediately that they couldn't do a traditional horror flick. It was Lloyd's idea to change the whole premise of the movie and make it a comedy, with the monster as the hero, and this would shape both the future of Troma's films as well as the horror genre for the decades to come. The film that came of this was eventually called The Toxic Avenger and went on to become Troma's biggest-selling movie of all time, making the Toxic Avenger himself (more affectionately called "Toxie") into Troma's Mickey Mouse.

Lloyd, now 53 years old, is the mastermind behind Troma. "He's just sort of the spirit behind the studio; that's what's really captured people's imagination about Troma and that spirit is in everything we do, every movie we make," says Patrick Cassidy, writer and producer of Terror Firmer. "In every movie [that Lloyd has directed] you can see certain trademarks; there's a certain spirit of independence, a take-no-prisoners attitude. He makes these movies for very little money and does amazing things with them." Lloyd's vision, when he started the studio, was to create a sort of universe of Troma characters. The fictional town of Tromaville is what came of Lloyd's vision, a town of questionable morals whose residents include the Toxic Avenger, Tromie the Nuclear Rodent, The Penis Monster, Killer Condom and other colorful individuals.

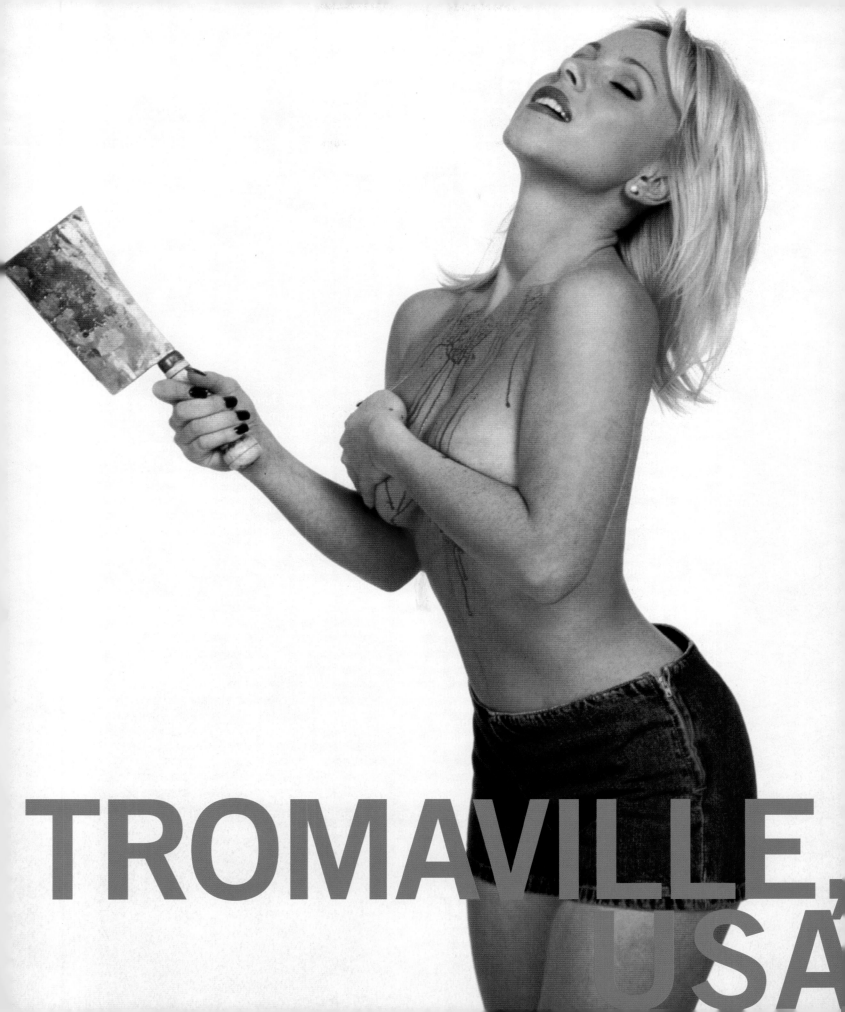

TROMAVILLE, USA

One reason Tromaville can be seen as an unmistakable whole is the fact that Troma's characters often turn up in multiple films. Five hundred-pound action hero Joe Fleishaker appears in no less than five Troma films. Toxie has cameos in at least two other films besides his own series. Another interesting thing to watch for in Troma's films is the reuse of props, even scenes in two or more movies. A fake leg from one of the Class of Nuke 'Em High series has been reused at least three other times. The rubber larvae creature originally used in Sgt. Kabukiman NYPD also turned up in Tromeo and Juliet. And finally, a car crash scene from Sgt. Kabukiman NYPD found its way into Tromeo and Juliet as well—who cares that the two cars don't really even look alike?

Troma has fun with their work. Lloyd and his team genuinely enjoy what they do (it's definitely not for the money). In Lloyd's new book, All I Need to Know About Filmmaking I Learned from the Toxic Avenger (Penguin Putnam, 1998), he maintains that what can be gleaned from all his work is that if he can do it, then anyone can do it. "That's his attitude and that's why we bring people in off the street to work here. People can just walk up and say, 'I want a job,' and all of a sudden they're working here," says Cassidy, excitedly. "That's kind of the Troma aesthetic."

Troma's most recent release, Terror Firmer, is a film inspired by Lloyd's book, featuring Ron Jeremy, Lemmy from Motorhead and Kaufman himself as a blind director trying to make a low-budget horror flick. It is a kind of history of the Troma film. Well, maybe that's a stretch. It's the story of a Troma film crew on a shoot that is sort of set up by a sexually conflicted serial killer, but it does also feature many historically accurate examples of life on a Troma film shoot. Lloyd's character will go to almost any lengths to stretch a day of filming into two days worth. The filming goes on despite problems such as crew and cast departure, resulting in those minor inconsistencies that give Troma's movies their character.

It's the very same method of filming depicted in the film that allowed Terror Firmer to be made for a measly $400,000, yet turn out to be one of the best Troma movies to date. The film just premiered at the Cannes film festival this year and met with an amazing response (no doubt due to the scenes of the fat naked guy running through the streets of Manhattan). "We had three screenings in Cannes and they were all packed," says Patrick Cassidy. "It's like that all the time, actually. We go there and we get tremendous grassroots support. People from the highest levels of the movie business to the bum on the street, they love Troma because we have this spirit and it's all about making that stuffy businesslike atmosphere more fun."

Possibly the most important aspect of Troma's guerilla marketing campaign at the Cannes festivals is the Tromettes. Early on in his career, Kaufman, filmmaking genius that he is, realized that to make any money off his movies he needed a selling point: sex. Hence, there are few Troma movies to date without nudity or violence. Or Tromettes. The Tromette is the archetypal heroine of a Troma film. She is often depicted as a big-breasted lady in minimal amounts of clothing who will kick your ass. Their appearances at Cannes, flanking Lloyd as he walks the streets, is at least as highly anticipated as the films themselves, if not more.

As the millennium comes to a close, Troma is in it to win it; they have big plans, most of them involving your sister and a gallon or so of fake blood. Hey, if Lloyd Kaufman can do it, anyone can do it.

—Writer's note: This article was actually fine, but then Roger published a photo of a fat naked dude running through Times Square as part of the story and said it was me.

STUPID STUFF

CONGRATS, JOSH MCGEE

The *Ex-Girlfriend Issue* provided us with many interesting responses from readers, but only one was sent priority overnight. It contained four different envelopes, each containing the story of an ex-girlfriend and tokens from the relationship. Such items included invitations to the prom, dried flowers and Kate's red bowtie from when she worked at Steak and Shake. The silly bastard with stamps to burn was Josh McGee of Knoxville, TN. (He's in a band!) Accompanying the memory packets was a letter explaining himself with a footnote regarding a picture of Lily McCabe. Thinking she'd be flattered, we shared Josh's dementia with her, and asked her to respond:

Dear Josh,

In you letter, you so sensitively described me as "fucking hot," and I can't deny how flattered I was. In response to the package you sent I'd like to offer you some advice for future love. You seemed to have only dated girls that already were involved, and you need to stop doing this. There are many completely single, independent women out there, and since you're wondering, I am one of them.

I also noticed from your letters that you've never been in love. To remedy your sad situation (every great singer needs love) WYWS has offered a roundtrip bus ticket to D.C., where you and I can discuss relationships in person and then go out on a date. They will plan and pay for (and photograph) one date, and if we click, I may let you take me out on another. Sleeping arrangements are pending.

With love,
Lily

You heard the lady, McGee. Get in touch with us at *WYWS* headquarters and we'll arrange for your bus and pre-order some "Cheese Wing Bacon Onion Fajitas" at Philly O'Funday's. Call to confirm at 301. XXX.XXX and ask for Roger in the travel office. We're not kidding.

Originally printed in WYWS Issue #17

Two issues ago, Josh McGee shared the details of every girl who'd ever dumped him. He also requested a date with one of our employees, Lily McCabe, and after hearing the runaround that Katie from the Steak and Shake gave him, we decided to hook him up.

Originally printed in WYWS Issue #18

First, Josh's friends dropped him off at the Lexington, Kentucky, bus station at midnight. It would be 14 hours before Josh would sit on anything besides the ass-sweat soaked sponges of a Greyhound seat.

Upon arrival the next day, Josh was just as delirious as we'd planned. Delighted, we tossed him in our 1987 Tercel and rode out to headquarters to begin the weekend fun.

We hired a "Patzilla" (pictured right) to make sure Josh was not a threat to safety. Josh still had the same goofy smile on his face as when he arrived, so we deemed him harmless.

Josh had a lot of time to kill before his big date, so we had to keep him awake with lots of distraction. He kept making The Face right up until the date, even during his first cab ride ever.

The young lovers finally met at the zoo, then went to dinner and the D.C. opening of *Pornstar: The Ron Jeremy Story*. The kiss and a smooch goodbye were all J-Money would wind up with, but he eventually slept soundly knowing Lily thought he was "really nice."

We were glad to have him here for the most ghetto magazine sweepstakes in history. Good luck, Josh, and anyone interested in going out with Patzilla, please write our offices.

PNS
c/o WYWS

Bethesda, MD 20814

Dear WYWS,

My name is Josh McGee, and I am twenty years old living in Knoxville. Enclosed in the following package is pictures, memorable, and other bullshit from four of my ex-girlfriends. I separated each ex-girlfriend's crap form the other and enclosed with each envelope is a little biography of each one, why we broke up, and how I feel about them now. I wish I had naked pictures to send you guys, but I never got that far with them.

Also I have enclosed a picture of myself. If you decided to us any of my stuff for any reason hopefully, girls will see my picture and be like, "Damn, that guy is a such a cuttie. I'll make him feel better because all those other girls broke his heart. What a hottie!" Well, hopefully they'll say that. Yeah, in my fucking dreams.

Well thanx again. I just started reading your magazine and I think it is fucking awesome!!! Probably the funniest thing I have read in a long time. Keep up the good work.

Later days,

josh mcgee

josh mcgee

ps. who is this chick?...she is fucking hot....

Cori

Cori was the love of my life. She was everything I wanted in a girl and more. I met Cori my sophomore year of high school. I was in study hall in the same class were she had World History. We started talking to each other and became really close friends. I didn't see her all summer because she went back to California. She was from California. In my junior year, Cori and I had the same ecology class. I was thinking to myself, "I need to ask her out. I really need to." So I wrote her this long ass letter saying how much I care for her and how much I like her. Plus I wrote her this long poem. I gave it to her and after class she said "Yes. I would love to go out with you, Josh." I was in the clouds. I was so happy. We dated and then one day she wrote me this not breaking up with me. She just saw me as a friend and that was it. I was like, "Horseshit!! Why the fuck would you toll with my heart for so long just to say we are friends?" So we broke up but I still kept trying to get her back. I asked her to prom and she said "yes." We went to prom and had a good time, but for the longest time I wondered why she would not go back out with me. It was really fucked up. I never treated her bad, I always made her feel good, I just wanted to know what happened. I finally found out. She felt bad she was cheating on her boyfriend in California. WHAT THE FUCK!!!! One the narf* is in California. It is like a different area code or something not to mention a different fucking state. Two when the fuck did she have a boyfriend. She never fucking told me that. Another episode were Josh is the one used and left heartbroken. Fuck it...

*narf- one who wears skater clothes and thinks they are skaters....but they are not. wanna-be's

Cori moved back to California were she goes to art school. She smokes too much weed and grew her arm pit and leg her out. Gross Mang!!!

I have a lot of shit from Cori. As she was the love of my life and all that bullshit. There is a photo she gave me her sophomore year, and our prom picture (notice the stain on her dress right above her wrist). Other prom memorable

Letters from her when she was at Governor's school and when she moved back to California.

Notes she wrote me when I told her "I loved her" and when I gave her flowers. So much for saying "I love you"...it leaves you heartbroken and a lot of nights of masturbating...awesome....awwooooo!!!!

Josh-
Hey. love you.
bad picture.
♡Cori

WHAT HORSESHIT

I am four

SHE GAVE ME THIS PHOTO OF HER AND A BUNCH OF BULLSHIT POEMS.

Dear Josh,

I guess I have been weird lately. I don't really know what to say to you. You are one of the best friends I have here. You have always been the one there for me. Thankyou for that. I am sorry things aren't the same as they were but I still love the person you are. Never think I don't care for you. It has been a confusing, frustrating past few months for me and I hope that can help you understand me better. I have alot to straighten out and it really just kills me that I don't know where I am going to be after governor's school. Maybe California, maybe not. I don't know. I am so sorry I didn't know what to say to you when you told me how you feel. I still really don't know what to say. I am flattered. All I have to give is friendship. And your friendship means alot to me, really. Thankyou so much for taking me to prom. I know we'll have fun. I hope these words clear some clouds up for you.

LOVE,
Cori

LETTER WHEN SHE WENT TO GOVERNOR'S SCHOOL FOR ART...

Cigarette in her hand
smoking softly away the time
And as the ash turns into
a former buzz as the day
is broken.—Ships inside
a dark, silent, grassy
wave, so where had gone
our childhood?

CORI WROTE ME THIS AFTER I TOLD HER SHE WAS THE LOVE OF MY LIFE

☠ even though your mouth is shut, your still fucking beautiful—glassjaw

Jennifer S.

I met Jennifer S. towards the end of senior year of high school. She was in my pre-calculus class. I always thought she was cute the first day I saw her. My friend Matt and I went to Party-City to get some fake blood for this concert we were about to play. She rang us up and she started talking to Matt. I asked Matt who she was and how he knew her. He told me, "Dude, that was Brad's younger sister Jennifer." I said, "Holy shit are you serious? She is hot." So after that I was trying to thick of was of asking her out. She was friends with my friend Erica. I found out when her birthday was and made her a birthday card saying how much I liked her and we go out some time. She gave me her number. Everything feel into place after that moment. We dated and we went to our senior prom together. I like Jennifer a lot, but she basically used me for a prom date. She never talked to me again after that night. I did not do anything to make her stop talking. She just stopped. Wine her, dine her....leaving me behind.

Jennifer moved back to Florida were she goes to a community college in Melbourne. She has no friends. How about them apples?

The pictures or Jennifer are her senior picture and form our pre-calculus party. I think she failed that class. Then just memories from our senior prom.

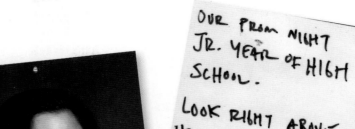

OUR PROM NIGHT JR. YEAR OF HIGH SCHOOL.

LOOK RIGHT ABOVE HER WRIST... ABOVE THE FLOWER... THERE IS A STAIN ON HER DRESS.

"From This Moment On..."

The Junior Class
of
Bearden High School
request the honor of your presence
at the
Junior – Senior Prom
on Saturday, the eighth of May
Nineteen Hundred & Ninety Nine
at eight o'clock in the evening
at
The Tennessee Theatre

"From This Moment On..."

Saturday, May 8th
8:00 - 12:00 A.M.
at
The Tennessee Theatre

* THIS WAS AT OUR PRE-CALCULUS PARTY
YES WE WERE MATH DORKS... BUT
I DID LIKE HER.

"From This Moment On..."
Bearden High School Junior-Senior Prom
Saturday, May 8, 1999
The Tennessee Theatre

Ticket Sales: Tickets will be sold in the West Mall during lunch period.
April 5 - 15 - $20.00 per person
April 19 - April 30 - $25.00 per person

Dress: Formal attire is required.
Tuxedo or suit and tie for Males!
Prom or "dressy" dresses for Females!

Pictures: Pictures will be provided by McEachern's
Package options and prices will be distributed in advance.

Music: Music and entertainment will be provided by Sound Force.

Food: Assorted party foods and punch will be served.

Souvenirs: Prom favors will be given out as you leave the theater.

Parking: Parking is available at no additional charge in the State Street Garage.

Directions: Take I-40 East.
Take the James White Parkway Exit.
Take the 2nd Exit (#441), "Cumberland Ave."
Turn right at the 1st traffic light.
Go 2 blocks (through 1 light to the "Stop" sign).
Parking garage is on the right! Park and walk up Clinch to Gay Street.
The Tennessee Theatre is on the left!

Prom is a school-sponsored activity;
even though it is not being held at the school, all rules apply!

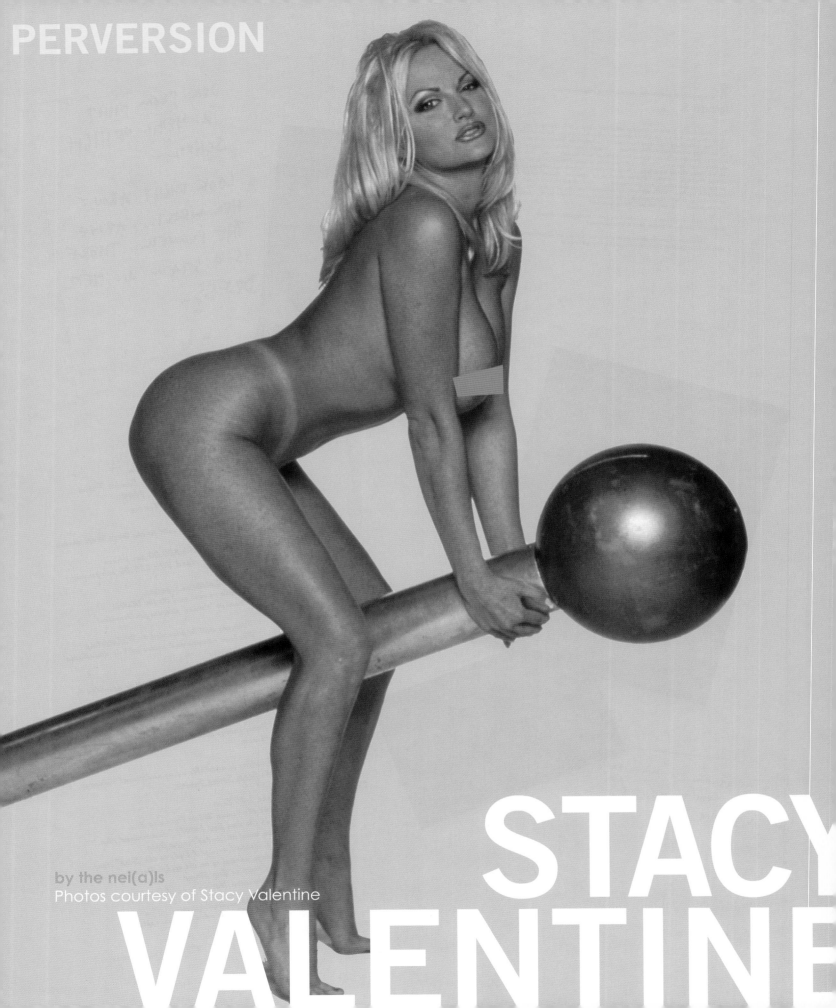

PERVERSION

by the nei(a)ls
Photos courtesy of Stacy Valentine

STACY
VALENTINE

PINK DESTINY

A young child once asked me, "Daddy, do porn stars believe in God?" I simply stared at the child, confused. Porn can be a dirty business, and more than a few of its stars have gotten lost in the hypnotic whirlwind that surrounds it, but where does God fit in? Porn stars are cast in a difficult lifestyle. They are indeed "stars," in that they are as easily recognizable as Gary Coleman or Emanuel Lewis to their fans. Yet they are recognized for something that most of us, myself in particular, hold very private. In an effort to see how these unique performers hold on, we set out to dig into gorgeous VCA contract star Stacy Valentine's beliefs (even though we wanted to dig in elsewhere).

To get a look deep into the very soul of this erotic bombshell, we decided to sneak in the back door (I know what you're thinking… and you're dirty). Psychological mind games will give us an opportunity to gather information, and then analyze it from a safe distance. The very first hoop we asked her to jump through was to play Hangman with us, the theory being that the word she chose would reveal some sort of missing piece that no mere question could tap from her blue eyes and 600cc breasts.

At the outset, we fumbled, guessing before she was ready, and she became threatened and indecisive. The word she had chosen no longer appealed to her. She quickly came up with a replacement four letter word, which we, a Harvard student and a graduate cum laude with honors from Emerson College (so what if no one's heard of Emerson College—fuck off), were stumped by, even after her hint: "Feminine, think feminine." Fearing that our effigy would be lynched like a horse thief, we frantically searched for a direction and then simply demanded to know what letters lay behind those empty spaces…

"Do I believe in God?" she said, in humorous disbelief at the lameness of our opening question. "Not necessarily. I believe that there is something out there. I'm definitely spiritual, but to pinpoint one specific person, I think is ignorant. I think there's a force, there's something out there, and there's a balance. Because of the way I live my life, whenever people hear I don't really believe in a God, they're like 'Well. You're going to Hell.' But the way I live is that I try to be as kind to other people as possible. I try not to hurt anyone, or harm anyone. I try to maintain the 'do unto others…' and live my life that way."

I never thought that we'd find the golden rule in the land of golden showers. When asked for an appropriate revenge for the ultimate trespass, she held herself to a lady-like stink bomb in an open car window. Tactful and effective, her Leo qualities are beginning to show. But how does her karmic outlook carry over into her on-screen life? Surely, there are times when the guy she is working with deserves, and receives, the Shocker? "I don't ram 'em, no. I'll slip in a finger, not to be mean, just 'cause it's dirty and nasty. It gets guys turned on to think they're with a real freak.

"Eye contact during blowjobs is another thing, it sends guys through the roof. But with the ass, it's like I said, 'Do unto others…' because I'm sure that soon my ass is going to be real close to them, and they're bound to ram me back with something a lot bigger than a finger."

Yes indeed, much bigger. But neither John Holmes nor Dick Rambone are bigger than love. What does love mean to someone who makes their living bent over a piano bench, with a mouthful of hairy beanbag? "People ask me what the hardest part about watching *Girl Next Door* [a documentary on Stacy made just before she signed with VCA] and most people think I would say the plastic surgery. But the hardest part, for me, is when that woman asks me to explain the difference between sex and love, and I could tell you exactly what sex was, but I didn't know what love was."

But all that has changed since she has met her new guy. Take notes, boys: "I do know love now. I was married twice and I wasn't in love those times and I wasn't really in love with Julian (unpopular ex-gay porn star boyfriend featured in the documentary). This person I'm with now is my soul mate, and that's it. He's great. He's someone I have a lot of fun with.

"We play on the computer, and I listen to him play the guitar. He plays whatever I want to hear. Last night he played 'Semi-Charmed Life' and 'Breakfast at Tiffany's.' You know, easy ones, 'cause he just listens to it and we goof around." A far cry from the days of dating fellow porn star Julian. We ask her if she wants to talk any shit about the cob-nobler turned straight porn stud. In true form, she explains only what she knows, and not what she thinks. "He was under exclusive contract with VCA and Vivid, and the girl he dates now shoots her own line of gonzo, you know, like, amateur stuff? Yeah, so VCA and Vivid both found out he was shooting her movies on the side and he was fired from both. So, good luck to him, he just pissed off the two biggest companies in the industry."

Since he has left, that would leave open spots on two of the hottest rosters in town. Do we have a shot at the big time? "If you have a 12-inch cock and can fuck all night, then stay the fuck away from me. I don't want some big fat cock fucking me all night. I would rather bust a nut three times a day. I don't know what these girls are talking about with this longevity stuff. If you seriously want to get into the business, go in a room with 30 of your guy friends and jack off. If you can keep your dick hard and cum with those 30 guys pointing and laughing at your sorry asses, you've got a 50 percent chance."

Not the recruiting line you'd expect from the 1998 winner of Hot d'Or's "Best American Starlet." No, Stacy Valentine is dedicated to the highest-quality screen sex, and works hard for VCA. In fact, she rarely has time to play.

"The holidays are my time to really jam on work. I found out that Santa Claus doesn't exist," she whispered. "The phone's not ringing because everyone is away and I have time to focus without distraction. I'm not much of a drinker, I really have to be in control. I did enough drinking before I was 21 to last a lifetime. Once we were on our way to Oktoberfest, and this guy challenged me

to tequila. He did 11 and not only did I do 11, I did 14. I stood up, took one look at my friend, and she knew right away. We got into the bathroom and I puked my guts out. If I do drink, it's got to be real pee-water, like Coors Light. When I was in Amsterdam, though, I was so high my friend had to tie a string to me so she could pull me down when she needed to talk to me."

Reefer, excellent. That's illegal here, of course, and we want no part of that. If you mess with drugs you are destined to do hard time, and that's no joke, Jack. Is Stacy concerned with what destiny has in store for her? "I have too many things happening to worry about something in the future. I have no idea what my destiny is, but everything happens for a reason, there is no such thing as coincidence. If I lose my keys, I tell myself that if I had them and left when I originally planned, I'd have gotten in a wreck." Ah ha. It would seem we've got a believer in the Fates on our hands. What does fate have in store for the new year? What precautions has this destiny-minded fantasy girl taken?

"I'm not sure what I'll be doing on New Year's. I'm not going to be stupid, though, I'll get a few little things just in case. Water, kitty litter, tampons— a lot of women are going to forget tampons. I'd hate to be without those."

Us too, Miss Valentine, us too. And kitty litter for that matter. Stacy uses Fresh Step for her three cats. We suppose that it's good that George, Gracie and Beavis the Bastard will be well taken care of in the post-apocalypse, but will we? No one knows except Stacy, who refused to comment on whether she will be staying with VCA when her contract expires.

She is a Leo, and as she says, "You can't control a cat, and you can't control a woman." Independence aside, she is a true-blue team player. You may catch her butt-naked, sweeping ants off an outdoor location, or setting up the spike back on her high school volleyball team. She isn't in this porn game for money or the spotlight. "I got into this industry to have sex, plain and simple."

Simple as Hangman? I should hope not, since we dropped the ball and were left to swing by the neck until dead. What words lay behind the gallows? What tightly guarded secret password into the psyche and soul of possibly the most beautiful woman in all of cinema? Pink Destiny. Pink Destiny indeed, a very pink, very juicy… destiny. Best of luck, Stacy, we love you.

I remember picking up the first issue of *While You Were Sleeping* at Tower Records on Newbury Street around 1998 and thinking that Roger looked like a weird raver. But the magazine was really funny and I loved all the pictures of quality graffiti. So when I moved to D.C. from Boston for college, I decided to email him and see if I could get an internship at *WYWS*.

Roger got back to me, and soon after, I was taking the Red Line out to Bethesda twice a week to hang with him and Neil Mahoney. It was an amazing foundation for me to be around people who did what they loved for a living, and to this day, I tell people it was one of the most formative experiences of my life. When I wasn't eating California Tortilla or transcribing articles about porn stars, I was sitting in Roger's office and scouring through his huge binders of pictures from my favorite eras of graffiti (early 1990s SPORTS/IMOK crews of course). On top of all that, I had the opportunity to interview El-P at his house, interview Mister Cartoon with Roger on the phone from my dorm room, and meet some of my graffiti heroes like COOL "DISCO" DAN and GKAE.

Almost every job I've had since that internship came from Roger or someone Roger introduced me to. I'm thankful that I had the opportunity to intern there and learn from him and the rest of the *WYWS* crew.

—*Judd*

I have many *WYWS* memories, from seeing so many of Roger's teenage friends within the pages—and wondering the legality of that—to Roger telling me to write for *WYWS* early on, and me (stupidly) never actually doing it. Roger ended up employing so many of his friends; I still kick myself! Looking back at those early issues, and what *WYWS* eventually became, it's amazing it all started with a kid that used to sell flowers on the side of the road in Bethesda.

—**Dave Brown**

I met Roger in 1996, just before the first issue, at the Baltimore hall of fame. He was there painting with EVER, and I was with SUPER and BREAST, two of my super early partners in Baltimore.

I painted the *WYWS* office with SEAZ and DALEK. I'd come in, Roger would give me a ton of caps, and we'd rap about what was going on in the scene and whatnot. We did an illegal spot on 14 & U. We just went illegally and did a whole production, it was *Alice in Wonderland*—me, Roger, Cory and KIER. One of the owners of the shops said something like, "You don't have permission, so if the cops come, I'm going to tell them you don't have permission, but otherwise I'm not calling the cops."

It was cool having a local magazine because everything pretty much came out of Los Angeles or New York. Everybody loved the magazine, especially in Baltimore. There were no publications coming out of Baltimore, and there was a *WYWS* issue that featured Baltimore, with an interview with SHAKEN and CHASE. Roger gave a lot of shine to Baltimore, so I know people up there really liked it.

I thought it was great. I was still traveling back and forth. I lived in D.C., but I was still painting freights in Baltimore because I was more comfortable there. Unless it was an event Roger was putting on, I wasn't involved in the scene too much in D.C. But anytime Roger had something going on, I was always up for it.

Roger pretty much kept the scene alive in D.C. by putting it in his magazine and then books.

—*Tim Conlon*

I sold back issues of this god-awful magazine out of Roger's garage in Bethesda, Maryland. Between packing up mags and shipping them around the world, Roger and his goons would threaten my safety (sexually) and/or suggest I hit on the cute neighbor girl who lived across the street. Either way, no one could have provided a better high school internship than *WYWS* magazine/Roger Gastman.

—***Noah Livingston***

LITERATURE

JOHN TAKES GABE TO THE STORE FOR GROUND POUND
by Gabe Banner
Photos courtesy of John Pound

Anyone who grew up in the mid-1980s remembers the Garbage Pail Kids, a collection of not-so-nice trading cards that captivated kids with their grotesque humor (and, of course, their fine artwork). Their creator, the almighty John Pound, is not only responsible for over 400 of the close-to 700 GPK in existence, he is also the man who brought you the lesser-known Meanie Babies and 1992's Trashcan Trolls. "I was sad to see [the Garbage Pail Kids] stop, really, it was one of the most fun and satisfying projects I've had to work on. I've always liked things that are just kind of silly or stupid. There is some special joy in producing art that is crazy and stupid but well done."

Since the Garbage Pail Kids series ended in 1988, John Pound has worked on other projects in a similar vein. Most recently, Pound has done a few paintings for Shorty's Skateboard Company in Santa Barbara for a series called Shorty's Nasty Wrasslin Bastards. The series of 10 paintings is very much in the spirit of the original GPK, but it's intended for "older kids." For some odd reason, characters like the "Masked Penis From Venus" and "Stoned Cold Steve Olsen" just didn't make it into Topps' original lineup.

"It's a small niche of skills that I seem to get called upon to perform," jokes the soft-spoken Pound. He began his career painting comic book covers and illustrations for magazines, but has since fallen into the role of the go-to guy for the barfing baby market. Heavily influenced by underground comic artists of the 1970s such as Robert Crumb and Rick Griffin, Pound's early work resembled their brand of psychedelic art.

Starting his artistic career in his late teens, Pound had a couple of semesters at the Art Center College in Hollywood in the early 1970s before deciding that he just wanted to get out and learn on the job. "I was impatient there," says Pound. "I thought I was going to take the world by storm." And while the Garbage Pail Kids were not exactly what Pound had expected to do, everything worked out for the best in the end.

The actual paintings Pound did for the GPK series were twice the printed size and were done using acrylics with some airbrush for the background. He did them in such volume and in such a short period of time that he likened himself to one of his paintings in which a kid is standing on a conveyor line, barfing into cans as they go

JOHN POUND

—Writer's note: John Pound was actually super cool, and I was excited to do the interview. He didn't seem to understand the concept of an interview though. It took us hours to get through, because I would ask him a question, he would answer, and then he'd be like, "So how about you? Tell me your story." And I kept trying to tell him, "Look, no. This is getting retarded now. No one cares about me. This is about you.

by and looking really bored. "In some ways I feel like I've had to put myself into each of those characters, almost like being an actor and feeling what it would be like to be in that situation," says Pound. "One thing I kind of felt was that a lot of these characters, even though they might be having something awful happening to them, it's almost like they're having a good time despite the situation."

The very first Garbage Pail Kid was a painting Pound had originally done for another Topps project called Wacky Packages. There is a dedicated contingent of Wacky Packages collectors that is almost as large as the GPK series posse, but they seem to be of an older generation. In 1985, Topps asked Pound, along with three other artists, to do idea sketches and a color example for a possible sticker series (which would come to be known as the Garbage Pail Kids). "I really got into it, and cranked out a lot of ideas and sketches, which ended up being the closest to what Topps wanted for the project. They asked me if I could do 44 paintings in 2 months. 'Well, I'll do my best,' I said."

Most of the cards, says Pound, are just what he feels to be the "generic kid. My mom had a nursery school when I was growing up, so I saw all these little kids around all the time as I got older, and they've kind of influenced me." However, he then goes on to explain the paintings as "rude and nasty, you know, barfing, pimples, snot, grinding up things in the meat grinder [at this point John laughs maniacally and it really scares me], being electrocuted… Sometimes they were victims, sometimes they were perpetrators."

Parents didn't think the kids sounded generic either. There was a huge backlash to the Garbage Pail Kids, which Pound was fairly oblivious to. "I guess I just wanted to entertain people," Pound says, "I look at it that way." Eventually, it was not the public reaction, but a lawsuit with the creators of the Cabbage Patch Kids that ended the Garbage Pail Kids series. However, even after being shut down, the Garbage Pail Kids retain their cult-like following to this day.

Originally printed in WYWS Issue #8

PAT THE PARTY JERK

BLING BLING
by Trevor Michaels

I was watching MTV Cribs the other day when I realized that in order to keep up with today's trendsetters, one must "bling." Everybody, everywhere is "blinging." Juvenile, and his Cash Money Millionaires, are "blinging"—their teeth, their Bentleys, their gold necklaces, their wardrobes and their studios in the basement. Kobe is "blinging"—the contracts, the house, and the clothing line. We are in a "bling-bling" era. As I sit here, sipping my Natural Light 12-ounce from a can that cost me $9.99/case, I am about to tell you how normal cheese-dicks like you and I can "bling" with the best of them on our "pennies a day" budget.

A wise frat brother once said, "Porn is always the answer, unless the question is, 'What is not the answer?'" Hence, a logical answer to the question, "How can I bling?" is porn. Yet, simply carrying around a tape of The Butt Detective or the latest issue of Over 40 (a personal favorite) will not grant you the status to "bling."

On one episode of Cribs, Dale Earnhardt Jr. stood in front of his garage and said that all of the rappers and ballers were "blinging" Mercedes and Bentleys. Then he paused, and as he lifted the garage, asked how many of those people have this in their garage, a real NASCAR. As he revved the engine, I finally understood what "blinging" was all about.

It's about having something that no else has. Now, combine that with the versatile answer "porn" and what do you get? Personal porn! Personal porn is home movies of you and your gal or flicks of your gal naked. You can take them wherever you go in your pocket, leave them in your car in the sun visor, or throw them in your wallet. As soon as you need to "bling," you simply pull them out. Pictures are also easily posted on the internet for use if that bitch ever fucks you over. All we need to do is get the girl to be comfortable with you taking the pictures. Here are some helpful tips.

1. MAKE HER FEEL LIKE A SWIM-SUIT MODEL

Compliment her appearance, body and confidence. If her toes are painted, tell her they look great. Tell her she has great lips and a radiant smile. Try and pick small things on her body to compliment so that she begins to believe that her entire body, when combined with all these little pieces, is beautiful. This will give her the confidence to bear all in a well-lighted place.

2. PRETEND TO CONFIDE IN HER

After all those compliments on her appearance, the girl is most likely thinking that all you want to do is jump her bones. You need to make the girl feel like you and her share something deeper than the physical attraction. This is usually described by chicks as "connecting." In order to "connect," I recommend letting a girl give you advice on a subject that appears very personal and sensitive. Subjects such as family, friends and future are personal favorites. Actively respond to her advice, saying things such as "You are so right" or "I am going to do that tomorrow." By then end of your chat, you should have her believing that your view of the relationship has meaning and value. Thus, when you are coercing her to let you take the photographs, it will be more believable when you say that the pictures have deeper meaning than the novelty of porn, and believe me, they will!

3. THE PURPOSE

Unless the girl is a blatant whore, then getting her to be comfortable with you taking pictures is going to take some talking. If the girl lets you take the pictures easily, the flicks probably have no "blinging" value since half the block is going to have the same pictures, comprende? You need a prepared answer to the inevitable question, "Why do you need to take naked pictures of me?" This answer is going to vary depending on the type of girl with whom you are dealing. I recommend answers such as "To remember how beautiful you are as person" or "You just look so natural at this moment.

4. THE T-FACTOR

With girls, trust is always a factor no matter what the situation. When you confided in her your deepest fear (Tip 2), you let her feel as if you trusted her. But, in order to get her to let you take pictures, she must trust you. When you promise her the pictures "will never be shown to anyone else," use a soft tone; don't act like you are engaged in an argument. If you must, tell the girl that her face does not have to be in the pictures, and then proceed to take pictures of her face anyway. (This does not work if you are using a digital camera.)

5. CLOSING THE DEAL

As soon as you feel that the girl has taken at least one step over the border, make sure to let loose the closing argument, the summation of why she should let you take the pictures. I like to call this the "Crazy, Sexy, Beautiful" approach. (Please note that this approach can be adapted to any situation that involves coercing a female.) First, tell her that it would be so cool if she did something crazy for once in her dull life. Make her believe this is that "crazy thing" which will brighten up her life (and "bling" up yours), and offer her a whole new perspective on life. Make sure she has not forgotten how sexy she is, that she has the body of a swimsuit model. Finally, re-state the trust factor by telling her how beautiful she is. Make her think that taking the pictures does not porno-tize her, but rather is a meaningful, trusting, beautiful progression in your relationship.

May personal porn be your Bentley.

Originally printed in WYWS Issue #15

THE DISTILLERS DON'T TALK

by Shawna Kenney
Photo courtesy of The Distillers

soluscrow
06/20/2001
By The way, for those that have ill to say about her, I have seen beautiful and I have seen tragically ugly... and Brody... well, Brody is Razorblade Godliness... I guess we Goths like it Rough;)

Foffle138
06/18/2001
Wuttup. When I first heard the Distillers, I thought they sounded like Rancid with Courtney Love singing instead of Tim. Then I went to see them and missed most of their set. Then I borrowed the CD... and I had them all wrong. They're really good, even though some songs sound like Brody's trying to see how much screaming she can get away with. Oh well. Cheers, keep up the good work.

Nitwit57
06/16/2001
WOW! THESE GUYS SUCK! The only reason this band is even on a label as big as this one is because that beast is married to Tim... Chick bands suck.

CHRISSPENCE15
02/19/2001
I JUST WANTED TO SAY FUCK YOU TO ALL OF YOU ASSHOLES AND POSERS OR POSEURS. I CAME HERE TO SAY EPITAPH RECORDS SUCK. ALL THE BANDS EXCEPT A FEW SUCK, DROPKICK MURPHYS AND F-MINUS ARE OK. FUCK UUUUUUUUUUUUUUUUUUUUUUUUU

Just a sampling of the daily brilliance found on the Distillers' website message board (which the band members say they are on "all the time," by the way). Regardless, if you like your punk rock crusty, bloody and oozing angst, the Distillers is your band. Singer Brody Armstrong (yes, that would be wife of Rancid guitarist Tim Armstrong) may be rich, bright and beautiful, but she's angry as hell about something and blessed with a Sid Vicious-esque voice that'll let the world know about it—in song, anyway (she's quiet in interviews).

Sick of being compared to Courtney Love, the 21-year-old singer says she was weaned on Nirvana in her home of Melbourne, Australia, claiming, "Kurt Cobain's music had more of an influence on me than Courtney's ever did." (She's not eager to talk shit about Love, however... rumor has it they may be label-mates soon...)And don't call her a riot grrl. "We play punk rock. It shouldn't be about what's down there," she says.

"It's annoying to me when a girl might look great but she can't fucking strum," she continues. "Or get a real Mohawk," laughs 18-year-old guitarist Rose. "Like the Dvotchkes from New York. They're like this punk rock oi-band with fucking mohawks three-feet long. They've got fucking tri-hawks but just got their hair and ironed it. No shaving!" laughs the Detroit native.

"That's so they can go to work and be cool on Monday," adds new drummer Andy Outbreak (also in the Nerve Agents). "I don't care, as long as you can cough up some talent to back it up," Armstrong adds.

And cough she does. Armstrong's unique vocals and Casper's three trusty chords made the band's first Hellcat Records release a sobering kick-in-the-eardrums and guarantee their follow-up will be more of the same. In the meantime, ya just have to catch 'em live (where they quite capably pull off every song, by the way). Bring earplugs. Wear your ripped Crass shirt and bondage pants. And no fake mohawks allowed.

Originally printed in WYWS Issue #15

AVAIL

by Fat Rich
Photo by Chris Boarts

Let's talk about midgets. I love midgets.
I have a friend who is afraid of midgets. He loses his mind when he sees them. He panics and shakes and almost has a heart attack. I don't really think about midgets much. What do you think about them?

I have a theory about midgets. People either love midgets or they hate midgets. If I had an army of midgets, I could create a stronghold in the northwestern part of the United States. You see, people either run away from midgets when they see them or they embrace them.
Like little footballs.

Like footballs but more like Nerf balls.
I guess your theory is OK, but I'm staying neutral like Sweden.

I think you mean Switzerland, but I'll excuse your geography.
My friend who goes into the panic attack, claims that the town he's from has an actual midget colony.

There's midget colonies everywhere.
What do you mean, a gated community for midgets?

Not a gated community, a couple of blocks where the mailboxes are shorter, the doors are shorter, things are more proportioned for midgets. They do exist.
So it's like being in Japan then?

In your bio, it mentions that you guys have actually recruited a dancer to aid your live show.
Yes, it was something that was very

tactful. We had a band meeting one day and decided that we couldn't do this on our own, we're a bunch of honkeys.

So you recruited Beau?
Yes, we pay him five dollars a day.

Now I heard a rumor that Beau has been AWOL from the Navy for the past 15 years?
Not 15, about 25 years.

So what's an average day like in Richmond, Virginia?
An average day is waking up to gunshots and people getting shot in the backyard. Dodgin' bullets on the way to the liquor store at 8 a.m. and coming home and drinking the rest on the time. When it calms down, we go sit on the front porch.

Is there anything you'd like to get off your chest?
I love you.

You love me. Look at that, I'm picking up guys. Having been from Northern Virginia, I had observed that a lot of the men from that area have a high sexual prowess?
You think?

Let's just go along with this, its make us all look good.
Yes, it's absolutely true.

But along with this, there is something missing. Some might call it intelligence.
Don't you mean teeth?

Well, that too. Isn't it strange that a band that started out as a swing cover band a la Big Bad Voodoo Daddy and Squirrel Nut Zippers, is now trying to be a punk band?
We were trying to either go pop punk because Green Day was getting popular or do the whole Dave Matthews Band thing, 'cause he's from over there in Charlottesville. But that stuffs all too technical for us, and cause we are from Virginia, we don't have much technique.

So you got rid of the whole horn section?
The horn section is gone and we hired Beau.

So what is Beau's job in the band, besides losing teeth?
Losing teeth, growing his goatee, situps, push-ups.

Would you punch an alien?
Have I? Yes, I have.

I'm not talking illegal aliens here, we're talking about aliens.
Oh, damn. No, I wouldn't. Would you?

Well it depends, if you're talking Predator aliens I'm thinking I might get my hand bit off. If it's an E.T.-type alien, I'm thinking he's no competition.
You never know. E.T. could pull out some shit on you. You gotta watch your back with E.T.

Originally printed in WYWS Issue #1

DR. KNOW OF BAD BRAINS

Interview by Gabe Banner
Photo courtesy of Bad Brains

Gary Millers, aka Dr. Know, of the legendary punk group the Bad Brains is a busy man these days. With the Bad Brains back in action under the name Soul Brains and the tribute album released, a lot of people want to talk to the Doc. Gabe Banner was lucky enough to get a few minutes of his time.

So you're a doctor?
Back in the day, when I was in high school, senior year, I had an ambition to become a medical doctor. I went to Maryland University for a semester until my financial situation wasn't able to make me go anymore. That's right around the time we hooked up the band, around 1977, 1978. Because I had more musical experience than anyone else, HR dubbed me the doctor of music. And that was it. It just stuck with me.

Who were you influenced by musically?
Being black and living in Washington, D.C., of course Go-Go music. In 1974, 1975, we used to go to the Go-Gos at the rec centers and stuff. A Hundred Years Time and EU was around then, and of course, Chuck Brown. Also Earth, Wind and Fire and Stevie Wonder and all that music that we listened to in those times and a lot of fusion stuff like Chick Corea and John McLaughlin. We just kind of sat down and as inexperienced musicians we tried to emulate. We were very analytical of our music though and we just came up with our thing.

What do you think about the state of punk rock today?
I think a lot of them be frontin' these days. All the music back in the days was a way of life. Reggae, rap, punk—now all that shit is commercial and it's like let's jump on the bandwagon. Not all the bands but as a general thing you can hear it in the music. Broth-

convicted to anything. The music was about awareness and brotherhood and sticking together and trying and bring some good things into this world. Everybody's singing about girlfriends and all that bullshit instead of about conscious things, unity. You got to realize Reagan was the president back in those days. It was different times.

How did you end up getting banned in D.C.?
It wasn't just us that was banned in D.C.—the music that they were calling punk. We had played a couple of gigs. There was a show and the show was upstairs. There was a restaurant downstairs and the gig was upstairs and in those days everybody used a pogo. They got 50 people pogoing and the floor, which was the roof of the restaurant, was bouncing and this and that and the owner was like, "Yo, you can't be doing this, "and everybody's all punked-out dress-wise and they just didn't know how to handle it. So that promoter called the next promoter and then the next one called the next one and it was like, "No, we can't be having this." D.C. was very conservative at that time. It was just what happens with anything when it's something new and people don't know how to accept it or handle it so they'd rather not deal. So they was like, no more of this music in none of the clubs. So we was like screw that, and we at that point had rented a house out in Forestville, Maryland, and it had a basement, so we said screw that, we're gonna do our own gigs, 'cause you can't stop the music.

What happened when you guys got back together for the God of Love tour?
HR bugged out, man. He couldn't handle it. For whatever reason, he just bugged out and got negative and physical. I guess he was doing something he really didn't want to be doing at that time. He said he did, and then once we

tively and you can't be doing that so it's better not to do it if brothers ain't into it. He just had to deal with his issues that he had to deal with, which we all have to do. I think he wanted to just play only reggae. We're all brothers and I think he said he wanted to do it just to do it for us. And now he's doing it for himself and not for us and that's the difference. We were supposed to do the Beasties tour on that God of Love thing when he got negative and shit and punched his brother and punched our manager Anthony. He wouldn't punch me or Darryl—he's fucking 6-foot-4 and would knock his ass out.

What happened in Kansas?
HR cracked this kid in the head with the mic stand. The kid was heckling him and then—crack. It sounds kinda funny but, you know, he could've killed that kid. That was fucked up. He got arrested for assault. The kid was pushing his buttons; he couldn't take it.

Who would win in a steel cage match of all the past Bad Brains singers?
HR, hands down.

So did you ever steal any bombs when you worked at the factory?
Damn! You got all the info! How'd you know about that?

Don't worry about it.
Yeah man, me and H. That was in Virginia. That was some heavy shit. We worked in the fabrication department making the parts for MX missiles and shit. We was rolling up in there in our punk rock gear. We had to get up out of there right quick.

Can you prescribe medicinal marijuana?
Absolutely.

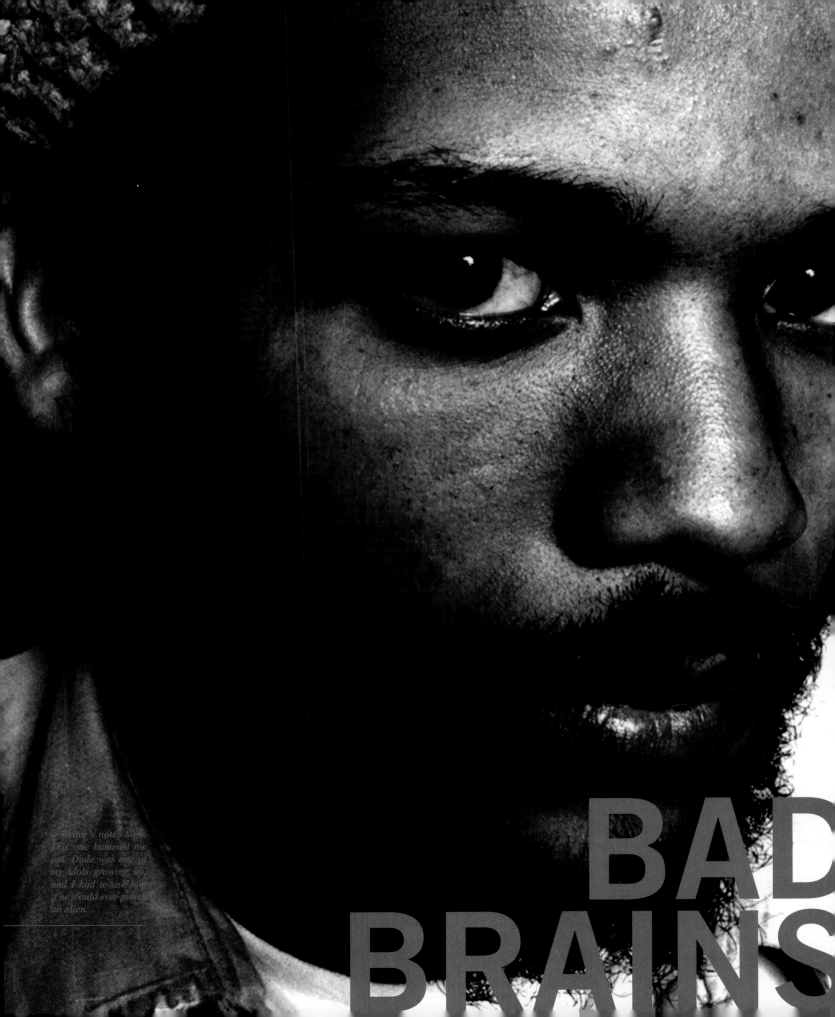

BAD
BRAINS

—*Designer's note: No.*

SEBASTIAN BACH

Interview by Gabe Onrubia
Photo courtesy of Sebastian Bach

What happened to Sebastian Bach, frontman of everybody's favorite 1980s rock band Skid Row? Gabe Onrubia finds out.

Do you still play all the Skid Row hits?
Yes. I will always do those songs because I spent 10 years of my life on them, and I didn't make them famous just to stopping playing them. I never wanted to stop, but I got kicked out of that band.

I heard you can tie your dick in a knot?
When I get on Howard Stern's show, crazy shit happens.

I'm sure you have crazy stories about the old days—girls, drugs, orgies, fights. I know you had it all.
I don't know where to start, you're asking me about 15 years of drugs, girls, fights, and it's hard to know where to begin. I can remember Axl Rose, when we were on tour with GNR, and they had rented the MGM grand plane. It doesn't even exist anymore. Back in 1991, 1992, MGM had this plane. It was the size of a 747. I kept asking him, I was like "Hey. Axl, can I come on the plane?" and he's like "Uh... maybe tomorrow." I go, "Dude, I got a big ball of opium, it's real sticky," and he goes, "Get on the fucking plane." So we were high in the sky and we didn't even leave the plane.

Are you ever gonna cut your hair?
I don't know, I just like the way it looks.

Anybody ever mistake you for a girl?
My whole life. I used to get in fights all the time at school because guys on the playground would go, "You look like a fucking girl."

You've been all around the world with this new band. How are the ladies treating you?
All the girls that were into Skid Row when we were on the 18 And Life Tour were like 12 and 13. So now they're 22. All I ever hear is, "I was too young to get into your shows but now I'm 22 and I can." The fucking crowd looks like a Victoria's Secret catalog now.

Where are you originally from?
Freeport, Bahamas. I lived there till I was six. My kindergarten picture is like 40 black kids and me. I was the only white kid in my class. I was also the tallest, so right in the middle there's this dorky white kid in the whole sea of blacks. I'm sure that probably contributed to something.

What were you doing before you were a rock star?
Trying to be a rock star. I was lead soprano in my church choir when I was a little boy. I've always been singing.

What did you do with all your money? Did you blow it like MC Hammer?
I didn't have as much as him. To tell you the truth, the business matters in Skid Row meant that there were so many people taking a cut from that band, I get paid more to headline JAXX with my solo band than Skid Row got when we were playing giant stadiums in front of 75,000 people. I don't know where the fuck all that money went, but it wasn't to us.

If you ever feel like getting laid, do you just go out?
I am a married man. I fuck my wife, but we aren't against threesomes. We don't fuck around on each other but there have been other people

in our bed with us. We keep things pretty wild.

That's good, an open marriage.
It's not open unless we're both in the room.

What's the stupidest thing you've ever bought?
That's easy, my first car. I was like 21, and I went to my accountant and was like, "I'm gonna get a car," and he goes, "Get whatever you want." So I go, "What do you mean?" and he goes, "Get what the fuck you want." I go, "Can I get like a Benz?" and he goes, "Go ahead." So I go into this Benz dealership and pick out a 560 SE sedan, four-door, fuckin' grey leather interior. 90,000 bucks. I fuckin' bought this fuckin' thing and I was paying four-grand a month on payments and insurance and I could have bought a house like in the Bahamas or something. That was really dumb. Really stupid.

Do you still have that?
Fuck no. I traded that in for a Jag and then I smashed the Jag into a guardrail on the New Jersey Turnpike, turned it into dust. There is no grosser sound than a silver-blue jaguar crumpling into the fucking guardrail. It sounds like a chandelier being smashed with a baseball bat.

Are women still flashing their titties at you?
Yes.

Are your band mates gonna be getting laid tonight?
I would assume so.

Do you prefer weed or coke?
I don't do coke. I hate it. I love weed. I smoke it as much as possible. But not before I go on stage, afterwards.

Have you ever been to jail?
Many times. I'm a convicted felon for assault and battery. I was up for 30 years, and I've been arrested for swearing on stage. I got assault with a deadly weapon. I kicked a guy in the face with my boots, they had three-inch heels on them and if you kick someone in the face with heels it is considered assault with a deadly weapon. It's called "shod foot." I got busted for shod foot.

If you went to jail, would you cut your hair?
I think they would.

Rumor has it that back in the day you had all these tassels on your jacket and they could hear you jerking off on the top bunk of the tour bus because the tassels would jingle.
Probably. Is there a guy on the planet that doesn't jack off? If there was no lubrication, I would use some strawberry yogurt.

Healthy.
Fragrant as well.

Do you still own the "AIDS Kills Fags Dead" shirt?
No, I donated that to the asshole hall of fame.

I heard that Jani Laine from Warrant called you soft?
Hey, man, he's the god of rock, so he's entitled to make his judgments. If only I could be as hard as "Cherry Pie," then I'd be doing' something, right?

Do you think I'm attractive?
Yes.

SEBASTIAN BACH

KURUPT
by Sean McMillan
Photo courtesy of Kurupt

The day I went to interview Kurupt, it poured. This really cramped my style in terms of making a good first impression, because I arrived at Black Entertainment Television (BET) soaking wet. Luckily, though, BET was in such disarray when I arrived that I had to wait a good hour before I even saw Kurupt's manager. By this time, I was dry, but wrinkled. I was escorted to the Green Room. Actually, "green" was purely euphemistic. It was covered in plates of old food, spilled drinks and pasta, all of which had been trampled into the carpet to render an effect that I can only describe as "brown." At least it made me feel better about my wrinkled clothes.

The Green/Brown Room was occupied by Mama Kurupt, who was laden with jewels, and Papa Kurupt, a heavyset man who was kicking back and watching the TV. I excused myself from this domestic bliss, and continued through BET's studios. On one of the sets, the filming for Rap City, starring Kurupt, was going on. I crept onto the set, not wanting to disturb the chaos of lights and directors and extras and cameramen, but the second I came into view, everyone stopped and stared at me. There was a moment of complete silence. I used this time to ponder whether they were staring because I was the only white person in the room, or whether they were admiring my T-shirt, emblazoned with "Pussy Rules."

For Kurupt, at least, it was the shit. As we walked back to the Green/Brown Room, he agreed wholeheartedly. "Baby, I love it when a girl eats another girl's coochie. It's better than drugs." Damn right. I decided we were off to a good start. With Mama and Papa Kurupt sitting next to us, and Kurupt's plane leaving in just over an hour, I got the interview underway.

Since we were on the topic of sex, I asked him when he'd had his first taste of coochie. "When I was twelve. Wilt the Stilt ain't fucking with me." Considering that Mr. Chamberlain is rumored to have bagged over 30,000 chicks, I was impressed. Since Wilt ended up dying of AIDS, I also expressed some concern. Not to worry. Kurupt is strictly a Trojan man.

Now 27, Kurupt spent his early youth in Philadelphia. Then, as a teenager, he stole a car and ended up in L.A. Cali was good to him. "Guns are real easy to get there. You just go out on the street, and holler at your homies, 'Let me get on of those pieces.' I was 17 when I got my first gun." Surprisingly, the police haven't completely approved of Kurupt's lifestyle, and he's landed in jail several times. Today, he doesn't even drive. "The police pull you over too much." This was disappointing. No hydraulics for Kurupt? "Switches, naw, the youngsters and the Gs get that, man. I can't be in the streets now or I'd either be dead or killing everybody."

Since I'd already met his mother and father, I inquired about any children. He told me that he had two daughters, but before I could ask if they were cute, he cut me off with "I'm just gonna beat up on anybody that wants to be their boyfriend." I suggested chastity belts, but he had a better solution. "Any guy that tries, I'll stick my little brother Dave on them, man, David will beat them to death." Good old Uncle Dave.

Having covered sex and family, we moved right onto drugs. Kurupt is intimately acquainted with that scene. His first drug experience was when he was 13. Since then, he's moved from weed to mushrooms to ecstasy. "But that's as high on the food chain as I go, brother." His drug of choice is weed. He's not a purist, though, and prefers to buy it rather than grow it, since it's easier. If given the chance to design any drug, he's decided to call his Oral Sex. "It would make you feel the biggest and baddest ever. It would sort of feel like ecstasy, but it wouldn't drop you down so hard afterwards. The after effect would be beautiful. Make you feel as good as if you were high on 15 orange joints, and it wouldn't harm you, either." I'm waiting for production to start.

In case you aren't familiar with his music, Kurupt keeps it real and sticks to the basic topics. Actually, topic, but I'm sure it's one you can all relate to. "I love it when they be eatin' coochie. Ain't nothing like a bad bitch that's eatin' cunt. I walk into this place called Peanuts out in L.A. Man, this girl steps up to be and says, 'Oh my God! Snoop Dogg and Tha Dogg Pound! What are you doing here? I'm trying to get some pussy, myself.' I said, 'What the fuck, I like you.'" He ended the story there, but I couldn't help thinking that more interesting things happened that night. It can't be bad, living in Kurupt's shoes.

Since he had a plane to catch, we had to wrap it up there. Kurupt left me with some parting pearls of wisdom. "Some people are addicted to drugs, some are into girls. But hos ain't really an addiction, they're more like a pleasure. They're a self-gratifying vocation. It's a way to make money, and it can be whatever you want it to be to ya." Sound words of advice.

For more tips, check out his new album, Tha Streetz is a Mutha, out now on Antra records.

KURUPT

Working on WYWS back in the late 1990s and forward was a bit like painting in the streets. There were just no rules. You want to make a collage with graffiti, roadkill and gory comics? Cool. Porn stars, crackheads, dumb-ass antics—all fair game. Keep in mind this was a few years before shows like Jackass appeared.

I think Roger's life experience, growing up in the D.C. punk rock and graff scenes, mixed with his laid-back open-mindedness, made this freedom of expression and content possible. I know as time went on, the magazine made changes to its direction, but at its core, WYWS was always an I-don't-give-a fuck publication.

—SICK156

GARY
COLEMAN

SHAWNA KENNEY FINDS OUT HE'S STILL THE MAN

by Shawna Kenney
Photo courtesy of Gary Coleman

Diff'rent Strokes moved my world, baby. Nothing could tear me away from it (not even my racist uncle who wouldn't let us watch it at his house because of the interracial family! Grrr!). Every week (and during reruns years after), I tuned in to see what mischief Arnold, Willis and Kimberly would get into. Whether Arnold was getting caught eavesdropping, or Kimberly was teaching that bigot she had to go to prom with a lesson, week after week, we watched and laughed hysterically at those five predictable little words that came out of little Arnold's mouth: "What you talkin' about, Willis?"

No one could have predicted such an unfortunate real-life outcome for the cast. Little did we know that Willis (Todd Bridges) would end up in jail on cocaine possession, Arnold (Gary Coleman) would get sued for slapping an out-of-control fan, and Kimberly (Dana Plato) would rob a video store, pose for *Playboy* and eventually die of a drug overdose in the late 1990s. Ah, such is the life of child stars, we've learned. Life is not as innocent as those *Diff'rent Strokes* years. But we sure did enjoy 'em.

We met at RJ's Ribs in Beverly Hills (Gary's choice). He kept us waiting a good 45 minutes and for a while I was afraid my childhood idol had stood me up. Just as I was about to curse the show and the day Norman Lear created it, Gary came running in, just as short and cute as ever. I walked over to him and extended my hand. A smile crept across his face, then faded when he looked at Rich and asked me, "Is that your boyfriend?" I said, "Yes," and finished introductions. Gary seemed displeased that I'd brought another man along. We found a table in the back and Gary ordered his "Bucket of Bones" and a bib from the waitress and just began talking away.

I handed him a copy of *While You Were Sleeping* and my book, *I Was a Teenage Dominatrix*, and he read the title out loud. "*I Was a Teenage Dominatrix*? How come I couldn't meet you then? And before boyfriend?" he asks, pointing at Rich. "He's actually not a bad-looking guy, though," he adds. How nice, Arnold approves. I assure Arnold that my boyfriend is a great guy, and then ask him if he's ever been to see a dominatrix himself. Gary seems appalled. "No. I would not pay. For free is one thing. Paying for it is completely another." He looks at the *WYWS* for a moment and offers a few words on graffiti: "Just like there's noise pollution, that's eye-pollution! Graffiti should be outlawed. It should be heavily fined. There should be separate jails just for graffiti artists so the real criminals can go into the real jails. Graffiti artists should be made to clean up their work. Maybe the cities that have this problem should have walls they can draw on so normal, working people don't have to look at an eyesore."

We're off to a good start. The conversation turns back to domination and then strip clubs and Gary goes on and on about prostitution and how it shouldn't be legal because women are equal and men should not be able to buy another human being. He's more of a prude than I thought! I tell him I'm a huge fan of the old show and he says that huge fans never sought him out to date him, and that although a company named Ugo recently auctioned off a date with him (the winner, a 6-foot-2 former model, paid $4,000 for the privilege),"Nothing happened there, either." He says the press was everywhere and nothing could ever happen on a date like that. Understandable, but what about the rumor that he's a 32-year-old virgin? "Still a virgin and counting," he laughs.

"I DON'T BELIEVE IN [ONE-NIGHT STANDS] AT ALL. THAT'S DANGEROUS AND YOU CAN CATCH A DISEASE THAT WAY."

He says that state of affairs is "accidental," and came about because he went through the "girls are icky" stage until he was 13. After that, he was just too busy working, which left him with no time to devote to a girl. Now he says he's decided that if a woman can't fit her busy schedule around his busy schedule, a relationship just won't happen. Plus, "Women just don't pay attention to me," he says matter-of-factly. He adds that he's too short for most women and "too tall for the rest."

He's resigned himself to being single, and calls marriage a "way for women to get into your pocket." How sad. My Arnold all alone with no prospects for getting any? Ever?! Perhaps a one-night stand with the right woman? "No, I don't believe in that at all," he snaps. "That's dangerous and you can catch a disease that way." But then he tells me he'd jump on me "in a second" if "that big guy with blonde hair wasn't sitting there."

So there's no woman in his life. He says he spends most of his time working his two jobs—one as a morning radio DJ for a station in Tuscon, Arizona, and the other as a video-game reviewer for Ugo, (the company that set up the date and also auctioned off many of Gary's possessions for a grand total of $15,000). "They wanted to help me with that, and I thank them for it," is all he says of the deal. He is still estranged from his parents, who he says are the ones, with the help of his management, who ruined him financially. Reportedly, he earned a total of almost $18 million during the *Diff'rent Strokes* years, which made him, at one point, the highest-paid child actor of all time. Where did it all go? "47 percent was divvied up between six people, before 35 percent taxes. There ain't gonna be a lot of $18 million left after you divide that up," he says.

Speaking of money, one would assume his parents must still be well-off from all that loot. He says that they claim they're not, but he suspects that they have a "Swiss bank account some-where." Since they were his adoptive parents, I ask if he's ever searched for his biological ones. "I did it once, and the only person they found was some crazy lunatic. It's not a concern or part of my adult life. I've always been my rock... and will continue to be. "

As a result of his two kidney transplants, he still has dialysis three times a week. He says that this is a pain in the ass, but doesn't affect his ability to work or take care of himself. There are no plans for a third transplant. "Having a kidney is like having a pet, and I don't like pets," says the rock. Surprisingly, because this is something I have always worried about, it seems that his height only interferes with his love life. He drives a 4x4 truck with no special devices (just a pillow), and is able to reach the top shelf of grocery stores with a little method he calls scaling (stepping on the bottom shelf).

Of his former co-stars, he says, "Todd's life is very much on-track with his wife and his kid and that makes me proud." He hadn't spoken to Dana for years before her death (he thought her *Playboy* spread was nice, though he vehemently denied ever jerking off to it), and his main concern seems to be for her teenage son. "I hope her son is cared for and loved and looked after by people who are considering his needs," he says. Apparently, Plato's son wants to act and Coleman, consider-ing his own misfortune, has "nothing but red flags for that." He hopes that the boy will get into the business in the "proper way, as opposed to being screwed by every adult out there that wants to take advantage of the fact that he's her son."

Photo by Dave Shubert

For now, Gary lives a basically unfettered existence in L.A. He says he's carved out a niche for himself here and knows the places he can go without being harassed by fans. His only vices are model trains, video games, off-roading, bowling and miniature golfing. Though he gets knocked out in the new Kid Rock video, he says he could kick Kid Rock's ass "easily," and could do the same to Emmanuelle Lewis as well (aka the kid who played Webster, whom he says he met several times during those golden years but hasn't heard from in years). Much to my envy, he says he also visited the *Silver Spoons* set several times but "that train was never working."

He adds that doing *Diff'rent Strokes* was fun, but that the last four years were hell. "Conrad Bane [Mr. Drummond] had the show written for him. It was called *45 Minutes From Harlem* at the time. Everyone auditioned except me—they flew me in to do it. We were just supposed to be a mid-season replacement. Had I had any idea of what I was doing to my life I would've said, 'Wait a minute, we've gotta talk about this.' But it was too late. A lot of people were making money and getting fat, dumb and happy."

The famed "whatchootalkin'bout" line was something the writers came up with for Gary and he says he's sorry he ever did it that way and will "never ever do the line in a show again" because he hates it. He prays they don't start showing re-runs of *Diff'rent Strokes*, especially since his residuals aren't worth anything anyway.

He doesn't even watch TV at all these days. He's been offered an array of interesting jobs, from professional wrestling (WWF and WCW) to porno roles, and he's turned them all down. Be-

ing a security guard was what paid the bills for a few years. "Income is income," he says. "I actually liked being a security guard. It made me feel useful. But I haven't been able to do that because that woman, Tracy Fields [the autograph-seeking fan he hit], caused my license to be pulled."

He says the Fields case is ongoing, and he's sure he'll have to pay a fine. "She was being obnoxious and out of line, and had I not been a celebrity she'd be lying in an alley somewhere," he says of the incident. "As celebrities, we don't get to defend ourselves or our honor." Later on, he says, "It was a great day in my life when that show got cancelled." Aww, too bad Gary didn't enjoy the episodes as much as I and millions of other kids did. Considering everything, he turned out to have the least scandalous life of all three kids on the show. He ended up with a pretty good head on his shoulders as well.

Gary licks each finger and removes his bib, and our brief encounter is over before I know it. We hug goodbye and he's out the door in a flash, hurrying to meet an electrician who is coming to work on a broken electric train at his house. I wonder if we'll ever meet again. I wonder if I should've given him my phone number so that he and Rich and I could all be friends. I'm wondering if this was real at all. Was I really just hanging out with my childhood idol? I look down and see my auto-graphed Polaroids and the bill, and then I know it wasn't a dream. Ribs are expensive.

Originally printed in WYWS Issue #9

—Editor's note: I have been obsessed with Gary Coleman my whole life. I wanted to feature him in WYWS, but he wasn't doing much with his life at the time, and he wasn't easy to dig up. Miraculously, Shawna found him, and I was psyched to say the least. The Big GC and I developed a long-standing relationship, and I wish I could find the emails where we would go back and forth about writing an advice column for WYWS. A year or so later, I got the idea—probably the best idea I had in my entire life—of renting Gary Coleman to go to the Magic tradeshow with us to promote WYWS. That little fuck thought he was going to Magic: The Gathering, and when Sean picked him up at the airport in a big suburban filled with chicks, Gary kept trying to get them to take their shirts off. During Magic, Gary worked hard and pushed WYWS to the masses. The few days with him were priceless. I will cherish the moments forever.

Photo by Patrick Hoelck

I wish I could tell you I had good memories of writing for *While You Were Sleeping* but I don't. And it's not that I have any bad memories either, I just really have no memories at all about a great many things in my life from that time period. As I mention in my book, *Skinema*, I was hooked to the gills on pills, generally blacked out and drunk for the better part of a decade. It's a real shame because seeing some of the photos of myself with actresses, porn stars and whores from those days it seems like I had a really good time. It's a good thing I wrote so much otherwise I'd have no way to look back on any of it. And even that doesn't help jog many memories.

When Roger sent me a PDF of some interviews I'd done that he wanted me to talk about I emailed him back and said, "Roger, I didn't write these. I've never interviewed Danzig." He replied, "But your name is on it, Chris. I'm certain you did it."

I was not so certain. But indeed, my name was on it. So unless someone was impersonating me and spelling their name with a silly hip-hop dollar sign like I used to, I must have written it. Sadly, I can offer you no insight on the material.

Only one thing stands out in my mind when I think of *WYWS*: interviewing Cerina Vincent, the beautiful former Power Ranger and star of *Not Another Teen Movie*. My memory is not of what we discussed or how she looked or how we may or may not have had some alcohol-induced chemistry, it is about getting my second DUI after leaving her company.

Back then, when I was drinking and driving (which was pretty regularly), I'd always take back roads home, but that night I took La Brea, then Wilshire then Western because it was around Halloween and Burger King had all *The Simpsons* Halloween Kids meal toys and I only needed the Lisa Simpson in the ghost costume to have all of them. So despite knowing better, I took three of the busiest main roads home, hitting three Burger Kings and all they had were fucking Apu toys.

The cops pulled me over in front of my favorite Mexican restaurant, El Cholo. I remember watching the waitresses in their festive attire all coming out to watch me attempt the sobriety field tests. I very much wanted to order a margarita.

I'm not sure what's more comical/sad to think about: the fact that the legal limit is a .08 BAC and I blew exactly .08 on the nose; that I got stopped and arrested just a few blocks from my house; or that the only reason I was on the heavily patrolled Western Ave. at all was because I was hunting Simpsons toys at Burger Kings.

I spent the weekend in the Downtown L.A. jail with gangbangers and murderers. One fellow showed up covered in someone else's blood and never washed it off. Another gentleman was so out of his mind he forgot to (chose not to?) pull down his pants when he squatted to shit. Three days the cell smelled of his lovely aroma.

Ever since, I've pretty much hated both Lisa Simpson and Apu.

—*Chris Nieratko*

Jelly's biggest disappointment in writing for *WYWS* is that he never got laid from it. That was *WYWS*'s initial pitch to Jelly, a once-successful and very horny Los Angeles writer, who lived (and lives) for the sweet hope of strange.

"*WYWS* is the dopest mag out there," Jelly was informed in the parlance of the times. "Once the bitches know you is Jelly, you be scorin' mad pussy, yo."

Alas, said trim was never delivered. This, despite the fact that Jelly interviewed porn stars aplenty in a wildly popular series for *WYWS* that involved cooking, playing Lite Brite, and slipping into a hot tub half nude to play chess with various L.A. video vixens.

Jelly even recalls with great anxiety two blonde, girly-girl celluloid sluts disrobing and making Rice Krispy squares *au naturel* in his kitchen for the series.

Imagine: Two of the most attractive bimbettes in the XXX stratosphere, licking marshmallow cream off each other's silky skin, and Jelly forced to watch without ever being offered a taste!

Which is why Jelly is currently suing *WYWS* in federal court for breach of contract, emotional distress, and medical and other expenses incurred by a near-fatal case of blueballs, causing Jelly to seek relief in various Asian massage parlors and Tantric goddess temples, which has left him nearly penniless.

Adding insult to injury, Jelly now has to read about graff-gal TRIBE's tantalizing escapades with some other chick on that Bret Michaels reality show *Rock of Love*.

Indeed, Jelly became so distraught by the fact that this unthankful little minx never even bothered to give him a handjob (which would have made Jelly quite happy, BTW) that he immediately self-medicated with a bottle of vodka and a handful of Percocets, seeking the ultimate oblivion.

But death be not proud, or even successful. Jelly now pens this diatribe from the bowels of a mental institution in Barstow, California, where he is regularly juiced to keep him from dreaming of all the cooze *WYWS* promised but never made good on.

Damn your skateboard-lovin' graffiti-encrusted hide, *WYWS*! Jelly will see your ass in court.

That is, just as soon as he finishes one final round of electroshock treatments for the road.

—*Jelly*

WYWS was my coming-of-age story. I was but a simple 19-year-old college kid when I got a call one day from my mom, who had gone to pick up her dry-cleaning and spotted the "interns wanted" sign in the magazine's storefront window. I had never heard of *WYWS*, but she thought I would like it because it was, in her words, "cool and kinda fucked up."

Like any good internship, it was a learning experience. I learned that professionalism means being prepared to work under any conditions, like returning from a three-bong-hit lunch only to throw on a giant foam hot dog hat and head off to meet the Oscar Meyer Weinermobile for a guerrilla promotional standoff. Or getting blackout drunk to prepare yourself for the misery of eating Spam straight out of the can, and then mustering just enough brain stem consciousness to write about it.

I learned the proper phone etiquette for talking to porn stars and brothel owners. I learned how to have meaningful philosophical debates, which somehow always ended up being about Gary Coleman.

Mainly, though, I learned how to be OK with various degrees of creepiness. A typical day consisted of researching topics like virginity and serial killers (sometimes in conjunction with one another), reading fan mail from federal inmates and listening to the then-23-year-old Roger say things like, "I haven't touched any 16-year-old girls since I was 22." I hope that was true then, and even more so I hope it's true now. But if not, I guess I'm OK with that.

—*Simon Steinhardt*

ROGER LODGE
THE BLIND DATE HOST GETS PUT TO THE TEST.
Interview by Intern Devorah Klein
Photo courtesy of Roger Lodge

Where would you take me on our date, the airport or a hotel lobby?
I would say the airport because there are so many different levels of emotions there. Sometimes it's the happiest place in the world, and sometimes it's the saddest. I mean, it's just an amazing exploration of human emotion. God, that must be the biggest hunk of crap I've ever said in my life.

So we're at the airport and we run into my ex. What do you do?
I would do whatever is appropriate at the time. Obviously, I'd say hello because that is part of your past. I would just say, "Hi," and move on.

They say that every girl's crazy for a sharp-dressed man. What will you wear on our date?
Armani. Gotta be Armani.

That night, we go to a costume party and I really want to win. What's your winning idea, Roger?
I would dress up as the San Diego Chicken.

I'm not into "ethnic" food. Where do you take me to eat?
The Target snack bar.

We're eating at this Target snack bar and I go to the bathroom. I'm gone for 20 minutes, what am I doing?
Good question. You're calling your friends to tell them what a great time you're having with me.

I'm turned on by sports statistics. Talk dirty to me.
Uh, sports statistics. Uhhh, shit, I don't know how to answer that. Um, shit, I don't know, skip that one.

Fine, but there will be no more skipping, Rog.
OK.

You're an astronaut and I'm the moon. What do you do when you land on me for the first time?
Explore the undiscovered.

Suppose you are the ex-host of a talk show called *Sci-Fi Vortex*. What's the final frontier... on our first date?
Some place with a view, a merlot and a great conversation.

I'm the hoop and you're the basketball. How do you score?
I'd take my time and run the offense. It's not necessarily scoring that's important, it's how you play the game. Anybody can score if you give them enough time.

Are you the kind of guy that likes long walks on the beach or dry humping on the couch?
Long walks on the beach, without question.

So you and I are dry humping on the couch—are you having fun?
I would never insult you by trying to dry hump you on a date.

Rog, you have won my heart. I'll be the one at the Target snack bar wearing a chicken suit, and remember, you're wearing Armani.

Originally printed in WYWS Issue #14

BLIND DATE
by Ian Sattler
Photo courtesy of Ian Sattler

One of the best parts about writing for WYWS was that Roger had such an "anything goes" mentality towards content. I think when he realized that the magazine could evolve from just covering graffiti a light went off in his head that he could do whatever the fuck he wanted. And if he could do whatever the fuck he wanted, then we could do whatever the fuck we wanted. It was just a case of if it was cool it'd make it into print. This was great because it lead to that random vibe WYWS had and certainly kept us entertained and readers on their toes. We were all pretty much willing to do anything if it was funny, and knowing that it'd end up in WYWS only egged us all on further. For me personally, my favorite example of this mentality was when I ended up on the TV show Blind Date.

I was sitting in my office in Los Angeles one day, shortly after I'd started contributing to WYWS on a full-time basis, and I got a message from somebody saying they're calling from Blind Date. This show was on TV all the time back then and I assumed it was a joke until the woman mentioned that my friend Tammy had given them my name. Tammy is wonderfully insane, drunk and a pioneer in the field of copping prescription speed. She'd been pulled off the street in Santa Monica to audition for the show and I guess freaked out the staff so much that they asked if she had any friends like her (i.e. "crazy") that might be willing to come in. She gave them my number, and refusing to be outdone by her, I immediately set an audition time.

My game plan going in was to just unleash as much sleaze and testosterone on them as I could to show why I'd make for good TV. I then proceeded to lie about being in AA to the woman doing the pre-interview so we could bond over our experiences getting sober. That got me through to the on-camera test where I explained that I had the stigmata tattooed on my feet because I have a Jesus complex and I closed the deal with an analogy comparing women to cats in their inability to make up their minds and also my ability to own and domesticate both. I was told I'd be out on a "date" in a few weeks. I called WYWS on my way out of the building.

I spent 12 fucking hours filming what would be cut down to half of an episode. They attempted to pair me with what they thought was my opposite to create filmable conflict. I ended up with a Southern Belle who had an audio version of the Bible on the front seat of her car. You quickly realize that you aren't on a date but some sort of demented field trip with an entire crew and two cars. The crew was just as much a part of the day as the girl. We spent tons of time between segments standing around, going to get ice cream, arguing over directions to the park where the girl and I was supposed to be filmed blowing bubbles together. At one point, my date got into an argument with the African American camera man where she said something sort of rude and he made a comment about how where she came from her people would have chained his family to rocks. I missed all of this because I was smoking with the sound guy and listening to stories about when he worked on The Real World: New Orleans. She filed a complaint the next day with the show and I never heard from her again. On the other hand, I still play in a Fantasy Football league with the guy who was the field producer that day. My episode ended up being pretty boring aside from the animated Boba Fett action figure they put in, but it was a fucking awesome run that, like so many other things, was fueled by a desire to get up in WYWS.

CHRI$ NIERATKO DROOLS OVER WENDI KNIGHT

Photos courtesy of Wendi Knight

Porn stars are a special breed. Most people would never consider changing their image, surgically altering their body or giving up their beliefs for their jobs. For the women of the adult film world, this is generally the case. Just today, I was told Houston had her labia cut and tucked and her implants redone. Don't get me wrong, I love porn chicks, but sometimes enough is enough. I guess that's what excited me about Wendi Knight. Sure, she's had her tits done—who hasn't?—but there's something really authentic about her. The more I talked to her, the more it became apparent. Wendi is a small-town Texan, who went through home schooling and married the first guy she slept with. She likes doing porn, but is not really into the image or the fan signings. She's had sex with two guys in her personal life, and not many more on screen. And that's probably what makes her great. She's a part-time slut who looks like Carmen Electra and her favorite thing to do when not working is... fishing. And she loves to get drunk. Sounds almost too good, doesn't it?

How did you get into porn?
Seymore Butts and Shane were making an appearance at a club in Dallas. I used to watch her movies all the time so I went to see her perform. I ended up becoming friends with them. I called them because I was going to Vegas. Seymore and Shane had broken up and he said come over and stay at his house for the week and if I wanted to shoot I could, but if I didn't, then no big deal. So I did. I was married.

How did your husband take to that?
He loved it—which is why we're not married anymore. The first one I did, I was so freaked out by it. When I got married, that was the only person I'd ever slept with. The second person I ever slept with was on film. It was a big shock to my little system.

Two months later, I started dancing at the club. I would just come out and do a movie here and there. When I was dancing, I was making bank, and he was like, "I wanna quit, I wanna travel with you." That was a bad idea.

How did you meet the guy you're with now?
I met him through some good friends of mine that were in the business and he runs Metro.

It's safe to assume that he's fine with what you're doing.
I'm not doing guys anymore, only girls. That was my decision. I think I freaked out about the disease thing. Everyone's going back to no condoms and that makes me nervous.

The first scene you ever did was a DP?
Yep, with Mark Davis and Tom Byron, no condoms, just an hour-and-forty-five minutes of anal. It was crazy. It was a Seymore movie called *Behind the Sphincter Door*.

What was that like? Only having sex with your husband then going and doing a DP with strangers?
It was definitely a change. I did the DP and I didn't do one for a really long time. I kinda blocked it out. I really don't remember a whole lot of it, which can't be healthy. I was like, I'm never doing that again. The one time was cool, and then, of course, Seymore calls me four months later, "Hey I want you to come shoot," and I'm like, "OK."

What is it that sucks you back in?
The thing was that when I was growing up I went to home schooling and was really protected. I was totally such a dork, and this was something different. Even more than the money. People always think that you must have tons and tons of money, but the money's not that great.

WOW... WENDI!

Are you ever out having dinner and get noticed by people?
Not at dinner, I've been in the grocery store or some place like that, but they're always really cool. When I danced, I'd get it all the time. I would dance during the day and we had 12 girls and the girls almost all hated me because I did my boobs.

It seems like in both professions girls are very catty. You must get it even worse dating Mr. Metro and suddenly your face is on box covers.
Pretty much everyone in the business is, which is something I hate. They're so nice to me, but I think it's because of [Mr. Metro]. I don't like that because I never know who's being real and who isn't.

Where I come from, if you don't like someone, you tell them or just don't deal with them.
None of my family knows. They're really religious, Southern Baptist. If they ever find out, I will just die. Actually, the only one I really care about is my grandmother. I don't want her to know 'cause she's so old. I never even told her I was dancing. I can just see what she pictures a strip club as, and it's nothing like that. No one in my family that I know of would ever watch porn or anything like that so I am probably pretty safe, but don't speak too soon.

Is Mr. Metro psyched you made the decision not to do guys anymore?
When we first started goin' out, I was like if you have a problem with it just tell me now because I don't want it to blow up later. He was like, "No, that's what you were doing when I met you," so I was like, "OK, cool." Then I started having a problem with it. I didn't want to do guys anymore. Then I had a problem that he didn't have a problem with it. I quit for eight months. I didn't do anything. I needed to go back to work and he was like, "Well, I don't want you to do guys anymore." I was really happy.

You said you wanted to have kids. Let's say you have a boy and in high school he finds one of your pornos, how are you gonna explain that?
I'd just be honest. With a boy I think it would be easier for me because with a girl I wouldn't want her to do that. It would be hard for me to explain to her that I did this, but it's not OK for her to. I think with a boy it would be easier. Just pawn him off on dad, let him explain it.

You're gonna have to say something when he sees a guy that's not daddy with his dick up your ass.
I don't know what I'd say. I would probably get kicked out of the PTA for sure. Hopefully, if he's seeing that, he's at least 16 or 17. I don't think I would lie, I think I would tell him. Even if he didn't understand, you know in 10 years it's going to blow over.

What does your mom think you're doing out here?
My mom and I don't talk a lot. She's very controlling and what she says goes, so we don't get along very well. She hates it because she's really nosy and she doesn't know anything that's going on in my life. My grandmother actually raised me most of the time. She thinks I am here with Greg, and she likes Greg.

What does Greg do in her eyes?
What was the lie? Some kind of magazine or something. I don't know. He just met everybody at Christmas. I was sitting in the corner of my Christmas party just laughing my ass off because I just threw him in the fire and I am like, "Tell 'em what ever you want to." He's great, he's such a bullshitter. He did good. I was very proud. I sat him in the living room and went to go chat. My cousin who is a home missionary sat down next to him.

What's the worst thing that's ever happened to you on the set?
I have had some bad situations but nothing really bad ever happened. I'm really freaky about stuff. If anything ever happened that was really gross, I think I would be devastated. If I have to do an anal scene, I never eat.

Do you poop regularly?
Yes, at every meal. I think that's a good thing. I think that's why I stay skinny.

After lots of anal sex, do you not need to use lube anymore?
I never use it. I'm a spit person. That's so gross, right? I never need it, never. I get so turned on. For scenes yeah, but not at home.

What do you think the best part of this job is?
How easy it is because even if I did work on a regular basis, I would only work five days a month. It can't get any easier than that.

What's your wildest unfulfilled fantasy?
What I really want is a live-in girlfriend. Someone who's my best friend, really cool and low maintenance. I want someone like that. Not even to have sex with Greg, just have sex with me. I want her to be there when I get home to hang out and have sex with me and the dogs. I'm just kidding. I want someone a little younger, maybe 12, I'm just kidding. Just someone who'll just fuck me like crazy.

When you have girls at home do you share with Mr. Metro?
He just gets blowjobs, never anything else. Isn't that sweet!

Originally printed in WYWS Issue #10

—Designer's note: Whoops!

JELLY'S QUEST FOR A CHICK CALLED TRIBE

Portrait by Carlos Batts
Graffiti photos courtesy of TRIBE

It's close to 1 a.m. on a Wednesday night, and I'm sitting in the Del Taco at Highland and Santa Monica in L.A., waiting for this chick called TRIBE. They tell me she's a legend. And if I'm to believe half of all the rumors out there about her, they're probably right. First off, she's supposed to be fearless. There are tales of her walking up to buses in the middle of the day, dressed in high-heels and a short skirt, turning the city's wheels into a rolling ad for herself. And there's more than one story going around about how she's done throwups right in front of the police and then talked her way out of it by batting her big brown eyes at Mr. Charlie until he let her off with a warning.

"If you're a graffiti writer and you know what's up, you know TRIBE," a San Diego graffiti writer told me. "She's a bomber, dude. That's all there is. I was at a writers' convention in Arizona, and I did a fuckin' five-color piece, my shit was rocking. TRIBE didn't give a fuck. She just did a throwup right next to me. She's ghetto, dude."

I emailed TWIST in San Francisco, and in a terse message, he confirmed TRIBE's status. "I have heard of her," wrote TWIST, whose work can be seen everywhere from the alleys of San Fran and New York to the cover of *Juxtapoz* and the walls of the galleries and museums. "And she is quite legendary."

The streets of Los Angeles scream her name on overpasses and billboards, rooftops and walls—in places you'd never expect a girl to have the *huevos* to creep and crawl—there's TRIBE's mark. Sure, she gets points for doing what the guys do in a mainly male-dominated game, but even if she had it hangin', she'd still get mad props. Hell, check the notorious L.A. crews she runs with: MSK and TKO.

Some other TRIBE rumors: She was in the pen under a false name; she's been in jail in Tijuana; she's been known to knock boots on rooftops; she has a handful of sugar daddies; she drinks like a sailor; she racks spraypaint from stores; she has three cars; and on and on.

Most of these sound like the products of overactive imaginations, high-testosterone levels, the lack of getting laid, or all three. Some are true. Some are false. Some remain tantalizing possibilities. All of them are part of the TRIBE mystique, and none of them would be out there if she weren't a great writer.

"A lot of guys won't admit that a woman kicks much ass," explained TOOMER, TKO's founder and eminence grise. "Fuck it, dude, I admit she kicks some ass. She gets spots that make motherfuckers' balls go in. Real scary-ass spots, you know. I can name 400 people in L.A. who haven't done anything remotely close to what TRIBE has done, but still run their fuckin' mouths. For one person to go out and do all the stuff she's done is a lot, let alone for a little girl in the tough areas she's bombed like South Central, Watts, Compton, Inglewood, Hollywood, downtown, you name it. She never had no help from nobody. She does her own dirt, and that's pretty cool. She racks her own paint. She's been locked up for racking before. She didn't call up collect every five minutes crying about being in jail, either. She figured she was in jail, fuck it. No other females bomb like that. There's girls that paint a little bit, but not one consistent like her. She's pretty much got it locked down for herself on the West Coast. If we're talking' about bombing, in the dictionary it would say TRIBE in big fuckin' capital letters. It's the truth. She's a crazy-ass bitch."

TRIBAL
WARFARE

TOOMER's best TRIBE story concerns a time a group of them were partying in Tijuana. TOOMER and some others were walking along, and TRIBE drunkenly demanded TOOMER's can, and TOOMER gave it up after an argument. The Mexican cops rushed the group, arresting a couple of them and surrounding TRIBE.

"She said, 'What the fuck do you think you're doing? I'm an American. I have rights,'" laughed Toomer. "I told her, 'Shut up. This ain't America. You can't be talkin' like that to these cops, they'll fuck you up.' She said, 'I don't give a fuck. I'm an American citizen. I demand to see your emperor!' To make a long story short, she went to jail. I had to go to San Diego, get money and go back and bail them all out. She was in the station, still goin' off."

Didn't she understand that Tijuana is corrupt as hell? "Dude, she's oblivious!" said TOOMER. "Sometimes I don't think she even knows that graffiti and tagging are against the law."

All of this is going through my mind as I wait for TRIBE, watching this old homeless guy falling asleep over a burrito. I expected a real man-eater to waltz through the entrance of Del Taco. After hearing grown men discuss her with awe in their voices, I picture some rough hoochie-mama straight out of a Too Short video.

But at least on this evening, TRIBE looks particularly inconspicuous. Accompanied by a couple of fellow writers, she rolls up to the Del Taco in a white Mustang. Dressed in a blue pullover, jeans and sneakers, she's the girl next-door if you live in most parts of L.A. Small and petite, she has long brown hair with blonde streaks pulled behind her head in a ponytail. Her eyes are large and brown, accented by some makeup that gives them a strange Vulcan curve upwards. And her lips are full, with a stud

piercing below her lower one. She seems like the kind of homegirl most guys would want to take to the movies; a nice girl, not the badass criminal everyone makes her out to be.

The small photo album she's brought with her offers evidence to the contrary. In it are pictures of pieces from all over L.A. One of them shows her done up in tight white pants, a white tube top and high heels. It almost looks like a different person, more like the man-eater I'd expected. "I was 13 when I started, one of my girlfriends gave me the name TRIBE. I wanted to go tag with them, but I didn't know what to write. I was looking at all these girly names but then she named me TRIBE."

Flipping through the photos, she starts to discuss the various times she's been "sweated" by the cops. "I've been caught a lot, but that's the benefit of being a girl, usually they let me go," TRIBE says. "Most of the time, I was a juvenile, so my mom would come pick me up. One time I was in Frisco with REVOK and we got sweated together. The cops shined the light on us, and I just told my homeboy to take off. So he ran, and the cops stopped me. I have paint all over my hands. They asked me, 'Who were those guys you were with?' They didn't even look at my hands. They automatically thought because of the way I look I wasn't bombing. So I thought, 'Cool, I have an advantage here.'"

TRIBE laughs at the memory, but being a girl, excuse me, a woman in the mail-dominated world, also has its downside. "Sometimes the guys will say, 'She's good—for a girl,'" TRIBE explains. "Or, they'll talk shit about you. Most guys think girls are for one thing, so it's hard to get respect as a writer. That's kind of why I chose the name TRIBE at first, so no one would know I'm a girl. I've been writing for eight years now, and I like to dress up and go out and

have fun. Because of that, everyone says, 'Oh she's this. She's that.' Everyone's all up in my business. They need to stay out. If I was a guy and I was partying, it'd be cool. No one would talk shit about me. But some guys are just jealous. They're just haters."

What about the other rumors? Being in jail in Tijuana, or here in Cali under an assumed name? Both, she admits are true. And rocking buses in high-heels and making love on rooftops? Hey, she's not ashamed of that either. "It's not like I plan to go out bombing in high heels, but if I'm out like that already, I might do something. As for Tijuana, I don't really consider it another country. I was drunk, so I didn't care. I figured my friend would bail me out. Sex on rooftops? Yeah, I like to try new stuff. But that was with my boyfriend of three years. That's no big deal."

For right now, if you're wonderin' fellas, TRIBE's not in a relationship. The only thing she's serious about is her rep as a writer. She's earned a BA degree from the Fashion Institute of Design and Merchandising in L.A., and she's interested in legit outlets for her creativity—legal walls, fashion, etc., but she still loves doing graffiti. "I've always liked to draw, but I like the adrenaline rush of vandalism," she says. "Even if I have money on me, I'll still rack. Anything I'm not supposed to do, I like doing."

Enough of the chit-chat, TRIBE's ready to move. It's almost 2 a.m., and this is when she's normally out bombing. I agree to follow her and her homeboys ZES and REVOK in my car, and soon we're out in the cool spring night, speeding toward the 24-hour Home Depot. TRIBE says she's got to rack some cans, so she and her boys amble into the store. As I'm present strictly as an observer, I keep my fat ass planted in my car and wait for them to return. When they walk out, I see TRIBE holding a can of paint. She's bold, that's for sure.

After this, I'm following TRIBE south. She stops before a little strip mall and points. Up above a Thai restaurant are some of her big, fat pieces. One of her boys jumps out and hits a wall. Then everyone is back in their cars, riding south again. We pass a cop shop bustling with black-and-whites. Just past it, a sign reads, "Rampart Blvd." Could this be the Rampart Division they're always talking about on the news? The LAPD station notorious for beating the crap out of suspects Rodney King-style? Must be.

Not far from there, TRIBE pulls up to a blank wall near a freeway overpass. She and her boys slam it hard without a word of explanation to me. I sit there for a few minutes, watching them work, until the thought of Officer Friendly sweating me makes my hair stand on end. I'm too old for this shit. I decide to head out, and let TRIBE do her thing.

When I call TRIBE a day or two later, she tells me she and the other writers went all night, till sunrise. Any trouble with the cops? TRIBE says she did get sweated once, while she was in a tunnel by herself, with the other writers on the outside. "The cop stopped me and asked me if I was alright," she says. "I said yes, and he left. I guess he didn't see the paint can in my hand." Classic.

Originally printed in WYWS Issue #10

—*Editor's note: Since this story, TRIBE has gone on to much bigger and better things—she's a successful DJ, rapper and was a contestant on Bret Michael's* Rock of Love Bus. *On the show, she rapped for Bret while reading the lyrics off the back of a paper labeled gonorrhea and genital herpes. Later, she took a shot out of another girl's vagina, a girl named Gia who happened to be a girl I went to high school with. In 10th grade, Gia stole my Danzig long sleeve T-shirt and got high off Glade in my bathroom. Now she's an amateur porn star and has had like eight abortions. Both TRIBE and Gia got kicked off on the first episode. It was a pleasure and an honor to see my life come full circle like that.*

HOW TO CHEAT

by Patrick Boyd and Lauren Gifford

I don't care who you are or how smart your Harvard ass is—everyone's cheated on a test in school at least once, if not habitually. If anyone tells you different, they're lying and you should beat the shit out them. If you're in cheating denial, it's time you came out of the closet, and gave some pointers to those who aren't as good at getting away with it. That's why we, at WYWS, are doing our part and have consulted with some professional cheaters, who go to some very elite colleges and know a little something about not getting caught. So, in advance, you're welcome, you degenerate cheating shitheads.

ANSWERS IN THE BATHROOM

This method is best used in college, but can be useful in high school, depending on your teacher. The important part is to leave your notes in the bathroom before your exam. After the test has been handed out and you look it over and see what parts you aren't sure about. Next, you ask to be excused to use the lavatory facility and you check your notes for the correct answers.

HOLE IN THE PANTS

This is where you cut a hole in your jeans near your upper thigh. You then write the answers to the exam on your leg and while taking the test you move the hole around to see the notes. This technique was better implemented in the 1980s when people actually wore ripped jeans, but seeing how the 1980s are back with a vengeance, go for it. You may just become the most fashionable kid in school, with an A on your test and the girls on your dick.

TEAMWORK

Everyone knows that teamwork is the best way to get things done. When taking a multiple-choice test, have your friends tap the answers on the table. One tap equals A, two taps equals B, and so on. Not only is everyone a winner, but this method of cheating builds team spirit as well.

GIRLFRIEND

As you can tell by the name, this technique requires a girlfriend, or a smart female who wants to be down with you and your dumb-ass rebel friends. Make sure your girlfriend takes the class before you and tells you the answers to the test between classes. It is up to you to decide which to pick first, the class or the girlfriend. But remember, it's easier to switch girlfriends then classes.

NEW TEACHER

Our experts believe that the best classes in which to cheat are those taught by the new teachers. New teachers haven't had time to get burnt out, they're just excited to have a job, so excited that they could care less how you pass their class.

At times, these techniques can work the other way, with older teachers. They get so tired of teaching and catching little brats cheating that they too could care less. They can't wait to actually accomplish something with their lives, rather than teaching a bunch a kids who can't get answers right without cheating.

HIDE ANSWERS IN THE CALCULATOR

Most college and some high school math classes require students to use the TI87 calculator. Not only can students hide cheat sheets in the calculator's handy-dandy case, they can also program them into the calculator itself.

Originally printed in WYWS Issue #11

—Writer's note: Unfortunately, I think this article had an expiration date in the late 1990s. Teachers caught on to calculators; no one has team spirit anymore; and I hate to say it but I definitely ended up smarter than 99 percent of my girlfriends after that. There are still a few good methods out there, but I'm not in school anymore and wouldn't want to crush the chances and dreams of some motivated future entrepreneurs.

THE LOST GAME

by Trevor Michaels

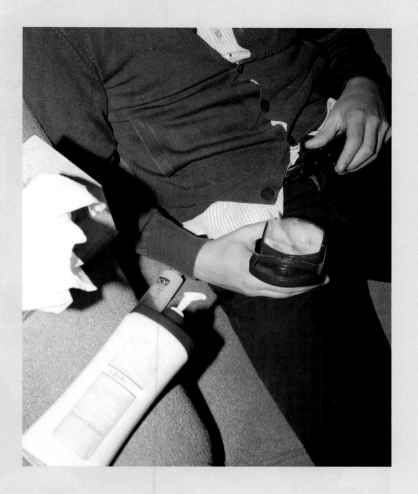

So you tell a girl she is like a "tiny heaven." It's a solid line regardless of the geniality. In high school, this line was guaranteed to get you in the backseat of a car. Now, at institutions of higher learning, you're lucky if the girl laughs. I ask you this: What the hell has changed? I am completely disillusioned with the whole picking up girls idea because it doesn't ever work. Politely, it's a bunch of crap.

I went to Boston the other weekend and threw out more game than Michael Jordan in the playoffs, and what happened? I ended up in Chinatown at five in the morning drinking cold tea with my buddies. Not that I minded the late-night brew, but I would have rather had some tender loving from some New England cat. I mean. I must have hit on over two-dozen broads. It's not like I have a bucktooth and a peg leg. The highlight of my night was when I hit on a close friend's sister. When I asked her how she was, at least she said, "Fine, thanks," before getting up and walking away.

I used to have no trouble hooking up. Hell, I could get girls to take their shirts off by saying, "I heard you were going to take your shirt off!" It worked all of the time. Granted, some of those tasteless lines that were so effective have become outdated and unproductive as we mature. But hey, it's not just the women who have matured—our lines have progressed too!

So here I am, stuck at this school, and so disgruntled that I have lost the urge to masturbate. Who is responsible for this unenviable situation? Women! If we are going to put in the effort, they could at least be nice to us. Why as women age do they become harder to pick up? Do I need to go back to the playgrounds? At what point did they become too good for us? Did they learn something in college that has changed their whole perspective?

My theory is that women learn that they can use ass to control us. Still, what gives them the right to treat us poorly just because they have a unique gift? Further, I ask, is it really worth all of the time, effort and pain we endure in the quest? I am beginning to question the value of good cat myself.

The game has changed, and I am looking for some new moves to get me to the hoop. I'm usually the one offering the information. If you're still in high school, I have tons to offer, but it seems I am lost in my own world and am the one in need this time. So, please send me any tips or lines that have successfully bagged a mature, slightly intelligent woman. Till next time—hopefully, I will have gotten laid by then.

Originally printed in WYWS Issue #5

NOISE

AFI

by Linas Garsys
Photo courtesy of AFI

I left the Bethesda office not knowing what tomorrow would bring. I was headed to the Van's Warped Tour for an interview with some vampires. To gear up for undead craziness, I had submitted myself to a crash course on vampire self-defense (a lot of bad comic books, and I watched The Lost Boys several times) and packed appropriately (a bible, a rosary, a stake, and some garlic). The next morning, as I headed out, I feared for the worst. But I sucked it up and sat down with lead singer, Davey.

—Writer's note: I treated this interview like they were actual vampires. Every question was like, "Is it hard to drink blood on tour?" and they laughed through the whole interview. The thing about all the interviews for WYWS was that none of them were serious and we didn't ask questions that anyone else would ask. I wouldn't say they were immature interviews; they were just ridiculous and fun.

"WYWS made me start paying closer attention whenever the walls were speaking to me. My life has been greatly enriched ever since."
—Davey Havok

Who is the boy who destroyed the world?
Well, that's me.

Did someone stop you, or are you still plotting?
I destroyed a different world. I can't mention it's name or it will destroy this one.

Would you punch an alien?
Yes, I'd definitely punch an alien, especially if it's a typical media stereotype alien.

What's it like being the only goth band on the Warped Tour this year?
[Loud laughing] It's really nice because before we came on this tour it was really sunny, but we managed to bring a pretty big storm today. We usually bring some light cloud covering. A lot of the other bands aren't too happy about the lack of warmth, but there's not much that they can do about it.

So what's it like playing in the sun, being up before nighttime?
We're not really used to being awake in the daytime. It's much worse playing in the sunlight. Its frightening and uncomfortable.

Can you cross running water?
Depends on how fast it's going.

When was the last time you drank blood?
The thing about the Warped Tour is that they really cater to all sorts of different types. They have vegetarian food, vegan food, food for the meat eaters, and they even have tested blood, which is really nice. I actually had some about three hours before we went on and I'll probably have some later for dinner. They really take care of you.

Do you prefer the blood of virgins?
Absolutely!

Are there advantages to being undead?
There's all sorts of things. The ability to leave your body, shape change, and summon the clouds when you have to play a daytime festival. It's really convenient. I'm lucky to be able to go into the sun now. The first few hundred years I really couldn't go outside at all.

I guess you haven't seen your folks much since you became undead?
No, they died centuries ago. They were great people though. My dad was a leathersmith.

How do you think they would feel seeing you decked out in pleather?
They were pretty openminded to the times. I think they wouldn't mind.

Do you get Halloween presents?
Yes, throughout the year. I get them in the summer, and I get them on Halloween. The other night in Toronto, I got a little scarecrow, a magic wand and a clown on a noose. It was really nice.

So is the van big enough to hold all the coffins?
We don't sleep in coffins when we're on tour. We sleep in the trailer hanging upside down from the ceilings.

Ever have candy apples with razor blades?
I actually had a horrible experience with a candy apple the other day. I went to the Six Flags theme park in California. All I wanted the whole day was a candy apple. I finally got it. When I took the second bite, the stick broke and the candy-apple smashed all over the ground.

Would you rather eat a live person or fuck a dead person?
Both.

***Blacula* or *A Vampire in Brooklyn*, which one is more legit?**
Both are completely misrepresentative of the real culture.

***Blacula* had street cred!**
It does have street cred, and it's beautiful 1970s trashy film.

How many names for the devil do you know?
Satan, Lucifer, Son of Man, Morningstar, the Bringer of Light—if I had known this was a test I would've studied.

You win the Publishers Clearing House Sweepstakes. On the same day that Ed gives you the check, aliens land saying they're gonna blow up the world. What do you do?
I guess, make out with Ed McMahon. How did I score on that?

Not too good.
What! Why?

It's from Heathers. The best answer would have been "you get a lion and a bomb, and you and the lion die as one."
So the one about the sax and the lake would've been better?

Yep. All right, we're picking teams...

Originally printed in WYWS Issue #11

DAVEY
HAVOK
of
AFI

LITERATURE

BRAWLIN' BROADS
SIMPLY THE BEST VIDEO IN THE WORLD.
Interview and photo by Neil Mahoney

Everyone I have showed this tape to has had no clue how to react. They all describe it, the exact same way: "A bunch of trailer park girls, kicking the shit out of each other."

In a room framed with blue sheets, these girls meet face to face and swing their arms like the tornados that threaten their homes. After a few minutes of bare-knuckled hair pulling, shit talking, scratching and thumping, one of the contestants submits and another walks away in triumphant splendor. Like *Jerry Springer* without off-duty cops to break up the ass kicking, and without pixilation when the boobies come floppin' out, *Brawlin' Broads* begs to be analyzed by media experts as the important step in media evolution that it truly is.

Holding all this together like two globs of red-necked glue are the Boone Brothers. These two "Trailer Park Kings" introduce the fighters, rate their ugliness by the number of beers it would take them to nail the bitches, and belch and grunt their way through the hour-long presentation of brutality and tongue-in-cheek charm. After a few Pabst Blue Ribbons, a mouthful of pork rinds, and a Home Run Pie, I had a chat with them in San Francisco.

—Writer's note: Of all the dumb things I was exposed to at this magazine, these hillbillies—and the guy who had blown his hand apart making rocked-powered robot monsters out of Cadillacs and military scrap—are the only people I wonder what they are doing now. That said, I have made no effort whatsoever to find out.

How did you guys start making these things?
Mitchell: The guys that run Mayhem Productions out of Antioch were down in Bakersfield and they were doin' some documentary or some shit, and we ended up hooking up with them by chance, hanging out at some bar and talking about doing some shit. We sort of came up with the idea. "You know, you guys should do somethin' with some chicks fuckin' brawlin'." It developed from there. They called us up and were like, "Fuck, you guys wanna host this shit?" And we're all like "Yeah, sure. Does it involve liquor and bitches?" "Well, count us the fuck in…"

Where do they find your contestants?
Martin: From what we gather they went into the Deep South, and found all these trailer park beauties.
Mitchell: They were working on it for a year just to round up the fights. It was kind of just fuckin' luck, a little cash, a little speed, a little beer.

What were you doing before this?
Mitchell: We both drive a tow rig. Just pickin' up broke-downs for the most part but we do a nice chunk of repos, maybe a couple a week. Fuck, we still do it now!

Did you get some stank on ya'll hang-low by hooking up with these lovely ladies?
Mitchell: Martin sure as shit tasted some of that fuckin' spoiled fruit.
Martin: Jealous bitch.

There is one fight that is over before it really starts, do you know if they ever fought off camera?
Mitchell: Nah, they never did fight. We're trying to get something goin' with them for number two. A lot of people are calling saying…
Martin: "Hey, man! That was a tease, man!" Fuckin' blue balls.
Mitchell: Exactly. "You get us scratchin' the knob and then all of the sudden…"
Martin: All rub and no fuckin'! Shoot!
Mitchell: A lot of those chicks are just fuckin' wayward. So it's like whether or not we can get 'em back together. Maybe they'll find us after we sell a few, they'll come knockin' looking for money.

BEWARE ATLANTA.

RECIPE FOR A BOONE BROS. BOILERMAKER
Needed: Shot glass, standard beer glass.
Preparation: Pour some of your favorite ale in the beer glass and fill the other with 10 or so ounces of cheap bourbon. Drop shot in beer glass and guzzle until you look like one of these guys, or these chicks look hot.

Originally printed in WYWS Issue #11

BRAWLIN'
BROADS

MISS CLEO
by Simon Steinhardt

Hi, I want to speak to Miss Cleo.
She's not here right now. Can I take your reading?

Can you speak with a Caribbean accent? It gets me going.
I can give you a reading but I'm really not Caribbean so I don't know if I can...

Do you know why I'm calling you?
No, I would think because you want a reading, how about that?

Well, actually that's incorrect. I'm going to deduct points for that one.
Are you calling just to call or what?

I'm calling to ask some questions, I need to know some things. I actually wanted to ask Miss Cleo some questions.
Well, how do you know she's gonna know the answers?

Because she knows everything—she's Miss Cleo.
I'm sure she knows a lot, but what were you wanting to know about you?

Whatever you see. I gotta make this kind of quick; my brother needs to use the phone.
Well all right, you have a fresh start coming in your life right now. Focusing around business and success, OK?

OK.
There's a young guy, dark hair, dark eyes around you?

OK.
And he's someone that's going to favor you and defend you and promote good vibrations around you. What's um, what's your brother's name?

Neil.
No, that's not your brother, that's somebody else. [She is correct. Neil was the editor listening in.] OK, there's a plethora of money coming in for you.

OK.
Right now you're juggling your money, and much more would be achieved if a decision was made, so expect to receive some kind of reassuring news or a small sum of money or a gift.

Oh OK, so it's not gonna be like, a lot of money?
Well it could be, but I also see other large money.

Like a billion?
I'm not sure as far as amounts. I do see amounts coming in for you, and things starting and going in the right direction for you, and you having a lot of success and prosperity. And more than you expect.

OK, well I got to go now.

In the weeks following our call to Miss Cleo, we received a total of 22 calls with offers of free readings and horoscopes, and continue to as of press time.

Originally printed in WYWS Issue #16

TV GUIDANCE

I usually disagree with sitcom moralizing, but there are some TV lessons that should never be ignored. For example, TV has warned us time and again how hard the path to professional artistry can be. So for all you aspiring Basquiats, pay attention to what TV foresees in your future: It's never too late to change majors.

—Ian Sattler

Originally printed in WYWS Issue #19

SCENARIO #1: YOU HAVE A GREAT IDEA TO SELL YOUR CRAFTS WITH A FRIEND, IN HOPES OF PAYING OFF SOME OF THOSE ART SUPPLY BILLS.

As Seen On TV: On *Who's The Boss?*, Tony and Angela go into business selling their tie-dyed T-shirts at a fair. A difference of opinion causes the two to split off and form rival operations. In the end, Tony is an unemployable drunk and Angela a washed-up infomercial whore.

TV Guide Says: Even if somebody wants to buy your stupid homemade wares, you're never going to make enough if you have to split it with a friend. To make matters worse, business between friends usually ends poorly after some combination of poor sales, sex and crying. And for God's sake, selling stuff at an art fair is for fucking hippies.

SCENARIO #2: YOU DECIDE TO JUMP START YOUR ART CAREER BY SHOWING STUFF TO A CELEBRITY YOU IDOLIZE, IN HOPES THAT THEY WILL TAKE YOU UNDER THEIR WING AND FINANCE YOUR PROJECTS.

As Seen On TV: Instead of worrying about Jo's mullet and her dream of becoming the warden at women's prison, the *Facts Of Life* girls are worried about Tootie's obsession with Jermaine Jackson. Things get out of hand when Tootie is invited backstage at Jermaine's concert. At the show, Tootie tries to present Jermaine with a bust of the singer that she sculpted out of clay, but Mr. Jackson's security guards think Tootie's bust is a bomb, and smash it in a bathtub, leaving Tootie devastated, and us wondering what the hell is going on.

TV Guide Says: You take the good, you take the bad, you take 'em both and there you have... a restraining order. Only crazy celebrities like Mariah Carey like fans to send them artwork inspired by an obviously unhealthy obsession. Thinking they'll like your art enough to contact you about it is like thinking a hooker liked your action so much that she'll give you a birthday freebie.

SCENARIO #3: YOU TRY TO JUSTIFY MOVIE MAKING AS AN ART FORM BY SHOWING YOUR FAMILY AND FRIENDS YOUR STUDENT FILM.

As Seen On TV: Poor Vinnie Delpino. Not only is his best friend an attention grabbing 16-year-old doctor, but he also can't get laid to save his life. In a desperate plea for validation, Vinnie decides to screen his first movie, *Revenge Of The Teenage Dead*, to the Howser family. Vinnie is laughed out of the room and back into the shadow of *Doogie Howser, M.D.*, forever.

TV Guide Says: I used to see art films with tons of hot naked chicks in them on Cinemax at my mom's house before I moved into my own apartment—an apartment I'd never be able to afford if I had spent my time trying to make my own non-pornographic movies.

SCENARIO #4: YOU THINK THAT HANGING A PIECE OF YOUR ART IN YOUR FAMILY'S LIVING ROOM WILL HELP BOLSTER SUPPORT FOR YOUR IMPENDING CAREER.

As Seen On TV: On the second episode of *Good Times*, J.J. hangs his painting of a black Jesus in James and Florida Evans' living room. Next thing they know, the family has a string of good luck. If this windfall is due to the presence of black Jesus, what will happen if J.J. enters the painting in a contest that could win the family rent money? For a show that made a practice out of unhappy endings, you can be sure it's nothing good.

TV Guide Says: This explains how I won the lottery after I hung my "White Devil" painting on the porch. This example also shows that the only time your family will care about your art is when it makes them money.

While you were sleeping

QUIK
THE STORY OF A GRAFFITI KING
Interview by Roger Gastman
Photos courtesy of QUIK

So, what started it for you?
Actually, seeing gang graffiti on the walls, like the Apaches and Black Spades, and Latino motorcycle stuff and Black motorcycle gang stuff. In 1969, once my parents started letting me go to the ball games myself, I just started scribbling with little dry markers. By 1970, I had graduated to little cans of Testors Paint. I manipulated my dad into buying them, pretending I was going to spray paint my model boats and planes. Also, my grandma would take me to the ball games in Yankee Stadium in the Bronx. I'd see the 4 train go by and see AJ 161 top-to-bottoms, and was like, Wow, I really want to do that. I've got these photos of me from that time, in my choir outfit, confirmation robe, my little smile; you can almost see the halo over my head. That was all about getting to go to church just so I could go bombing. I would either spray my way to church or back. My parents would give me 50 cents to take the bus. I would just take the bus either way, and spend the other 25 cents on pizza or something, and just spray along. And also you got to meet girls. So between spray painting and the girls, going to choir was my big excuse.

Did graffiti help you get girls?
Definitely not. It helped me get into a lot of fights. A lot of us make jokes, like, damn, being a graff dude you only attract dudes, you attract like one gal per 100 dudes. But my ex-wife, she would go through the tunnels with me. Now she's a corporate executive for a bank. I have photos of the things she helped me with. I used to take people who were not part of the graff culture, just to show them how weird we were.

So you graduated high school, and went to college in D.C.?
Yeah that was 1976; I wanted to be a forest ranger. Growing up in New York, I spent a lot of time in nature, and even at the end of the 1960s a lot of my mentors were hippies. I had a respect for nature. I had done a lot of hiking and canoeing, and nature was really important to me, and it bothered me that mankind was fucking it up. I had a friend of mine, a graff dude, who said he went canoeing, took his chainsaw and chopped down a tree. The place he told me he went to was a place I used to go as a kid, and I thought that was horrible, that they go on weekend adventures and chop down trees where I used to go and chill, make campfires, have sex, and just be groovy. I wanted to protect nature from that Neanderthal attitude. But at American University, it was more environmental science than forestry. I was too much of a pothead, and I was not into science. I realized that if I was a forest ranger, I'd be the only Black forest ranger in the northeast, and all the other guys were rednecks, just like mounted police. I started doing more painting in class and tagging around the city. I kept going back to New York, tagging and bombing, because college on that level was not interesting. I eventually got kicked off campus when I threw a console TV out of a 5th floor window. It made a huge crashing noise!

I heard you partied with the pimps and hookers a lot.
I was big time down with hanging out with prostitutes on street corners from New York. We used to hang around with the pimps, strictly the *Super Fly*

QUIK

stuff. There was just something about that seedy underworld, and looking at those characters. Just the pimps, there was something about their naive Southern ways, coming to New York with their big brims and big cars. In D.C., the pimps weren't as friendly, but I used to hang out with the girls. You know, you would watch their back, smoke a joint with them, run and get them a soda. Then you got your freebie at the end of the night, or you got your discount. I didn't mind that.

How old were you then?
18, but we had been hanging out for years so they kinda got to know us. The strange thing was I always looked like a Neil Young dude, whereas my best friend looked super Black and wore the uptown Grandmaster Flash Lees and black pocket T-shirt. So it was just a trip that we were odd dudes from Queens and were accepted by that culture. But I realized that it was my craving for the old blues, the Sugar Shack thing that I never experienced that drew me to that crowd.

What's your favorite memory of a hooker?
There is one in particular, maybe my first one. The gal was like 6-feet tall. The parking lot is still there. I did it in my mother's red Duster, and I remember getting home and I had a pubic hair in between my teeth.

Did your mom ever find out what happened in the back of the car?
Well, we're Americans, so that's where you do most of your business anyway. I think my parents

figured out what was going on with this car fixation on the weekends, other than bombing. I went out with my ex-wife for years. We would go to movies, and the car was the date, it was your hotel room. You get a big car, do it in the car, park at a golf course. Then after I took care of my business it was time to go bombing. Time to meet the fellas.

So what happened after you decided you didn't want to be a forest ranger?
I went back to New York to go to Pratt Institute. Art school of course hated me, but what was cool about Pratt was there were PHASE 2 tags all over the place. Of course I bombed that school and they wanted to throw me out. Every time I would do my work, they would give me a failing grade. If they said to do a 9-by-11 self-portrait, I would bring in something huge, in 9-by-11 proportions. They said if I took that to an ad agency, I wouldn't get the job, so they would fail me. I thought art school was a crock of shit, because I was pulling out whole cars top-to-bottom every evening, then coming home and doing my homework. I would look at the people next to me and think their work looked real good and they were gonna make lots of money on Madison Avenue, but there was something about what I was doing that they'd never get. I quit art school and started working at IBM to make lots of money to fuel my addictions for sex, drugs, cars and rock and roll. I got sick of IBM because I realized that after 20 years I'd have a car and a house three times as big as my dad's, but there wasn't anywhere to go with it.

"I THINK I'VE GOTTEN MORE PUSSY THAN PEOPLE HAVE SOCKS. BUT IT'S NOT ABOUT THAT ANYMORE. ALTHOUGH YOU'VE ALWAYS GOTTA KEEP YOUR OPTIONS OPEN."

What did you do then?
I went back to art school. By then, we had hit the papers, with FUTURA, ALI and ZEPHYR. The same fucking art teachers would ask me to do the same homework, and do it 9-by-11. I'd bring these giant paintings in, and they'd be like, "Hey, graffiti is hip. You're our resident graffiti artist," and I'd get an A. Whereas a few years before, they had failed me. I was like, "Fuck this," and once again, I left. Luckily, FUTURA forced me to meet a gallery dealer at a DONDI opening. He made an appointment to see my work in my house. The guy came and he bought a couple of paintings. Then it started again in Holland in 1983. We started doing shows and I ended up [moving] over there.

Your paintings are graffiti-influenced?
I'd say they are all graffiti-inspired. My painter part of me is just being QUIK, but I like to do other things. I paint a lot about the racism in America. I think that's why I'm one of Holland's favorite neo-graffiti artists. Dutch humor is really dark, and I think they see that within my work there is a lot of humor, but it's dark. I've just found that I have a far better audience for my work in Holland.

Do you have some groupies?
I might have one or two.

Do women throw themselves at you at art shows?
That has happened.

Fresh 20-year-olds?
That has happened.

Do you turn them down?
Even that has happened. There is only so much a man can handle. I love my ex-wife. I have a daughter. I think I've gotten more pussy than people have socks. But it's not about that anymore. Although you've always gotta keep your options open.

Do you still paint?
Not since my near-catastrophic accident.

What accident?
I was fleeing a very pimp-like art situation. I was just fed up. I didn't really have the energy to drive home, but I had been out bombing, and I had a couple beers under my belt, and I simply fell asleep at 4:30 a.m. What it all adds up to is I'm just too old to bomb.

Do you still have the urge?
Constantly. I still watch the train yards. Sometimes the thrill is gone. The last time I did a full-out bomb, I was with SACH and IZ. We were in our early 30s; it takes a lot out of you. They wore out before I did. But I did sleep very well that night. It did feel strange that I've done this 10,000 times, because what's 10,001? The times of 300 throw-ups a night, that's over for us guys.

You said you hung out with a lot of white trash guys?
[When] we were toys, we would hold the paint for them. They would cut the fence, go in, spray paint, then they would finish and we were allowed to go in. They went home, they didn't watch our backs. We would find whatever little spaces were left to hit. That's how I learned a lot about going through the yards. I guess it was post-1960s, and even my father dug the fact that graffiti was uniting races and religions, so as long as everybody was getting down to go bombing. It wasn't such a black versus white thing as most American culture was. That's why we felt comfortable underground. My father really dug that we got together to do graff. My dad would give me gas money to go bombing.

How does your family think that you went from illegal graffiti artist to where you are now?
They have been somewhat receptive to the fact that I've had some sort of artistic career. Unfortunately for them, it took place in Holland. They did see my art blossom and take off. When I first quit IBM they were upset. My family had some old traditional values. A lot of my family went to all-Black colleges, and I was like, no, this is my life. I want to be a forest ranger and rock to Jimi Hendrix and Black Sabbath and that won't be happening at Morgan or the other Black colleges. I got a lot of flack for that. In a sense, they didn't support my dream. Now I got a daughter who is half-ass proud of me, my ex-wife is half-ass proud of me, and they are the two most important people to me.

What about wild situations that graff has put you in?
Lots of mild situations like rafting down to Delaware. Maybe going into the mountains in California with HAZE, while deer are jumping out of the woods. There are so many I can't explain it all. There was a hotel on Delancey, and I remember I had been in every single one of those hotel rooms at some point in time. I remember meeting my first pussy that looked like 10 packs of bubble gum chewed up and spit out. I don't have a hair from that one.

Anything else?
Stay away from my daughter, all you motherfuckers, if you know what's good for you.

Originally printed in WYWS Issue #9

—Editor's note: QUIK was in the Bethesda area, visiting a relative, and got in touch with me through the evil DR. REVOLT. A lot of people exaggerated their stories for WYWS interviews, but QUIK didn't need to. His perversions are 100 percent authentic. I wonder how many pubic hairs are in his collection today.

All I can remember is waking up in the bushes off the redline, and, yes, I would punch an alien.

—*POSE 1*

WYWS was my connection for American entertainment. I loved every minute of it. Great to see it back!

—*BATES*

WYWS made me realize that everyone born after 1988 will have a photo of themselves naked on the inter-web at some point in the future.

—*Ben Woodward*

Roger had *WYWS* when we [AWR] were still kids, fucking around, writing, getting high, whatever. I think he was from Boston or Milwaukee of some other sort of shitty patch of land. I was intrigued with the fact that he had his shit together enough to actually publish a magazine.

I bugged him to put me on writing for the mag, and he sent me off to report on a few events, one of note being the Houston 500 gangbang. It was fun and I was hungry to try to distinguish myself from being a juvenile delinquent.

I don't know too much else about Mr. Gastman, other than he is vegan edge (all those SXE dudes are pretty tweaked), he reeks of date-rape, he is a perennial sneer-er, he owns one hat, dresses like a jock dad, used to have the Beastie Boys "Girls" as his outgoing message on his cell phone way too late in life, is probably a heavy sex-choker and although I have no concrete evidence—having never seen him wearing anything but jeans, a T-shirt, ballcap and Skechers—looks like one of the most hairy-bodied people south of Little Armenia. And I'm pretty sure he's racist, sexist and a gun nut.

—*Alex aka 2TONE*

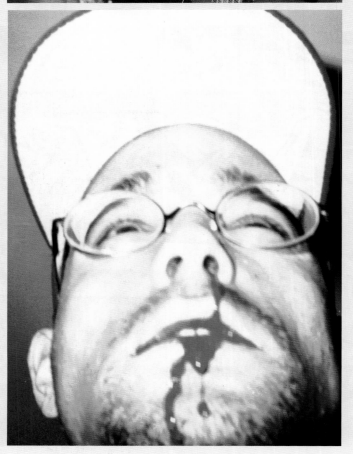

The best issue I ever saw was the first issue I ever saw... I can't recall an issue number or anything but it had an interview with Alisha Klass. It was awesome. There was a little bit of graffiti and a super hot babe talking about shaving her ass, having "ass-gasms" and getting fucked up the butt and loving it! Maybe I had a sheltered upbringing but this was a totally new idea to me... Also, once my even more sheltered roommate read it he was offended and disgusted. An added bonus in my opinion. I loved that fucking magazine! RIP *WYWS* and Alisha please return to adult entertainment!

—**Bill McRight**

I remember when you made me hook up with a burn victim and threatened to write about it… Eat a dick.

—*Mike E.*

I remember Roger coming to visit me in New York in the late 1990s. He took me to parts of the Bronx I had never been to, under bridges, by train tracks, I met graffiti artists and saw their work. It was amazing. Roger was already producing *WYWS* at the time and selling caps and still living with his mom in Maryland.

—*Julie M.*

WYWS provides nothing but sweet memories. I had the honor of gracing issue 4's cover. The photoshoot took place in a backyard, and we posed against a fence holding paint rollers. The basic direction was to look pissed off. The fence was later replaced with a painted wall (pretty intense post-production work for that debut in 1998). I remember seeing the magazine in Tower Records on Rockville Pike when it came out. Roger's closets at home were filled with spray paint and caps, neatly organized. His walls were painted too. I spent time in the Bethesda office and helped with design work here and there. Roger would give me a lot of stuff—Obey stickers, extra issues of the magazine, postcards featuring Ron English's work, and random collectables like sheets of uncut Garbage Pail Kids. He was always promoting what he believed in.

—*Anna M.*

GRAFFITI

6 FEET 6 INCHES OF DALEK
by Roger Rock
Images courtesy of DALEK

What the hell are Space Monkeys? Where did they come from? Do they bite? Are they house broken? Who cares, they are fuckin' cool. They are the creation of 32-year-old James Marshall. The graffiti artist better known as DALEK. Now, what the heck is a DALEK you are wondering? "It came from the Dr. Who British television series," says the artist. "The DALEK's are a race of robots that were created to destroy mankind. A superior race of artificial beings." Sounds sweet, doesn't it?

Don't worry, DALEK is house broken. He won't destroy your house or try and hump your leg. His 6-foot-6 frame is fueled by a diet of soda and junk food. A true child of the 1980s, he once sported a rat tail until one of the older skateboard kids he hung around just came up with a pair of scissors and cut it off "because he said it looked gay." Born in New London, Connecticut, young DALEK didn't stay in one place very long. DALEK's father was in the military, so he got used to moving around a lot. "I went to high school in Japan. It was 300 kids in a reinvented torpedo factory from WWII. They took the torpedoes out and put in some chalkboards and taught us. Back then, big, tall white people were still gods in Japan and as Americans we got away with whatever we wanted to. We rolled around on skateboards, reeking havoc."

What kind of havoc did he reek? "It's pretty mean, but me and my friend mugged this Japanese businessman. He was in a bar, flashing around his wad of cash. He was being an asshole all night, saying how Americans were all pieces of shit. We spent most of our time hanging out in the Japanese environment so we knew what was up. When he got up to leave, we followed him out. He passed out on a park bench. We took his wallet and broke out. We spent all his money the next day. We would steal a lot because the Japanese are honest and they're not really looking for you. We stole beer, food, skateboard stuff, whatever we needed."

That was a good story and all but what does that have to do with art and Space Monkeys? DALEK didn't even get into art until he was 22. "I went to school in Virginia [VCU, for a degree in sociology and anthropology] and met a bunch of artist kids. They would buy beer and go sit in their studios painting and drinking. I found that interesting, so I started hanging out with them. I started taking art history classes and painting abstract. That's how it all started. I never really had done art before other than when I was a kid. I drew fucking airplanes and dudes smoking cigarettes." Just proves it's never too late to get started.

After graduating VCU, DALEK was off to further his education at the Art institute of Chicago. There he got himself a BFS in photography. It was at this art school that he re-discovered graffiti. "I knew about graffiti when I was in high school. I had friends that tagged, I just didn't care for it. It wasn't anything that I was interested in at that point in my life. When I went to school in Chicago, it was just the right time in my life to start playing with it. I think that without graffiti, the Space Monkey never would have come into existence. It wasn't anything that evolved on paper. It evolved out of trying to find my own identity painting on walls. I wasn't interested in painting pieces. There were so many people doing crazy letter styles that were so advanced that I just didn't think I had anything to contribute in that arena. Doing characters was

DALEK

more natural for me. That was where I could bring through the qualities I had. It evolved from messing around on walls and one day the very first version of it just came out on the wall. I was painting with TDEE in Connecticut, he said, 'Hey, that's kind of cool, you should work with it.' He was the main person I talked to, so I took what he said pretty seriously. As more people liked it, I realized that I was on the path of doing something."

And the Space Monkey was born. Pass the cigars, tell the neighbors. "I'm just trying to make mankind aware that they're destroying themselves. They're not doing any good. The human race is a fucking worthless joke. Space Monkeys are kind of a comical out-take with serious undertones of how ridiculously stupid humanity is. How hollow we all are."

DALEK plans to let nature take its course and continue his "kind of cartoonish route" of the Space Monkey as an iconic image. "I'd like to evolve it a little more into a type of comic element. Create a storyline and work with it more commercially. Using it in only a fine-art capacity is kind of limited."

However, it's the painting that keeps DALEK sane. "I think if it wasn't for painting I probably would have been a lot worse person then I am. Painting has helped level me out and it's given me a reason to live so to speak." It has also taken time away from one of DALEK's other favorite past times, drinking. "I used to have a pretty good drinking career. I kind of slowed that up." Every drunk must have their tale, and DALEK is no exception. "One night I woke up with my roommate punching me in the chest, screaming, 'The ambulance is on the way just stay awake! He though I was dead. I had drank a whole bottle of Jack and blacked out. I had assaulted a few people but I had no clue." But wait, it gets better. "My sophomore year of college my friends came over and we were drinking vodka. I had a cold and had taken a bunch of Dimetapp. All I remember is waking up and it was pouring rain. I was laying in a mud puddle. My car was crashed into the fence behind my house. The engine was still on and the car was still in drive. It wasn't going anywhere. It was just lodged in the fence. I turned the car off, went in the house, and went to sleep. I woke up in the afternoon and realized that I was laying in my bed, covered in mud. I went down to the cafeteria and my friends informed me that I had driven them to parties all night. I asked them why they didn't stop me from driving and they said I told them I was fine to drive. Luckily, no one got hurt."

Drinking and womanizing come hand in hand, so I'm told. "I love talking about sex. I'm going to get myself in trouble talking about sex. I've dated all kinds of psycho girls." So how many women has it been? DALEK is not one to brag but says, "It's under 100." DALEK doesn't want the ladies out there to get the wrong impression. "It was mostly when I was younger. I don't sleep [around] with girls anymore. I'm about a nice, solid relationship with a good healthy girl." And boobs play a very important part in finding that special someone. "As long as they fit the girl. I hate squishy tits. If they're nice and firm, then they're all good. If a girl's got big, soggy tits then send her home—and bad nipples, god hates bad nipples. It's just the way it is."

DALEK'S 5 TIPS ON LADIES

1. Ignore them, they like that.
2. Don't do shit for them. (They'll just forget about it two minutes later.)
3. Never tell them the truth. They'll throw it back in your face sooner or later.
4. Don't call them... unless you need something. They will just ramble about something you could care less about.
5. Never poke fun at their shoes. That's where they draw the line.

It may take a few relationships to master these steps, but eventually you will be gold. Trust me. —DALEK

FIVE STEPS TO DRAWING YOUR OWN SPACE MONKEY

STEP 1

STEP 2

STEP 3

STEP 4

STEP 5

For now, DALEK is busy building a career. He devotes all his time to painting. The Space Monkeys have come a long way from that wall in Connecticut five years ago. They have grown and grown again. DALEK has started working more with acrylic, house paint, paint markers and some spray in taking the Monkeys on to canvas. He's creating the layers he sees in the outside world that intrigue him. "The layers of paint, buff and dirt [that are] created by the aging. Especially old signs where you see text and it's been faded and repainted and faded and painted over with other text. It's creating stuff that has layers of history and text work. Using imagery all in order to relay my little message of love."

It's been a long trip from the days of doodling airplanes and dudes smoking cigarettes. The Space Monkey is here to stay. Get used to it. "I love to paint. The more I grow as an artist and the more I meet other artists, I'm more inspired to paint. I see what other people are doing and it stokes me out. It makes me think that that's what I want to do with my life. It's what I want to focus on. I plan on trying to make a life out of painting." Good luck James, and when are the currently genderless Space Monkeys going to get some boobies?

Originally printed in WYWS Issue #10

LITERATURE

HEY, YOU CAN'T SAY THAT!
KEVIN SMITH ON VIRGINITY, JASON MEWES AND ORANGE-STRAWBERRY-BANANA SLIM-FAST

Interview by Jelly
Photos courtesy of Kevin Smith
Illustration by John Pound

You'd think Kevin Smith could say and do anything he wants on film. After all, his first film, *Clerks*, included necrophilia and a girl who had sucked 37 cocks. Subsequent films *Mallrats* and *Chasing Amy* continued to offend all the right people, but Smith really went for broke in *Dogma*, when he cast Alanis Morissette as God.

So did his foul-mouthed history or his amazing commercial success grant the 31-year-old Smith a free pass with the MPAA on his latest flick *Jay and Silent Bob Strike Back*? Hell no! The tighter-than-tight assholes on the ratings board first gave the movie an NC-17. Seems they didn't like the part where Jay pulls a long pubic hair from his mouth after eating out a nun, saying, "Oooh, she had '70s bush!"

"I've seen R-rated movies where people are brutally butchered or raped," Smith explained as we relaxed in his L.A. bungalow. "We just have people sitting around talking about fucking, and they're like, 'No, no, no, you can't do that.'"

Smith cut the scene to get an R, but don't worry, kids. Even without the pubic floss, Smith has so many references to ball licking, cock smoking and clit sucking that he more than makes up for it. If that isn't enough for you, then here's an interview that's most definitely NC-17:

Everyone says your partner Jason Mewes is a terrible interview, why is that?
He's the diametric opposite of what he is in the movie. He doesn't like to talk. He's very shy. If you know him, he'll take his cock out for you, and be like, "Look, meat and veg!" But when you first sit down with the dude, he covers his mouth a lot and doesn't make eye contact. If you ask him a question, he'll be like, "Yeah" or "I don't know." But conversely, if you know him, there ain't a part of him he won't expose to you, whether externally or internally. I've seen Jason Mewes' dick more than I've seen my own dick.

How did you hook up with him?
He was introduced to me by two other dudes who were really good friends of mine, Walter and Bryan. I worked with Walter at this recreation center in Highlands, NJ, when I was 18, right after high school. I was hanging out with Walter and Bryan pretty hardcore, and then after my year with the program was up, I moved on to another job, but I'd still hang with them. They started talking about Jason Mewes after I left the rec center. Like, "Jay, he's so fucked up..." I didn't know Jay personally, but I knew of him. He was like an urban legend in that town. People would point to him and go, "That Mewes kid, he fucked a dog." You'd find out later, he didn't fuck a dog, he just blew it a little bit. You'd hear that kind of shit about him.

ORCA
CIGARETTE PAPERS

KEVIN
SMITH

Did you always find him funny?

He's sort of an underappreciated comic genius. See, he's not self-aware. He doesn't think of himself as funny—he just is. The day I realized he was a comic genius, we were at the rec—me and Walter—sitting around reading comics. The kids hadn't shown up yet, it was very quiet, and the door fuckin' explodes open. Mewes marches in like Groucho Marx and proceeds to fellate anything remotely phallic in the room. So if there's a pool cue, he's sucking it off. Grabs the phone receiver and he's suckin' it off. And never once lookin' at us as if to say, "Isn't this funny?" I don't know if he even knew we were in the room. He just had an agenda. Like he's walkin' around town, goin', "It's 3 o'clock, I should go to the rec and suck everything off." So he comes to this standing Asteroids machine, and there's no joystick on it—just a roller ball. He comes to it, sees the roller ball, shrugs and starts goin' down on the roller ball. I was like, he's brilliant, in some warped kinda way.

I used to say, "You're fuckin' weird, dude. Someone should put you in a movie." Then when I got into film, I said, "You know what? I should be that somebody." So I wrote a character for who he was at 14 or 15, when I first met him. Except for back then, he was straight edge—a clean livin' kid. He was one of those kids who talked incessantly about pussy, but had never seen it. He'd talk about all the things he would do to pussy, how he rules pussy and shit, but had never seen a naked woman in person other than the birth canal he emerged from. He'd scream to the rafters, "I love pussy!" But if a girl came anywhere in a 10-foot radius of him, he'd clam up.

In 1992, I went to film school up in Vancouver. I was gone six months, then I dropped out. When I got back, he was completely debauched. He'd discovered booze and weed. He was a stoner. And he was startin' to notch his belt up pretty high. He was no longer the kid who talked about pussy and didn't know what it was. Now he knew what pussy was.

When did you find out what pussy was?

I lost my virginity when I was 13 to a girl named Norma. It was weird 'cause I was raised hardcore Catholic, and I had created in my head the line of what constitutes virginity. So I'd been inside Norma, but I'd never come inside of her. So I thought I was still a virgin. Years later, I had what I considered to be real sex, when I was 17. There was a girl named Carrie who I actually came inside. Then someone pointed out to me that that was a fucked up definition of virginity. Then I realized I had lost my virginity a lot to Norma.

How did you meet this Norma?

I went to this dance, and I met Norma there. She was really beautiful. We started hanging out, and we were dating pretty much through the first year of high school. I remember she had a waterbed, so I lost it on the waterbed in a dark room with all this music playing. It was pretty cool.

Was it your idea or her idea?

It was kinda mutual. We'd been through all the heavy petting and whatnot, and it was just one of those things. I remember her being like, "Do you wanna go inside me?" And I was like, "Hell yeah."

Was she a virgin?

I don't know. I would hope. We were both pretty young at the time.

And Mr. Mewes—how did he lose his virginity?
I remember because he told us about it in detail. There was this girl we had kinda introduced him to at this party. He was real shy about it. And we were like, "Get in there man. She likes you. Go ahead and kiss her and stuff." She took him into the bathroom to kiss. Found him later that night, and he said he'd had sex. We were like, "Dude, we sent you in to kiss the girl. How did you close the deal?" And he told the story of how she was like, "Let's do it." He was fumbling around, and the whole time she was bitching him out, saying stuff like, "Oh, God! What are you doin'? You're not doing it right. Are you in yet? This is terrible! Alright, hurry up." That's how he lost his virginity—in a bathroom at some person's house.

I see you're into Marlboro menthol ultralights, you've got a whole box sitting there. Do you smoke weed, too?
Nah, I could count on two hands the amount of times I've smoked weed. I don't really drink, either. I'm not really anti-drinking, nor do I not drink because of some horrible past of being an alcoholic, I just don't like the fucking taste of it. And I like having my wits about me. But cigarettes are my vice. That, and I like to eat all the shit that's bad for you. If it has sugar, I'll eat it. Any Hostess snack you could throw my way. Any candy bar you could throw my way. I'm a big chocolate milk fan. Chocolate milk runs in my veins. Of the four major food groups, I do the grains and cereals, the meats and the dairy, but you can't get a vegetable or fruit down my throat. The stuff that's good for you is the stuff that I stay away from.

Do you pig out in front of the computer?
I don't usually do it there because I'm busy typing. But in front of the TV, that's a different story. Last night I was watching Firestarter with Drew Barrymore, and I downed a whole box of Cinnamon Toast Crunch.

Dry?
Oh, no, with milk. That's dangerous. You just keep going until you go to pick up the box of cereal and there are like three pieces left in the bottom.

So what's your favorite cereal?
Lucky Charms. I will sit there and kill a fucking industrial-sized box of Lucky Charms. Sometimes my wife will look at me like, "God, will you put the spoon down!" How 'bout your favorite food?

Fig Newtons.
You do the Fat-Free Fig Newtons?

Yeah, but they're not as tasty as the ones with fat.
That's the thing, if it tasted too good, it's probably fattening.

Originally printed in WYWS Issue #14

KEVIN SMITH PUTS SLIM-FAST TO THE TEST

DARK CHOCOLATE FUDGE
It's very rich. I guess the overriding taste is chocolate. But it's not like Quick Chocolate Milk. It's kind of like chocolate is the aftertaste. That's all right.

FRENCH VANILLA
Vanilla's not bad. In recent years, I've become a fan of vanilla. I always thought that vanilla was the lack of taste, but it actually has a taste all its own. Is this a soda?

ORANGE-STRAWBERRY-BANANA
I don't know about this one. Maybe I need to shake it up... Ugh, that's pretty bad. It tasted like there's a hint of that orange-strawberry juice that Tropicana makes. I'd have to say of all of them, this is the worst.

ALF EXCLUSIVE!

by Fat Rich

My quest was simple. Interview Gordon Shumway, better known as ALF, for an upcoming feature on aliens. No problem, I say, figuring I'll just call the Screen Actors Guild and get his agent's number. This is the point where all things went sour.

I called up the Screen Actors Guild and, to my amazement, ALF was no longer a member. According to my source, ALF was kicked out of the guild. After the failure of the ALF movie, the only line of work he could secure was TV commercials. But during the filming of a Purina Cat Chow commercial featuring Shumway, Mindy the Cat, who had the lead role, went missing.

No charges were filed against ALF, but the shame of the incident left him unemployable. No motive was made clear on ALF's part, but many have speculated that he was jealous that the cat got the leading role. Others have said that he was just hungry.

I was up shit's creek without a paddle. I called the editor and delivered the news. He wasn't too happy. "Look asshole, that's not good enough! Find him! I already have 60,000 covers printed with the words 'ALF exclusive' real big across the front. They don't call you Private Fat Dick for nothing."

The hunt was on. I started with a little background. Gordon Shumway, aka ALF, was born on October 28, 1756 on the planet Melmac. Son to Bob and Flo Shumway, and brother to Curtis. ALF's profession prior to his crash landing on Earth, was an orbit guard. Their job was to protect the planet, but they were horrible at it and the planet was destroyed in a nuclear explosion.

Somehow ALF escaped in a spaceship, but sucked at flying and crashed on Earth. More specifically, 167 Hemdale Street, Los Angeles, CA, home to the Tanners. For some strange reason, the Tanners befriended the furry little bastard and even gave him his nickname ALF (Alien Life Form). First there was Willie, the dad. He and ALF had a love-hate type relationship. ALF would love to do things like try and eat the family cat, Lucky. Willie had a son named Brian, and he and ALF would become the best of friends.

I had little in the way of clues. I got a hold of Brian Tanner. He said he hadn't heard from ALF since the Mindy the Cat scandal, but he gave me a lead. It was the name and number of the L.A. Humane Society. He told me to ask for Hector Hansen.

Since I had no other leads, I gave Hector a call. Hector sounded like a cross between Cheech and Chong, and Ricky Martin. He insisted we meet in person. He was very hush-hush.

Hector had been searching for ALF for six years. He explained his love for cats and showed me some startling statistics on the severe decline in the cat population in L.A. He contributed these losses to ALF. Pointing out that the decline began around the disappearance of ALF from the public eye. Hector had photos of a crime scene at the local catnip factory. He claims ALF uses it as bait to lure the cats in.

On the way home, something Hector said gave me an idea. ALF used catnip to catch cats. Why shouldn't I use cats to try and catch him? The next morning, I woke up refreshed. After a little research, I found out the rarest cat was a Mexican Hairless Cat. Since this cat is so rare, it must be a delicacy to any Melmacian. I called 15 pet stores, but none of them had even heard of the thing. As a last resort, I called Hector.

"Ever heard of a Mexican Rat Cat?"

"Hairless or the furry kind?"

"The hairless one."

"Why yes, my precious Tulip is one."

It took almost an hour to persuade Hector to let me borrow his cat. My plan was simple. Hector had told me that the main area of cat disappearances was on the eastside of town. I thought I'd just tie the cat to a dumpster in some back alley, make some meows, and wait till Shumway appeared and grabbed him from behind. After I had him in custody, I would trade freedom for an interview.

After three hours of waiting, all I had to show for my efforts was the fact I smelled like garbage. Just when I was about to pack it in, I saw something sneaking up the alley. I ducked into cover and kept my eyes peeled hoping for the best.

The best was not to come. What did come was some guy in a chef's hat with a meat cleaver in his hand, wearing a T-shirt that proudly stated "Number One Chinese Restaurant." All those stories my Uncle used to tell me about Chinese restaurants and passing cats off as Peking Duck must be true. Just as he was about to deliver the fatal blow to Tulip, I came running out of the dumpster yelling, "Health inspector!" It scared him off. I decided to untie Tulip and call it a day.

I was at a loss. A dead-end. I had nothing to go on. Everyone I phoned had either hung up on me, or was as useful as a used Trojan. Just when I was about to throw in the towel the phone rang.

"Hello?"

"I hear you've been asking questions."

"Who is this?"

"That's of no importance. You want answers, meet me at the Cool Cat Club in half an hour."

"Shumway, is that you?"

No answer.

Desperate for something, I took the stranger up on the offer.

The Cool Cat Club was a cheap strip joint with good drink specials. I got a table near the stage. Twenty minutes and two lap dances later I was beginning to think I got stood up.

All of a sudden, I heard a racket coming from the kitchen. I ran in to find some Chinese cook pointing out the back door. Grabbing the nearest thing within reach, I ran into the alley. I realized that the soup ladle wasn't going to be much use, so I chucked it. I heard another commotion from around the corner. Slowly and quietly, I lurked up to take a peak. To my disappointment, it was nothing but an alley cat. I walked back through the kitchen and back to my table. Still no sign of the mystery man. I ordered another round and requested another lap dance from Betty Whitetrash.

From here on things get a little hazy. All I remember is waking up in Betty's apartment with her underwear on my head and $100 less in my pocket. I snuck out of there and did the walk of shame back

ALF QUOTES

- "Does Bob Hope still have teeth?"
- "On Melmac we have first class, second class, fish, and ham."
- "No Problem."
- "I'll take care of it."
- "Ha, I kill me."
- "Here kitty, kitty, kitty."
- "It was an accident."
- "Before you get up for that final snack, I want you to know I'll be right back."
- "I'm a peoples' alien."
- "Yo, Lucky, my man."
- "Holy stork invasion, Batman."
- Wayne Schlagle, Michigan Life and Casuality."

home. I had no story and no leads. I was at a loss. I checked the machine and there were two messages. The first was from my editor screaming about the deadline. The second message, however, held my interest.

"Schmuck, that's the last time I invite you to a classy joint like the Cool Cat Club. I was in back trying to enjoy some dinner when your fat ass interrupted. I had bagged me an alley cat. Do you know how rare a delicacy alley cat is? It's like truffles, a needle in a haystack. I was going to grant you rights to the first all-exclusive ALF interview but you had to go piss me off. That's it! Interview off! No deal jacko! And just to let you know, I had nothing to do with that whole Mindy the Cat thing. I'm innocent I tell you, innocent!"

Originally printed in WYWS Issue #12

MELMAC FACTS

• Melmac is smaller than the Earth, but larger than a gopher.

• Pocket lint, dental floss, and battery-operated hamsters are among Melmac's chief exports.

• Melmac's national anthem is "Dance Till You Drop" by Homer T. Swipe.

• Melmac was once the intergalactic convention site for the federation of incredibly strange food groups.

• Melmac's only merchandising failure was rubberized scissors.

• Melmac's deepest lake is lake Glub-Glub. It was named after the last thing its discoverer said.

• The smallest creature on Melmac is a squish, named after the sound it makes if you accidentally step on it.

• Melmac's biggest box-office hit was *March of the Wooden Lips*.

• Tyrone Split was the biggest game show winner in the history of Melmac. He was 7-feet tall and weighed 327 pounds.

• On Melmac, Brussels sprouts can sing.

• Instead of money, Melmacians pay for things with fur. This way, if they spend too much, they go bald.

• During the holiday season, Melmacians dress up as vegetables and dance with their neighbors' pets.

• To run for president on Melmac, your middle name has to be the name of a cheese.

• In 1923, Melmac won its first blue medal in the intergalactic Olympics for freestyle fainting and guppy chucking.

• You can't own land on Melmac unless you are over 1-foot tall.

• Melmac's national flower was Roger, the turnip.

• Melmac was discovered 23,000 years ago when Harold Twink accidently took the wrong exit from Neptune.

• Before Melmacians existed, huge creatures used to roam Melmac. They looked like a cross between a dinosaur and an insurance salesman.

• Melmacians wore fresh fruit under their arms when they showered.

• Melmacians couldn't pronounce the word "Ohio" until 1956.

• The biggest clothing craze on Melmac was see-through socks.

• Cats taste very much like hamster.

• On Melmac it was illegal to juggle your cousins.

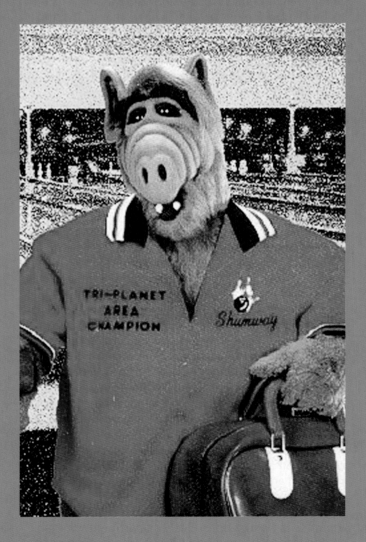

WORDS ALF JUST DOESN'T UNDERSTAND...

Racketeer: "I was really embarrassed to find out this had nothing to do wil Annette Funicello playing tennis."

Recycle: "Isn't that when you ride your bike on the same route two days in a row?"

Ruthless: "So sue me! I thought it meant Dr. Ruth's show got cancelled."

ALF TALKS ABOUT THE TUBE...

"Why are all of the agricultural shows on at 5:30 in the morning when the farmers are already outside working?"

"My favorite show is *Gilligan's Island*. But how come all five passengers packed so many clothes for a three-hour tour?"

"An alien can learn a lot from watching TV. For example, I never knew that before 1953 this entire planet was in black and white."

"If I've learned anything from watching TV, it's this: Those who can, act; those who can't, host game shows."

ALF ON DEATH...

"If you really can't take it with you, why does your life insurance policy only pay off after you're dead?"

"I've heard that on Earth, traffic accidents kill a lot of people. On Melmac, the biggest cause of accidental death is inhaling next to a talent agent."

"I guess I'd attribute my long life to the fact that I haven't died yet."

ALF'S UNCLE GOOMER...

"My uncle Goomer was a brilliant inventor. I remember when I was just 116, he crossed a pigeon with peanut butter and got a bird that stuck to the roof of his house."

"Sixteen years ago, Uncle Goomer got an Icky. No, it's not a disease... it's an award. He got it for being the host of Melmac's shortest-running game show, *Bowling for Lard*."

"Uncle Goomer's acting career ended when his voice changed and left him sounding like William F. Buckley."

ALF ON LIVING...

"I finally figured out the difference between apartment living and owning your own home. If you live in an apartment, you have to pay to take a ride in the clothes dryer."

"If Willie hates to mow the lawn so much, how come he waters it so often?"

"Why do humans spend twice as much money planting a garden as they save by growing their own food?"

ALF ON FOOD...

"It took me three months to realize that when the whipped cream can says 'Shake well before using,' they mean the can, not me."

"I wish cats really did have nine lives. I love leftovers."

"My idea of a balanced meal? As much food as I can carry in both hands without dropping it."

ALF ON TRANSPORTATION

"Willie told me that, in the 1960s and 1970s, all cars were named after animals. I'm surprised no one came up with a car called the Gopher, for people who like to run their cars into the ground."

"Why do earth cars have so many different gears? On Melmac we only had three: fast, really fast and yikes, we're going to die!"

"Lynn was saying that, in high school, you have to take Driver's Ed. What I want to know is, who's Ed and where do you take him?"

MELMACIAN RIDDLES...

Q: What's green, moldy and covered with meat?
A: Stan, the barber.

Q: How many Melmacians does it take to screw in a light bulb?
A: One. Why would it take any more than that?

Q: What do you get if you cross a fungle with a cat?
A: EEEW! How could you even consider that?

Q: What can you use a broken glazbarr for?
A: A paperweight. Ha!

IN THE BACKYARD...

"Yesterday I saw Willie cooking on a grill in the backyard. He called it 'barbecuing.' On Melmac, we did the same thing... but we called it 'thinning the cat population.'"

"Willie was in the backyard last week and he said he was 'spraying for bugs.' I thought we had enough bugs before he sprayed."

JOSH'S SECRET
Story and Photo by Josh Slater

When I was a little kid, I thought the perfect way of getting paid was Tom Hanks' job in the silver screen classic Big. His job in Big was to be a professional toy tester. Definitely a 10-year-old's dream, but my recent real-life job consistently gives grown men cream dreams.

I had the honor and privilege of being one of the select few who helped dress the Victoria's Secret models at their annual New York lingerie show. I know what you're thinking, and no, I didn't sell my soul to the devil and sacrifice a little girl on a homemade altar while listening to Slayer to get this job. I got it the old-fashioned way: through a friend.

The night of the show, my job was to help one of the models (or "girls" as they're called in the biz) put on a metal snowflake and then guide her to the runway, making sure she didn't run into anything. I was paired with an Aryan-looking chick who was about 6-foot-10. I called her "Caroline," but she quickly cored me ("Karo-oh-lean"). I could tell we were going to be BFFs.

After waiting and waiting—and drinking glass after glass of free Moet—it was show time. I had to apply the snowflake to her back, which looked more like a giant ninja star. So picture it (like Sophia from the Golden Girls used to say): I'm on my knees tying this crazy-looking backpack to sweet "Kar-oh-lean" with my nose pretty much up her ass. Not a bad day's work. I then followed her to the runway, protecting her and her back piece like a rent-a-cop on a power trip. Right around the entrance to the runway was pretty much a moshpit of all the "girls," their makeup people and other assorted hangers-on. So I had to play Moses in a sea of models. This led to one of the most surreal moments of my life.

As I was doing my best Kevin Costner imitation, I felt my elbow hit someone's breast and realized that I accidentally elbowed non other than Tyra Banks. In shock, I turned around, and because I have long, skinny arms, I elbowed another tit. This time, it was non other than the Teutonic giantess Heidi Klum. I could have dropped dead right there, but I didn't want everyone looking at my massive erection.

Originally printed in WYWS Issue #18

TV GUIDANCE

As you well know by now, we at *WYWS* are always in trouble. From smashing pumpkins to scribbling something with spray paint, we're totally pro-property damage. But way before I met the other *WYWS* staffers, I had my television teaching me how to nurture my own creative sensibilities whilst destroying things that didn't belong to me. However, the sitcoms made it clear that there is vandalism etiquette, a right and wrong way to have fun at someone else's expense.

—Ian Sattler

Originally printed in WYWS Issue #20

SCENARIO #1: DESTROYING YOUR HOME.

As Seen On TV: That pesky Steve Sanders! He's always talking the Walsh kids into all sorts of dumb shit. Here, Steve comes up with the bright idea of throwing a party at Brandon's house, and since it's going to be sold soon, Steve **thinks it would be hysterical to destroy the house by spray-painting hip phrases like "party" all over the walls.**

TV Guide Says: Just because it's close by, doesn't mean your house is a good place to start a career as a vandal. Brandon was in a pretty bad spot when he found out that he'd be living in the house he'd just trashed. Poor Brandon, all of this and Kelly is fucking some loser artist-guy. Brandon should've gone out and spray painted "cock junkie" on Kelly's house instead.

SCENARIO #2: DESTROYING YOUR NEIGHBOR'S HOME.

As Seen On TV: Steve and Elyse Keaton, with all of their hippie ideals and moral posturing, had to be the worst parents on television. So it should come as no surprise that in the first part of a very special two-episode *Family Ties* tale, **the Keatons naively try to convince their black friends, the Thompsons, to buy the house across the street. The Thompsons politely insinuate that they might not be welcome in the upper-class-cracker neighborhood, but the Keatons insist. By the second episode, the Thompsons' house is broken into and the words "go home" are painted on the walls.**

TV Guide Says: Vandalizing your neighbor's house is stupid because the troublemaker down the street (aka you) will undoubtedly be the first person they suspect, but painting racist slurs is fucking retarded, especially if your name is Alex P. Keaton and you drive up and down the street sporting a GOP bumper sticker—that must've been a dead giveaway.

SCENARIO #3: DESTROYING NO ONE'S HOME.

As Seen On TV: Maybe it was just that *Leave It To Beaver* **was from a gentler time, but the Beave's mischief was vanilla at best. Take the episode where the cops find him and Lumpy throwing rocks** through the windows of an abandoned house, and the kids are forced to run for it. Pretty lame, right?

TV Guide Says: Lumpy and Beaver? Who the fuck names their kids Lumpy and Beaver? Beaver had the right idea, but his only problem was the cops who happened to be creeping by had nothing better to do than bust a couple of white bread boys with stupid-ass names.

SCENARIO #4: DESTROYING YOUR SCHOOL.

As Seen On TV: Jessica Biel's character, Mary, is the bad girl on *7th Heaven*.

When Mary finds out that her basketball coach is forfeiting the rest of the season because the girls' grades aren't good enough, the shit hits the fan, the girls go wild, break into the gym and destroy everything in sight.

TV Guide Says: 7th Heaven has got to be the stupidest shit on TV. Jessica Biel even posed naked in some magazine in an attempt to get fired from the show. But for all of its religious propaganda, 7th Heaven hit the nail on the head when it comes to vandalism. Your school hates you, and it's time you did something about it. We suggest any of the ultra-flat Rustoleum colors.

GROUP HOME LIFE: 10 THINGS YOU SHOULD KNOW

by Zee Oh
Illustration by Linas Garsys

SHIT

If you're a danger to yourself or others, you will be put on suicide watch, which means a staff member has to be with you at all times. For an undefined amount of time, you will have to sleep on the living room floor next to the night staff, and a staff member will accompany you in the bathroom anytime you have to shower and/or shit. The latter can be used to your advantage to get back at staffers. Especially after chili night.

SWALLOW

There are two rules at meals: One, you have to take a minimum amount of everything prepared, and two, you have to eat everything on your plate. This means that on a pretty regular basis you will have to eat shit you hate. In my case, that meant I had to eat tomatoes and ground sausage. Your best bet is to swallow these things whole. Don't risk actually chewing your food or you will throw up and still have to finish your dinner. Been there. Done that.

SHAVE

Razor blades aren't allowed and you will only get access to electric razors once in a while. When you finally get access to an electric razor, don't go crazy. Do not, under any circumstances, shave your eyebrows off. Do not draw them back on with a ballpoint pen or Sharpie.

LEARN

If you're in a high-security group home, you will not be allowed to attend school and will be group-home schooled instead. Group-home school is a joke and you will not learn anything. Luckily, you have group therapy for that.

Even if you didn't have a drug problem, you will probably have to sit through non-anonymous Narcotics Anonymous sessions. Pay attention. The things you learn here will come in handy later in life. See the "Lie" section below.

WORK

Work project is group home speak for slave labor. For a minimum number of hours a day, and all day on Saturday, you will be forced to do manual labor. If you have a choice, do not volunteer for the chicken coop. Pulling weeds or moving railroad ties beats chicken shit any day.

BREATHE

On the rare occasion that you're sick enough, and they take you to a doctor, and that doctor leaves you alone in a room with a nitrous tank... do I really need to finish this sentence?

RESTRAIN

If you mouth off or start freaking out, you will get restrained. This means that three to five overweight staffers will lie on top of you and hold down your feet, legs, back, arms and head. Unless this is one of your fantasies, show some restraint and see the "Shit" section above for a better POA.

RUN

Shoes aren't allowed, which means you will have to wear sandals, at all times, even in the snow. This will actually work toward your advantage because, if you do decide to run away, you can do so barefoot and won't feel a thing. However, in all my time at the group home, only one kid successfully escaped, so I don't recommend it.

SHOVEL

If you do run or get restrained, you will end up at the compost heap. This means shoveling a massive pile of shit and rotten food back and forth until they tell you that you're done. If you refuse and it starts to snow in the meantime, do like Kathy did, and dig a hole in the pile and lay in it to keep warm. That'll show them.

LIE

If you have been there for two years, and they still won't let you out, don't freak. This will only mean being put back on suicide watch and having to stay there longer. Instead, tell them whatever they want to hear: "Yes, I will respect my parents." "No, I won't do drugs." "Yes, I understand how shoveling shit fits into the therapeutic process." Make sure to write this stuff in your journal too, because they will read it while you're out on work project.

Then, when you finally get out of the group home, get tattooed, get your tongue pierced, do massive amounts of drugs, stop going to school, shoplift, pawn your camera for drug money, date thugs from Oakland, get into fistfights, and do everything else you learned about in group therapy and weren't allowed to do in the group home.

HEAVY METAL PARKING LOT

by Ben C.

Images courtesy of Heavy Metal Parking Lot

Have you ever had sex while laughing at a redneck with hockey hair saying, "They should make a joint so big it fits across America?" I have. After my mom goes to sleep, my girlfriend comes over to watch Heavy Metal Parking Lot, the best 16-minute documentary ever made.

In fact, you may have seen us necking at Washington D.C.'s last artsy theater, all the way through HMPL's 15th Anniversary. Yes, Jeff Krulik and John Heyn, the two masterminds behind the cult phenomenon, have re-released the movie, plus a slew of other short films inspired by HMPL such as Harry Potter Parking Lot, Monster Truck Parking Lot and Raver Bathroom. But let's say you're not hip to all this HMPL talk, let me catch you up.

In 1986, John and Jeff, two 20-somethings with the time and access to video equipment, asked each other, "Why hasn't someone made a documentary about the two silliest things in the world: hillbillies and heavy metal? Reading that Judas Priest was coming to town, John called Jeff, who swiped a camera from work, and the two headed down to Landover, Maryland's Capital Centre. "We had no idea what to expect," Jeff, now a freelance TV producer in his 40s, explains. "We weren't metal heads but we knew it was a scene. We watched MTV and listened to the radio. We all knew the different stereotypes of music fans. In hindsight, I wish we had done more." We all do. But they did manage to capture some of cinema's more memorable characters. Examples: The zebra-print guy, Ms. "I'd jump Rob Halford's bones," and, of course, Shirtless Graham—"as in a gram of dope."

You couldn't write it funnier. So why aren't Jeff and John as famous as the Farrelly Brothers? There is still a glimmer of hope. Recently, girl band American Hi-Fi straight-up jacked HMPL for their video "Flavor of the Week." In college, we call that plagiarism but Hollywood calls it "paying homage." As John explains in a slightly disgruntled voice, neither he nor Jeff knew the video was being made. It just appeared on their doorstep one day like, Hey, dudes, we hope you don't mind that we stole your great idea and are now getting rich off of it. Of course, John and Jeff do mind, but there's not much they can do now, except try to ride the Hi-Fi publicity wave.

At the end of HMPL's anniversary show, they show the music video, demonstrating how they've finally infiltrated the MTV world. "We're happy to be superstars in the underground," John, now married and editing instructional videos, says. "What we crave at this juncture is some mainstream success," Jeff continues, explaining how they plan to capitalize on this whole hair-rock comeback. If red-necking is suddenly chic, shouldn't every city-boy ironically rocking a mullet own a copy of HMPL?

Get yours here: www.heavymetalparkinglot.com.

Originally printed in WYWS Issue #14

PLAYIN' SPLASH WITH JASSIE

SIN CITY STARLET JASSIE SHOWS JELLY HOW TO EAT HER CATCH OF THE DAY

by Jelly
Photo by Carlos Batts

With her raven tresses in curlers and her lithe, 19-year-old bod clad in white cotton undies, Sin City girl Jassie is eager to play with Jelly's fishing pole. In town for Erotica L.A., she didn't have time to visit Jelly's pad to fix him up something to eat. So Jelly grabbed a bag of Starburst Fruit Chews and headed to Jassie's hotel room, with a Lite Brite and Splash under his arm to cook up some fun.

Splash is first. The little fishies go around the electric pool in a circle. Whoever hooks the most guppies triumphs. Jassie bends over the pond doggie-style; her petite derriere high in the air. It's all ol' Jelly can do to keep from fainting.

"Yay, I win!" cries the star of the XXX-rated flicks Quiver and Flash! "Now, I'll teach you how to play Lite Brite." Off goes her top. Jassie feels freer without it, and Jelly doesn't mind. With her nipples pointing straight up, Jassie's perky breasts look sweeter than the Starbursts.

"See, I spelled my name," she says, and Jelly's impressed with her artistic abilities. "Now what do you wanna play?" asks Jassie, half-naked on the unmade bed. There's a twinkle in Jelly's eye and a song in his heart. His eyes roll heavenward as he thanks the Creator. Life is very, very good.

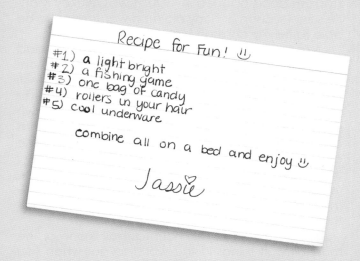

Recipe for Fun! :)
#1) a light bright
#2) a fishing game
#3) one bag of candy
#4) rollers in your hair
#5) cool underware

Combine all on a bed and enjoy :)

Jassie

GRAFFITI

TWO HEROES
by Chris Pape

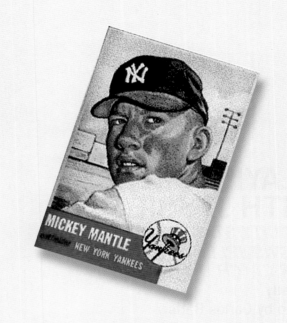

"It's so hard to be a saint when you're just a boy out on the street." –Bruce Springsteen

When I was 8 years old, my father took me to the cathedral on 161st street in the Bronx. If you don't know what that is, it's *the* stadium; I won't embarrass you by naming it. In 1968, when you went to the ballpark you put on a sports-coat and a tie, men in charcoal grey business suits wolfed down cartons of cigarettes, the smoke hung lazily in the air, drifting around girders that had been in place since the stadium doors opened in 1920. It was Mickey Mantle's final season and my old man wanted me to be able to tell my children I saw him play.

We took the number 4 train uptown; my dad read the sports page while I listened to the rhythmic sound of the subway wheels. When we arrived, had our tickets torn, and walked up the ramps, an usher took us to our seats and wiped them down with a large fuzzy mitt. The Mick wasn't playing that day, but it was still a nice day at the ballpark, a little cold but the sun was out. The Yankee brass knew that most of the parents were there for the same reason my father was: Ruth, DiMaggio, Mantle— the passing of the baton, word was sent down in the late innings for Mantle to pinch hit.

Hitting a 90-mile per hour fastball is one of the most difficult things in the world to do, when you consider that if you're successful in one in every three at bats you're considered a star in baseball. The great author Roger Kahn once stood in against Sal Maglie of the Brooklyn Dodgers. Kahn had played some college ball and knew his way around the batting cage. His description of that event is one of sheer terror. Maglie went into his

wind-up and threw an 80 mph slider right at Kahn's head; at the last mili-second Kahn jerked his body backward, his feet jumped into the air. Kahn had dirt on his suit and was pissed off that Maglie had thrown at him, but anger turned to embarrassment when the umpire called it a strike. This is what Mantle faced over and over since his call up in 1951. Now he had 10 more games, perhaps 30 at bats to go and hit a towering shot, one more prodigious blast for the fans.

--

I'm in a car on the FDR highway with ZEPHYR and JAYSON, my eyes are slightly glazed over and I'm thinking back to 1969 and Mickey Mantle and the cathedral in the Bronx. It's March 2000, and we're on our way to visit STAYHIGH 149, the legendary graffiti writer. Three middle-aged men bound together by our love of the New York graffiti movement. Each us had caught the graffiti bug at a young age in the early 1970s and had unique careers. ZEPHYR was the great stylist in the group, while JAYSON had the unique distinction of being up in two different generations. I was the odd man out, my subway career seemed somewhat pedestrian next to theirs, but I gained later fame for my works in the Freedom Tunnel.

When I was 13 and roaming around with my brother on the IRT line, we would go from station to station checking every coin slot in the soon-to-be-defunct candy and soda machines. I had noticed graffiti springing up everywhere, covering the trains like ivy. Tags at first, marker, then spray paint—early on it was just motion tagging until someone discovered the train yards, and the writers had time to expand their vocabulary in a more artful manner.

149 St-Grand Concourse Station

2 4 5

STAYHIGH
149

Photo by Craig Wetherby

There were many important firsts—first outline, first stars, first candy-cane stripes, first 3-D—it seemed endless what you could do on the side of the train. In 1973, at the age of 23, STAYHIGH 149 painted the most ambitious and classiest painting to date. It was on the side of a number 4 train—the same train that shuttled passengers to Yankee Stadium. He spray painted his name from top to bottom in white and added his iconic saint figure smoking a joint.

To a 13-year-old that was just beginning his graffiti education, I was dumbfounded. The proportions were exact and it seemed to stop right in front of us so I could touch it. My brother and I jumped on. The white paint covered the windows beautifully and I kept saying over and over again that we were riding on a cloud. There might've been better trains but this one was mine.

In the next two years, STAYHIGH 149 would become the undisputed king of the city. A good deal of STAYHIGH's fame came from the media. *New York* magazine featured a photo of him in 1973, as well as SNAKE 1, PHASE 2 and NOVA. This one magazine helped launch a movement that would last another 17 years, 'cause everybody wanted to be like STAYHIGH, and then he was gone. Although, he left us one last present, his new name, VOICE OF THE GHETTO, which he bombed everywhere in three toned uni-wide magic markers.

--

I've practically made a living tracking down old-time writers, not financially, but spiritually. SANE was perhaps the best of anyone, and even he couldn't find STAYHIGH. After looking for 20 years, I wound up finding STAYHIGH in the *New York Times*, photographed at a gallery show with KASE 2 and BAMA. I set about trying to get the interview, and the phones started ringing. The people I talked to all asked the same question: Did STAYHIGH realize his legacy? The answer was yes and no.

ZEPHYR, JAYSON and I arrived at STAN 153's apartment in the Bronx not quite knowing what to expect. The disappearance of STAYHIGH had become part of the reason we loved him. Almost every old school writer had been accounted for, but none that had the weight that STAYHIGH had. He was so popular that people actually claimed to be him, and one went so far as to get a tattoo of his tag. We walked up the staircase to STAN's crib and were greeted warmly by BAMA and STAN. There were some loose-leaf paper pages with STAYHIGH tags that made his presence felt, but he wasn't there. I settled into STAN's couch and sifted through the drawings.

STAYHIGH entered the room like a basset hound, his chin leaning in everywhere as he shook hands and looked for markers, bobbing and weaving until he finally sat down. We talked for a while about him possibly doing some work for Zoo York Skates. He was clean and lucid and looked me in

"THE PEOPLE I TALKED TO ALL ASKED THE SAME QUESTION: DID STAYHIGH REALIZE HIS LEGACY? THE ANSWER WAS YES AND NO."

the eye and struck me as quite bright. I bring this up because a lot of older writers aren't, and because I had to interview him. He was generous enough to sign books and seemed genuinely humbled by all the attention. ZEPHYR gave him a copy of the *Faith of Graffiti*, the same book that featured the big red train with his signature piece. I gave him a mocked-up sign of the 149th street station with the hopes that he would sign it. There was some down time as we set up for the interview and I started thinking of Mickey Mantle again.

--

In the 1950s, as the Mick finally became accepted as DiMaggio's replacement, he was involved in a teeth-removing, alcohol-fueled bar room brawl that even the Yankees couldn't keep out of the newspaper, and a few weeks later they shipped off Billy Martin as a warning. The Mick kept drinking and the affairs become more lurid, but at the stadium, the Cathedral, all the Mick's sins could be washed away with one sweet stroke to the short right field porch.

On that cold autumn day in 1968, I would finally see what it was that I was supposed to hand down to my kids as the Mick came in to pinch hit in the eighth. After years of knee surgery his gimpy walk to the plate was agonizing to watch. I could see him, this big bull of a man with no long sleeves on under his September uniform, looking, praying for one last piece of redemption, and suddenly he became my hero.

--

Back at STAN's house, STAYHIGH and I sat together on the couch with BAMA. I asked the main questions but told everyone to jump in if they had something to say, and they did. What began as a straightforward interview turned into a roundtable discussion with STAYHIGH as the focal point.

It's always amazed me how much of our past our heroes forget. There's a legendary story about SUPERKOOL 223 and STAY HIGH waging a week-long, all-out battle for king of the city. It turns out that the story was actually STAYHIGH throwing down the gauntlet to every major writer. He claimed that within one week he could kill more fronts of the subways than anybody else. Back in the day, the front was a pivotal position because it would eventually rotate into the first car on a train, and when that train roared into 149th street station, home of the writer's bench, you got major props. So, imagine a week going by and STAYHIGH hitting every front in the yard, going from the 2s to the 4s and hitting every train available. Imagine you're a king—SUPERKOOL 223, LEE 163, PHASE 2—and you're all sitting at the writer's bench on the Concourse when the week's up. Imagine your horror as you're hit with one STAYHIGH after another, each tag with the reminder "no comp," or even worse, "ya dig." Not a question, but a statement! You gotta dig me, it's nothing to be ashamed of.

As we had just begun, I had to ask him where he'd been for the last two decades, and he deflected the question citing personal problems. This is where any good journalist would pounce on him, it's the story. But I didn't. In the 1950s, it was OK for a ballplayer to get drunk and punch a guy so hard that he spit his teeth out like Chiclets, as long as he had the Yankee machine behind him. STAYHIGH 149 didn't play for the Yankees and he came of age in the 1960s, where getting high on dad's bourbon no longer cut it.

Sometimes, our heroes fail us, but they might not have wanted to be your hero in the first place. The Mick had the stadium for his own redemption—where STAYHIGH's sins were washed away remains a mystery. Mantle was inducted into the hall of fame in 1972 based on his cumulative stats, and maybe that's where STAYHIGH's redemption lies. Maybe it's the black-and-white photo published 27 years earlier in *New York* magazine to a city of transit cops that were looking for him. Maybe it's the big train, or the fact that he wrote so much that almost everyone has a heart or a halo accompanying their names in some bastardized form—I proudly include myself in that group—or maybe, just maybe, he's the VOICE OF THE GHETTO and all that that implies.

Mickey Mantle hit a homerun in the eighth inning, only I didn't see it. Everyone was standing at the stadium, and I couldn't see him. I met him years later and he was sad and drunk. When he died, I remember being touched by his funeral. I met STAYHIGH 27 years after riding his train and he impressed me. Warm, knowledgeable, generous to all of us that love him—you could do worse for a hero.

Originally printed in WYWS Issue #11

LITERATURE

COREY FELDMAN
Interview by Neil Mahoney
Photo by Adam Wallacavage

Bikini Bandits, the much-hyped series of naughty boobs 'n bullets web flicks, has finally produced the worst feature-length movie you will ever see. But, since you'll get to witness one of the last appearances of Dee Dee Ramone, it's definitely worth enduring this 69-minute Winger video. Its other "star" is the refocused solo musician Corey Feldman, who continues to amaze his generation with career choices. Catch him on tour all summer supporting his new album *Without* on Crazy Bastard Records.

It seems *Bikini Bandits* and your cameo in Moby's video are pushing a new self-conscious take on celebrity in general. What does this mean to you?
I would say [Bikini Bandits] is the worst piece of crap I have ever been involved in. I am definitely ashamed, shocked and dismayed to have ever lent my name or likeness to such a piece of shit... Essentially, I think [the rest] is bullshit because I don't want to continue my career playing myself—it's kind of a worthless existence. To me, it's always about doing things that are more challenging and about trying to hit the next plateau in your career. So I do it all with a big smirk. For now, I am doing certain things to make somewhat of a statement [that] I don't take myself or anything else too seriously and at the same time take it all seriously enough to let everybody know that I am not going to continue being patronized, labeled or categorized by my past. So, in one sense, I've done several things this year to kind of capitalize on my past, but to let everyone know that it's the last time that I will be doing it... On the acting side of things, I suppose I am disappointed that I got stuck in the rhetoric of disheveled iconism at a very young age. However, I have risen above it, and, hopefully, the rest of society will get the message after all of this and see me as the actor that I am, as opposed to just the celebrity.

Your new album has a track called "Megalo Man" about Michael Jackson. Tell me about the "MJ" phase of your career...
Well, you see, what happens is when he sticks needles full of drugs in young boys' arms, it's very easy for them to fall into a kind of admiration stage, where they feel they need to dress like him, and dance like him, and sing like him. But that's just strictly the mind-manipulation process that he puts the kids through.

Holy shit.
No, I'm just joking. You were just like, "Whoa, I guess I just I got some juicy shit!" Listen: In the 1980s, what kid didn't dress like Michael Jackson? I don't think that was just a phase in [my] career, as much as it was a phase of society kind of going, "Hey, this guy is the coolest thing since sliced bread." But then we all grew up in the 1990s and stopped believing in Santa Claus, and we said, "Oh, alright, this guy's just another wacko, another artist." You'll hear what I really think on the album.

What's it like having celebrity's access to beautiful women?
Well, understand this: I certainly don't go out with women that want to be with me because of who I am. The bottom line is this: I've always had the strict advantage that if I am in a club, and I see a hundred hot chicks floating around, I know for a fact that if I look at the hottest girl in the club, I can have her. I know that sounds really egotistical, but at the same time, it's just kind of a matter-of-fact thing. That becomes the game, whereas most guys who aren't celebrities are like, "Can I get a chick? Can I get laid tonight?" For me, it's got to be the top. It's really the same game on either side of the spectrum; it just depends on the level that you're reaching for—we're all just trying to get laid, right? But now I am engaged, so I don't have to worry about those kinds of things anymore.

She's super-beautiful. How'd you meet her?
I met her in an L.A. nightclub, and she was there for her 19th birthday. I had just broken up from a really bad relationship, so I was trying to gather up a bunch of girls. See, usually me and my brother and our friends will find a bunch of chicks and say, "Hey we're having an after-party," and invite like 20 or 30 people back to the house, and we'll see who wants to have fun, who wants to hang out, what's going on, you know what I mean? So, I was going to invite her as one of the candidates, and she stopped me and was like, "Hey! You're Cory Feldman, right?" And I said, "Yeah," and she goes, "You know I've been a fan of yours until... well, until today." I said, "Good fucking answer." Because she said that and it was clever, we hit the dance floor immediately. I bought her a drink, we danced, then I took her home, and we made passionate love all night long.

Wow. Well, that should about do me, anything else?
I just hope everyone enjoys all the new work that I'm putting out. Enjoy the past too, but let go of it a bit—that's my wish.

I'll do what I can to make those wishes come true.
Thank you. I appreciate that.

Originally printed in WYWS Issue #19

COREY
FELDMAN

RICHARD TRENTON CHASE
by Ben Shupe

Nevada. An oasis of rock and sand in a world we call shit. This magical land is filled with hookers, aliens, fat Italian guys, an occasional Elvis impersonator, and a couple homosexual magicians who like to molest white tigers. What a party. If you'd been there in August of 1977, you might have witnessed **RICHARD TRENTON CHASE** naked, covered in blood, and being chased across the desert floor by the Nevada police.

Once apprehended, there was a little explaining to do. He told one cop the blood was seeping from inside him. A minute later, he recanted his story for another officer: It wasn't human blood; it was blood from a deer he shot three months ago in Colorado. So, he sat in jail while authorities could determine the make of the blood. Later, he was released and forced to pay a fine when they discovered that the blood was actually from numerous cows that 27-year-old Chase had slaughtered from a nearby ranch.

Richard's childhood was as normal as any red-blooded American serial killer could have. At age 10, Chase found a love: cats. He loved to bury them in his backyard. Rick's teen years didn't treat him kindly either. He was arrested numerous times on drug charges and couldn't comprehend why his father never hired a lawyer to defend him.

Rick developed several "medical" conditions. He complained that his heart would stop beating, his stomach was turned around backwards, and his blood would frequently stop flowing.

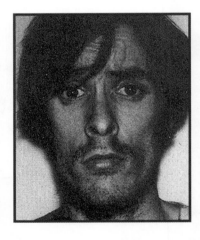

Chase believed injecting rabbit's blood into his veins would cure his ailments. Hell, sometimes he'd just slit their chests open and suck them dry like a bag of Capri Sun. After one of his rabbit cocktails, Rick woke up in the hospital, where he told the doctors about the rabbit. It seems the rabbit had eaten battery acid, which seeped through the walls of the stomach and into the bloodstream. The hospital decided to keep Richard for observation at Beverly Manor, which is where he earned the nickname "Dracula." Many a morning, the hospital staff would find him awake in bed with fresh blood covering his face. Oh, the poor little birdies that lay drained of all their blood right outside his window.

A few months and a few dozen birds later, Chase's mother made a convincing plea to release the troubled Richard into her custody. When Chase started coming out of his room stark naked and proceeded to strike up unintelligible conversations with house guests, the family thought it best if he found his own place. In a quest to stop his blood from turning into powder, he began butchering and drinking dog's blood. Again, Chase found himself with blood poisoning, so he found a new source for blood, which was, of course, humans.

He bought a gun and a 1974 El Camino soft-top. Chase's first human victim was a man he shot through a kitchen window while he was eating dinner. Next was poor unsuspecting Teresa Wallin, who always left her car unlocked and her front door open. This carelessness made it possible for her husband to come home to find her half-naked and laying in the hallway. There were two bullet holes in her head, her left nipple carved out, and her intestines spewed out like a busted piñata. There was also a little present in the bedroom for the husband: A big pile of shit in his wife's panty drawer, and urine all over his socks. How nice.

A day after the Wallin incident, police were called to some yuppie subdivision. Guess what they found? Evelyn Miroth, legs spread eagle, intestines rearranged. The ones that didn't fit back inside were left on the floor next to her. Her son and boyfriend were also dead, and the latter had been cut up like a Thanksgiving turkey. Ms. Miroth had been babysitting her nephew, but no baby was found at the crime scene. The authorities were lucky enough to find the baby later, hacked to chunks on the sidewalk of a church two blocks away. Chase was stupid enough to keep the kid's clothes with him, so when the cops found him, they found enough evidence on him, even without finding his blood-soaked apartment.

His insanity defense failed miserably. Prosecution moved too swiftly in the conviction of six first-degree murder charges. Chase was sentenced to die by lethal injection at Vacaville Prison in California. December 26 rolled around and Chase was still curled up in his normal fetal position with the pillow over his head. This time, the guard noticed that the pillow was covered in blood. The guard removed the pillow to find Chase bleeding from the ears, eyes, nostrils and mouth. It seems that Chase had been stashing his dosage of Sinequan, an antidepressant he was supposed to take daily. An autopsy revealed that Chase had consumed 36 times the lethal dosage of his prescription in one sitting.

Originally printed in WYWS Issue #6

SPAM
by Simon Steinhardt

About a week before I wrote this, a press release came to us, courtesy of Hormel Foods, regarding the opening of a museum in Austin, Minnesota, dedicated to SPAM and other Hormel products. Roger asked me to write a quick blurb about it and suggested, half-jokingly, that I eat SPAM for the story. I told him that there was no way that I would ever eat SPAM unless I was unequivocally wasted. We had a hearty laugh about it, and then a week later, out of the blue, Roger told me to get some 40s and some SPAM. Shortly after consuming the aforementioned items, I sat down and wrote this:

I got drunk and ate SPAM. It's kind of soft and salty. If I wasn't drunk, you prbably would have to kick me in the balls to make me eat SPAM. I drank to 40s, and some Sutter Home wine, but not much of the wine, and then Roger took some pictures of me eating SPAM. I'm still drunk, but they want me to writ this aticle. If I had to compae SPAM to another thing, it would be salty tuna fish in a can. If you eat canned food any-way, you probably have very little money so you don't care if it tasted like salty ass ham in a can. I'm really glad I got drunk before I ate SPAM because there is no way I would have eaten salty ass ham tuna when I am sober. St. Ides make the best 40s, I don't know why, There's gonna be a SPAM museum in Minnesota soon, it's gonna be weird, and I bet that most of the popel who go there will never eat SPAM. It tasted like shit, but at Least I can say that from experience, because most people are big pussies and won't eat SPAM. Morty won't eat Spam, but he wants to go to the museum opening on September 15. Who eats SPAM anyways? I bet they won't go to the museum. Oh yeah, I'm wearing a hot dog hat from the costume shop, it's cool, I can wear it sideaways and it's still cool, but I'm wearing

it normal right now, although I wore it sideways when I finished my first 40. I would suggest that if you are going to eat SPAM you should get drunk or do some drugs that'll make you forget that you ever ate SPAM because it is deplorable. Oh my got, I'm laughing so hard right now. People try to fuck with my hot dog hat, but they can't even front. Can't front on the SPAM, yo. We are all wearing weird hats today, but mine is the coolest, just because it is on myh head, which is the coolest head in the office, word is bond yo. Yeah, so SPAM isn't something you would eat every day and shit, but it';s not so bad when you get trashed in the afternoon. Oh shit, I can't believe I ate SPAM a feew minutes ago, but it wasn't that bad considering that I barely tasted it. But this SPAM muse um sounds tight, it's gonna have SPAM trivia and the Monty Python SPAM sketch which was the shit back in the day. Word is bond yo. So suck a might dick if you think SPAM sucks because you are gay if you don't like SPAM. Even though it tastez like crap, you better eat it if you want to become a real man.

I was still trashed when I got home from work that day, and my dad started talking to me about our new lawnmower. I tried to go pass out, but I threw up instead. I eventually did pass out, but my mom came home and woke me up and was about to start lecturing me about how I sleep too much, but I told her I was sick and explained what happened. She finally went away. I then endured the most painful, sickest night of my life. I can't say that SPAM was completely to blame for this illness, but I have a strong suspicion that it figured heavily into the equation.

Originally printed in WYWS Issue #14

BURRITO MEMORIES:
Mr. Food vs. El Tepeyac Café

by Ian Sattler
Photos by Roger Gastman

Four years ago, Roger asked me to come back to *WYWS* and reclaim my mantel as "Mr. Food." To be honest, I was unsure at the time if I wanted to do it. I was coming off my second divorce, my blood pressure was dangerously high, and I was still banned from competing in any sanctioned food challenge within the United States. But I knew I could still eat like a champion, and as long as I was competing against myself, I could take on any dish I wanted. I have never regretted that decision, but I came close the night we went to El Tepeyac Café in Los Angeles, California.

Word on the street was that El Tepeyac served a five-pound burrito called the "Manuel Special." I wasn't too worried about the prospect of defeating a giant burrito as they are the food I trained with the most on my way to becoming a professional eater. I should have known something was wrong when we got so lost on the way to the restaurant that even our GPS didn't know where we were. After a while Roger, Zio, WISE and I found the spot and took a table in the very middle of El Tepeyac.

The next warning sign came when I discovered that the Manuel Special seemed to fluctuate between five and seven pounds, depending on construction and filling. I settled on a Manuel Special filled with steak and waited for it to arrive. The tricky thing about burritos is that they look smaller than they are because the tortilla wrap condenses whatever ingredients are inside. The Manuel Special looked *huge* so I had to take into account that it was even bigger in terms of actual crap I had to eat.

My secret strength as an eater is that there is a serious lag time between when my stomach is full and my brain understands that my stomach is full. In other words, I have to eat fast enough to keep my stomach ahead of my brain. I tore into the Manuel Special like it was my enemy. I was carving off huge chunks and shoving them into my mouth while trying to block out the other people at the restaurant who were now focused on my quest.

This is where I hit another surprise—the burrito was excellent. I usually try and block out taste in these situations, but the Manuel Special was super tasty and also filled with a lot of peppers so I had to get past the heat as well. I finished the first half of the burrito in about 20 minutes and then the unthinkable happened… I hit the wall. I was already full and I had at least three pounds of burrito to go. I was

honestly shocked. I kept plugging away but was seriously discouraged when I found what appeared to be half of a steak hidden under a pile of lettuce.

I sat back and rocked from side to side as I tried to clear any room that was left in my system. More time passed and I managed to get down to about a quarter of the burrito. I was panicking inside my head and started to make noise about stopping and how this wouldn't even go on my official win/loss record.

Then, like a perfect corner man, WISE leaned into me and said, "What would Joe Gibbs want you to do?" The thought of the Washington Redskins legendary head coach was like a shock to my system that found room in my stomach where there had been none. I finished the burrito in under an hour and was deemed a champion by the restaurant's owner who presented me with an "I Ate The Whole Thing!" victory T-shirt.

I may have finished the burrito, but my ordeal was far from over. I literally couldn't move on the way back to Roger's house. I slept on the floor and woke up the next morning with both of his dogs sleeping next to me and realized that I must have smelled like restaurant dumpster and Manuel's Special. I looked like I was hung-over and my hands were shaking slightly. I felt terrible until I saw my T-shirt lying on the couch. I was still a champion. I was still Mr. Food and I had many more *WYWS* food challenges to destroy.

I believe it was the summer of 2003, I was in my junior year at the Corcoran where I was majoring in graphic design. All of our professors recommended getting an internship over the summer. We had some recommendations from our professors, however, most sounded pretty lame. Spending my summer as intern in some political or law office, type setting Word documents in Garamond sounded awful. I wanted to do something that could be fun and creative, plus I thought I was a pretty awesome designer and wanted to show my skills!

I had been into *While You Were Sleeping* for a bit, because of the graffiti aspect. By 2003, *WYWS* was really getting big. It had hot shit, photoshoots with hot chicks, sick fashion, hilarious and often perverted writing, and graffiti from all over the place. I wanted in. I wanted my name in. I wanted to flex some design muscles. Screw the internship at the greeting card office in VA.

So I put some samples together and sent them over to Roger. We meet a week later and I ended up getting the internship. The first day on the job I showed up ready to go with a retarded-looking smile on my face. I meet with Dave, one of the graphic designers for the mag, and was told Roger would be with me in a minute. He had a real important job for me. I could see him through the glass in his office, talking on the phone and looking around for something.

He came out of his office about 30 minutes later, and hands me a picture. Doesn't say a word. I look down, and it's a picture of a chick, blonde, with curly hair-metal band groupie hair, and huge tits. I am a little thrown off and just look back up at Roger, wondering what is the purpose of this. A gift? Payment? Are we bonding? All he says is, "This chick has really great boobs, I would like to use them in the magazine but you can see too many veins." He points and says, "See right those blue veins, I need you to scan this in and Photoshop out the veins or something." Then he walks away.

I learned over that summer that this was just a typical day at the offices of *WYWS*. Man that was a great summer! I even learned something about design and the magazine industry—well, that's what I told my professors anyway.

—*Gabe*

I've known Roger since 1996. I went to go meet up with a mutual friend of ours, CERT, at the Bethesda metro station and Roger pulled up in a 4runner, and we went and hung out. That night, we went to Roger's mom's place, and he had all sorts of graffiti stuff and it was all very cool for me because I didn't have any of that stuff in my room. I was still hiding it from my parents.

Very shortly after, Roger started *WYWS*. I think I bought the first copy at a store, and I showed it around to all the writers from PG County. It was really cool that there was a magazine from around the way that was representing the scene.

Almost around that same time, I was doing a lot of street promotions, and booking acts for this club down on U Street, where we were doing open-mic hip-hop nights. I started doing some partnership stuff with *WYWS*, like they sponsored our event Power Moves, gave us stickers, and we had some magazines there—we were representing everyone's brands together, showing love for what he was doing, and in turn it made us cooler because what he was doing was cool.

Then, a few years later, when the investment was made in the magazine—Roger had already been at it for a couple years, and already had six or seven issues out, and this guy liked what he was doing and was from around the way and wanted to invest—I got put on as an official employee for *WYWS*, doing street promotions, putting up stickers, you know, basically just talking about the mag to folks, letting people know about it and representing that on the street.

Everybody loved the magazine, especially the first seven that were put out, which were very heavily graffiti-focused. The writers loved those most. When they started to bring in the fashion and other stuff, which is all extremely cool and raised the value of the project, the writers were all kind of like, Aw, man, there's less graffiti in there, but in turn, you were being turned onto other stuff. I think that was a credit to Roger being a tastemaker, bringing things to you that you should know about, things people are talking about and interested in, and even some stuff that was way ahead of the general public's grasp. Just adding all that extra stuff in there, I appreciated the magazine more. D.C. got less play, but I think it was a good thing that made the brand a lot more interesting, a lot more valuable. *WYWS* was three, four, five years ahead of other magazines.

I think Roger's just incredibly focused—to have an idea, to nurture it through all the phases, and then into production, and post-production—that's the thing that really excited Roger probably more than anything, and I share that with him. That sense of accomplishment at the end of a project is very, very similar to pulling off a really dope burner or wall you've worked on all weekend with your homies. At the end, you feel that sense of accomplishment, that it's solid, and it's done and it's documented. I think he probably gets that from the work that he's doing now.

It takes a certain person to combine resources, to project manage, because a lot of people are very creative, but a lot of people cannot do the things that Roger's doing because they don't organize, dedicate or commit themselves to a certain level. Working 16 to 20 hours a day on a project is not uncommon for people like Roger who really produce great things. People who only work seven or eight hours a day are only doing the basics. If you're really driven to do what you want to do, you've got to put in those hours.

No bullshit, a lot of people player hate on Roger for his success and the things he's done, but the reality of the situation is, they should all be kissing his ass at this point. People who have said those things about him are not doing things that are more important than him.

I think if people only look at what Roger's been doing as business, it would be very shortsighted, because where Roger's strength lies, at this point currently, is in collecting these artifacts of culture and documenting them. And some of this is extremely significant, like the graffiti that happened 10 years ago was no where like it is today, in terms of documentation and telling of the story and tracing of the roots. A lot of the major things that can be pointed to as legitimate pieces are Roger's pieces, the *Freight Train Graffiti* book, *The History of American Graffiti* is going to be the lexicon, and so *WYWS* was just the beginning of that.

—*Cory Stowers*

Class Pictures

2001

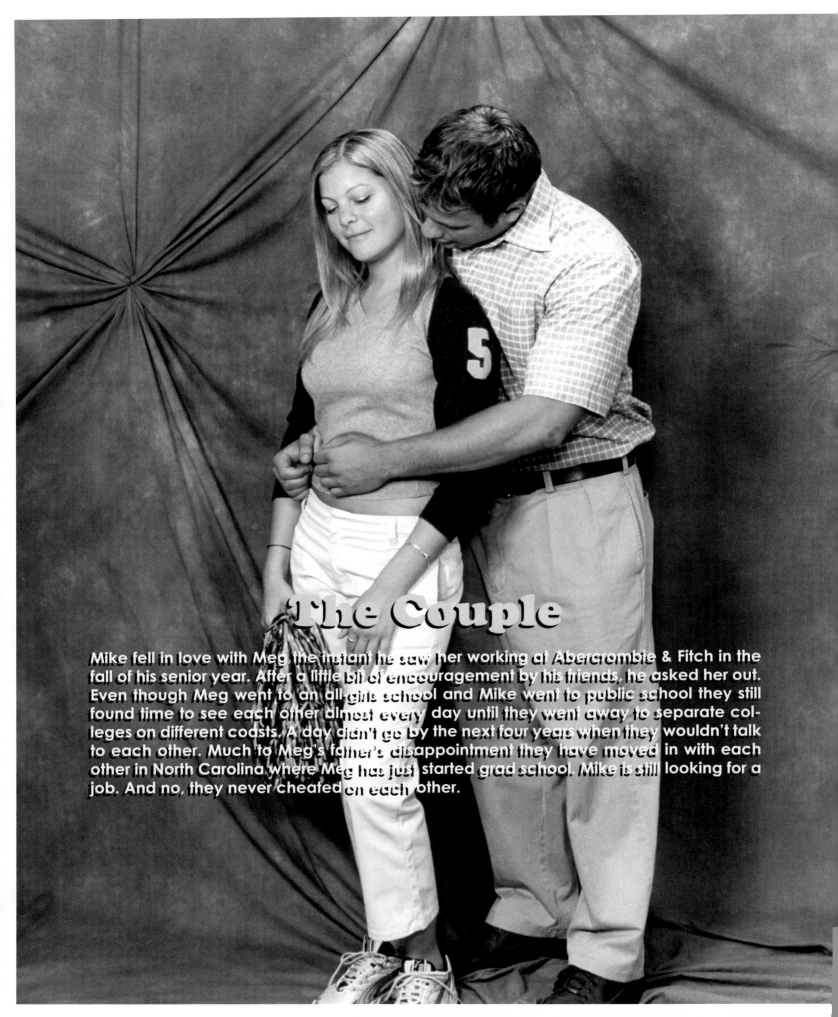

The Couple

Mike fell in love with Meg the instant he saw her working at Abercrombie & Fitch in the fall of his senior year. After a little bit of encouragement by his friends, he asked her out. Even though Meg went to an all-girls school and Mike went to public school they still found time to see each other almost every day until they went away to separate colleges on different coasts. A day didn't go by the next four years when they wouldn't talk to each other. Much to Meg's father's disappointment they have moved in with each other in North Carolina where Meg has just started grad school. Mike is still looking for a job. And no, they never cheated on each other.

Drug Dealer & Druggie

After learning about supply and demand during his freshman year social studies class, Chris decided to quit his after-school job at the sports store and start putting that knowledge to use. Currently under investigation by the DEA for drug smuggling, Chris has taken up tennis and moved back in with his mom. Neal's drug habit never seemed like a problem. "I can quit whenever I want, I'm not an addict, it just gives me something to do 'cause this town sucks," Neal was overheard bragging to a friend before over dosing on _____ during P.E. He was suspended for 10 days. He is currently living a sober life in Minnesota after extensive rehab programs.

The Bully

"Mushmouth," as his friends call him, didn't manage to graduate, but he did manage to beat the crap out of almost all of the students in the three schools he was expelled from. On Mushmouth's 18th birthday he started a food fight in the cafeteria and when the vice principal grabbed him from behind he didn't look, he just swung. That was the last straw. Mr. And Mrs. Mushmouth kicked his butt out of the house, leaving him to fend for himself. Mushmouth thought about joining the Navy, becoming a boxer, and several other things while couch surfing the next few months. He currently lives in L.A. where he is a bodyguard to the stars, a la Pamela Anderson's *VIP*.

The Slut

Lollipops weren't all Tonya liked to suck on. She wasn't all that picky, if you were the star of the team, had a nice car, were a few years older, your parents were out of town, or you took her to dinner, she was yours for the night, the week, the month, or until the next flavor came around. Her junior year of high school her parents came home a few days early from their second honeymoon and found 17-year-old Tonya in a not-so-pleasant position with two "older" boys. Statutory rape charges were pressed and then later dropped by Tonya's parents after they found she had lied to them about her age. They figured it would be wrong to ruin their two lives for their daughter's lies. Tonya was sent to an all-girls boarding school and has been happily living an alternative lifestyle ever since.

The Jock

A varsity starter for all four years for the field hockey and lacrosse teams, Christine led her school to state championships three of those four years. She accepted a full ride to Duke to play both sports. She is currently in her last year of college and faces the tough decision of whether to attend UVA law school or join the Olympic training team for the 200__ games in _____. *Playboy* has contacted her three times, and three times Christine has told them to "Go to hell!"

The Super Senior

Rich got along so well with high school he decided to stay an extra two-and-a-half years. His tour of duty spanned five schools and several states. After being asked to leave from his last boarding school because the principal was scared for his and his students lives, Rich landed back where he started, public school in his hometown. Being an almost 20-year-old senior begging your earth science teacher in a class full of mostly 10th graders for a passing grade isn't a pretty picture. After finally graduating, Rich tattooed, worked in a coffee shop, and was a bike courier before heading to Boston for art school where he still is. No one knows for how long.

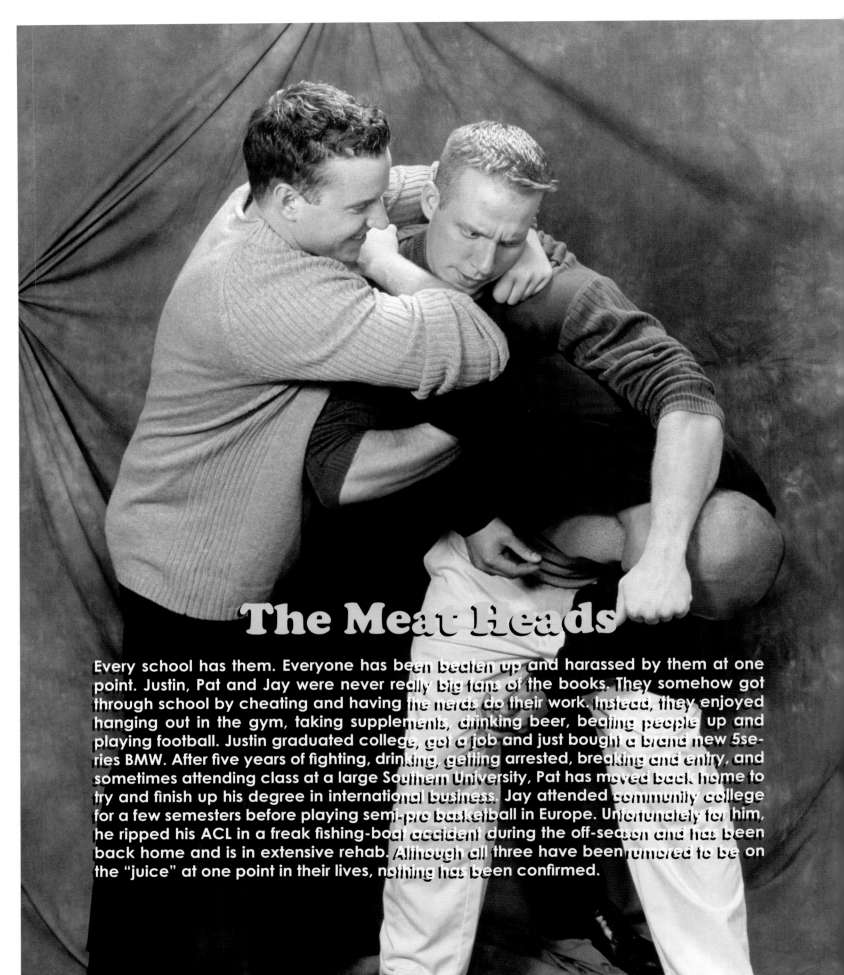

The Meat Heads

Every school has them. Everyone has been beaten up and harassed by them at one point. Justin, Pat and Jay were never really big fans of the books. They somehow got through school by cheating and having the nerds do their work. Instead, they enjoyed hanging out in the gym, taking supplements, drinking beer, beating people up and playing football. Justin graduated college, got a job and just bought a brand new 5-series BMW. After five years of fighting, drinking, getting arrested, breaking and entry, and sometimes attending class at a large Southern University, Pat has moved back home to try and finish up his degree in international business. Jay attended community college for a few semesters before playing semi-pro basketball in Europe. Unfortunately for him, he ripped his ACL in a freak fishing-boat accident during the off-season and has been back home and is in extensive rehab. Although all three have been rumored to be on the "juice" at one point in their lives, nothing has been confirmed.

The Clique

Kelly, Amanda and Kristin might not have ever committed a murder but behind their backs the entire school called them Heather, Heather and Veronica. Kelly was, of course, the head cheerleader, and to make the cliché even more perfect she dated the captain of the football team, one year her senior. Kelly's heart was broken when he went away to college and she found out that he had slept with half of her JV cheerleading squad and her younger, not-so-light-weight step-sister. Recently having graduated from college, she is engaged to a wealthy doctor who is almost old enough to be her father. Amanda was the goody-goody of the trio. Something like Donna from 90210 minus the David. She's not very close with Kelly and Kristin anymore. While at college, Amanda found morals and graduated with a degree in teaching and travels to third world countries teaching students that are in desperate need of an education and a positive role model. Kristin never made it to college. She went to work for her father's real estate company right after her graduation present, a first-class trip to Europe with Kelly and Amanda. Kristin is currently in the middle of huge divorce settlement with her husband, also a wealthy real estate agent who cheated on her with, ironically enough, Kelly's not so light-weight step sister. They are all looking forward to their five-year high school reunion.

PAT THE PARTY JERK

WOMEN AT WORK
by Trevor Michaels

So you're fresh out of school and you've just landed a new job at an office full of women. Let's say, for example, you work at the headquarters of a major clothing manufacturer in the Midwest (rest-assured that my rules apply for offices of all sorts, from Arby's to Goldman Sachs). What's the first thing you should do? As if you didn't already know: **Sleep with the girl in the adjoining cubicle.**

But, Pat, Mister Party Jerk, isn't that going to cause problems, isn't it going to hurt productivity, or worse, get me fired? Friends, take it from me: **If it won't get you fired, it's not worth doing.**

Seriously, what's more important to you: your job or the sex you have on the job? A 1997 study by researchers at Columbia University's School of Human Behavior indicated that 84 percent of all men have imagined making love to their female co-workers while masturbating. (The study also showed that 18 percent of all men regularly use a shampoo bottle for anal pleasure while showering.) Would you rather brag to your friends about the fantastic increase in the number of wool mittens your department shipped to Gary, Indiana, or about the time you laid rod for two-hours straight to the secretary with big bangs and tight-rolled jeans? I don't need to answer that question for you.

Now, it's one thing to close the deal with a female co-worker, but it's quite another thing to manage the aftermath in a manner tactful enough to keep yourself employed. If there is one lesson that transcends all aspects of the romantic world, then it is this one: **Men must learn to deny, deny, deny.**

A firm, straight-faced denial will often save your job and won't be too difficult to pull off if you don't waver. People would rather believe a good liar than try to prove him wrong (just look at the love O.J. received). A simple no goes a long way. Men must also learn how to divert an accusation. For example, if your boss accuses you of sleeping with the new high-school intern because he found a collection of her cotton floral panties bunched under your desk, then you should reply, "What makes you so sure they're her panties, anyway?"

And when the girls in this corporate harem cross paths, then you've got to get creative and remember that when girls make accusations, they aren't exactly looking for the truth so much as they're fishing for compliments. If Viki, the girl you banged in accounting, asks if you banged Hillary in merchandising, then you say, "Oh, the fat girl? You mean Saddlebags? Of course not, she's a linebacker. Why would I sleep with that mammoth when I can make love to someone with a luscious body like yours?" Though corny and transparent, this technique will save you from hours and hours of tedious arguments and bickering.

This brings up a very important point that you should write down and frame on your nightstand: **Lying is an art that can propel you to great heights.**

Don't fool yourself, the office is a place where the appearance of propriety is more important than propriety itself. So if you can cover your tracks, then the workplace will become less of a drab and sanitary location to perform someone else's mindless work and will become more like a setting with all the ingredients for a pornographic scene. You'll whittle away the time imagining every desk as a place to prop a secretary's ass in the air and the drawers as cum depositories.

Before you know it, it'll be time to retire. They'll throw you a pathetic party around your cubicle, and while they're singing "Happy Retirement," you'll be running a tally in your head of the dozens of women you lured into the men's room for a passionate morning screw. Then, you'll say to yourself proudly, "I'm at the height of my profession."

Originally printed in WYWS Issue #12

Sex, Death, Money & Robots

This cartoon wonderscape was provided by the unmatched, silky-soft hands of Richard Colman. His smiling style of anti-superheroism and romantic melancholy often elicit furrowed brows paired with the laughter of shared experience. Through his work with the *Playerhaters* traveling gallery show, the Coca Cola *Art of Harmony* mural campaign and projects with Boston Area Charities, Colman's army of collectors continues to grow as he approaches new projects in Europe for the Summer of 2002.

Photos: Rosina Teri Memolo
Assistant: Monica Keys & Chris Henzel
Hair: Khnong Tran for P.R. & Partners
Makeup: Ferdinand Aulia for P.R. & Partners

JACK AMSTER:
MACK DADDY OF THE CENTURY.
by Shawna Kenney

These days, Hollywood nightlife isn't raging over the Garage, the Derby, Dragonfly, Martini Lounge, Coconut, Cherry or the Key Club, but the 95-year-old Jack Amster. Self-described "jazzy dancer" and permanent guest-lister at all the above hotspots, the Hungarian-born scenester came to L.A. from N.Y. as a ready-to-retire machinist 40 years ago. Having been charmed by the legions of pretty girls, themselves enchanted by stardom, Jack himself is now the subject of the documentary, Jack: the World's Oldest Club Kid.

Jack was getting his freak on at the Dragonfly a few years ago when 29-year-old filmmaker Mae Lynch decided to make him the subject of her first documentary. Much to his delight, Jack has since been on Howard Stern and Roseanne, and invited to numerous Playboy Mansion parties to hobnob with Rod Stewart, Hef and hordes of bunnies.

His evening starts with careful preparation in his apartment, inside the beautiful 1920s art-deco style Montecito Building, a historic hotel-turned-senior facility, which he calls a "dump." He adds, "There's too many old people here, and a lot of them are crazy." He shits, showers and shaves to the tunes of Too $hort's You Nasty CD, picks out a cream-colored shirt to match his polyester pants, throws on his crystal amulet necklace, and combs his half-gray/half Grecian Formula #5 hair.

In the bathroom, the anti-bacterial denture cleanser sits comfortably next to a bottle of Pussy Enhancers Luscious Warming Oil in Hot Cherry Jubilee Flavor. "That stuff doesn't work," Jack informs. "It's just a gimmick." He admits he's only tried it on himself, but he can indeed "still get it up" and claims he had sex just a month ago. "I like to go down on a woman," he explains. "But I don't like the word vagina. It sounds like an organ, like liver. I call it cunt."

"OK, enough. Stop bullshitting, Jack!" says Mae, herding him out of the apartment and on to the seedier end of Hollywood Boulevard for a Tommy's Famous Chili Burger. "I like McDonald's," he says. "This isn't that good, not for supposedly being famous. That's bullshit," he says, waving his hand at the red-and-yellow "World Famous" neon sign. Then he whips out a 4-ounce bottle of Finlandia vodka from his pocket, dumping half of it into his wax-paper soda cup. "Alcohol's too expensive in the clubs," Mae explains. "So he gets these from the 99-cent store beforehand."

Next it's on to Club Cherry, a trendy place with topless go-go dancers and DJs spinning everything from trance to 1980s goth. When Jack shows up, the velvet rope is undone and he waltzes past the doorman without so much as a glance. The tiny senior citizen heads straight to the center of the dance floor and sways to the music with little side-to-side steps, holding his hands up in front of him, making hourglass shapes in the air. Fearless, he heads to the closest group of girls he can find, and his standard rave-like moves morph into "freaking" up and down the body of the tallest, most-scantily clad twenty-something of the three. She giggles and dances away from his hungry hands at first, then angrily moves her crowd to the other side of the club when he refuses to quit. Mae stops groups of club-chicks for pictures with Jack, and most are more than happy to oblige the photo op with such a sweet innocent old man. He's careful to keep his "I loved her tits!" comments quiet until they're well out of earshot.

After 45 minutes of his way around the floor, he declares, "Most of these women are men," and he demands that he and his posse head to the Sunset Room, where he knows there's a Playboy party tonight. There he's met with smiles of recognition, and the babes flock immediately. "Jack, we've missed you," "Why haven't you called me?" He makes his rounds and heads out to the dance floor for another couple of hours.

During breaks, he is glad to talk to anyone, answering questions about everything from the sublime (how he escaped the draft board in WWI) to the bizarre (he supposedly has the cure for AIDS, which he confidentially gave to some doctors in San Diego) and hilarious ("My brothers never liked me—I think they both even fucked my wife!"). He hands out copies of his manifesto-of-sorts, a typed sheet of paper titled "Attitude," which explains his secret to longevity. From the looks of his DMV Senior Citizen's ID, you have to hand it to him; he just may have tapped some inner pipeline to the proverbial fountain of youth.

In a strange twist of fate, Lynch is now Amster's legal guardian, checking in on him, and insuring that there's food in his apartment. "I leave him Popeye's chicken. He's not allowed to use the stove anymore after leaving it on all the time!" She makes sure that he makes his check-ups on time and gets out a few times a week. "He'd like to go out every night," she says, exasperated, "but I just don't have the energy."

She's sure the state wouldn't appreciate the fact that their outings consist of club-hopping three days a week, with her trying to keep his drinking to a minimum and him sneaking bong-hits from well-meaning fellow partiers, but she says, "It's what he likes. What can I do?"

Originally printed in WYWS Issue #16

Safety First Guarantee

THIS CERTIFIES that I undersigned a female about to enjoy a sexual intercourse with .... am above the age of consent, and is my right mind not under the influence of any narcotic or drug. Neither does he have to use force, threat or promise to influence me. Having no fear of him whatever, do not expect or want to marry him, don't know whether he is married and don't care. I am not asleep or drunk and am entering this relation with him because I love it and want it as much as he does, and if I receive the satisfaction I expect I am willing to play an early return engagement.

FURTHERMORE I agree never to appear as a witness against him or to prosecute under the Mann White Slave Act.

Signed before going to bed, this .... day of ...., 19........

Name ....

Address ....

JACK AMSTER

Ahhhh, *WYWS*! I have just one word: pivotal! No, actually, sick is more fitting! Then again, funky fresh works well... Cool comes to mind... Weird, oddly entertaining, somewhat interesting but not so much, come to think of it, fuck that mag! Piece of shit... Thanks for nothin'. Roger... dick.

—EASTO

WYWS was just the beginning of the long story that would become a great friendship between Roger and I. I saw some things while working for *WYWS* that I will never forget. Truly a magazine that was born and died before its time.

—Eddie Donaldson

While you were sleeping, Roger was eating. Perhaps that could be a title for a new magazine of Mr. Gastman's. The man is a food connoisseur of sorts. However, thinking back to my encounters with the magazine that I am writing about and you are reading about right now, I distinctly remember a particular issue with an unsettling, yet intriguing cover. Unless of course you like to hunt rabbits or slurp a rabbit stew from time to time. A cover story that I was particularly fond of because yes, Florida is weird and fucked up and it happens to be the state in which I was raised. The issue to which I am referring is issue 19 with the cover story, *This Is Florida*, by Colby Katz. The photos reveal an honest side of Florida. The Florida I have experienced. Growing up in the Sunshine State, the place of orange groves, beaches on both coasts and beautiful sunsets is anything but pretty at times. That is one thing that bothers me about perceptions of places, both promoted and perceived, the fact that the acceptable, jovial and aesthetically pleasing side is all you seem to get. *While You Were Sleeping* seemed to get it right. I liked the honesty. I mean, who doesn't like seeing heads wrestled into thumbtacks, blood-drenched faces, women hand-balancing dogs in a room fit for a David Lynch film, a depressed teen with a slight black eye dressed for a wedding or prom standing in a vast expanse of green. Hey, Roger, pass me a slice of pie, please. Oh, and yes, I will take extra cream on that.

—Rocky Grimes

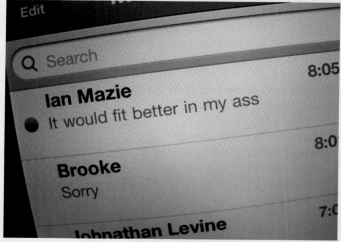

My now husband, Justin, was living with Roger in Bethesda while he was running the magazine. Everything about that house was *WYWS*—boxes of magazines in the garage, stickers, T-shirts and prints all over the place; friends, artists and writers coming in and out of town for Roger, sleeping on couches, in the basement, everywhere.

Roger put me to work a couple of times calling vendors, advertisers and setting up appointments. I can recall the boxes of spray paint in the garage and helping him organize it from time to time. I also remember doing a photoshoot for one of the issues of the magazine—come to think of it, I want a copy of that issue!

Roger would eat, sleep and breathe *WYWS*. Everything revolved around that. He was so passionate about it. I still wear my *WYWS* T-shirt proudly!

—*Kelly*

In the early days of *WYWS*, Roger would send me bricks of stickers, some T-shirts and stacks of issues. It was unreal what people would do for this shit—namely girls. Show them a sticker or give them a free issue and the tits came out. "Let me film you taking out your boobs and saying, *While You Were Sleeping*." No release papers, no signature bullshit, nada.

Looking back on it now, its absurd, almost unfair how easy it was. Back then, it made sense, but now it's like, WTF were these broads thinking?!

—*LEAD*

I was still in high school when I started interning for Roger at *WYWS*. Within a day, I was chugging Red Bull, transcribing shit interviews, and packaging and shipping fat caps. Within a couple months, I was a staff writer and photographer and Roger had gotten to me. I spiraled downward into a life of petty crime, theft and destruction of private property. You learn a lot about yourself in the ghetto of South East D.C. at 4 a.m. Bar Mitzvahs don't make you a man, but getting shot at for spray painting someone's wall… well, that doesn't either.

Here I am, 10 years later, thanks for the scumbag training, Roger.

—*Jeff Schroeder*

WHAT A MOTHER!

FORMER DEVO FRONTMAN MARK MOTHERSBAUGH KICKS IT WITH JELLY AND DROPS SOME SCIENCE ON GRAFFITI, POSTCARD ART, THE REAGAN ERA AND WEIRD SEX WITH GROUPIES.

by Jelly

Art images courtesy of Mark Mothersbaugh

Mark Mothersbaugh is a real motherfucker, and I mean that in the nicest way possible. Miles Davis claimed to have coined the term as the ultimate in superlatives, and it certainly seems to apply to the former DEVO frontman. Not only did he help found one of the most influential and unique acts of the punk/new wave era, but he also slept with one of the women I've lusted after since I was a little snot-nosed Southern kid in the 1970s: Laraine Newman of *SNL* fame. To this day, just the thought of her pale, contortionist's bod, long auburn hair and luscious overbite sends me into epileptic fits of lust. And Mothersbaugh had her for a couple of years back in the day. Damn his black hide!

That's not all Mothersbaugh has done to earn my eternal envy and admiration. Along with other members of the DEVO crew, he's responsible for some of the most memorable songs of my youth, songs like "Whip It," and "It's a Beautiful World" (now being used in a commercial for Target). He scored *Pee-wee's Playhouse*, and his company Mutato Musika has done ads for McDonalds wherein they've inserted subversive subliminal messages like "Biology is destiny" and "Choose your mutations carefully."

To top it all off, the motherfucker's an accomplished visual artist whose work has been lauded by art mag *Juxtapoz* and exhibited at various galleries. Indeed, Mothersbaugh is a one-man factory of inventiveness, churning out his "postcard art" at dizzying speeds, while composing music for all the films and commercials Mutato Muzika sucks into its vast cerebral vortex.

Mutato HQ is an odd green circular structure with mirrored windows situated on Sunset Boulevard just across from Tower Records. The building has no signs, and like millions of others who've passed it by, I've long wondered what the heck was going on behind its pistachio façade. Now I know: It's where Mark Mothersbaugh oversees all creative activity on spaceship Earth as part of his alien reconnaissance mission.

Life is strange. One minute I'm watching Mothersbaugh in a compilation of DEVO videos to get in the mood for this interview, and a couple of hours later, there he stands before me, a bit older and grayer, in stainless steel horn-rimmed glasses and a gray T-shirt. So here's my interview with the motherfucker.

Looks like your building got tagged, big-time, dude.
Yeah, these taggers have gotten really diabolical. I saw the guys right before they did it, and they just looked like a couple of frat boys. It was about the end of the day and I saw them out there pointing at the wall. I was like, I wonder what they're doing out there. By the time I got outside, the paint was fresh. The bad thing is they had an ugly tag. That's the problem with most taggers, they're shitty artists. They have unimaginative and uninteresting looking stuff. It's just a stain.

Maybe you could critique their work for them.
At least a lot of the original taggers, people like FUTURA 2000 and even Keith Haring were doing interesting things and had their own style and had something still worth looking at.

Well, there's *some* cool stuff out there...
About 99 percent of it sucks.

Did you study art in college?
Yeah, fine art at Kent State University. When I originally went to college, I was just trying not to go to Vietnam [pulls out a pocket full of his art postcards]. I do these every day.

Nice. How many of these do you do a day?
It depends on what day it is. If it's a day when they're blowing up the World Trade Center, I might do 20 or 30. Some days I only do a few. Since I never did them originally to show to people, I didn't care if I mixed mediums or if they got filthy or stupid. I liked the stuff that was kind of stream of consciousness. I'd do it and then I'd be like, "Where did that come from?" Now, I've been using Photoshop. Like in this one, the background is Photoshop, and then I drew on top of it.

How long have you been doing postcards?
For about 30 years. It keeps me from going out and driving my car into the side of a playground full of kids or something. I put them together so that they sort of tell a story. They're usually observations of whatever happened that particular day. You'll probably end up in them.

MARK
MOTHERSBAUGH

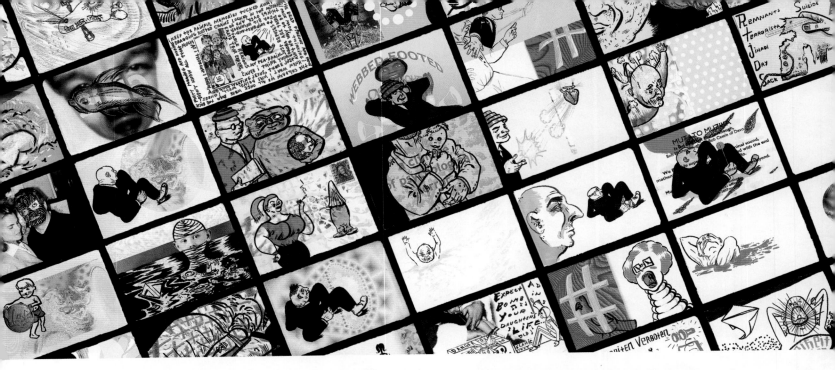

Is it true you did the music for the new Wes Anderson film?
Yes. In fact, Anderson just vacated the downstairs where he'd been editing his movie The Royal Tenenbaums. They were working down there right up until Friday, now he's back in New York. Doing a film with someone like Wes Anderson is a really enjoyable project.

How did DEVO end up doing commercials and film scores?
We just fell into it. In the early 1980s, I wrote some music for this Hawaiian Punch commercial, and it won a bunch of awards. Then a friend of mine, Paul Reubens, asked me to score his TV show. I started doing Pee-wee's Playhouse at the time it came out. I thought, "Well, I can still do stuff with DEVO, and every other week, I can do something for Pee-wee." It kind of went from there. The first time we scored a movie was for Revenge of the Nerds Part Two.

Then we started doing a lot of commercials, and we found out you could just put weird stuff in them. These people in the ad world were these hyper, overly enthusiastic types who never reflected what they were doing. The things that were important to them had nothing to do with the music, so they'd let me do whatever I wanted as long as I followed a few simple rules. Then we started throwing in subliminal stuff. I was sure that someone was going to freak out, and say, "Did you put something in our commercial that says, 'Sugar is bad for you,' and it's on TV now?" But they didn't.

Can you say what commercial that was for?
I won't if I don't have to, but Gummi Life Savers comes to mind, without really mentioning anyone. Every time we'd do something like this and play this music for people in these meetings, I'd blush. But no one ever paid any attention. They'd just be bobbing their heads, and tapping their pencils, like good ad agency people.

Do you think people pick up on those messages?
I hope so [wicked laugh]. We were wrongly accused of putting them in our first little movie we made about DEVO. This is like the mid-1970s, and there's no such thing as MTV. We were showing it at the Akron Art Institute, and these people came up afterwards and said, "I know what you're doing. I heard the word 'submit' and the word 'obey.' I saw them flash on the screen." We were like, "Uh, yeah, that's right. So do it!" Then we were looking at the movie going, "Where the hell did they see that?" Ever since then, I've had it in my mind that I liked the subversiveness of it. Usually, people do it for all the wrong reasons, like if they're trying to get you to drink whiskey or something. Whenever I've used it, it was always to try to balance out whatever message was overtly being pushed on people with the commercial.

Do you think there's any irony in the fact that such a radical rock group as DEVO now works on corporate advertising?
DEVO has always embraced pop culture. I was influenced by pop artists like Andy Warhol and Roy Lichtenstein—artists who appropriated Brillo Boxes and tomato soup cans. With DEVO, we always liked walking that fine line of commercial art and fine art. We created our own stupid icons like red hats and yellow suits, and we sold T-shirts and stuff on our album sleeves. At the time no one was doing anything like that.

You guys were also critical of popular culture. The idea that there's devolution instead of evolution is a pretty critical concept.
We were just being even-handed reporters of what we saw going on around us. We saw things falling apart.

Did you get laid a lot from being in DEVO?
That was one of the best things about the whole experience, because the record company never paid you what

you were supposed to get. It was really wild times before AIDS showed up.

Do you have a lot of residual drugs in your system?
Every now and then, if I go on a fast or something, I discover a few more. It'll be like, "OK, that was that all-night party at Timothy Leary's house and Larry Flynt showed up with Althea and they were throwing film canisters of ecstasy out into the crowd."

Did that really happen?
Oh yeah. Larry Flynt used to be really interesting while Althea was still alive. He was in a wheelchair, but he had a really good outlook. And he was a defender of First Amendment Rights. So you'd go over to his house and there'd be Russell Means, the Indian activist who shot the FBI guy, and Madalyn Murray O'Hair, the atheist, her and her kids would be there. It was this weird rag-tag bunch of people hanging out with Hollywood hipsters.

I remember sitting at a party—my girlfriend at the time was Laraine Newman—and we're sitting in a room with Terry Southern, Tim Leary, Angie Bowie, and G. Gordon Liddy. I remember sitting between G. Gordon Liddy and Timothy Leary and somebody was passing around, like, an ashtray full of cocaine. I watched Tim Leary do some, and he's talkin' to G. Gordon. And I passed it over to Liddy, and Liddy was doin' it. There was always something goin' on. The early 1980s were pretty wild.

In the 1970s and 1980s, there was this clear demarcation between being part of this corporate mass and not being part of it. You get the impression that still exists?
Back in the 1970s, if you said that we're devolving, people would go, "You're fucked up. You're assholes. You guys have got a bad attitude." And now you say the whole world's devolving to kids today and they go, "Yeah!" and they pump the air, give the victory salute and run off to see System of a Down, Blink 182 or something.

What I really appreciated about you guys in the 1980s is that you were one of those groups fucking with the whole Ronald Reagan Cold Warrior ethos that was so in vogue then.
In this country, we'd been fed this propaganda that there was this big, ugly machine that we were just keeping at bay with all the money we were spending on defense. Then with the fall of the iron curtain, all of a sudden you realize that behind the curtain, what was there? Some tiny guy shaking his fist. They had nothing. There were a bunch of potato planters over there. They posed no threat in reality, but you and me, we had nightmares.

When I was a little kid, I remembered dreaming that I looked out the window and the Russians and the Nazis had joined together and they were going down the street collecting all our neighbors and making them march in front of this tank. And I remember seeing Mrs. Larson with her pink bathrobe on. Then I got chased by them afterwards, they were hunting me down and I remember sliding and I did a curly and just kept going 'round in circles while these Russians came over and that's when I woke up.

Who was Mrs. Larson?
My school friend's mom. She was hot. I saw her bent over once with this robe on, her ass was pointed towards me, and I remember I had this urge I could barely control to just run over and push my face right into the back of her pink robe, right into her ass. I never did though.

Too bad.
Yeah, tell me about it.

Originally printed in WYWS Issue #16

ATMOSPHERE

Interview by Ben Fasman
Photo by Dan Monick

When I would drive cross-country to visit D.C., I'd cruise America for days on end, biting the ends off of Twizzlers and using them as straws for my Dr. Pepper. Once, after days without human contact, I took a detour to the Mall Of America right outside Minneapolis. I hoped to sit in the food court and watch cheerleaders rock silver eye shadow, high tops, bad skin and fast cars. Instead, I found the Mall ain't shit. When I met Midwest-coast hip-hop superstar SLUG (Sean Loves Ugly Girls) from Atmosphere, I thought he'd be able to tell me why their fancy mall sucks so hard, but instead I heard about people shitting themselves and Christina Ricci tribute albums.

I've heard rumors about girls kissing each other in the front rows at your shows...
Yeah, I used to only see that in Minneapolis. I thought it was this weird isolated thing, but recently I've been seeing it in L.A, NYC—over the place really. I'm not saying if you come to an Atmosphere show you're definitely going to see chicks kissing, but... I guess it's just not all that rare to see chicks making out these days, and, for some reason, it seems to gravitate around our shows. It's weird, I always knew that Dibbs [Atmosphere tour DJ] put sublimi-nal shit in his sets, but I always thought

What kind of subliminal shit?
I really shouldn't be telling you this... Well there's this noise called the "Brown Zone." It's too low for the human ear to register, but for some reason, it has a physical effect on you when you hear it... it loosens your bowels. It makes you shit yourself. Dibbs brings all these gadgets to the shows, and the sound men have no clue what they do, but he runs these sounds through the whole set. (That's fucked up that I'm telling you this.) I haven't positively seen any shittings yet, but then again, I doubt anyone would come up and admit it.

You've been categorized as "nerd rap," "backpack rap," and I even saw one website classify you as a "rap-emo hybrid." You have a lot of songs about girls, but are you a nerd? Do you own a backpack?
Yo, that's a writer's tool. I ain't really mad at it. Writers have to come up with some way to describe shit to people who might not have heard our stuff, so while I don't want to be that guy that gets this new label put on him, I understand that game... and writers gotta get laid too. If that writer wants to be fucking famous and get laid, he's gotta write cool and be smart about it. So go ahead. Get your pussy.

Exactly. It's all about women being attracted to the quality of my writing. What other projects are you working on?
Me and Murs did a record together that's a tribute album to Christina Ricci. We had to cut it down to an EP, though. We're letting this really old guy put it out, so it's going to be really hard to find, just because we wanted to be dicks and make a good record that no one has. Anyway, there's 10 tracks, and the songs aren't all about her, but they're all for her. Like, if she listened to them, she could find the reason why that song was about her, whereas to the average listener, it's a little bit more ambiguous. If you stop and think about it though, you'll figure it out. Lots of Addams Family references.

Are you going to get a copy to her somehow?
Look, I want to fuck Christina Ricci. So does Murs, except I think I got him beat because I read People magazine religiously, and she's never with any black dudes. So I think I may have the edge on that one.

BAD LUCK 13

Interview by Baby Patwick Kennedy

Photos courtesy of Bad Luck 13

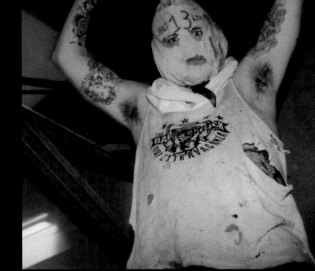

Big sister 13, mommy older, daddy in jaily, uncle put needley in arm, melty powder on spoon with lighter Smoke powder thingy on shiny foil. Lay next to crib all sleepy, turn colors. No hit baby. Bad Luck 13 tattooey and scary, beat people with pipey. Fire! Flames pretty like sunshine, hurt like bumblebees. Throwy bottle at babyhead. No play in grow-up clubs. Grow-up clubs and pig-gies make Bad Luck 13 go awayey. No playey. Blood come from face like when kitty step on thorn and say meow like when baby cry from belt whipping. Hur-y. Me talky to JAG, big sheet overhead like flamey cross men. He sings songs and breaks things like when Ddaddy go to room with bars on windows. Ask question, get answer. No hurt. No ouch. No more tangles and tears. Throw rat-le against baby mirror. Cry and spit up baby food. Pray for Jesus with baby hands. Bad lucky play for lots of years, more years than baby boy. Like to hide. No real names. Danger like red light on street. Hit by car is hit by Bad Luck 13.

Where from Bad Lucky 13 bandy?
We hail proudly from parts unknown.

Shiny badge man say you do bad things.
We have warrants out for us in New Jersey for aggravated arson, and two counts for inciting a riot. In Baltimore, we have warrants for grand theft, inciting a riot and harassment. In Springfield, Virginia, we have them for inciting a riot and aggravated assault, and you can add attempted murder in D.C. In Philly, we are banned from all clubs. If the police find out we are playing, they shut it down immediately. We've played maybe three clubs more than once during our career.

Do you get scrapy and bleedy?
Right now, we have these injuries pending: our bass player has a broken hand; our guitar player has a double hernia; I have seven stitches in my forehead, and someone else has six stitches in their face.

I get stings from bees since I was fetus thingy. What else happens to you?
Broken leg, second-degree burns, concussions, countless stitches, many broken fingers, two lost teeth, broken rib.

Big people see you and clap hands and run like beetles on our kitchen floor.
And there have been too many audi-ence-member injuries to name. Do I care? None.

Describey. Jesus has a beard like you. Woolyface.
The Mentors meets Bolt Thrower. G.G. Allin meets CZW Wrestling. We played a CZW on top of an 18-wheeler. We're putting the hard back in hardcore. I don't hate any bands in particular. I hate everyone.

Mommy make goal: make pie for baby boy. You have goaly?
Well, hopefully, some kid will listen to our music, and kill himself or others.

Originally printed in WYWS Issue #13

I feel as if WYWS and Roger are greatly [respon]sible for the success of the supergroup tha[t is Bad] Luck 13 Riot Extravaganza. After Bedtime[...] we have risen to the top of the fame, and with[out WYWS] I wouldn't be writing this, sitting in my ma[nsion in] parts unknown, on top of my throne made [...]

INTERN-VIEWS

Interviews by Jeff Schroeder
LaChat photo courtesy of LaChat
Brody photo by Carlos Batts

LaCHAT

Intern Jeff Schroeder never stops talking. We figured letting him do interviews might shut him up, but no such luck. After he interviewed Dirty South MC LaChat, and then asked the same biased questions to Australian punk rocker Brody Armstrong from the Distillers, we cut the three hours of tape down to the following columns. Now, go take out the trash and feed my meter, Schromo-sexual.

Let me just tell you about myself: I'm 17 years old, 5-foot-9 and 130 pounds. I got a 1999 Saturn with 15-inch stock rims. It's tight. Think you might be interested?
Interested in what type of way?

You know, what's your type of man— big? I'm just wondering where I stand.
Nah, they ain't got to be big, they ain't got to be small. It's all about their way of thinking.

If I got consent from my mom, do you think we could have sex?
I'd have to meet you first.

I don't think you really need too—you know I got a Saturn, I'm a 130-pound white boy, you know how I roll.
That's all I need to know, huh?

I heard about a feud between you and Bone Thugs.
That came from Three 6. They thought they brought out the style that Bone Thugs-n-Harmony got. Everybody in Memphis was feuded with them about that.

What's the difference between fronts and grills?
Fronts, them the ones you can take out, grills are like permanent. I got 12 permanent, top and bottom.

What's the song "Slob on my Cat" mean?
It's a replay to "Slob on my K—t."

It's when a guy is eating your pussy?
Yeah.

So how many times a day do you think you get your cat slobbed?
Uh, I don't get it done that much.

Do you have any pets?
Yeah, I got five pitbulls. One an inside pitbull, and the other four are outside pitbulls.

There's a really good line from "Slob on My Cat" that goes, "One ate my pussy and the other ate my butt." Does that happen often?
Nah.

Sorry to say I don't slob on the cat.
Everybody slobs on the cat.

Nope, no, sorry.
Make sure to include that in the interview, say "Everybody slob on the cat."

Listen, I've been working on a little flow: "Bring ya a hot dog/ My cunt be steamin' my buns/ Tongue my marinated meat curtains/ Explore my ass with your thumbs/ You got my cooze twitchin'/ So, you just stay down south/ Cuz I'ma cum so hard/ that I shit in your mouth."
I like that, it's hot.

BRODY

Let me just tell you about myself: I'm 17 years old, 5-foot-9 and 130 pounds. I got a 1999 Saturn with 15-inch stock rims. It's tight. Think you might be interested?
You got a Saturn? You need a truck or something. Put some rims on a truck. You don't need a Saturn no more.

That's what my parents bought me, there's nothing I can do about it.
Yeah, well you should trade it in. I push a Tahoe. It's a 1999, so it's boxy. Not like the new bubble shits.

How much was your stereo?
They took it out recently 'cause it was broken. So I'm looking at this big gap where my CDs used to go in. It's driving me fucking nuts.

Do you lick ball sack?
Yeah, of course, my husband's.

You got any kids?
Yeah, I have kids. Ten. Hopefully no more.

That's a shitload of kids, you're a baby factory!
I'm a baby machine.

Aren't you worried about stretching out your shit?
Nah, I'm tight! I'm tight.

I found out there was a little feud between you and the Bone Thugs.
Yeah, I stole their raps and sold them fake guns that I got from this porn shop.

Who's the best lyricist out there?
I really like Juvenile.

He's kinda faded, kinda washed up. You can only say "back your ass up" so many times. What does the song "Slob on my Cat" mean?
What do you think it means?

Eat pussy probably. Does that happen often?
All the time. Every day.

Would you get with a man that wouldn't "slob on the cat"?
No. What if women went around not slobbing on the knob?

I wouldn't like that. But what if the guy ate your ass instead?
No.

Listen, I've been working on a little flow: "Bring ya a hot dog/ My cunt be steamin' my buns/ Tongue my marinated meat curtains/ Explore my ass with your thumbs/ You got my cooze twitchin'/ So, you just stay down south/ Cuz I'ma cum so hard/ that I shit in your mouth." Did you rip me off?
Did you rip me off?

No. That was a J-Schro original. Did that do it for you?
Yeah, that's OK.

ANDREW W.K.

by Chris Nieratko
Photo courtesy of Andrew W.K.

Being a freshman in high school you don't get invited to many parties unless you have tits. Big tits. So instead of waiting to become sophomores, my friend Dave and I stole a beater 1976 El Camino from our friend's backyard and drove that bitch to the mayor's son's party like we were straight seniors. The only problem was the car had no steering, no brakes, no lights, no coolant, and worst of all, no radio. When we pulled up to the mayor's house we ran over three bushes, two small trees and hit an oak to stop, which made the hood pop up and pour out gray-and-black smoke. We got out of the car like Cheech and Chong to a round of applause. We were the hit of the party and every girl wanted to get in our pants. That might be my favorite high school memory and I think about it every time I listen to Andrew W.K.

What have you stolen in your life?
At every job I ever worked at, all I stole was cash. The best scenario was a parking garage I worked at. There were two guys, one working on each end. You'd organize with the other guy to take a four-hour break. You'd take whatever you could during those four hours. Most of the time it would work like gold. He'd be gone for four hours and I'd get about $100, $200 a day and then go to the fanciest restaurants downtown, and then I'd go play pinball at the arcade.

Did you have long dirty hair and look like a suspicious person?
No, I didn't look quite so suspicious. The earlier jobs, I was a borderline skinhead. The parking garage job, the reason that it all worked was that it was corrupt. The city contracts companies to work the parking garages and the companies are stealing so much money from the city. I would get a call like, "Your drawer was $100 short." I knew that it wasn't because I would be so careful. Other people in the office would just take it. People would take entire bags of deposits. The city shut it down.

Were you ever taken downtown?
No, never. I've done such bad shit: straight up mail fraud, check fraud, forgery. I've spent hours making fake checks. I forged baseball cards and sold dozens of them to a local antique-asshole-weird guy that I was friends with for a long time.

How did you scam Expedia.com into using your song "It's Time to Party"?
You've got ad agencies and they go around saying they need a song to go along with a certain idea. A good buddy of mine knew someone who worked at the ad agency and we gave them them a CD and it worked out great. In my ad, there's a dad with his family around him and he's typing, planning a trip for his family on Expedia.com. He types in "two adults." Then starts thinking for a minute. It flashes to his teenage son and it's a really good use of the song. The house is getting torn up and he types in "three adults." I'm happy, I don't give a fuck, give me money for my songs. They keep sending money every month. It's insane how much you can make.

Originally printed in WYWS Issue #17

THE MYSTERY ALIEN POD
by Caroline Ryder

There are a lot of things wrong about the place I work. One of them is the crazy, old Bulgarian dude in the building who wears a bunch of gold jewelry and always yells "hello" every time you walk through the lobby to go to the restroom. One time, he invited me into his office, then he talked about rape and licked my wrist. I was totally grossed out. He is 84 years old. He pulled a gun in the bakery next door one time, and they had to call the cops.

There are other things wrong with the office where I work. Like the giant roaches, the homeless people who live and piss in the parking lot, the Armenian pop songs that people blast really fucking loud, the broken strip lighting that flickers like you're in a mental ward, the women's bathroom which stinks like old Chinese food.

But mainly the worst thing about working in my office is that Roger doesn't appreciate the gifts I bring him. Like one time I found a Christmas tree on the sidewalk. It was February. It was pretty big. I think it was silver. It would have looked really good in the reception area, like Christmas all day, every day. But Roger got mad and made me put it in the dumpster. It scratched the shit out of me.

Roger said it was really weird that I brought the tree to the office. So subconsciously that just made me want to bring even more stuff in. Like a tube of toothpaste I found in a bush. A fake Louis Vuitton scarf I found in the parking lot. Everyone was like, "Ew, it's probably got homeless piss on it." Whatever! One time, I found a really fucked up cat with no fur and no tongue. I almost brought it in, but ended up taking it to the vet instead. We had to put her down because she was so fucked up.

The best thing I ever brought into the office though was the alien pod. I found it on the lawn in front of my house. There was this huge tree with really evil spiky leaves that grew in the front lawn. The pod landed underneath it. It looked like one of the pods in Alien. There was ooze and sap dripping from it and it was green and about the size of a big human head, a bit longer though. It looked like it had fallen out of a spaceship and was about to hatch. There were weird bugs crawling all over it, and it was spiky and sticky and sharp. I came in holding it in my arms and said, "I found an alien pod, I think we should adopt it and see if it hatches."

Roger got really mad. I think he was scared, to tell you the truth. He told me to take it outside immediately. I was really sad to say goodbye to the pod. I put it down next to the back door. Then about a half hour later I went to check on it and it had disappeared. Probably beamed back up to space or something.

A few days later, the entire office was called to a meeting and given the following memo:

"This memo is regarding the alien pod that was brought into the office by one Caroline Ryder on 7-20-09. While we have a very loose policy on pets, language and pretty much everything else, alien pods with sap and who knows what the fuck else dropping from them and living inside of them will not be accepted beyond the doors of suite 100. Since Ms. Ryder is in fact an alien I understand her attraction to this pod. But she must keep her personal feelings toward this manner away from the work place. This goes for everyone."

Then he put a photo of the pod underneath. I promised never to bring another alien pod into the office again. I often wonder what happened to it though, and where it went. Probably to a distant galaxy, or a trash can somewhere. Maybe it ate a homeless person. RIP pod.

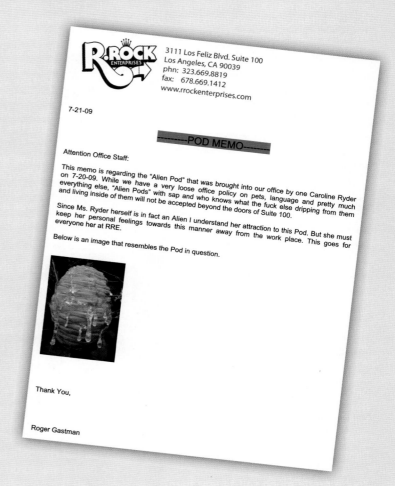

RROCK ENTERPRISES

3111 Los Feliz Blvd. Suite 100
Los Angeles, CA 90039
phn: 323.669.8819
fax: 678.669.1412
www.rrockenterprises.com

7-21-09

----------POD MEMO----------

Attention Office Staff:

This memo is regarding the "Alien Pod" that was brought into our office by one Caroline Ryder on 7-20-09. While we have a very loose office policy on pets, language and pretty much everything else, "Alien Pods" with sap and who knows what the fuck else dripping from them and living inside of them will not be accepted beyond the doors of Suite 100.

Since Ms. Ryder herself is in fact an Alien I understand her attraction to this Pod. But she must keep her personal feelings towards this manner away from the work place. This goes for everyone her at RRE.

Below is an image that resembles the Pod in question.

Thank You,

Roger Gastman

NOISE

by Shawna Kenney
Photo by Piper Ferguson

Did you ever do graffiti?
Yeah, I did! I got arrested my very first go. The Clash was playing in a place called Camden. Outside the nightclub we were horrified to find one of the Vibrators had written "The Vibrators" on this fresh white wall. So it was Topper's first job in the Clash after he passed the drumming audition to act as lookout while I went towards the wall and wrote "The Clash" all over the Vibrators! I just about reached the letter "A" when these two guys who looked like football fans came up and arrested me. They were plain-clothes cops and they walked right past Topper!

How long did you stay in for that?
I thought this was gonna be a giggle, but they found out I'd been charged with some misdemeanor up in the north, on tour, for stealing pillows from the hotel. We were in an uncomfortable bus, so everyone nicked all the pillows. The cops stopped us to search for drugs and they found all these room keys and pillows. They had to charge somebody.

I read that you were a pretty bad student. What do you want to tell your kids now that they're school-age?
I was appalling. I tell them that "school sucks." They know already that it sucks.

Is guitar the first instrument you played?
No, I started on the ukulele because I figured it must be easier, having four strings. I was in awe of music. Most kids might learn something in their youth, but I didn't have any musical knowledge at all. From the Rolling Stones onwards, I listened obsessively. At the time, there were a lot of "fret-wizards." Technique was king. I figured, How complicated could this be? It was much more complicated than guitar, different tuning and the chord-shapes were different. Thankfully, it made me move on to the guitar. That's the only instrument I can play. I play really rudimentary.

You're pretty much self-taught then?

The only person who really taught me about the guitar was Tymon Dogg, who is a fiddle player and now in the Mescaleros. I started out in the music world by collecting money for him while he was busking down in the London underground, the tube system. This is back in say 1971. If you went down to Piccadilly, you'd see Tymon Dogg playing a wild mountain fiddle, and me standing by him with a hat, going, "Thank you, thank you."

Before your music career, what was your worst job ever?
It's a toss-up between digging graves and cleaning toilets. They both have good things going for them.

Do you have a huge record collection?
Well, I did have the beginnings of a decent collection, but living in squats and being on the road and being in rented flats, sometimes we had to sell some records to eat and all that usual stuff. People always take your best records at parties. I have some shattered remnants of bits and pieces. Mostly it tends to be Herb Albert and the Tijuana Brass.

Did the Clash have groupies?
Well, we weren't so ugly, ya know? It's hard to compare with another group. Paul Simonon was a good-looking guy, so I think he brought a few ladies into the audience.

What do you do to chill out when you get home from tour?
Open a bottle of wine, find an interesting book, smoke a couple of spliffs, and just chill. I like to read because it's the opposite of being on the go. Reading is the perfect antidote.

What about writing your autobiography?
It's something like being a stool pigeon. It's like, "Yeah, then we went there and did this with so-and-so." It's like, I ain't gonna tell the police anything! I figure the best thing to do would be to strip away all the pomposity and just write

the best anecdotes I can remember, and then just get it down so it's a non-stop chain of anecdotes, rather than "I woke up and was feeling bad about my mother..."

Is punk dead?
Punk is alive and kicking because I am signed to a punk rock label.

What do you remember about the Sex Pistols opening for the 101ers?
They were new in town and we'd been on the circuit about 18 months. These were only pubs, maybe 400 people could fit in 'em. My whole group went out front and sat in the audience to watch them. They came on and people are standing at the bar. It was a rainy Tuesday, and nothing else was going on. They kind of re-wrote the history of rock-n-roll right in front of me!

Were you blown away?
Absolutely! Except other people couldn't see it. Immediately, the whole scene was divided, if you dug the Sex Pistols or you thought they sucked. You couldn't stand on the line. It was one or the other. We were all squatting in huge families. It divided whole squats.

How did the audience react that night?
They didn't react at all. It was like they were in a coma of surprise or delayed reaction. Remember that I was ready for something, and these other guys just stopped into the bar for a beer on their way home from work.

The straightedge thing never got big in England?
No. People like their beer and cigarettes over here.

You credit marijuana for your youthful appearance?
I do.

Originally printed in WYWS Issue #15

JOE
STRUMMER

THE DESTRUCTION OF CHARM CITY

AN ILLUSTRATED HISTORY OF BALTIMORE GRAFFITI.

**by STAB and KEST with additional help from
SHAKEN, REVOLT, Erik Warner, WILD and John Ellsberry**
Photos courtesy of the artists

Just up the road from our nation's capital, near the northern end of the Chesapeake Bay, is an armpit called Baltimore. Now, for those who immediately take offense to that label, I use the term "armpit" affectionately. I grew up in Baltimore, and I love a good armpit. Quite frankly, it's probably one of the most underrated erogenous zones in the western world. And that sums up Baltimore to a T. Consistently overlooked due to its proximity to New York, Philly and D.C., this sleeping giant has secretly held its own for two decades and has remained an undiscovered fountain of youth for street art.

In 1979, a seasoned subway artist named DR. REVOLT moved into town from NYC and, in the time it took him to collect his BFA from the Maryland Institute College of Art, sparked the graffiti movement in Baltimore. His pieces were the first real graffiti the city had ever seen.

Prior to REVOLT's arrival, Baltimore had never been bombed save for BEAU, who had been writing his name on local walls since the late 1960s. BEAU has always been, by everyone's account, the first person on a mission in Baltimore, and during the early to mid-1980s, you couldn't find a place where there wasn't a BEAU tag a hundred feet from you. But BEAU was a lone gunman and a mystery to most.

Along with early bombers BIG PIG (aka MR. ED) and CUBA, REVOLT wreaked havoc on Baltimore's walls and highways, influencing generations of Baltimore writers to come and putting them on to the New York style.

In the years after REVOLT left B-more and headed back to the Big Apple, writers such as CUBA, BIG PIG and DILLINGER picked up where he left off. CUBA founded the MOBTOWN crew, which included BOULEVERSTA, QUEST, PANIC and TRASH1, among others.

It was 1982 and the center of Baltimore's thriving punk scene was a ramshackle flophouse downtown called the Loft. The Loft was a second-story inner-city barn, high and hollow, where the shows were cheap and all ages were welcome. The Loft hosted bands touring the East Coast and provided a home away from home to local ones. It was also the gathering place and practice gallery for the MOBTOWN crew.

The Loft's owner, a guy named Jules, let writers put up pieces there during the day and then put on the hardcore shows there at night. Many of the writers in MOBTOWN played in various local punk bands at different times during the scene's heyday, including Fear of God, Reptile House and 21 Deal Men, to name a few.

Although the Loft was the stomping grounds for the MOBTOWN crew, other writers frequented the place as well. It served as Baltimore's writer's bench for many years, and despite the constant attempts by the man to shut it down, the Loft flourished and became the birthplace of Baltimore style.

Due to their stern adherence to the punk scene, MOBTOWN brought a distinctly punk aesthetic to graffiti. Writers like JINK, VOID and BOULEVERSTA brought a sharper, angrier look to their tag styles.

With the inclusion of artistically talented writers like ANOK and AMUCK, the crew soon formed the basis of what would become the trademark Baltimore style. "We did it because we liked to see things where they weren't supposed to be," says AMUCK. "We thought it was punk. We wanted to fuck things up. That's it."

By 1984, MOBTOWN had all but hung it up. CUBA, who had helped make MOBTOWN the real deal, left town for the graffiti-drenched mecca of San Francisco. One of the first bombers from the East Coast to make a permanent West Coast jump, he is credited as one of the first non-cholo writers to hit the Bay Area.

After CUBA left town, ZEKOIZ and DOOM from Baltimore's west side formed GHETTO STROLLERS INC. (GSI) and began to frequent parties at the Loft as well as catching serious wreck on the midwest and northwest parts of town. Along with PLAT, TRON, TUFFY and MIRAGE 2, GSI set the pace for the oncoming movement.

Even without the original heads still in the game, graffiti in Baltimore really began to jump off and spread outward from the concentrated downtown area in late 1984. STAB from the east side along with AZTEK from the north end joined MOBTOWN and helped revitalize the crew, while younger writers like JAMONE, from Baltimore's south side, started to come up.

JAMONE—better known as SHAKEN, Baltimore's all-time bomb king—began his ill-fated career in 1984 and hasn't spent much time out of trouble since then. From early on, he was on a mission to become an all-city king and became known for his recklessness and his sheer numbers. SHAKEN's tags blanketed Baltimore's downtown area in the mid-1980s. At one time, every corner of every major cross-town thoroughfare was blessed with some of SHAKEN's handiwork. This was called "spotlighting" by Baltimore's old school, a method of getting up taken on by many writers to come.

After getting caught in early 1986, SHAKEN dropped the tag JAMONE and started the KAN'T STOP WRITING crew with JAZI, REZ and WEB (Baltimore's first female writer), which eventually grew to include KEY, JUSTONE, MEEK, KORUPT, RANK and a host of others. 1986 and 1987 were, without a doubt, the years SHAKEN and the KSW crew made a name for themselves as a serious bombing team.

The buses played a major role in many Baltimore writers' rise to infamy. Most writers, being of high school age, rode the buses to school every morning, so the insides became a mode of communication between writers. Not to be outdone on any level, the buses became SHAKEN's domain as well. He methodically destroyed each and every one of them, bringing his name and his crew's

name out of the inner city and into suburbia. Suddenly, even Baltimore's most affluent neighborhoods had a graffiti problem.

The authorities responded with ferocity and methods that made it seem like they were fighting espionage. Kids were pulled out of class and locked up. Informants were placed. Handwriting analysis was used. Sentences were handed out.

"I was still a fugitive when summertime rolled around, and I was painting with MASK, who had a style crazier than heavy metal," SHAKEN explains. "You could tell by looking at his stuff that the guy smoked a lot of pot, drank a lot of beer, and listened to way too much Slayer. I remember one time, I was in this dude's basement huffing this stuff called 'ethyl blast,' which gave you all sorts of crazy dreams, and I started dreaming I was on the roof of this futuristic prison, which was about a hundred stories high. There was a guy on the roof with a net trying to catch pigeons and somehow I convinced him to help me escape. He led me down this hall, then out of nowhere I started hearing these pig noises, and instantly I snapped out of the dream. It was this dude's dad screaming at us, 'What the fuck is going on!' After I woke up a little more, I realized that the kid's room looked like a bomb hit it. In my dream, I had climbed the guy's entertainment center (which was the prison in my dream) and proceeded to knock the whole thing over, destroying the TV, VCR and a whole bunch of CDs. In the process, the entertainment center hit my friend in the head and knocked him out."

As 1986 went on, GSI evolved into the SUPREME TEAM and reinforced its talent with NAZE and MASK, who bought grand experimentation and extremely technical styles to both writing and painting.

Baltimore graffiti continued to grow: Brothers CHAS and BAZ emerged as ORGANIZED CRIME TAKEOVER; Baltimore's MODE resurfaced as META-SIN and romped the east/northeast with SAKE and JBROCK in a click called CRUSHING OTHER VANDALS; and a young talent named KUZIN wrecked the southeast. KUZIN continued to bomb hard throughout 1987 and into 1988, joining STAB and VESPA's newly formed FUNHOUSE crew.

The early 1990s saw CAR's DST crew doing serious damage to Baltimore's streets, while SHAKEN, JASE and WILD teamed up to take over Baltimore's highways and the access walls surrounding the light rail and subway lines. SHAKEN became Baltimore's public enemy number one, and spawned quite a fan club in the graff community, making the covers of both the *City Paper* and *Baltimore Sun* and inspiring city officials to make an example of his case. Throughout the 1990s, SHAKEN was a fugitive more often than not. He got bounced in and out of jail five times, landing there for an extended stay in October 1996.

Twenty years after Baltimore got its first taste of graffiti, it has developed into a thriving mecca for graffiti fiends. The freight scene is huge and walls rarely get buffed or gone over. Writers who started back in the early 1980s are still around, still painting, and helping to bring younger writers up.

The PA crew (DAVER, ARON, JESER, SIEK, CISE, METASIN, STAB, etc.) is one of the strongest crews out right now with members of the original MOB-TOWN crew painting with some of Baltimore's fresh new talent. JASE's BA crew has a constant presence with the likes of SUPA, EKO, WILD and SKY. And even in SHAKEN's absence, the KSW crew is still out bombing hard with plenty of new writers. Most impressive of all, original heads like STAB, MASK and MODE have resurfaced to represent their generation. Lurking beneath the surface, Baltimore graffiti is alive and well.

DR. REVOLT
by Fat Rich

I seem to have this recurring problem with interviews I cannot for the love of Christ figure out how to get my tape recorder to work. I bought a new tape recorder and adapter from Radio Shack that you plug into the phone and still all I seem to get is my voice. This first occurred when I tried to interview REVOLT. According to Roger, this guy is supposed to be the shit, and everybody swings from his nuts, but at the same time, he is supposedly older than dirt. I tired to give him a grueling interview. Unfortunately neither the grueling interview technique nor my tape recorder seemed to work. I asked him if his senior citizens discount comes in handy, and his reply was simply, "Not yet." Somehow I think he is lying. The guy is a self-proclaimed "Doctor of Teenage Lobotomy," and you've got to figure that he's at least passed the half-century mark. He continually refused to tell me his age, confirming my suspicion that he falls in the that category we like to call "over the hill."

REVOLT is supposedly famous in the graffiti world for painting a lot of trains. That amounts to a whole pile of nothing in my world of fast cars and faster women. He did tell me, however, that he "got a hummer once on the in betweens of a moving B-Way express train." Interesting. wonder how much that cost him? I informed the good DR of my misfortune when I came into contact with Canadians. I asked how he got along with our northern, how shall we say, less intelligent neighbors. "So far so good, aye!" Just when I was thinking that these one-line answers were not cutting it, REVOLT pops me the question: "Did you blow bubbles when you were a little kid?" My reply: "I don't think so." This is where his comic genius comes out: "That's funny, I saw him last week and he said to tell that kid Fat Rich what's up." After the three seconds it took to recover from my fit of laughter, I continued with the inquisition.

Roger took me to meet some other old graffiti writer one time. His name was ZEPHYR. Anyway, he told us how some of the old New York writers used to hang out with Madonna before she was famous. Could this DR. REVOLT be one of those lucky bastards? "I wouldn't know, I've met her and I've been in her apartment." This guy just seems to disappoint me with every response. How many hot dogs do you think you could eat in one hour? "Oscar Meyer or Tofu Pups" Great God in Heaven, what I would give for a straightforward answer. One of my last attempts at a question: If I was an attractive girl who didn't know shit about graffiti, could you give me a good reason to sleep with you? "Tender Vittels." What the hell are Tender Vittels? Maybe I'm just a moron, but I just don't know what the hell this guy is talking about. Although he agreed with me that almost all graffiti writers are just big dorks, he insisted that social security was a scam. My final question was, how do you do graffiti from your walker? I know the hip isn't quite what it used to be. Always quick with the comebacks, he replied, "I use it as a ladder to paint." I give up. All I can say is I am glad that he is not my fucking doctor.

BALTIMORE'S STENCIL BOMBERS

Photos by John Ellsberry

Even as REVOLT's influence was being felt back in 1979, Baltimore's streets came alive with another group of fast-moving illegal artists: the stencil bombers. The original stencil bombers were a handful of kids from in and around the Maryland Institute College of Art who collectively referred to themselves as BOMB (Baltimore Oblivion Marching Band). Although Paris and New York had a stencil art movement to some degree, in the Baltimore area, the BOMB crew was the first to exploit the medium. Using stencils cut out of cardboard, plastic or acetate, these guys and girls hit Baltimore from 1979 through to their high point in the mid-1980s.

Around 1979, certain BOMB members decided to take their art to the streets as what BOMB original John Ellsberry describes as "guerilla art." Ellsberry, one of the original stencil artists who now paints murals for the city of Baltimore, and his brother Richard were responsible for many of the classic stencil art images seen around Baltimore in the early 1980s, perhaps the most enormous of which was the Bob Dobbs Head. The Bob Dobbs Head was the icon of a religious cult out of Texas called the Church of Subgenius. Richard Elsberr's version of the 1950s-style Ward Cleaver-lookin' head smoking a pipe stands six-feet high, significantly larger than the majority of stencils, which were six inches to a foot high on average.

The Bob Dobbs head is only one example of the possibilities the stencil medium offered; the subject matter had no limits. Insects, automobiles, personality spoofs, single images and storyboards graced the walls of Baltimore during this time period. Other infamous stencils were the "Black Hole" stencil, the "Followed?" stencil, the "Fox Trot" stencil, the "Red Cross" stencil and the "Chain Link" stencil. The "Black Hole" was actually just a big black circle, which at a distance appeared to be a hole, spray painted on various surfaces around Baltimore by artist Bonnie Bonnell. "Followed?" by David Bakker

was a prevalent image around Baltimore's streets depicting a detective with the word "Followed?" above it. The "Fox Trot" and "Chain Link" stencils, by Ruth Turner and John Ellsberry, respectively, were both examples of stencils that spanned large and indefinite areas. The "Fox Trot" was a stencil of foot patterns that were used in repetition to create dance steps. The "Chain Links" were exactly what the name suggests; left open-ended on either side of the stencil, they allowed Ellsberry to do as many links in a row as he wanted. If chased, he could leave and come back to finish the job with no problem. He used the chain links to "chain up" structures that looked dilapidated, as though they would fall over if they were not chained up. The "Red Cross" stencil, by artist Randy Hoffman, was used as a way of identifying "safe houses" to other stencil-crazed artists. It was painted on the sidewalk outside houses belonging to friends of the BOMB crew.

John Ellsberry's work was more political than most, featuring, among other images, his "Reagan Master" stencil, an image of Reagan's head with the word "master" stenciled over it. The Reagan Master stencil was designed to "evoke feelings of distaste" for the former president when he was running in the 1980 election. Around this time, REVOLT and his crew started catching tags over top of the stencil art. "There was a big of a grudge match going on for a while," says Ellsberry. The stencil artists felt that graff was more vandalous and violent than their art, although both were illegal.

When the "BOMB versus the taggers" grudge match existed there were certain things that the stencil artists would do to try and get back at the taggers. "We didn't want to be overly vindictive so, for instance, instead of going back over them with a stencil, I cut out stencils of a T and an A and put them on either side of REVOLT's tags, making them into TREVOLTA tags," says Ellsberry.

The beef went on throughout the early 1980s but never became very serious. There was a certain level of respect and tolerance among the graff heads and the stencil artists, some of whom went to school together. Perhaps the most important stencil art in Baltimore was done by an original BOMB member known as tENTATIVELY, a cONVENIENCE. His work, which began appearing on Baltimore's walls in 1979, was a direct criticism of the shallowness of the art world. tENT criticized how much importance the art world placed on simple principles in a four-foot-by-three-foot stencil that read:

"Sayings of a Famous Artist:
To be a Famous Artist One has to be Recognizable.
The Easiest Way to be Recognizable is:
1. To Be Repetitious.
2. To Have a Highly Visible and Easily Readable Signature.
This Text is my Recognizable Repetition.
Hopefully, This is a Clear and Blatant exposure of Some Fame Mechanisms."

"This text wasn't meant as encouragement for people to become famous through becoming stupid," says tENT, "it was meant to show how moronically simple it is to accomplish a goal that so many people in the art world attach so much importance to."

Unfortunately, most of the stencil art was buffed about 15 years ago and there is very little photo documentation of this chapter in Baltimore's street art history, but the memory remains as one of the facets that set Baltimore apart from the crowd.

Originally printed in WYWS Issue #7

SPACE 1026
Photography by Adam Wallacavage
Styling by Chi-Eun Kim

hile you were sleeping, these guys were out rocking stupid large pieces. 'nuff said.

COOKING WITH PORN STARS

VIVID GIRL RAYLENE INVITES JELLY OVER FOR HOMEMADE FAJITAS AND SOME OF HER "SPECIAL SAUCE"

by Jelly
Photos by Wild Don Lewis

Raylenes Chicken Fajitas
1 ½ Lbs of Chicken or beef
½ Green - Red & Yellow Peppers
¼ Red onion
1 ½ packets of fajita Powder Mix
3 tablespoons of olive oil
½ Cup Water

Cover - Cook until done
add Rice & Tortillas
Get your own Salsa Its a secret

love
Raylene xxxo

The magnet on Vivid contract girl Raylene's fridge that reads "Dip me in honey and throw me to the lesbians" was a sure sign that I was in the right place. Truly, I was in Jelly-heaven as I stood in the huge kitchen of the porn queen's sprawling Northridge, CA, home and watched the Jennifer Lopez of adult film cook me up a mess of fajitas, all while dressed in a skimpy, form-fitting outfit from Latin Thug Wear. Actually, for my money, Raylene looks hotter than J-Lo!

Raylene can stuff a corn tortilla like a true Mexican-Jewish senorita. As for sex, all you have to do is pick up a copy of a Raylene classic like *Bad Wives* 2 or *The Trophy*, and you know she can fire up some spicy lovin' in the sack. I also discovered that Raylene is a cool, sweet individual with a bong collection that's out of this world! According to her, she's in a serious relationship right now, but she declines to offer up a name. "No one knows we're seeing each other," she giggles. "It's a secret."

Whoever he is, he better put a ring on that gal's finger quick before someone else does. Hell, a lady who can cook like a Latina Martha Stewart, enjoys bud, has more curves than the Indy 500 and can freak you until you pass out from excitement, that's a catch! Just the glimpse ol' Jelly got of Raylene's bedroom during a brief tour of her abode made the Gelatinous One's eyes roll back in his head. Painted in dark purple, with a canopied, four-poster bed, candles all around and various witchy-woman decorations (Raylene practices Wicca), they nearly had to call 911 to drag me out of there.

Here are some snaps of Raylene fixin' the Jellster some grub. Raylene swears this is her last year in the biz, but don't despair fellas, she's got a CD coming out with her band The Holy Order of Mary Magdalene, produced by none other than top Hole-head Courtney Love. Till then, you'll just have make these fajitas at home, pop in a Raylene video and lick your plate clean.

Originally printed in WYWS Issue #16

Raylene dips that big fajita in some of her special salsa and swallows it down.

We're not sure what looks more tasty—Raylene or her lovely fajitas. But don't try to put the moves on her right after dinner, boys. For Raylene, food and sex don't mix. "When I'm done eating, I don't wanna jump right into the bedroom and go pounding away," she laughs. "The only aphrodisiac for me is alcohol." (Raylene's drink is Captain Morgan, straight up.) What about on the set? "I try not to eat before I go into a scene, but it's hard 'cause there's always so much food around. Something light yet full of energy is best—maybe Red Bull and an energy bar?"

Hey, good lookin', whatcha got cookin'?

Raylene uses all-natural ingredients in her meals, and she advises guys to keep it natural when makin' sweet love to your woman. "There has to be a natural flow," she explains while mixing in some fresh garlic and cilantro to her salsa. "There's nothing you can do to make sex more interesting than be natural. Don't be too pushy. That's a turn-off." As for artificial ingredients, Raylene says you can front, but you're not foolin' anyone. On Viagra: "I know a lot of guys that use it. They can say they don't, but I can always tell."

Raylene's fridge, like her T-shirt, is burstin' at the seams!

Whenever Raylene flashes those pearly-whites, you feel the star-power. How could any man, or woman for that matter, resist her? But Raylene, who loves guys and gals equally, says girlfriends don't always work out. "I'm really into girls," she says. "But it's hard to find a girl who's as interested in me as I am in her. A lot of girls do it for work. It's easier for them. But for me, it's not work. I'm absolutely enjoying myself. Some days are harder than others, but I couldn't do it if I didn't enjoy it."

Choppin', Grindin', Rubbin' and Humpin'.

Raylene asserts the myth about porn stars taking their names from L.A. road signs is a myth. Though there may be a Raylene Street out there, she chose her porn name from a different source. "I had a crush on this girl in high school whose name was Raylene. That should say it all. I never got over her." As for porn stars being sex addicts, well, to that she can testify. "I haven't had a porno party in a looong time," she says. "But back when I used to do 'em, they would always end up breaking out into a big orgy. Porno people are crazy! You'd think they'd get enough sex on the set, but no."

OK, boys, come and get it!

Mmm-mmm, looks good enough to eat. But before you dive in headfirst, know that Raylene says sex with a fan is a pretty rare event: "If I want to hang out with you, that's one thing. But usually it doesn't go any further. I can recall only one time it did, and that was with my assistant, another girl. Two boys got to watch. They weren't really fans, they were just boys we were hanging out with in the club, but they were sooo cute! We took them home, but we couldn't decide what to do with them. So we let them watch." Well, that's something. Like the good Rev. Jackson says, "Keep hope alive!"

MR. T

Interview by Ian Sattler
Research by Neil Mahoney and Josh Bernstein

In Hollywood, there are two ways to say "no." The first is "pass," and the other is "I'll do it for $40,000." We heard both from Mr. T's representatives whenever we requested an interview, but we weren't about to let some filthy Hollywood pimps stand between us and Bosco "Bad Attitude" Baracus. After all, this was the man who pitied fools, who clobbered the Italian Stallion, and made obnoxious gold acceptable for an entire generation of wannabe tough guys. We tipped off all our inside contacts, consulted Mr. T memorabilia experts, even shaved our pubic hair into mohawks in solidarity, but no matter how much blood we sacrificed, we were no closer to the chained one. Disheartened by the results, we resigned ourselves to running nothing but photos of cheap, schlocky *A-Team* merchandise, scored off of eBay. Then, at the eleventh hour, salvation came in the form of an offer from Ubi Soft Entertainment. The tough man would be hawking Ubi Soft's new Rocky® Boxing game, and they were prepared to grant us two minutes in the (interview) ring. The Gods answered, and Ian Satler went the distance.

Can you tell us a little bit about the game you are promoting here today?
Aww, man, any fool can play this game, that's how easy it is. This is the best game. You think Mr. T would be standing at some place that he don't love? We're going to take some of these games, and I'm gonna give 'em to the poor kids in the ghetto. You know what I mean? It's a simple game. Before I got out here I played with the game myself. And I'm electronical... uhh... defunct...uhh... kinda stupid... ya know what I mean? So anybody can play it.

Who would you like to throw down with if you were on *Celebrity Boxing*?
Nah... nah... I wouldn't get on Celebrity Boxing. Can you believe what this fool just asked me? Asked me something stupid about Celebrity Boxing. Man, that's for has-beens, man. Do you see what I'm promoting, man? Ain't nobody on Celebrity Boxing got no game!

If your name was on the dollar bill, what would it say instead of "In God We Trust?"
No, no, no. If my name was on the dollar bill, it would still be "In God We Trust." As tough as Mr. T is, and as bad as he is, he's a momma's boy and he loves his God. I'm a religious man, [and] my father baptized me, so the money will always say, "In God We Trust." 'Cause that's who I trust in, God. I don't trust in no friends 'cause they stab me in the back and try to steal my gold.

Would you ever work for Vince McMahon and the WWE again?
I like Vince McMahon. I have no problem with him, but I'm retired. I'm 50 years old. I had my fun in wrestling. I've been there, done that. So I'm doing good. I got a game about me—I got 1-800-COLLECT commercials, you know? So I'm a happy camper. I don't wanna do no movies; I don't wanna do no TV. I just wanna keep on doing 1-800-COLLECT and this here game. I love this game! I can give this game to the poor kids at the church. You know what I mean? Unghhh! That's the type of guy Mr. T is. So I made the producers of this game give some freebies to the less fortunate. I go to the hospital sometimes, and the kids would love to have a game to play while they're waiting to get well.

How was it working with Puffy and the Neptunes [in the "Pass the Courvoisier Part 2 (Remix)" video]?
Puffy and the who? There weren't no Neptunes, man! You trying to start some stuff, man!? You don't want Puffy to get after you, man! Puffy knows Mike Tyson. So you better not mess with Puffy. Alright!? It was cool to do it with Puffy and Busta Rhymes. They was cool. It was an honor to be with P-Diddy and Busta Rhymes. It was fun, and the kids love the video. So that was cool, ya know?

Do you have anything to say to the readers of *WYWS*?
Just enjoy the show.

Originally printed in WYWS Issue #19

TEST YOUR SKILLS IN THE MR. T TRUE/FALSE QUIZ

1. Mr. T nearly burned off his penis with a hot fire poker.

2. Mr. T broke bricks with his head while escorting women to pick up welfare checks.

3. Mr. T's movie D.C. Cab is not the best movie ever made.

4. Mr. T's legal first name is "Mister," his middle name "." and his last name "T."

5. Mr. T left the scene of an accident and claimed the car was stolen when a coked-up Leon Spinks wrecked a Cadillac.

6. Mr. T has been arrested twice, once for deserting the military.

7. Mr. T punched A-Team costar Dwight "Murdock" Schultz as a joke and accidentally separated Shultz's shoulder.

8. Mr. T was crowned "Toughest Bouncer in America," by competing in events like the "Blast," in which contestants ran through walls and doors.

9. Mr. T once jumped from a second-story window and chased two muggers for five blocks in his underpants, while firing a .357 Magnum.

10. Mr. T is just as terrified of flying as his character B.A. Baracus.

11. Mr. T and Sylvester Stallone included disco dancing as part of their Rocky II training regiment.

12. Mr. T was baptized by Reverend Al Sharpton.

13. Mr. T once lent his voice to an episode of Alvin and the Chipmunks.

14. Mr. T was the Iron Sheik's tag team partner during the first WrestleMania.

15. Mr. T has been the bodyguard for both Muhammad Ali and everyday prostitutes.

16. Mr. T loves going to day spas and having his fingers manicured.

17. Mr. T wears gold chains to represent the chains of his ancestors.

18. Mr. T once tried out for the Green Bay Packers.

19. Mr. T is the smallest of his parents' eight sons.

20. Mr. T has never killed a man.

STUPID STUFF

WOMEN'S SOCCER NEWS

This photo of the *WYWS* SheDevils was taken from the cover of the "Life" Section of *USA Today*. Said Editor-in-Chief Roger Gastman on the sponsorship of a women's soccer team: "That's the best $500 we ever spent."

DAVE THOMAS

Dave Thomas owns Wendy's, and he is a 33rd degree Freemason. I go to Wendy's very often—I average about seven trips a week. My favorite advertising slogan of there's is "See you tomorrow." It's funny, because I usually go every day.

Freemasonry is not a religion. It is a social organization like the 4-H or Rotary International. The Masons do not control the world. Masonry is not pagan, it is not Satanic. I go to Wendy's every day. Freemasons are obliged to honor the Deity they recognize. I never go to McDonald's or Burger King.

My favorite items at Wendy's are the Jr. Bacon Cheeseburger and the Spicy Chicken Sandwich. Freemasons do not have the Elixir of Life. I also like 99 Percent Fat-Free Frostees. Freemasons do not know where the Holy Grail is hidden.

Freemasonry is not a secret organization. Everyone knows that Masons exist. Dave Thomas is a Freemason. Wendy's is the restaurant I go to every day.

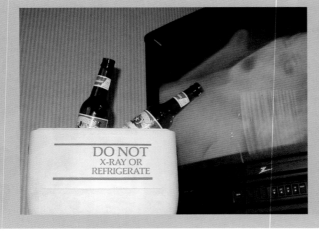

CARRY HUMAN BODY PARTS

Love to travel? What if it's free—now do you love to travel? I thought so. In case you were wondering, our nation needs organ couriers. They'll call you with a few days notice, ask if you can travel, and then tell you where you're going—so James Bond. You'll breeze through security and, once you make the drop, you've got a free hotel room and 50 bucks to blow on room service—beer and Spectravision not included. Ask hospitals in your area if you can donate your time to a worthy cause that saves lives. It's real, you can really do this.

MR. T QUIZ ANSWERS (from page 465)

1. True. A three-year-old T dislodged it from the potbelly stove that heated their house. "I escaped permanent damage to my penis... if it had been any bigger, my sexual life would have been ruined."

2. True. Of course he did; he's an animal.

3. False. It is the finest piece of cinema ever made, and one of the very few movies to feature indigenous Washington, D.C., Go-Go on its soundtrack.

4. True. He was born Laurence Tureaud; his father later changed the family's last name to Tero; while attending college he converted to Islam and went by Mohammed Tero, and once he returned to Chicago he changed it to Mr. T. Since then, he does not answer to any other name, and disregards any mail or phone calls not addressed accordingly.

5. True. Spinx was a victim of what Mr. T calls "Project Paralysis" and never escaped the traps of drugs and loose women. Sworn to protect him though, T went along with the stolen car story.

6. True. The other time was for unlawful use of a weapon, aggravated assault, theft of lost property, disorderly conduct, and failure to register firearms. In reality, Mr. T had no weapons or any property lost or stolen. The case was thrown out.

7. False. Murdock ruled though.

8. True. As practice, Mr. T would go incognito to condemned housing projects and run through the walls and doors left behind.

9. True. The men he chased had attempted to rob his father.

10. False. He loves to fly, and it shows.

11. True. Sly directed Stayin' Alive and loved that disco shit. FYI, disco was part of Leon "Booger Sugar" Spinx's training, too.

12. False. Mr. T was baptized by his father, Reverend Nathaniel Buddy Tureaud, Sr.

13. True. He had his own cartoon, too.

14. False. He and Hulk Hogan faced Rowdy Roddy Piper.

15. True. By his partial tally, there've also been eight bankers, eight airline stewardesses, five preachers, four storeowners, eight housewives, 14 secretaries, seven clothes designers, seven judges, four attorneys, five models, 10 schoolteachers, sixteen prostitutes, nine welfare recipients, and 18 children.

16. False. Neil Mahoney the editor does, though. Send gift certificates.

17. True. Mr. T explains: "The fact that I wear gold chains instead of iron chains is because I am still a slave, only my price tag is higher now. I am still bought and sold by the powers-that-be in this society—white people—but this time they pay me on demand, millions and millions of dollars for my services. Yes, I am still a slave in this society, but I am free by God."

18. True. Mr. T tried out for the Packers but blew out his knee.

19. True. Sometimes all eight bruisers would cruise for someone who had threatened family members. "[My brother] Nate hit him with the butt of the carbine rifle again and again, until blood started gushing down from his lips and nose [and] started knocking his head against the concrete wall. Jesse and Gus started... beating them at the same time."

20. We're not sure, but the book Mr. T by Mr. T says, "I would like to add that up until that point I had never killed anyone before. I will not say what I did to those two niggers who robbed and threatened to kill my mother, but I will say this: 'No one will ever see them again and I don't have no hurt in my heart anymore.'"

TOOMER AND CREW TAKE ON TJ
Story and photos by John Lacroix

Road trips are always the best unplanned. The phrase, "Lets go to Tijuana!" echoed in my ears as images of donkeys, whores and midgets passed through my mind. The next day, we were on the road. It was the first time I made my way over this particular border and the anticipation was uncontrollable. I was like a little kid on Christmas morning; every mile closer to the border was like a step closer to that tree, where amazing gifts of debauchery awaited me.

Of course, the magazine had a different agenda; they didn't care about piñatas, or pharmaceuticals, or even midgets riding donkeys through a whorehouse. They wanted to me to get the story straight. A story about how a Los Angeles graffiti crew literally took Tijuana back to the age of the conquistador and about how its obvious that this crew will own all of Mexico before the apple drops in 2003.

So lets get a few things straight about Tijuana. I'm no pussy, but I did have some fears of being raped and murdered by the Federales, only to have my camera sold to a shitty American tourist for 20 pesos in a pawn shop on Revolucion Avenue. As much as I didn't want my rotting corpse eaten by stray dogs, it was kind of cool to fantasize about. Most of what I knew of TJ was the horror stories and what I saw in movies. Early on, however, I realized that the stereotypes were gross exaggerations. TJ actually seemed like a pretty legit place to hang, which is probably why our guide, TOOMER, leader of the TKO crew, spent so much time here.

TKO is a crew with 10 years of history, based in the hoods of Los Angeles. TOOMER started it himself to get his own thing going. A new thing, different from what was going with all the L.A. gangs he was surrounded by. TKO did its share of bombing in L.A., but when heat started coming down on TOOMER, he needed to lay low for a while. It all started with parties down in Rosarito Beach, which is on the Baja peninsula just south of Tijuana. That was summer 2001 when TOOMER started making regular trips over the border. "I'm poor, I can't afford to go to Europe to party and paint, but I can just drive to TJ," said TOOMER. For the most part, it wasn't worth paying attention to the paint on the walls at that time. There were mostly gang tags and feeble attempts at throwups. But there was this event, some kind of pay-to-paint event that TOOMER ended up at. Needless to say, he was bored enough to check it out and something good actually came out of it. He met a couple of Tijuana writers who he instantly connected with. They were SPEED and PEEL. They became the first soldiers for TKO in Mexico.

SPEED was a well-respected writer in TJ already. Bound to a wheelchair, he has heart like no other. Racking cans in his chair bag, and zipping through the streets with reckless abandon. SPEED was getting up in places a walking man couldn't get to or wouldn't even have the balls to try. SPEED is a role model for all the locals and there's not a person who'd talk back to him.

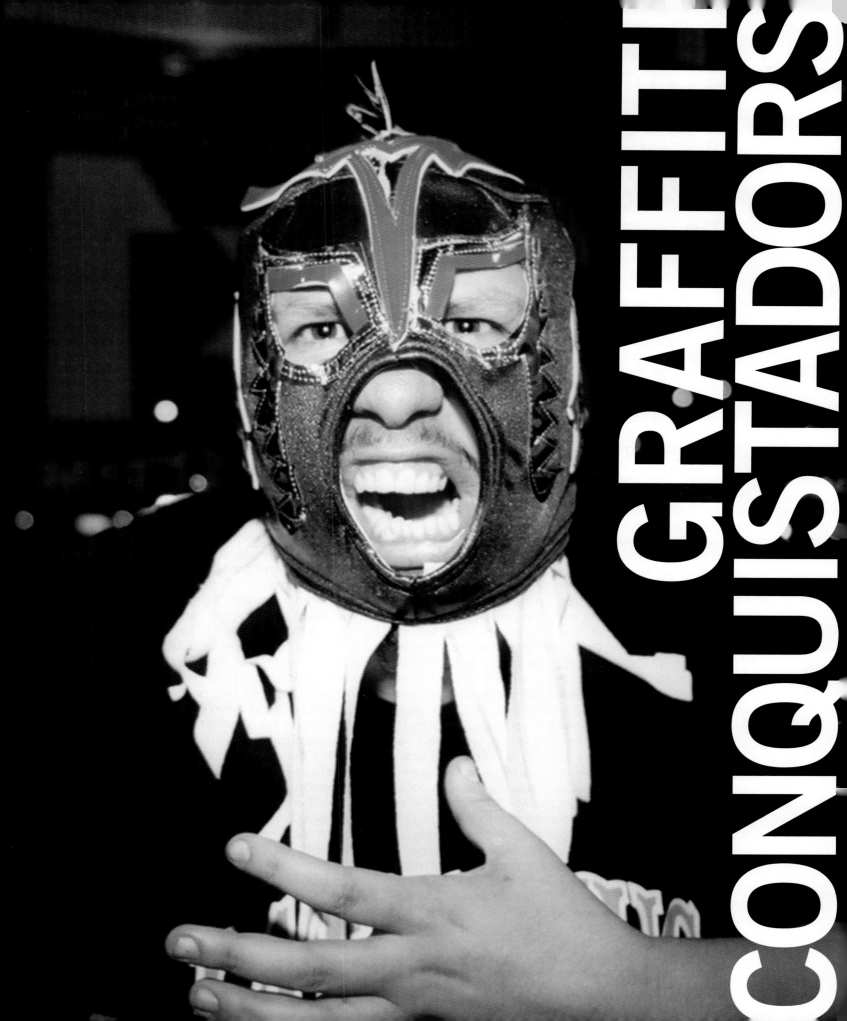

GRAFFITI
CONQUISTADORS

PEEL is public enemy number one as far as graffiti is concerned. He literally has a sickness, an addiction to bombing. As TOOMER says, "He has no respect, he makes me sick, and I love it!" This kid will tag up a donkey if it stood still for a second. PEEL is mellow and down to earth, and is what the new kids all aspire to be. When the local newspaper finally gave graff some recognition, they cited PEEL as causing the most damage. Together SPEED and PEEL bring the fresh blood and are the ambassadors to Tijuana for the rest of the world.

If you don't know TOOMER, well, you're missing out. Besides being able to tell a story like a born comedian, he's a big-ass scary dude you wouldn't want to mess with. He paints like he's possessed, making him, along with RESQ the most up. In addition, TOOMER can talk his way out of any situation. About 20 minutes after crossing the border, he took us to a spot planned for the next day's painting. There were a couple of big productions already there that TOOMER had organized, with writers JUST, BATES, SABER, DIME, WANE, TOAST and PERSUE up on this wall. Of course, we didn't get to enjoy the scenery too long. Cops were blazing down the dirt road as soon as we got there. Guns pulled and everything. If it wasn't for TOOMER, our gringo asses would have been taco meat. But after a quick search and a little story telling, we were free to hang out. No fines, no bribes and no prison, and the cops actually gave us some respect. Go figure.

TOOMER also knows all the party spots. He took us straight to the right places. My shopping list was important too, I wanted the antidote for Anthrax (just in case), piñatas, velvet paintings of Jesus, hookers, midgets, donkeys, wrestling masks and, of course, I wanted to commit crimes. We started our scavenger hunt at a club downtown. Not just any club—a hooker club. Within minutes what do we see? Yes, a midget… with a hooker. That was enough for that night. I think it was an omen. I was ready for bed.

The next day, we drove around getting evidence of the damage this crew has done. In less than 10 months time, TOOMER has trained an army in TJ. Every wall we saw was painted. Rooftops, roll downs, abandoned cars, busses and trains—they were all bombed. "You gotta learn to play the game, how shit works here. The cops suck, the gangs suck… you gotta watch your back!" says TOOMER. "It's like the movie, *Traffic*, drug lords really run the city." After those first few trips over the border in the summer, TOOMER went back and told his homies that he had it figured out in TJ. "Half of them were down and the other half thought I was crazy," TOOMER said, "but they realized they had to trust me."

We painted all day, ate some food, took pictures and hung out. We even went off to get some more of the items on my list, including donkeys painted like zebras and a piñata we named "Lucy." When painting, there were times when we had crowds all around us. It seems that people in Mexico respect graffiti. They have a different way of looking at it. It's not exactly legal to paint everything you see. Maybe Mexico has bigger problems to deal with, but it looked as if they hadn't even bothered to try and buff the city just yet. TOOMER has figured out how to get around all the problems and dangers and he invites anybody to get in touch with him if you want to paint TJ. Like he did with KE42, DUEM and FUSHA, guiding them safely to the best spots to paint more than a few times. Be warned though, it's not something you can go about alone. Despite TOOMER's connections down in TJ, even he has had his share of problems. There was the time a local gangbanger stabbed him while he was painting and then there was the time he blew up a stakeout by the Mexican FBI, where TOOMER says he really thought they weren't going to talk their way out of it. And that's just the stuff we can print. Remember this, pioneers are people who get there first. Conquerors are those who take it from them with force. Like Hernan Cortes, TKO members are the true graffiti conquistadors. Next stop, Mexico City.

Originally printed in WYWS Issue #16

STONED

by I.B. Stoney
Photo by Rosina Teri Memolo

You've seen them in someone else's copy of *High Times* and always wondered if they worked. Wonder no more, thanks to *WYWS*'s very scientific study of fake drugs. In order to make a direct comparison to readily available street drugs, we purchased three grades of marijuana "Herbal Alternatives" based on price (high, medium and low) with a special class for "Krypto," since it cost twice as much as its closest competitor. We also bought every kind of imitation hash, bogus magic mushrooms, ersatz ecstasy, and pseudo-opium we could find, and binged like fat comedians for a week. The following are the direct effects on our trip to the Fake Dope smorgasbord.

"SCHWAG"
Bulldog and Buddah's Blend
At nine dollars an ounce, there's no other way to smoke this other than in a crumpled beer can. These weeds look like they were mined from the bottom of a hamster cage. Smells bad, tastes bad, and all it does is make you sick.

"KIND BUD"
Panama Red and Sweet Green
Panama Red is scary. It's really soft and clumpy with this kind of sticky texture that makes me think they've sprayed it with something. It's almost cottony and smells a little like brown sugar. The Sweet Green is a rip-off from the get go. The bag is all stems and if I had any intention of touching this shit again, I would definitely find a new dealer. I'm not liking either at this point. It's a shame I have to try them all, because I am already ready to quit. And when I say quit, I mean my job—whose idea was this?

"THE CHRONIC"
Hydro and Wizard Smoke
Wizard Smoke is definitely the winner here. It looks gross, but doesn't taste as much like tomato leaves or weird herbs. The Hydro blunts were the first we tried of any of this stuff, and we are constantly checking ourselves. "Are you feeling anything?" "I don't know... I don't think so." Both do nothing, but the darker, dryer Wizards Smoke is less detrimental to my throat and mouth.

"G13"
Krypto
Since this Krypto stuff is supposedly the bomb, I wanted to puff like a high roller on the front porch with a big Bob Marley joint. Like some others, it has a pleasant odor, but becomes overly fragrant before long. I've decided that they price these weeds based solely on appearance—because while this one definitely looks like the real deal, none of them do a damned thing.

"HERBAL OPIUM"
I can only taste it on the way out, and it tastes real bad—like burning perfumed Styrofoam. I have a stomachache and feel like my anus will burst open any second with hot lava. I hate to swallow and keep spitting into my garbage can. The gooey gum stays aflame when you light it and looks evil. When I pulled it out it looked like a black marshmallow. Bad, bad, bad.

HASH
Jamaican
We just did bong hits of this stuff that smells like rabbit food. Looks like rabbit food, too. All I could taste was the bong,

which still tastes nasty from the opium, or maybe it's just that the bong itself tastes bad Regardless, I have a lump in my throat that will most likely be there tomorrow. Actually, feeling a littly buzzy though. "How you feelin', Dave?" "Irie."

TURKISH BROWN

The disappointment is overwhelming when you notice the amount of smoke going out of your body is nowhere near as much as went in. My head feels slightly light, as if I have been sniffing magic markers.

HONEY BLONDE

The hash definitely has some sort of effect... I don't know what it is. I feel a little bit warm and ditstant-headed, but without the drooling and headachey smells of the weeds.

MUSHROOMS
Magic Mushrooms

Absolutely nothing happens, they taste gross, and you shouldn't take them if you don't like to eat normal salad mushrooms. You shouldn't take them unless you're being paid.

MDMA
Cloud 9 and Voodoo Euphoria

I was really feeling Cloud 9 after 40 minutes or so, like a hyper, caffeine-feeling making me want to talk to girls and drink lots of beer. I couldn't find parking around my favorite bar, so I drove around blasting music until 3:30 a.m. When I returned home I was notified that Cloud 9's key ingredient, Ephedrine, "fucks with your dick." Horrified, I stayed up hoping that the jittery, tight-chested, short-breathed, imminent-heart-attack-feeling would go away. It didn't, so I went to bed and masturbated to make sure everything was in working order. Cloud 9 would clearly be the best of all the fake drugs, and the only one worth experimenting with. The next morning, I felt horrible, so I took four tablets of Voodoo Euphoria to spruce up my spirits. I split the package with a real Ecstasy buff to get another perspective on it, but she maintained that she "didn't feel shit." There would be neither Voodoo nor euphoria on my end either. Although we did play Wiffleball with the neighborhood children and I was sore for days.

Originally printed in WYWS Issue #18

while you were sleeping

GRAFFITI

BANKSY
Photos by B Plus

The votes are in and the polls are closed. In cities all over the globe, people are pretty tired of authority. At least, that's what art is saying. Case in point: On a certain wall in London, there's a life-size stencil of a girl hugging a bomb. Sure, it's a little strange, but in these anti-authoritarian times, this type of graffiti doesn't deface so much as it defines local decor. Elsewhere in this fair city, there is another stenciled wall, an Imperial Guard painting an anarchy sign, and you know, he isn't so out of place either. Around here, rebellion feels all right.

Rebellion isn't just for limeys, though. Even in normally tame countries such as the USA, people are starting to call into the question the powers that be. It's like they used to say way back when: Fuck the police and parents just don't understand. So these subversive stencils—the girl hugging the bomb, the guard touting anarchy—belong exactly where they are, in the big city where everyone knows that only losers follow the rules.

Although you'd expect graffiti about bombs and anarchy to be heady and yawningly political, BANKSY—the artist responsible for all this—isn't pushing any specific political ideology. True, as he'll tell you, his work is dubious of the activities of the ruling class, but even that message seems secondary. BANKSY's art is puckish, and it's obvious that he's more aroused by the fun of bombing, the running from the law, than he is in conveying any message. "You get addicted to [painting illegally]," he explains. "It's just short of having sex with girls." And while he does have sex with girls, he has no real credo or determination to change your mind. To his credit, he is not overly concerned with art or your reaction to his work.

However, you are going to react. It's there, it's in your face, on city walls from London to Los Angeles. And here, in the city, I suspect that a lot of people don't really mind having the characters around. Propaganda art has integrated itself into the cityscape; the protest is second nature, it's part of our reality. So if everyone already agrees stuff's got to change, how effective is a protest?

That's why BANKSY's humor is essential to his work. "I guess [my message] helps," he explains, "but I try not to think about it too much. I think the world is full of people who think too much." In essence, BANKSY seems to have co-opted the propaganda style mostly for the visual quality, not the semantics. "I like the way things look," he says. "I like the propaganda style. Just for the pictures."

First and foremost, BANKSY is an artist—no need to suffer when the world is full of walls to paint and chicks to pick up. Put simply, there are more important things to do than to spout philosophy.

BANKSY just wrapped up a stint in Los Angeles. The pieces you see here were created on that trip. "It's incredibly hard to do anything in a town like Los Angeles [with] the amount of cynicism here and smart assiness," he says. "You get contaminated by computers or something. Everyone who works with computers is really hard to impress. Whereas the people who work with their hands are better. The country-folk. They're less cynical."

What, then, is the impact of propaganda art in a place saturated with cynicism? Is the only option left for the propagandist to move his art to more naïve locales—say Duluth, Minnesota, or Lubbock, Texas? BANKSY agrees that perhaps the impact would be greater in a place less contaminated by computers, but he's content in London. BANKSY won't leave the city, and if his art is merely entertaining to cynical Londoners who are merely addicted to inspiration, well that's just fine by him.

Originally printed in WYWS Issue #20

U-HAUL
by Ian Mazie
Photos by Roger Gastman

It was a hot, humid and very sticky typical D.C. summer day when I arrived at my first U-Haul storage unit auction. The storage facility holding the auction was located in Prince George's County in Maryland, right outside of D.C. According to the news, someone gets shot in Prince George's County every day, sometimes twice a day.

The auctioneer was running way late, so we all waited in the customer service office, where I observed the competition. They all seemed to know each other. They greeted each other warmly and joked with one another and seemed like one huge family. They spotted me as they cooled off with water and paper fans. They looked me up and down and seemed suspicious of my camera, tape recorder and notepad. I decided to take a chance and approach them. In mid-strut, a very, very, very dark man cut me off. A lady who lacked knees and had three asses and sat in the middle of the group, yelled out at him, "Hey chocolate, what's up baby. Mmmmmm, mmmmmmm, mmmmm, the blackier the berry the sweeter the juice, the whiter the berry there is no use!" At that moment, I knew this was my type of place.

I introduced myself to the gang, and explained my article, the magazine and my own desire to be one of them. I asked them to show me the ways and tell me the tales of their freaky subculture. They told me about the "prizes" they have come across: money, gold jewelry, antiques, CDs, movies. One man, who warned me not to take his picture, because it was already up in the local post office, showed me his gold rings, all from storage units. He thought he had thousands of dollars on his fingers, but it looked like huge, gaudy, gold plated, badly finished, early 1990s costume jewelry. One man said he witnessed a guy find an Elvis Presley autographed photograph. One of the other men had found a bunch of South American currency (and I would assume cocaine, but that wasn't discussed in the interview). I was also told stories of famous paintings being found—surprisingly, when asked the names of the artists, I couldn't get an answer. I began to wonder how true these stories were, but I just smiled and nodded, so I wouldn't lose my new friends.

When I questioned the patrons about the scariest or grossest thing they ever found in a storage space, I was told by one man, "something fuzzy." He wasn't able to expand on his

answer, so I decided to move on with my questions. Another man, who brought his own chair, ignored my questions and told me his life story. He is going to be a rap-star one day, he assured me. He also nicknamed me his "girlfriend" for the rest of the day. The lady who lacked knees and had three asses told me she found "shit." I made her clarify, and she responded, "Poop." She grew a liking to me and insisted on following me around the rest of the day. I appreciated it at first until her ass kept on pushing me into walls by accident.

Finally, the auctioneer showed up, and the games began. He knew the gang and toured us around to 14 different units. We got about 30 seconds to check out each one. Many of the professional buyers brought flashlights. Then the bidding began. Most of the storage units went for around $20, some up to $75. Since we were near the University of Maryland, and in gunshot central, most the units had college kid's stuff or people's belongings who had been evicted.

I was eager to buy a unit and find a hidden fortune. Finally, my turn came and I got a storage space the size of my bedroom for $25. To my surprise, I didn't find gold or a big screen TV. I had bought a family: I got picture albums and middle school diplomas and little girl drawings. Anything that makes all the fun of the auction go right down the drain. One of the men I had interviewed had warned, "We make money off of other people's misery."

If I hadn't bought it, someone else would have, or else U-Haul would have dumped it all at the nearest dump or Salvation Army. Luckily, there were a couple of prizes in the unit, including fake gold, hair weaves, a Bill Cosby sweater, a Muslim praying rug, plenty of 1980s clothing and a laptop the size of a modern-day desktop.

I didn't win big, but by the end of the day, I felt accepted and I was even able to refer to the very, very, very dark man, by his nickname, Chocolate. Friends and memories are what made the day a success.

If any of you feel like buying a family's history or have hopes of finding some junk that can make you some cash then contact your local self-storage facility and ask when their next auction is. They tend to run monthly. Take my advice and try going to one in a more affluent area, stay away from messily packed units, fuzzy things and poop.

BEDOUIN vs. FRED "RERUN" BERRY

Introduction and photo by Teri Memolo
Interview by Bedouin

What's Happening!! was only supposed to be a four-episode summertime replacement show. It ended up running from 1975 to 1979 with Fred "Rerun" Berry as the unlikely star of the show. "[During casting] I could tell they didn't really know what kind of character they were looking for, so I made up one," Berry explains. "The baggy pants, suspenders and red beret… They said Fred, 'You read very well, but we're actually looking for a thin white guy.' I said, 'I'm Here!' And the rest is history."

The show was cancelled and went into syndication for the next six years. Then What's Happening Now!! was picked up in 1985, but Fred left the show after the first year. "I tried to renegotiate my contract to get paid more," Berry explains, "but they said fat and funny, but no more money. So I left the show. They blacklisted me, sued me, everything you could think of, and I survived it all. I'm still kicking."

At the time of this interview, Fred was doing his thing touring with Lakeside, The Sugar Hill Gang and Rolls Royce. He had spent the previous year opening up for James Brown, which Fred said was a dream job.

Fred was also serving as the director of the Rerun School of Dance—which had 25 dance students and six acting students at the time—and was doing personal appearances, stand-up comedy and emceeing shows. "My reason for wanting to be successful was so that I can give back," Berry says. "So I could reach back and grab somebody else and help them reach their dreams and goals. I used to be blessed now I'm mo' blessed. Because it's mo' blessed to give than it is to receive."

This interview was recorded on April 24, 2002:

Bedouin: Let's go back in the day to when you first got your start in the business.
Rerun: I started dancing on Soul Train back in the day. I met this guy at a club, name was Don Campbell, and I met him at a club called Maverick's Flat over on Crenshaw in L.A. He asked me if I wanted to be on Soul Train. I said, sure, you know. I didn't know he was going to sneak me on the show. He actually snuck me in the studio and we had to outrun the guard and everything, but I became a Soul Train dancer.

How old were you then?
I was about 19. After about a year or so on Soul Train, we got kicked off 'cause we asked to be paid. We formed a professional group called The Campbellock Dancers. Don Campbell made the dance up, so he called it the "Campbell Lock." That group went for about maybe two years, we traveled around, did a few little gigs.

So then locking was an original thing?
Exactly, but Don Campbell made it up. In the original group it was myself, they called me Mr. Penguin, Don "Campbellock" Campbell, the originator, there was Charles Robot, the first robot guy from Soul Train—[he was a] dark-skinned guy with the gold tooth—there was Slim, [who] took over the robot position with the Lockers, with the following group. There was Sambo Lock, Johnny McCloud was his real name—he was a precursor to all the b-boy stuff, that floor work, walls. He worked floors, walls, ceilings—you know what I mean! He was a precursor to all that stuff, but he got married and his wife didn't want him to [continue to dance].

What year was this?
This was around 1969 or 1970. We danced professionally two years as the Campbellock dancers. That group broke up and we re-formed a year later with Don "Campbellock" Campbell, Slim "The Robot," we had Flukey Luke, we had Greg Campbellock Jr., and we had Shabadoo and then eventually Toni Basil who also managed us—the Toni Basil from "Hey Mickey you're so fine you're so fine, you blow my mind." She danced with us for a couple of years. That group stayed together for about approximately five years.

And that was the group called "The Lockers"?
That was the Lockers—the group that got all the notoriety. We opened for Sinatra at Carnegie Hall, did a 14-city East Coast tour with Frank. We opened the MGM Grand in Las Vegas with Roger Miller and Dean Martin. We even danced at the Mormon Tabernacle in Salt Lake City, Utah—hey, hey, hey, that's an accomplishment, OK! We were considered a rock group because we only traveled with rock bands or R&B bands, and people like Sinatra. We were never considered a dance troupe.

What were some of the bands?
Funkadelic, Ohio Players, Grand Central Station, 5th Dimension... Don Kirshner's rock concert, American Music Awards, Black Gold Awards, Grammies—all that.

What are the top-10 things we don't know about Fred Berry?
I'm not broke, I'm not on crack, I don't have AIDS, I'm not gay, I'm not bisexual, I'm not hungry, I ain't no punk... I don't know what else to say... Oh yeah, send me the check.

What are the top-10 Things you would do if you were president?
Kill George Bush. I'm just joking. Definitely, I would fire just about everyone at the FBI and CIA because no one has been fired since the 9/11 attacks except for Jeff George of the Redskins, and believe me, 9/11 was not his fault. I'd fire the now-coach of the Redskins and hire Doug Williams who should have been coach of the Redskins after he won the Super Bowl. And the last thing I would do is make love to Hillary Clinton.

Before there was any magazine, Roger approached me to do the design. I think I was one of the only graphic design people he knew, and probably the only one with access to a scanner. The first issue was pretty low budget, and I think my payment for the first two issues was two zip drives, which is about $100. But at the time, I didn't mind, because I thought it was fun.

We were graffiti artists so the first issue had lots of graffiti flicks, but Roger also wanted to put other things in the magazine, like random photos he found on the street and other weird stuff. The first issue barely had any text, it was just flicks, photographs and one interview with ESPO. Roger came over and we just scanned photos and set it up on my computer. We tried to make the graphic design look really easy to read, and very simple.

The first issue also had an ad for his cap-selling business, which featured a girl laying on the ground with a bunch of spray-paint caps all over her body so it looked like someone busted a nut on her. "Blowing away the competition," the ad said. That was typical Roger.

I worked on the first two issues, and then I had to leave. I had a fulltime job at the time and was unable to devote enough time to the magazine without being paid for it. So it was unexpected and actually really awesome that, when someone came up with the funding, Roger asked me to design the magazine again. I jumped at the opportunity, and was very happy about it.

The first issue I came back on was issue 13. By this time, *WYWS* had developed a reputation, and built a following, and I was super psyched to start working on it again. Issue 14 featured Jay and Silent Bob on the cover, and had an awesome fashion spread with all these punk rock people and celebrities like Appollonia, DJ Muggs and the Circle Jerks. I thought it was the coolest thing ever because we were in the suburbs of D.C. but the magazine had a totally different vibe.

For issue 15, we went to Las Vegas for the Magic tradeshow, and Roger kept saying, "We are going to rent Gary Coleman." I guess Gary Coleman would hang out with you or promote whatever you are doing if you paid him money, and so Roger did. So we had Gary Coleman with us at this tradeshow, and it was a total success, because everywhere we went people were like, "Oh my god, Gary Coleman, oh my god!" So that definitely generated some buzz at the tradeshow.

Gary was a pretty cool guy, but I think he was sort of pissed off at me. I made the mistake of getting a little too crazy at the tradeshow because somebody had given me some little pills of some kind that I thought weren't very potent to take, so I was like "OK, fuck it I will try it." I was drinking beers, and I was acting like a crazy person, as you could see by the photos. In the issue, there is a picture of me lying on the ground. Right before this photo was taken, they woke me up with water. So I wake up, and there is a chick talking to me, and I'm like, "What's going on?" and everybody is laughing. I guess they had gotten me a transvestite stripper. Way to go, guys. I guess they thought that since I was so messed up that I might think it was a chick, and try and hook up or something. But at that point I just wanted to go home. I was being a party pooper, I know it, and I wandered back to my hotel room and went back to sleep. I guess I missed my opportunity with a transvestite hooker.

—*Dave Dawson*

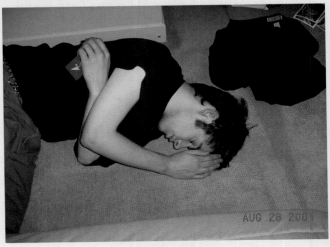

First OFF, WYWS is the whole Reason I Am currently serving Time in A Federal Prison. My Most Fondest memory of the mag would prolly be the 2000 Magic Convention in Vegas. A bunch of us went, Lets see, me Roger, DAVE, Mushmouth, And Flew to Vegas And had A cross over in Denver, There we met two girls And ended up meeting then Again in Baggage claim in Vegas, there were no cAbs, so I sprung for A Limo And we let the 2 broads cruise with us. So we get to the HARD Rock to unwind, and DANNY, DOSE, SEST, DOSE's girl All meet me there Also. Everyone is busy, so Roger has me go pick up GARY coleman, yeah the midget guy At the Airport since I had Talked one of the girls we met into Rent A expedition in her name, Long story. So me DANNY And 2 girls DRive out to meet GARY At the GATE. He's the LAST OFF the plane with a garbage bag for Luggage. Geesh. So we Laugh At him And then he tells us he thought it was A Magic the Gathering Convention And How he Loves D And D. We get in the truck and I place the two girls on either side of him, And He's About strange And I tell one of the girls to get Topless, and He's sold. So He kicks off His shoes And socks, yuck! Feet were so Ashy it looked like he had been TAP DANCing in Flour. Instantly the shirt goes back on. we get to HARD Rock, And everyone is CALLing him webster. Which made me realize how truelly Depressing his Life is. So we torent him For A Few DAYS And he leaves SAFLey. So At the time I'm married with A DAughter And Another on the wAy, And Sober. So we go to A Cypress hill show And DOSE And one of the chicks And SEST have me smoking weed And eating pills. Not Good, The next DAY DOSE is telling me how great the pills were And How he got to bang his girl in the ASS Then she comes up to me LATer Asking to stay in my Room because she has A UTI. Gross DOSE was Double DIPPing! So AFTER THAT TRIP I lost my sobriety And ended up here. I could write A whole Book Just About that Trip, but this is the short And skinny, Roger is A GREAT Friend, And we Didn't talk for A Few YEARS. He was one of the 1st people to write me when I got locked up, So THANKS FOR the memories And FRiendship, The 5 years is worth it.

Love
SEAN

P.S. Please send me babys mom THAT DOUGH FOR The ever PRINTS

SORRY SO MESSY

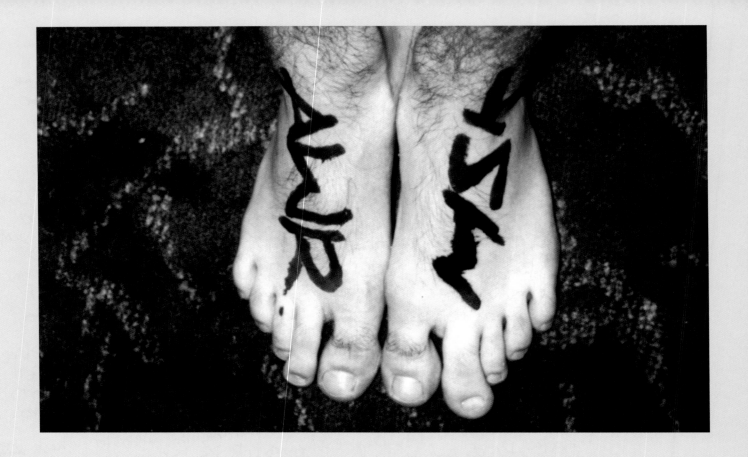

I started working for *WYWS* by accident. I was working as a shop manager at Jinx Proof Tattoos in D.C., and this dude came in, acting like he was too cool for anyone. I was introduced to him, and a few days later, I was re-labeling barcodes on his new graffiti book, working for a 12-pack of beer a day.

I soon realized Roger and I had a ton of mutual friends in the music scene. Once the magazine started to gain more exposure, and Roger was ready to start to take it to the next level, he asked if I wanted to be a part of it—and not just scanning photos for his graffiti archive or fielding phone calls from his nagging mother.

Working for this magazine, I managed to travel for free, get drunk for free, and evade the law on the regular (thank you Rich Colman and friends). I went to a graffiti convention in Ohio and met a dude with an abnormally long toe. I went to Vegas and Dez from Black Flag was buying me beers at an after-party. I got to see one of my friends get married, and as soon as he kissed the bride, he ripped open his shirt to her parents and displayed the "I Fucked You Daughter" shirt to them. I gave the City of Bethesda, Maryland, thousands of dollars in parking fines while working for *WYWS*, and used to drive the assistant editor to his DUI classes, while driving under the influence. Indirectly, I have an awesome wife and an awesome kid because of *WYWS*.

Someone told me once that "*WYWS* is bathroom reading at best." Why is that a bad thing? Who the hell seriously sits down to full-on read a magazine? Best bathroom read ever... I got to see *WYWS* rise to greatness and fall because of dipshits. New chapter, new book, right Roger?

—*Chris Henzel aka Mushmouth*

WHILE YOU WERE SLEEPING I SCARED YOU